SUSTAINABLE COMMUNITIES IN EUROPE

Edited by
William M Lafferty

EARTHSCAN

Earthscan Publications Ltd
London • Sterling, VA

First published in the UK and USA in 2001
by Earthscan Publications Ltd

ISBN: 1 85383 791 1 paperback
1 85383 790 3 hardback

Typesetting by PCS Mapping & DTP
Printed and bound in the UK by Creative Print and Design Wales, Ebbw Vale
Cover design by Richard Reid
Index compiled by Indexing Specialists, Hove

For a full list of publications please contact:
Earthscan Publications Ltd
120 Pentonville Road, London, N1 9JN, UK
Tel: +44 (0)20 7278 0433
Fax: +44 (0)20 7278 1142
Email: earthinfo@earthscan.co.uk
http://www.earthscan.co.uk

22883 Quicksilver Drive, Sterling, VA 20166–2012, USA

Earthscan is an editorially independent subsidiary of Kogan Page Ltd and publishes in association with WWF-UK and the International Institute for Environment and Development

A catalogue record for this book is available from the British Library

Library of Congress Cataloging-in-Publication Data
Lafferty, William M., 1939-
Sustainable communities in Europe / William Lafferty.
p. cm.
Includes bibliographical references and index.
ISBN 1-85383-790-3 (cloth) — ISBN 1-85383-791-1 (pbk.)
1. Sustainable development—Europe. 2. Economic development—Environmental aspects—Europe. I. Title.

HC79.E5 L34 2001
338.94'07'091732—dc21

2001023294

Contents

Figures, tables and boxes

Figures

Tables

Boxes

Foreword

Local Agenda 21 (LA21) is one of the success stories of the Agenda 21 process that was launched in Rio de Janeiro in 1992. I strongly believe that the exchange of practical experiences and good practices is a cornerstone for taking LA21 processes forward. As this book helps disseminate such information, I am convinced it will help to promote the LA21 movement in Europe. I therefore warmly recommend it to a broad readership.

Over the years, I have followed progress in this area, noting with satisfaction that local communities engaging in LA21 processes can and do make a real contribution to sustainability. I have seen many examples of this from the European Sustainable Cities and Towns Campaign which, since its launch in 1994, has been the main vehicle for promoting and supporting LA21 processes in Europe.

Through its Charter of European Cities and Towns Towards Sustainability (known commonly as the Aalborg Charter), the Campaign has promoted the objectives of Chapter 28 of Agenda 21. It has done this by calling on local authorities to consult with their citizens and achieve consensus on 'a local Agenda 21' programme for the community. With over 1200 local authorities participating in 36 European countries, the Campaign is the biggest single European initiative for local sustainable development and LA21.

This commitment to the objectives of the Aalborg Charter and the Campaign proved to be an important driving force for policy development and implementation by local and regional authorities across Europe. This development and implementation has respected the principles of sustainable development. Concrete examples show how participating in the Campaign has had a direct bearing on, for example, the development of LA21 programmes. It has also directly influenced: strategic action plans and sustainability programmes (CO_2 reduction, integrated environmental education, environmental audits etc); the definition of local policy frameworks; the allocation of resources for activities related to sustainable development; and the commitment made by all policy groups to achieve sustainability.

While the success of the Campaign is ultimately dependent on the political commitment and progress made by the participating authorities and their local communities, I am proud of the European Commission's role in helping to launch and subsequently fund the Campaign. In order to give the Campaign a firmer basis for its activities and, more generally, to strengthen cooperation between the Commission, networks of local authorities and other stakeholders, a 'Community Framework for Cooperation in the Field of Sustainable Urban Development and Local Agenda 21' is being put in place. This will, uniquely, provide a secure legal base as well as technical and financial support from a European level for the implementation at local level of Agenda 21 initiatives.

For a more comprehensive approach, it is also necessary to monitor the results of Agenda 21 processes. Following the advice of the Campaign participants, the Expert Group on the Urban Environment has developed a tool for monitoring progress towards sustainability at the local level and for providing objective and comparable information across Europe. This tool is based on European Common Indicators.

While the European Commission attaches great importance to supporting local communities in their work on LA21, through the Campaign and other related activities, it also takes seriously the commitment it made to taking action itself to implement Agenda 21. The European Commission recently adopted the Communication *Ten Years After Rio: Preparing for the World Summit on Sustainable Development in 2002* which sets out European Union (EU) priorities and actions in preparation for this event. The forthcoming EU Sustainable Development Strategy and the recently proposed Sixth Environment Action Programme, 'Environment 2010: Our future, our choice', will be important European contributions to this event.

This book, with its local focus, will constitute a welcome complement to these European actions, as well as to the many national contributions that will be made to the World Summit on Sustainable Development in Johannesburg in 2002. I hope it will prove to be a source of inspiration and support for the many actors involved in meeting the challenge of sustainability.

Margot Wallström
Commissioner, Environment Directorate-General
European Commission

Preface

The present work constitutes the final report of a project sponsored jointly by the Environment and Climate Programme of the European Commission's Research Directorate-General (project reference: ENV 4970466), and the Programme for Research and Documentation for a Sustainable Society (ProSus), Research Council of Norway. The project has been organised as a 'concerted action', indicating that the primary purpose has been to produce 'value-added knowledge' from ongoing research in 12 participant countries. The countries reported here are Sweden, Finland, Denmark, Norway, the United Kingdom, Ireland, the Netherlands, France, Austria, Italy and Spain. Germany was also originally part of the network, but could not, for personal reasons on the part of the German partner, deliver a final country report. The working title for the project has been SUSCOM: 'Sustainable Communities in Europe: A Cross-National Study of the Implementation of Agenda 21 at the Local Level of Governance'.

In presenting our final report, it should be pointed out that SUSCOM has only been funded for network activities. None of the participating researchers has been funded directly by either the EU or the Research Council of Norway. The contributions of the individual country teams have been based on research supported by the participant institutions. It has been the goal of SUSCOM to bring the different research efforts together, and to try to systematise the different national reports within a common dialogue and joint evaluative framework.

This final report updates and further develops a status report issued in 1998 (Lafferty, 1998). The purpose here has been:

1 to update the situation in each country;
2 to provide 'profiles' for each country reflecting a judgement as to what appears to be most distinct or interesting in the implementation experience of each case; and
3 to bring together in the introductory and concluding chapters the most significant collective perspectives emerging from the project.

The introductory chapter thus outlines selected 'information' and 'knowledge' goals of the project, as well as the different conceptual and evaluative frameworks developed. We feel that these perspectives alone have made a significant contribution to the understanding of the implementation task, providing other researchers and practitioners alike with important insights and perspectives on the global–local problematic. The concluding chapter then attempts to summarise the most significant (and robust) findings, and to draw major policy lessons.

As project coordinator for SUSCOM, I would particularly like to thank all of the members of the national teams who, through their respective institutions, have clearly contributed 'above and beyond the call' of a project of this nature. The spirit and level of involvement of the network have been of the highest order throughout. Special thanks are also due Katarina Eckerberg and Frans Coenen, who have served with the coordinator as a 'steering committee' for the project. In Brussels, we have had excellent contact and assistance from Angela Liberatore at the European Commission, and in Oslo we are indebted to several key people at the ProSus Centre: first and foremost Elisabeth Frydenlund, but also Gørild Mathisen, Trine Hognrø, Mette Samsing, Trygve Bjørnæs, Gard Lindseth and Daniel Fryer. In short, it has indeed been a concerted action – in the best spirit of Rio and Local Agenda 21.

William M Lafferty
Oslo, 12 May 2001

About the contributors

Carlo Aall received a graduate degree (CandAgric) in 1987 from The Norwegian University of Agriculture. He has also worked as an environmental officer for the municipality of Ølen (1988–90). He is employed as research associate and head of the Division for Environmental Research at The Western Norway Research Institute in Sogndal, and has also recently completed a PhD in Municipal Environmental Policy at the University of Ålborg. He has previously published numerous reports in Norwegian on the Eco-municipality Programme and Environmental auditing in Norwegian municipalities, and is working on all phases of local planning and implementation of sustainable development.

Chris Church is an advisor to the UK Community Development Foundation and to UNED UK on sustainable development, and specialises in work at the local and community levels, and on work linking poverty and environmental issues. He worked for Friends of the Earth UK from 1987–1990. He has worked with many local authorities on their Local Agenda 21 programme. He chairs the Board of ANPED, the Northern Alliance for Sustainability, a network of NGOs in all regions of Europe, and manages their local sustainability programme. He is currently working on two research projects funded by the Joseph Rowntree Foundation on the impact of local sustainability in the UK.

Francesca Di Pietro holds a PhD in Landscape Ecology and is now teacher and researcher in environmental planning at the Department of Town and Country Planning, University of Tours (France). Her research and lecturing are in agricultural landscapes, including rural land use and sustainable farming systems. They focus on the role of agriculture in country planning and management. Recent published articles deal with agro-ecosystems assessment and the evaluation of agro-environmental policy.

Katarina Eckerberg is professor at the Department of Political Science, Umeå University. Her research and lecturing focus on environmental politics and policy, including comparative international studies. Her publications include *Environmental Protection in Swedish Forestry* (1990, Avebury); *Process and Policy Evaluation in Structure Planning* (1993, Swedish Council for Building Research); *Comparing Nordic and Baltic Countries: Environmental Problems and Policies in Agriculture and*

Forestry (1995, Nordic Council of Ministers); and *From the Earth Summit to Local Agenda 21* (with William M Lafferty, 1998, Earthscan). Current research involves studies of sustainable rural development and the use of local sustainability indicators.

Cyria Emelianoff is a lecturer in urbanism and planning in the Department of Geography, Université du Maine. Her research bears on sustainable cities in Europe and urban ecology, the topics of her PhD and latest publications. She is currently working on Local Agenda 21 in France.

Nuria Font is an assistant professor at the Department of Political Science and Public Law, Universitat Autònoma de Barcelona. Her research and lecturing focus on environmental policy, citizen participation and EU policy. Her recent publications include *Democracia i Participacio Ciutadana* (1998, Fundacio Bofill), *Politica Ambiental en España* (with Susana Aguilar and Joan Subirats, eds, 1999) and *Local y Sostenible* (with Joan Subirats, eds, 2000).

Maria Francesca Gomila received her graduate degree in Political Science and Administration from the Universitat Autonoma of Barcelona in 1997. She has recently completed a Master's degree in Public Management, and is now working on her PhD. Since October 1997 she has been working as a research assistant in environmental politics at the Universitat Autonoma of Barcelona, with a special emphasis on the implementation of Local Agenda 21 in Spain.

Andrea Grabher is a senior research fellow at JOANNEUM RESEARCH, a non-profit research organisation owned by the regional government of Styria, Austria. Her research focus is on concepts and models for the sustainability transition process in local and regional governments, and companies, for example.

Laure Héland holds a Master's degree in Planning and has been working for several years on urban ecology and sustainable development in France and the United States.

Jesper Holm is associate professor in environmental regulation at the Department of Environment, Technology and Social Studies, Roskilde University. He also holds the chair as external associate professor at the Department of Political Science, Copenhagen University. He researches and lectures in environmental policies and regulation, and in corporate responses, democracy and environment. He is currently involved in two pan-European research projects on environment and innovation, in developing a new postgraduate Master's degree in environment and innovation, and in a research and development contract with business on ecological communication. His most recent publications include: 'Technological Innovation and Environmental Policy in Denmark – on technology oriented environmental policy and environmental oriented technology policy', National Macro Report for ENVINNO, RUC 1999, in Holm, Schrama and Seedlacheck, 2000, *Technological Innovation and Environmental Policy in Europe*, Kluwer; 'Standards, Modernisation and Ecological Space' (with Bente Kjærgård), in Bruno Dente, ed, forthcoming, *The Ecological State*.

William M Lafferty is professor of political science and director of ProSus, at the Centre for Development and the Environment, University of Oslo. He is also affiliated with the Centre for Clean Technology and Environmental Policy (CSTM), University of Twente, the Netherlands. His most recent publications include *Democracy and the Environment* (1996, with James Meadowcroft, Edward Elgar), *From the Earth Summit to Local Agenda 21* (1998, with Katarina Eckerberg, Earthscan), *Towards Sustainable Development* (with Oluf Langhelle, 1999, Macmillan) and *Implementing Sustainable Development: National Strategies and Initiatives* (with James Meadowcroft, 2000, Oxford University Press).

Corrine Larrue is associate professor at the University of Tours. Her major field of research and teaching is policy analysis, with emphasis on environmental and regional policies. She was coordinator of a comparative research project on the application of the subsidiarity principle in the implementation of environmental policy (4th Framework Programme, European Commission), and has recently completed work on 'environmental performance contracts' as a new tool for environmental governance.

Rodolfo Lewanski is associate professor at the Dipartimento di Organizzazione e Sistema Politico, Faculty of Political Science, University of Bologna, Italy, where he teaches courses in public administration and environmental policy. His main field of research and scientific interest is environmental policy, with specific reference to Italy. Among his most recent publications are: 'Italy: Learning from international cooperation or simply "following suit"?', in Arild Underdal and Kenneth Hanf (eds), *International Environmental Agreements and Domestic Politics* (2000); 'Italy: Environmental policy in a fragmented state', in Jansen, A-I and Hanf, K (eds), *Governance and Environment in Western Europe* (1998); 'Environmental dispute resolution in Italy', in Weidner, H (ed), *Alternative Dispute Resolution in Environmental Conflicts* (1998); and *Governare l'ambiente: Attori e processi della politica ambientale* (1997).

Gerard Mullally holds a Master's degree in the Sociology of Development (1992). He is currently a lecturer at the Department of Sociology and a research associate at the Cleaner Production Promotion Unit (CPPU) in the Department of Civil and Environmental Engineering, University College, Cork. His teaching and research are in environmental sociology, politics and policy. His current research interests include the implementation of Local Agenda 21 and the social organisation of sustainable tourism in Ireland. He is currently completing his doctoral dissertation in the University College, Cork, and is a member of the management executive committee of Cork Environmental Forum.

Michael Narodoslawsky is associate professor at the Institute of Chemical Engineering Fundamentals and Process Technology at the Technical University Graz, Austria. He has published widely on sustainability indicators and sustainable regional development, and participated in several EU-sponsored projects in these areas. He also heads the research association SUSTAIN, and is consultant to various national and regional administrative bodies.

Anita Niemi-Iilahti is associate professor of public administration at the Department of Public Management, University of Vaasa, Finland. The contribution to this book is a result of a senior research fellowship at the Academy of Finland (1998–99). Her teaching and research are in the areas of comparative (European) local government, including policy, organisation and reforms, and environmental policy implementation, particularly within the fields of agro-environmental policy and sustainable development in local communities.

Emiliano Ramieri received a degree in environmental sciences in 1995 from the University Ca' Foscari of Venice, and studied at the Universities of Bergen and Groningen. He is employed at the regional agency for the protection of the environment in Bologna, where he is working on geographic information systems. He is also collaborating with the Fondazione Eni Enrico Mattei in Venice (FEEM), where he worked as researcher for three years, in particular on Local Agenda 21. Within FEEM his research is into the impact of climate change on coastal zones. He has also worked on the development of sustainability indicators for urban systems.

Joan Subirats is senior professor of political science and administration at the Universitat Autonoma de Barcelona. His research and lecturing focus on public policy analysis, institutional performance and environmental and social policy. His recent publications include *Politica Ambiental en España* (with Susana Aguilar and Nuria Font, eds, 1999, Tirant lo Blanch), *Politicas Publicas en España* (with Ricard Goma, eds, 1998, Ariel), *Un Problema de Estilo*, 1992 CEC, and *Analisis de Politicas Publicas y Eficacia de la Administration* 1989, MAP.

Jane Wallace-Jones has a degree in biological sciences and a Master's in environmental management. She works in the Veneto Regional Agency for Environmental Protection on the promotion and design of projects regarding the diffusion of environmental management systems and other voluntary initiatives in local industry. She worked previously in the FEEM, Venice, where she carried out research on voluntary agreements, the implementation of Local Agenda 21 in Italy, and coordinated the organisation's scientific contribution to Local Agenda 21 for Venice in 1999.

Mercy Wambui Kamara received a Master's degree in technological and socio-economic planning from the Department of Environment, Technology and Social Studies at Roskilde University, Denmark. As a PhD student at the same department, she has been involved as a research assistant for the Danish team in various international concerted action projects on biotechnology and the European public. She is also a research officer in a new international research programme: 'Life Sciences in European Society'. Her fields of interest include the relationship between policy-making, science and politics, with particular reference to modern biotechnology.

Stephen Young is senior lecturer in the Government Department at the University of Manchester. He is a joint editor of *Environmental Politics* and of the Routledge series 'Issues in Environmental Politics'. His recent publications include *Cities in the 1990s* (with Gerry Stoker, 1993, Longman); *The Politics of the Environment* (1993, Baseline Books); and articles/chapters on local government, participation, wildlife and environmental issues. He has recently completed a project on the participatory aspects of Local Agenda 21 for the Economic and Social Research Council of the UK (ESRC).

Acronyms and abbreviations

4d	Dossiers et Débats pour le Développement Durable (sustainable development NGO, France)
ADEAN	Association for Development of Northern Alsace (France)
ADEME	Agency for the Environment and Energy Control (France)
AF	Association of County Councils (Denmark)
AFLRA	Association of Finnish Local and Regional Authorities
AKF	Research Council for Danish Counties and Municipalities
ANCI	National Association of Italian Municipalities
ANPA	National Environmental Agency (Italy)
ANPED	Northern Alliance for Sustainability
ARPA	Regional Environmental Agency (Italy)
BEVER	Soil Remediation Policy Review (The Netherlands)
BTCV	British Trust for Conservation Volunteers
BUGM	Programme for Funding of Municipal Environmental Policy (The Netherlands)
CBO	community-based organisation
CDF	Community Development Foundation (UK)
CEMR	Council of European Municipalities and Regions
CEPR	Centre for Economic Policy Research (UK)
CFDD	French Commission for Sustainable Development
CIBU	Centre for Internet-based Education (Denmark)
CIPE	Inter-ministerial Committee for Economic Planning (Italy)
CIPRA	International Commission for the Protection of the Alps
CISPEL	Italian Confederation of Local Public Services
CLOE	Local Operational Environmental Contract (France)
Comhar	National Sustainable Development Partnership (Ireland)
COR	Committee of the Regions (EU)
CPRE	Campaign for the Protection of Rural England
CPPU	Cleaner Production Promotion Unit (Ireland)
CSTM	Centre for Clean Technology and Environmental Policy (The Netherlands)
DEO	Development Concept for East Styria (Austria)
DETR	Department of the Environment, Transport and the Regions (UK)

DEYNA	Foundation for Development and Nature (Spain)
DGXI	*former* Directorate-General for Environment, Consumer Protection and Nuclear Security; *now* Environment Directorate-General (EC)
DGXII	*former* Directorate-General for Science, Research and Development; now Research Directorate-General (EC)
DN	Danish Society for the Conservation of Nature
DoE	Department of the Environment (Ireland)
DoELG	Department of Environment and Local Government (Ireland)
EC	European Commission
EIA	environmental impact assessment
EIM	Environmental Policy in the Municipality (Norway)
EMAS	European Eco-Management and Audit Scheme
ENDA	Environment and Development Association (France)
ENEA	National Body for New Technologies, the Environment and Energy (Italy)
ENVINNO	Integration of Environmental and Ecology-oriented Technology Policy: Stimulus and Response in Environment Related Innovation Networks (EU DGXII)
ESRC	Economic and Social Research Council (UK)
ERM	environmental research management
ESCTC	European Sustainable Cities and Towns Campaign
EU	European Union
EUROCITIES	association of European metropolitan cities
FEEM	Fondazione Eni Enrico Mattei (Italy)
FMCU	Fédération Mondial des Cités Unies
FoE	Friends of the Earth
FUN	Programme for Funding of National Environmental Policy (The Netherlands)
GAP	global action plan
GATT	General Agreement on Tariffs and Trade
GDP	gross domestic product
GNP	gross national product
HUP	Public Nuisance Act Implementation Plan (The Netherlands)
ICLEI	International Council for Local Environmental Initiatives
IDeA	Improvement and Development Agency (UK)
INE	National Institute of Statistics (Spain)
INU	National Institute for Urban Planning (Italy)
IUCN	The World Conservation Union (*formerly* International Union for Conservation of Nature and Natural Resources)
IULA	International Union of Local Authorities

KL	National Association of Local Authorities (Denmark)
LA21	Local Agenda 21
LASALA	Local Authorities Self Assessment of Local Agenda (ICLEI)
LEADER II	a community initiative for rural development (Ireland)
LETS	local exchange trading systems (UK)
LGA	Local Government Association (UK)
LGMB	Local Government Management Board (UK)
LO	Confederation of Trade Unions (Denmark, Norway, Sweden)
MATE	Ministry for Spatial Planning and the Environment (France)
MEE	Ministry of the Environment and Energy (Denmark)
MIG	Modernising Noise Abatement Policy Instruments (The Netherlands)
MoE	Ministry of the Environment (Norway)
MUP	Environmental Policy Implementation Plan (The Netherlands)
NALRA	Norwegian Association of Local and Regional Authorities
NCDO	National Committee on International Cooperation and Sustainable Development (The Netherlands)
NEF	New Economics Foundation (UK)
NEPA	National Environmental Protection Agency (Sweden)
NEPP	National Environmental Policy Plan (The Netherlands)
NGO	non-governmental organisation
NOK	Norwegian kroner
NPCA	Norwegian Pollution Control Authority
NUTS	nomenclature of territorial units for statistics
OECD	Organisation for Economic Co-operation and Development
PDO	Dutch Program ('Platform') for Sustainable Development
PIR	regional programmes (Italy)
POLLEN	local government-project of Bouguenais (France)
ProSus	Programme for Research and Documentation for a Sustainable Society
PRS	Regional Development Plan (Italy)
PRSS	Regional Plan for Sustainable Development (Italy)
RECITE	European Union project for environmental audit models
Rio+5	refers to the Earth Summit follow-up meeting in 1997 (see UNGASS)
Rio+10	refers to the Earth Summit follow-up meeting in 2002
SCP	Social and Cultural Planning Office (The Netherlands)
SEK	Swedish kroner

SIAU	integrated system of urban indicators (Italy)
SIVOM	*Syndicat Intercommunal Vocation Multiple* (France)
SLC	Sustainable Local Communities (Norway)
SMEs	small- and medium-sized enterprises
SOU	government official report (Sweden)
SSB	Statistics Norway
SSCN	Swedish Society for Conservation of Nature
STEP	Programme for Participatory Urban Planning (Germany)
SUSCOM	Sustainable Communities in Europe
TCPA	Town and Country Planning Association (UK)
UK	United Kingdom
UN	United Nations
UNA	United Nations Association
UNCED	United Nations Conference on Environment and Development
UNCSD	United Nations Commission on Sustainable Development
UNED-UK	United Nations Environment and Development UK Committee
UNEP	United Nations Environment Programme
UNESCO	United Nations Educational, Scientific and Cultural Organisation
UNGASS	United Nations General Assembly Special Session (Earth Summit +5)
UPI	Union of Italian Provinces
UTO	World Federation of United Cities
VNG	Association of Dutch Municipalities
VOGM	grants scheme for the development of municipal environmental policy (The Netherlands)
VROM	Ministry of the Environment (The Netherlands)
WCED	World Commission on Environment and Development
WHO	World Health Organization
WRR	Dutch Scientific Advisory Council to the Government
WWF	*formerly known as* World Wide Fund For Nature
XCPS	Network of Cities and Towns for Sustainability (Spain)
ZEAT	zone d'études et d'aménagement du territoire (regional zoning concept, France)

Introduction

William M Lafferty

LOCAL AGENDA 21: THE CORE IDEA

Local Agenda 21 (LA21) refers to the general goal set for local communities in Chapter 28 of Agenda 21, the 'action plan for sustainable development' adopted at the United Nations Conference on Environment and Development (UNCED – commonly known as the Earth Summit) in Rio in 1992. Chapter 28 is the shortest chapter in the 40-chapter plan, a fact which may account for its relative success.[1] While other chapters are heavily loaded with guidelines, recommendations and ambitious goals as to specific problem areas, Chapter 28 is a relatively simple appeal to local authorities to engage in a dialogue for sustainable development with the members of their constituencies. It is because 'so many of the problems and solutions being addressed by Agenda 21 have their roots in local activities', that the participation and involvement of local authorities is viewed as 'a determining factor' in fulfilling the objectives of the action plan. As the level of governance closest to the people, local authorities 'play a vital role in educating, mobilizing and responding to the public to promote sustainable development' (Agenda 21, para 28.1 (United Nations, 1993)).

Chapter 28 stipulates just four major objectives, three of them with very specific deadlines:

1. By 1996, most local authorities in each country should have undertaken a consultative process with their populations and achieved a consensus on 'a Local Agenda 21' for the community.
2. By 1993, the international community should have initiated a consultative process aimed at increasing cooperation between local authorities.
3. By 1994, representatives of associations of cities and other local authorities should have increased levels of cooperation and coordination with the goal of enhancing the exchange of information and experience among local authorities.
4. All local authorities in each country should be encouraged to implement and monitor programmes which aim at ensuring that women and youth are represented in decision-making, planning and implementation processes.

What we learn from these objectives is:

- The aim of the chapter is an identifiable result of a consultative process – 'a Local Agenda 21'.
- The effort in question should be both cooperative and coordinated across national boundaries, with the specific assistance of the international community and transnational NGOs.
- The sub-programme should make a particular effort to bring women and youth into the change process.

These signals are then followed up somewhat more specifically in three sub-paragraphs on 'activities'. Without going into detail on these, it can be said that they serve to expand on the objectives, adding a number of specific ideas and identifying the types of international organisations and transnational bodies that could become involved in the coordinating activities.

Based on these relatively sparse documentary sources, it can be inferred that an LA21 is a strategic programme, plan or policy which has emerged from a consultative process initiative by local authorities with both local citizens and representatives of relevant local stakeholders, with a particular interest in involving women and youth. The purpose of the strategic programme is to implement Agenda 21 at the local level, which by implication is to say that the purpose is to entrust local authorities with a particular responsibility for achieving sustainable development within their particular sub-national domains.

ICLEI AND THE AALBORG CHARTER

Several international and regional organisations have played a major role in following up, and filling out, the signals provided by Chapter 28. Foremost among these has been the International Council on Local Environmental Initiatives (ICLEI). Established two years prior to the Earth Summit, ICLEI played a major role in preparing and coordinating Chapter 28 of Agenda 21. Working closely with organisations such as the United Nations Environment Programme (UNEP), the International Union of Local Authorities (IULA) and the European Commission (EC), ICLEI has taken a clear and forceful lead since the summit in sponsoring and promoting LA21 activities.[2]

Two initiatives have had a major impact on our understanding of what LA21 has come to mean, namely the EC's European Sustainable Cities and Towns Campaign, and the survey conducted by ICLEI as part of the reporting exercise for the 1992 Special Session of the UN General Assembly (UNGASS or 'Earth Summit +5').

Beginning with a resolution by the European Council in 1991 to establish an 'Expert Group on the European Environment', a Sustainable Cities and Towns in Europe conference was held in Aalborg, Denmark in May 1994. The conference resulted in the so-called 'Aalborg Charter', a three-part document outlining basic values and strategic options for sustainable development in European urban areas, and launched a broad-based campaign for sustainable cities and towns in Europe. Part III of the Charter made a specific commitment to follow up Chapter 28 of Agenda 21, and also made a direct connection between the Charter, Agenda 21 and the European Union's Fifth Environmental Action Programme 'Towards Sustainability' (Commission of the European Communities, 1993).

The Aalborg Charter also proposed an eight-stage model for preparing and implementing a local action plan – an LA21 (Aalborg Charter, Part III):

- *'recognition of the existing planning and financial frameworks as well as other plans and programmes;*
- *the systematic identification, by means of extensive public consultation, of problems and their causes;*
- *the prioritisation of tasks to address identified problems;*
- *the creation of a vision for a sustainable community through a participatory process involving all sectors of the community;*
- *the consideration and assessment of alternative strategic options;*
- *the establishment of a long-term local action plan towards sustainability which includes measurable targets;*
- *the programming of the implementation of the plan including the preparation of a timetable and statement of allocation of responsibilities among the partners;*
- *the establishment of systems and procedures for monitoring and reporting on the implementation of the plan.'* (Aalborg Charter, Part III)

These stages can be interpreted as a logical practical extension of the objectives and activities proposed in Chapter 28 of Agenda 21. Taken together with Part I of the Charter (which outlines the notion and principles of 'sustainability'), there emerges a relatively concise understanding of what constitutes an LA21:

- An LA21 is a local action plan for the achievement of sustainable development.

- It is to be worked out through a broad consultative process between local authorities, citizens and other relevant stakeholder groups, and eventually integrated with existing plans, priorities and programmes.
- The 'consultation' in question is clearly meant to be a *new* and *different* process from existing protective and remedial environmental activities.
- The process has a clear *strategic intent*. Though the actual content of an LA21 is not spelled out, there is a clear presumption of both *change* and *instrumental rationality* with respect to achieving the Earth Summit goals.
- The action plan should be implemented with due provision for ongoing input, and revision, and it should make special efforts to engage women and youth in all phases.
- Chapter 28 of Agenda 21 is specifically addressed to local Authorities: the responsibility of national governments is thus *primarily facilitative*.
- The substance of any particular LA21 will be *relative to the specific nature of the local community* in question (its geography, demography, economics, society and culture), and it should be expected to *evolve dynamically over time*.

IMPLEMENTING LA21 IN EUROPE: DEVELOPMENT OF THE SUSCOM PROJECT

Trying to attach a specific meaning to the concept of an LA21 is important for a number of reasons. While a certain amount of conceptual flexibility is necessary in order to apply an idea like LA21 across a broad spectrum of local and regional communities, there is also a need for a common understanding of the features that are unique to LA21. If LA21 were seen as an equivalent to, for example, 'environmental policy', the concept would quickly deteriorate into a catch-all category with little potential for evaluation or for cross-national analysis.

In the spring of 1995 a small group of researchers met in Oslo to establish the criteria necessary for a joint research effort. Building on the 'constitutive elements' outlined above, two further sets of 'benchmarks' were agreed. Firstly the group adopted a list of six basic criteria for identifying and comparing LA21 activities:

1. A more conscious attempt to relate environmental *effects* to underlying economic and political *pressures* (which in turn derive from political decisions, non-decisions and markets).
2. A more active effort to relate local issues, decisions and dispositions to *global impacts*, both environmentally and with respect to global solidarity and justice.

3 A more focused policy for achieving *cross-sectoral integration* of environment-and-development concerns, values and goals in planning, decision-making and policy implementation.
4 Greater efforts to increase *community involvement*, that is to bring both citizens and major stakeholder groups, particularly business and labour unions, into the planning and implementation process with respect to environment-and-development issues.
5 A commitment to define and work with local problems within a broader ecological and regional framework, as well as over a longer period (three or more generations).
6 A specific identification with (reference to) the Earth Summit and Agenda 21.

Secondly it was stressed that activities which qualify as LA21 under these criteria represent a new phase in local environmental policy and implementation. Three different types or levels of environment-and-development activity were stipulated.

The first level refers to policies and initiatives which are primarily designed to either *conserve nature or improve and restore the environment*. They are initiatives which could have been taken prior to the publication of the report of the World Commission on Environment and Development (WCED, 1987) (commonly known as the Brundtland Report), and which are addressed to environmental concerns in a relatively narrow, more technical and more 'natural-science' type of perspective. Such activities are simply referred to as 'environmental initiatives': they are not presumed to reflect *any* of the above six characteristics.

The second level refers to initiatives which *specifically refer to the concept of 'sustainable development'* as expressed in the Brundtland Report; or which *use broad concepts such as 'global ecology'*, reflecting the general concerns of the Brundtland Commission without specifically using the terms and categories of the report itself. Such activities should reflect most or all the first five criteria above, and can be referred to as 'initiatives for sustainable development'. Most of these local initiatives would have been instigated in the period following the publication and dissemination of the Brundtland Report, that is between 1987 and 1992.[3]

At the third level, the project has identified *activities which make specific reference to the Earth Summit or Agenda 21*. Only these activities qualify, in the strict sense of the term, as an LA21. Such activities should reflect all six of the above criteria, and they should do so as a conscious attempt to implement the intentions of Chapter 28 of Agenda 21.

It should be stressed that this combination of 'guidelines' was developed to facilitate a common understanding of, and approach to, LA21. The differentiations in question proved necessary for the internal research dialogue of the research network, and laid a better foundation for more systematic reporting and comparative analyses. The original monitoring reports of the network revealed that there was *considerable* confusion as to what 'a Local Agenda 21' was thought to imply, particularly on the part of national governments in their reports to the United Nations Commission on Sustainable Development (UNCSD) (Lafferty and Eckeberg, 1998). It quickly became clear that if everything that had to do with either improving the environment or achieving 'sustainability' was to be categorised as an LA21, there would be no way to monitor and evaluate the impact of the Rio accords. The major differentiation that emerged in this regard was between, on the one hand, the first level of more 'traditional' environmental activities and, on the other, the second and third levels, both of which express the values and goals of 'sustainable development'.

Using these criteria the original network generated initial findings for Norway, Sweden, Finland, The Netherlands, The United Kingdom (UK), Ireland, Germany and Austria (Lafferty and Eckerberg, 1998). The activities and results from this phase were then channelled into a second phase, where the network was granted status as a 'concerted action' within the research programme on Environment and Climate (under the Fourth Framework Programme of the EC's Research Directorate-General – previously DGXII). The original network of eight countries was expanded to include Italy, Spain, Denmark and France, and the project was given the acronym SUSCOM.[4]

This book constitutes the final report of the SUSCOM project. It has been developed through a series of workshops and internet dialogues, whereby each country team has operated with two major tasks:

1. an updated overview of the status of implementation in each national case; and
2. a more case-specific focus on those aspects of the implementation process in each country which appear most distinct and relevant for a better understanding of the LA21 experience.

Building on a report issued in 1999, which updated the assessment for all 12 cases (Lafferty, 1999), the book provides overviews for each case, but concentrates mostly on drawing implications from research projects and outstanding features of each country. Whereas the descriptive aspect focuses on the practical lessons to be learned for a more effective realisation of LA21 in practice (the 'information goals' of the project), the analytical profiles for each country aim to cast light on underlying issues of broader academic and policy relevance (the 'knowledge goals'). While the former tend to emphasise specific 'barriers', 'incentives' and 'best cases', the latter relate to selected factors affecting policy implementation and the thorny issue of 'subsidiarity'.

In addition to maintaining an open website for the project, it was decided at an early stage that the concluding report should be subjected to more detailed feedback and discussion through a 'dialogue conference'. The format of the conference was to invite selected representatives – from government, NGOs, business and research institutions – from each country to read and discuss the draft chapters in open session.[5]

THE KNOWLEDGE GOALS OF THE PROJECT

As mentioned above, in addition to generating basic information as to the 'what and how' of LA21, the project has also aimed to produce insights as to the 'why and wherefore'. Three areas of more general relevance were thus identified as 'knowledge goals': *policy implementation, democracy and participation* and *subsidiarity*.

Policy implementation

Given the nature of Agenda 21 as an action plan, it was soon established in the research network that policy implementation would be the central academic reference point. Action plans have to be interpreted, structured, implemented, evaluated and revised. The prospect of realising the goals and ambitions of Agenda 21 is the type of task that policy analysts have been studying for decades. Given the ad hoc nature of the concerted action, with many different research agendas driving the individual national projects, it was decided that the network would aim to produce 'value-added' knowledge with respect to three key aspects of the implementation process: *global–local policy*, *central–local relations* and *environmental protection versus sustainable development*.

Global–local policy

LA21 is an integral part of a very particular type of global policy. It involves local authorities in trying to achieve the global policy goals adopted by over 150 governments at the Earth Summit. This means that the policy is external to existing knowledge on policy implementation. Most approaches to implementation analysis operate with either an explicit or implicit system model, whereby the factors affecting *policy input* are integral to an understanding of how *policy output and implementation* are carried through. Policy is seen as arising in a particular political and institutional context, and the structuring features of this context play a significant role in how policy is adopted and then put into operation.

In the case of LA21, however, it is clear that this did not exist as a policy issue prior to the Earth Summit. Chapter 28 of Agenda 21 was developed mainly by representatives of national organisations for local and regional authorities, international umbrella organisations for these authorities (IULA and ICLEI), or the administrative bodies related to UNCED. This gives LA21 (as a policy initiative) a particular 'outside-in' character. Whereas most implementation analyses begin with an understanding of the history of policy development within a given political context, an understanding of LA21 implementation must begin with an analysis of *interpretation and introduction into* the political process. This leaves considerable room for cross-national variation as to how, when and why the LA21 idea becomes salient and eventually integrated with national policies for either environmental improvement or sustainable development.

Some of the principal issues that can be raised are:

- What history, if any, was there of involvement by national associations of local and regional authorities in the preparation of Chapter 28 of Agenda 21?
- How much attention was given to LA21 by central authorities immediately after the Earth Summit?
- Is there evidence of attempts to specifically treat LA21 as a local manifestation of a global policy (for example, with North-South or East-West links)?
- What indications, if any, are there that LA21 contributes to the adoption of more ambitious local targets for sustainable development than those currently being pursued by national governments?
- Is there evidence of LA21 being influenced by policy initiatives from the EU?
- How has the introduction of LA21 been affected by factors of culture and existing party-political constellations?

Central–local relations

A second type of implementation problem is the debate as to how public policy is either *actually implemented* (the descriptive discourse) or *ideally implemented* (the normative discourse). A number of key concepts here are 'top-down' and 'bottom-up' steering, 'epistemological communities', 'target-group strategies' and 'multifaceted strategies of governance'. The project has focused on two major conditioning factors:

1 constitutional provisions for central, regional and local power sharing; and
2 more informal effects deriving from programmes of administrative reform, 'modernisation' and decentralisation, for example.

The goal here was to focus on the possible effects of these variables on LA21 initiatives. The core idea of LA21 involves a conscious attempt to combine a top-down initiative by local authorities with a clear bottom-up mobilisation of *local* stakeholders. The idea presupposes that these two aspects are mutually reinforcing, with the 'new dialogue' for sustainable development among local groups being channelled back into official planning and decision-making processes. Greater operative responsibility for target groups and affected interests must be joined with: budgetary and regulatory activity; cross-sector administrative coordination; and official monitoring and revision of long-term plans. LA21 can, therefore, be seen as a prototype at the local and regional level of its primary ambition at the national and global level: a 'new partnership for sustainable development'.

Major points of interest here are:

- The role played by central government as a facilitator of LA21.
- The nature of alliances between central, regional and local authorities in developing and implementing LA21.
- The effect of constitutional arrangements and administrative reforms on the profile of LA21 implementation.

Environmental protection versus sustainable development

It is an essential feature of the intent of Chapter 28 that the new dialogue, strategic planning and implementing programmes of LA21 should reflect *sustainable development and not traditional environmental protection.* This aspect has been a central feature of the internal dialogue within the research network. In line with the entire political and ideological thrust of the Earth Summit, it was necessary to distinguish between 'environment' and 'environment-and-development'. The types of issue which come into focus are:

- The nature of activities aiming to achieve cross-sector integration, both within the governing structures of local authorities and external to government in the form of stakeholder mobilisation and 'cooperative management regimes'.
- Innovative policies for sustainable production and consumption, both locally and with respect to global linkages.
- A greater awareness on the part of local authorities of the dependency between short-term economic dispositions and long-term consequences for environment and development.
- A broader application within local governance of the principles of resource management and biodiversity.

Planning and democratic participation

The second major issue that emerged during the first phase of the project had to do with issues of democratic planning and participation. LA21 is by nature a planning and democratisation reform, and much of what emerged from the preliminary country reports indicated the significant relevance of these issues. As indicated above, the core idea of Agenda 21 has largely been interpreted as either a strategic plan or a democratic reform, and it is often the interaction (and occasionally the conflict) between these two aspects which has characterised the implementation process.

Key questions to be raised here are:

- How and to what extent have LA21 activities affected participation, influence and power with respect to planning procedures and forms of local democracy?
- What new forms of participation have emerged through the LA21 process, and do they give promise of a more effective pursuit of sustainable-development goals?
- To what extent have LA21 initiatives incorporated new ideas of 'visioning', 'deliberative democracy', 'target-group steering', 'stakeholder democracy' and 'cooperative management regimes'?
- Has the new dialogue associated with LA21 functioned as a one-way consultation process (under the purview of local authorities), or have new foundations been laid for more interactive strategic partnerships and shared responsibility?

Subsidiarity

Finally, there is the very broad and complex issue of subsidiarity. Having devoted considerable time to the issue during the early phase of the project, the network gradually developed a double understanding of the principle: one with roots in a historical–philosophical discourse, and one with more immediate pragmatic–political relevance. In the first instance, subsidiarity refers to the idea that superordinate decision-making bodies should only exercise powers that are ostensibly necessary for securing a 'better' (more effective, more efficient, more morally correct) state of affairs for individuals and institutions at a lower level of organisation. The burden of proof in exercising this understanding of the principle is that the transfer of authority upwards gains its legitimacy from a necessary or desirable *additional contribution* that is not attainable through the efforts of lower-level domains.

The other connotation of subsidiarity is clearly more 'modern' and politically motivated. In many ways this understanding turns the first connotation on its head. Instead of arguing why it is necessary or desirable to provide subsidiary authority at a higher level of governance, its purpose is to argue for the moral necessity of keeping decision-making authority as close to local decision-makers as possible. What was originally a principle to justify a transfer of 'sovereignty' *upwards*, here becomes a principle to enhance democracy and protect sovereignty *downwards*: 'decisions should be taken as close as possible to the citizens affected by the decisions'.

Two aspects of this latter notion require further comment. Firstly, as derived and developed within the context of the EU, the lower level in question has been the nationstate. The debate has focused, in other words, on the division of powers between the supra-national bodies of the EU and the decision-making bodies of the member states. While there has been considerable discussion of the nature of regions within the EU, the principle of subsidiarity has not been seriously applied to either cross-national regional units or to sub-national units.

Secondly, the more political connotation of the principle also gives implicit expression to the first (more philosophical, legalistic) connotation. This is done through an underlying notion of either effectiveness or efficiency (CEPR, 1993). The decision that is to be taken closest to the people affected is to be *the best decision possible within the scope and functionality of that particular unit*. It should, in other words, be a democratic decision *that works*. The political principle of subsidiarity is (in the context of its origin during the debate over the Maastricht Treaty), not an open-ended admonition for radical local democracy, but a principle to protect *national* democracy from unnecessary incursions from the EU. The application of the principle thus carries with it the basic presumption of the more traditional connotation, that is, there exists an unavoidable need for transferring *some* powers upwards. The political (democratic) principle of subsidiarity only makes sense, in other words, if there is a preordained agreement as to the necessity of the pragmatic–legalistic (supra-national) principle of subsidiarity.

Given this understanding, the importance of the research project for the debate on subsidiarity emerged along the following lines:

- The commitment to the Earth Summit accords by the EU means that Agenda 21 achieves legitimacy as a form of 'supra-regional' legal subsidiarity vis-à-vis the Union.
- At the same time, LA21 becomes, by its very nature, a reflection of the political principle of subsidiarity, since the entire premise for Chapter 28 is that numerous aspects of sustainable development must be achieved at the level of the local (not the national) community.
- In a regional context, LA21 provides a legitimisation for establishing new transnational decision-making mechanisms to achieve effective steering of ecosystem problems not currently covered by existing political–administrative units (Regional Agenda 21).

All three of these dimensions mean that specific attempts to implement LA21 in Europe touch on both the potential benefits and practical problems of applying subsidiarity within the context of the Earth Summit action plan. Given the interdependent and holistic nature of ecological sustainable development, experiences in trying to realise Local and Regional Agenda 21 will reveal both the limits of subsidiarity as local democratic reform, and the necessity and desirability of subsidiarity as supra-ordinate capacity and entitlement. Sustainable development can only be achieved by combining democratic mobilisation and social learning at the local and national levels with more legitimate and effective steering at the regional and global levels. LA21 is therefore a specific admonition for political subsidiarity (Chapter 28) within an action plan (Agenda 21) designed to sanction and achieve global subsidiarity (through the Rio Principles).

These then are the major academic and policy-related themes underlying the different national efforts. Resources did not allow a concentrated research effort into each of the issues raised, but different aspects of the various problems emerged throughout the course of the project. More pointedly, it has been the specific purpose of this book to provide 'storylines' for each national experience; perspectives whereby the individual research teams tried to grasp the most distinct, interesting and relevant aspects of the implementation process. Value-added knowledge is thus provided in the form of substantive information as to how LA21 has actually been pursued, at the same time that the narrative for each country tries to relate the most salient aspects of the case to the issues raised above. The storylines are thus intended to reflect the national experience as viewed from the standpoint of ongoing research activities and commitments of the participant institutions, and do not reflect a common research design. The challenge for each team has primarily been to determine the profile of the storyline – so that this could stand alone as a contribution to a more pragmatic understanding of the LA21 experience – and then to try to present the storyline in such a way that a synthetic analysis of all cases could derive insights and perspectives for the knowledge goals.

This approach offers a fruitful model for the value-added ambitions of the concerted-action idea. This book is intended to provide a solid foundation for better practice in the area, as well as more specific cross-national efforts in the research areas of democratic studies, policy implementation and European integration.

NOTES

1 As adopted at the Earth Summit, *Agenda 21* is a document of approximately 470 pages. The official document is published as United Nations, 1993, but several other versions have been published; but it is interesting to note that, as of June 2000, none of these versions was available from internet booksellers. Fortunately, there is a version available on the internet at: www.un.org/esa/agenda21.

2 The activities of ICLEI are well-documented at the organisation's website: www.iclei.org.

3 As a concept for joining developmental with environmental concerns, the term 'sustainable development' was apparently used by Barbara Ward as early as the mid-1970s (Holmberg and Sandbrook, 1992). Dennis Pirage contributed to the further spread of the concept in his anthology on *The Sustainable Society* in 1977, and the International Union for the Conservation of Nature (IUCN) made it a central idea of its *World Conservation Strategy* in 1980 (see Dahle, 1997). It was not, however, until the idea was made the core concept of the Brundtland Report that it gained its current prominence and legitimacy (see Lafferty and Langhelle, 1999; Trzyna, 1995).

4 The 'work programme' for the project is available at: http://afux.prosus.nfr.no/la21/eu/program.html. It should be noted that a 'concerted action' is not a fully-funded research project, but rather a funding mechanism to promote 'value-added' knowledge within a network of established research interests. In other words, none of the members of SUSCOM has been specifically funded by the EC to do research in this area. Funding is limited to coordination and networking costs, with the assumption that the partner institutions are already carrying out research of direct relevance to the theme and issues of the research network. SUSCOM was not designed (or funded) to conduct original empirical research within the 12 participant countries. The fact that so much original data have been generated and reported within the framework of the project is testimony to the individual members of the research network and their institutions, as well as to the wisdom of the concerted-action model of funding.

5 The conference was held in Barcelona in November 1999. Representatives of 11 of the 12 countries in the research network were present (with nearly 60 participants in all). The German partner (the Wuppertal Institute) was forced to withdraw because of illness affecting the research team.

REFERENCES

Aalborg Charter (1994) Available at: www.iclei.org/europe/la21/echarter.htm

CEPR (1993) *Making Sense of Subsidiarity: How Much Centralization for Europe? Monitoring European Integration 4*, annual report, CEPR, London

Commission of the European Communities (1993) 'Towards Sustainability: A European Community programme of policy and action in relation to the environment and sustainable development', *Official Journal of the European Communities*, No C 138, pp5–98

Dahle, K (1997) *Forsøk for Forandring? Alternative Veier til et Bærekraftig Samfunn* ('Experiments for Change? Alternative Paths to a Sustainable Society'), Spartacus Forlag AS, Oslo

Holmberg, J and Sandbrook, R (1992) 'Sustainable Development: What is to be done?' in Holmberg, J (ed) *Policies for a Small Planet*, IIED/Earthscan, London

Lafferty, W M (ed) (1999) *Implementing LA21 in Europe*, ProSus, Oslo

Lafferty, W M and Eckerberg, K (eds) (1998) *From the Earth Summit to Local Agenda 21: Working towards Sustainable Development*, Earthscan, London

Lafferty, W M and Langhelle, O (eds) (1999) *Towards Sustainable Development: On the Goals of Development – and the Conditions of Sustainability*, Macmillan, London

Pirages, D (ed) (1977) *The Sustainable Society*, Praeger, New York

Trzyna, T (1995) *A Sustainable World: Defining and Measuring Sustainable Development*, IUCN – The World Conservation Union and the International Center for the Environment and Public Policy, Sacramento and Claremont

United Nations (1993) *Report of the United Nations Conference on Environment and Development, Rio de Janeiro, 3–14 June 1992, vol 1: Resolutions Adopted by the Conference*, United Nations, New York

WCED (World Commission on Environment and Development) (1987) *Our Common Future*, Oxford University Press, Oxford

1. Sweden
Problems and prospects at the leading edge of LA21 implementation

Katarina Eckerberg

Sweden could perhaps be labelled the leading country in Europe concerning the implementation of LA21. As suggested by a cross-country assessment of the status of LA21 in 12 European countries, Sweden appears to be in a category on its own. It shows the earliest start of all countries monitored and the highest proportion of local government units showing LA21 activity (Eckerberg, Coenen and Lafferty, 1999). One of the main factors explaining this success story is the comparatively high level of support towards LA21 from the national level of government, in the form of campaigns, finance and coordination. Since 1997 financial incentives for municipal action have increased with the government's investment programme for local initiatives towards ecological sustainability. This is part of the Social Democratic government's programme to build a Sustainable Sweden.

The rapid growth of LA21 in Swedish municipalities could thus be attributed to a top-down strategy from the national government, quite contrary to the notion of bottom-up initiatives and participatory approaches that characterise the LA21 concept. At the same time, the importance of grass-roots initiatives and involvement has been emphasised in the Swedish response to Agenda 21. In this chapter, the tensions and mutual dependency between the national and local level in designing and fulfilling the challenge of LA21 are explored. The following questions will be raised: how has LA21 been conceptualised by the national and local governments respectively? What role can the new national investment programme, aimed at the local level, play in furthering LA21 implementation? To what extent has LA21 implied new participatory approaches at the local level in planning for sustainable development, and thereby led to a revitalisation of local democracy in relation to environment-and-development policy? And finally, are there any tensions between the state programme and local initiatives that might create problems in the near future?

The chapter is divided into four sections. The first gives a general overview of the status of LA21 and introduces some of the main characteristics of its content as seen from the municipalities. Second, the national government's programme for Sustainable Sweden, and the local investment programme in particular, will be described and analysed in relation to LA21. Here, the national government's understanding of sustainable development will be compared with the municipal picture. Third, the extent to which local planning for sustainability has led to a greater use of participatory methods due to LA21 will be examined. The chapter ends with a section in which the problems and prospects of LA21 in a country at the leading edge of implementation will be discussed. The effects of the national investment programme will be contrasted with Agenda 21 work at the local level.

Methodologically, this research builds upon interviews with key actors at national and local levels of government, and with representatives from other organisations that are involved in the Agenda 21 process in Sweden. Four pioneer municipalities have been studied in depth over three years (Eckerberg and Forsberg, 1995 and 1998; Forsberg, 1999), and interviews were also carried out in another nine municipalities during 1999.[1] Various policy documents and reports from government authorities, NGOs and data from our own survey of the status of LA21 in 1998 (Brundin and Eckerberg, 1999), as well as in-depth interviews from the nine municipalities selected for a follow-up study in 1999 (Eckerberg and Brundin, 2000) are used.

THE STATUS OF LA21 IN SWEDEN: AN OVERVIEW

In late 1998, a research group headed by the author conducted a survey of all Swedish municipalities and the city-districts of Stockholm (achieving a 95 per cent response rate). In brief, the following questions were examined:

- What is the status of LA21 in Swedish municipalities?
- What areas and issues are contained in local work with LA21?
- What is the political impact of LA21 within the municipality?
- What support is received locally from the national level?

The Swedish government reported to the United Nations General Assembly Special Session (UNGASS) in June 1997 that all municipalities were underway with LA21 (Ministry of Environment, 1997). Even if this figure is exaggerated, there is no doubt that Agenda 21 has become a working concept in most Swedish municipalities. At the end of 1998, 56 per cent of them had formally adopted LA21 plans, the majority of which had been discussed in the municipal councils. The great majority have placed the coordination of LA21 directly under the municipal board, whereas only 33 of the 298 who responded had given this task to the environment and health board. This indicates that LA21 is perceived as something more than environmental work. More than 70 per cent of local authorities have employed a full-time or part-time LA21 coordinator, which means an increase from 1995 when about half of them had such a person employed. Most of the persons who are responsible for LA21 are environmental officers. There is a clear tendency to emphasise the 'green' aspects of Agenda 21 rather than the social and economic aspects, both at the local level and in national programmes. LA21 is largely perceived as a renewal, and an expansion, of environmental policy.

Most municipalities have not only planned for LA21, but have also taken action to meet its objectives. Four out of five municipalities have allocated special funding towards LA21 activities. Compared with the situation in 1995, the level of funding has increased somewhat, but there is a suggestion of a widening gap between pioneering municipalities and those who have cut back on staff and resources for LA21. About 30 per cent have reduced their inputs in terms of both funding and staff since 1996.

The activities included in LA21 have expanded over the past few years from being focused largely on waste and water management and 'green purchasing' to a range of issues including renewable energy, biological diversity, environmental management and auditing systems, and sustainability indicators. About half of the local authorities have initiated grass-roots activities, while quality of life and social welfare issues are manifest in about one-third of the LA21 cases. Almost all municipalities have tried to involve local citizens.

In almost 80 per cent of the municipalities, the initiative for LA21 comes from public authorities, but this does not mean that politicians and local citizens are inactive. In half of the municipalities, local politicians have shared the initiative, and in 40 per cent it has also come from the grass-roots. In our earlier studies, we noted that the pioneering municipalities are those that have managed to combine the presence of individual enthusiasts among local organisations and municipal officers with support from local politicians (Eckerberg and Forsberg, 1998). In general, the political interest for LA21 has not changed during the last few years but remains rather high. Moreover, there seems to be a consensus among the different political parties concerning these issues. The local elections that were held just prior to the time of the survey were not perceived to have had any substantial impact on the prioritisation of LA21 in municipal policy.

Education and information on LA21 are widespread in Sweden. Not only has it become an issue among the younger generation in many schools and day care centres, but the local authorities themselves have also made internal efforts. Local politicians have been reached in 55 per cent, municipal staff in 64 per cent, and managers in 38 per cent of the municipalities. As many as 46 per cent of the LA21 coordinators claim that they have educated all personnel, while 35 per cent claim to have educated all politicians. Even if these figures include education ranging from half-day sessions to ongoing efforts, it reflects a sincere attempt to spread the concept of LA21 within the municipality.

One way of evaluating the impact of LA21 is to examine the extent to which it has been integrated into the different municipal sectors. The most successful integration has occurred within day care centres, schools and centres of advanced education. Other prominent areas are environment and health, sanitation and waste, planning and building, water and sewage, property management and energy use –considered to be within 'traditional environmental policy'. However, only 11 per cent of the municipalities have integrated LA21 into roads and traffic policy, and even fewer have thought of LA21 within social and elderly care, or culture and leisure. Only a minority have integrated LA21 into the municipal budget process. Hence, LA21 is still far from making a political impact on the entire work of a municipality. One exception is structural planning: 52 per cent of the municipalities report that they have formally decided to integrate LA21 within the structural planning process. About 40 per cent of the respondents claim that this integration has been successfully achieved, while more judge that the integration has not taken place in reality, or only to a limited extent.

There is no doubt that Swedish municipalities have taken LA21 seriously. Progressing from an original planning stage, it is now being more actively implemented. However, our survey indicates a growing gap between pioneer municipalities, and those that are presently dismissing their coordinators and ceasing funding in the wake of UNGASS, the five-year follow-up of the Earth Summit (Rio+5) in New York 1997. There is no clear pattern as to the size, geographical location, socio-economic profile or other characteristics of the pioneer municipalities. Instead, it seems that local circumstances can create favourable conditions in terms of individual enthusiasts and political support towards LA21. The number of pioneer municipalities in Sweden remains roughly the same (between 40 and 60, depending on which criteria are used), representing up to one-third of the local authorities.

National initiatives: The investment programme

The investment programme was launched in the spring of 1997 by the Committee for Sustainable Development, a group of five young ministers who were appointed in January 1997 by the new Social Democratic Prime Minister, Göran Persson. He had announced in his inauguration speech in September 1996 that 'Sweden shall be a lead country in implementing ecologically sustainable development'.[2] The committee consisted of ministers from the Departments of the Environment, Education, Labour

Market, Agriculture, and Finance, led by the Minister of the Environment.[3] It was decided to allocate 5.4 billion SEK over three years for municipal initiatives towards reduced pollution of the environment, more effective use of energy and natural resources, increased use of renewable raw materials, increased recycling and more jobs (Rskr, 1996/97:13). This came about partly as a response to the criticism from the municipalities that little money had been provided from the national government to help towards local sustainable-development efforts. Another two billion was added in the spring budget of 1999, and, at the same time, Parliament decided to extend the programme until the year 2001. With some reallocations of funding in the 1999 budget, the total financial support to municipalities from this investment programme from 1988 to 2001 is 6.77 billion SEK (about 0.8 billion Euro) (Parliamentary Auditors, 1999).

Local authorities and associations of local authorities may apply for this funding, but are encouraged to seek collaboration with local industry and interested organisations. Finance is provided towards local investment programmes that contain measures supporting an ecologically sustainable development. According to the government directive, the reason why only municipalities can apply for the funding is the need for a holistic perspective. The investments at the local level should be seen as part of a larger national programme for building a Sustainable Sweden. Therefore, in addition to the 6.77 billion SEK for local investments, another 1 billion SEK was allocated towards 'eco-cycling' – the sustainable use, reuse, recycling and disposal of resources without damage to the environment – measures within buildings and infrastructure, and about 9 billion SEK was provided for renewable-energy and energy-efficiency projects for the period from 1997 to 2004. The new strategy from the government is to combine environmental goals with labour-market policy. It has been inspired by the need for creating 'green jobs' and strengthening the economy (Eriksson, 1996).

These investments can be compared with an annual national budget of roughly 1.2 billion SEK for public expenditure in the environmental sector. Only a very small part of this money goes to the local level in support for environmental work. The main funding for environment administration at the municipal level is provided by local taxes and revenues. The new money thus represents a considerable strengthening of the national government's role in Sweden's environmental administration, monitoring and nature conservation at the local level. Traditionally, the selection of environmental projects to be supported is performed by the Swedish Agency for Environmental Protection or by the county administrations. However, in the case of the new local investment programme, the selection of projects to be financed is made directly by the Committee for Sustainable Development through the Ministry of the Environment. This is a totally new approach in Sweden,[4] taking away the administrative function from the agency and moving it into the ministry. As such, it has been criticised for introducing 'ministerial rule' into Sweden, with all that this implies for a more politicised government administration.

The investment programme was, however, not the first financial support provided by the national government to local initiatives. Starting in 1994, a total of 100 million SEK was allocated by the National Environmental Protection Agency (NEPA) to local governments and local businesses for 30 per cent of their costs for projects towards ecological development. From 1994 to 1996, there was also a special annual fund of 7 million SEK for LA21 projects carried out by local governments and local NGOs. The demand for this funding was large, with the number of applications reaching over 500 in 1995.

According to the Programme for a Sustainable Sweden, three overall objectives were adopted, which also define the government's conceptualisation of ecologically sustainable development:

1 Environmental protection through 15 national goals for environmental quality, whereby human health and the state of the environment should be decisive for future development;
2 Efficient use of material and energy resources, and a reduction in the use of non-renewable resources;
3 Sustainable provision of natural resources through support towards renewable resources and eco-cycling principles (Rskr, 1998/99:5).

In addition to these goals, the local investment programme was to contribute to the objective of cutting unemployment by half by the year 2000. However, it is not clear what proportion of the reduction should be borne by the investment programme compared with other labour market policy measures. More specifically, a municipality can apply for funding towards measures that are aimed at:

- Reducing environmental pressure on nature.
- Increasing the efficient use of energy and natural resources.
- Supporting the use of renewable resources.
- Increasing recycling and reuse of materials.
- Protecting and strengthening biological diversity and cultural heritage.
- Improving the circulation of nutrients within systems.

In direct connection with the above measures, support may also be given to:

- Local industry as well as administration.
- Local educational efforts.
- Architectural values and refurbishing of deprived housing areas.
- Gender equality.

The latter types of support must, however, be in line with the overall goal of ecologically sustainable development and also be tied to a specific investment. The municipalities and their partners must themselves provide matching funds. The share of national funding in relation to the total investment cost varies depending on the type of measure, as well as on how much support the municipality applies for. For example, industrial measures receive a smaller share of the national contribution while broader cross-sectoral programmes receive more.

According to the Ministry of the Environment, priority is given to local investments that are part of an integrated programme for local sustainability as well as fulfilling the above criteria. Thus, the investment should both imply a durable and physical improvement of the environment and generate new jobs. A direct connection is also made to LA21:

> *'Local support is required in order for the ecological dimension within societal development to succeed'* and *'Local Agenda 21 work should be brought into the investment programme'* (Government Bill, 1997/98:1).

> *'The investment programme has a direct linkage to Local Agenda 21 work. Hereby a connection is made between the local level and national decision-making within the Cabinet and the Parliament'* (SOU, 1997:105).

During the first year (1998), all but two of Sweden's 288 municipalities applied for funding. About 2.3 billion SEK was allocated to a total of 460 such local projects in 42 municipalities. In addition, a sum of 50,000 SEK was given to small municipalities who would otherwise have difficulty finding the local resources required for developing a new application. In 1999, another 1.4 billion SEK was allocated to 47 municipalities. The total sum, including investments from the municipal level, reached 17 billion SEK for the two years. On average, the national share varied between 12 and 100 per cent in the 1998 allocation, with an average of 31 per cent of the total investment. In 1999 the national share of the total funding varied between 14 and 65 per cent, but the average remained the same (Parliamentary Auditors, 1999). Table1.1 summarises the allocation of national funding for both years.

To what extent can these investments be classified as, or connected with, LA21? To what extent do the types of measures that are supported coincide with the content of LA21 and to what extent have the municipalities, that have received funding, involved LA21 coordinators and networks in the design of their applications?

Table 1.1 shows that about 30 per cent of the already distributed subsidies are within the building sector; 30 per cent towards energy-efficiency and renewable energy; and the remaining 40 per cent to a mixture of

Table 1.1 *Allocation of national funding in the investment programme for local sustainable development*

Type of measure	*Percentage of national allocation*
Renewable energy (mostly support to bioenergy plants and district heating)	21
Multi-dimensional projects (mostly environmental adaptation of housing areas and recycling within new building constructions)	17
Energy efficiency (both within housing areas and the re-use of industrial energy)	10
Waste management (mostly biogas plants)	10
Water and sewage (support to eco-cycling)	10
Cleaning up of hazardous wastes, restoration	10
Traffic (mostly support to use biogas for fuel and create cycle paths)	9
Biological diversity and nature protection	6
Buildings and housing (refurbishing of deprived housing areas)	4
Supportive functions (administration, education)	3

Source: Parliamentary Auditors, 1999

investments towards communications, waste, restoration, water and nature protection, and information and education. This means that in the practical allocation of funding within the investment programme, there is a clear bias towards 'ecological modernisation'. The municipal LA21 coordinators are not convinced that this corresponds with the priorities made locally within LA21. Almost half of them either did not know or thought it was not at all useful, and only 5 per cent found that the investment projects coincided with LA21 work (see Table 1.2). Apart from activities related to environmental policy, LA21 includes a greater emphasis on schools, daycare centres, grass-roots projects, lifestyles and social welfare, and cooperation with Eastern Europe. Such activities are not found in the investment programme. On the whole, there is a discrepancy between the national programme, which emphasises environmental goals and eco-efficiency, and LA21, which contains a much broader range of activities. This difference is not as distinct in the above criteria for the investment programme as it is in practice; that is, in the prioritisation of measures that have been funded. According to the follow-up by the Swedish National Audit Office, there are many examples where local priorities in the municipalities' applications for the investment programme have been changed in favour of the national goals and criteria. This is not surprising, since the municipalities tend to go where the money is. Hence,

Table 1.2 *To what extent do the projects that have been allocated funding from the local investment programme coincide with LA21 work?*

Response	Percentage of municipalities
To a great extent	5
Partly	48
Not at all	10
Do not know	38

n = 282

those municipalities that have developed multifaceted programmes that combine local interests with the criteria for the investment programme are the winners in this competition.

On the connection between LA21 and the investment programme in terms of who has been involved in its design, the picture is more varied among the municipalities. Among the nine municipalities that we have investigated in greater depth, four had built on LA21 networks to elaborate their application for the investment programme. Two had not connected the application to LA21, while the remaining three municipalities had developed their application within other municipal units, but with a clear linkage to LA21. The majority had involved various local groups in the design of their application. According to our survey, there was a greater emphasis on local industry in the local investment programme compared with the involvement of various groups in LA21 (see Tables 1.3 and 1.4).

Several of our respondents in the nine municipalities studied point out that the investment programme has raised the status of LA21 work. Indeed, there is evidence in the follow-up by the Swedish National Audit Office that many of the most advanced municipalities succeeded in using the investment programme to support and bring forward previously planned activities. In these cases, there has often been a broad involvement of local organisations and industry, and even local citizens, in the development of the application for the investment programme. LA21

Table 1.3 *Which groups have been involved by the municipality in the 1999 application for the local investment programme?*

Response	Percentage of municipalities
Industry and business	76
Local NGOs, interest groups and movements	39
Local citizens	57
Others	45

n = 258

Table 1.4 *Which groups have been involved by the municipality in the LA21 work through special activities?*

Response	*Percentage of municipalities*
Children and youth	70
Educational associations	64
Merchants and trade associations	63
Industry	62
Environmental groups	51
Neighbourhood councils and grass-roots	50
Farmers and forest associations	41
Humanitarian and church organisations	31
Women	20
Minority groups	19
Universities and polytechnic schools	18
Trade unions	18
Others	18

n = 259

networks have been used and strengthened, and environmental work has been given higher priority both within the municipality itself, and within local industry. In some cases, the investment programme has also spurred regional collaboration among municipalities. Those municipalities with the strongest background in environmental work are also the ones that best manage to set local priorities and make the investment programme fit ongoing local activities (Swedish National Audit Office, 1999). Our interviews confirm that some pioneer municipalities have succeeded in combining certain LA21 activities with the investment programme, thus giving additional support to particular aspects. We have also found some evidence that municipalities that have connected LA21 to their application for the investment programme have been given priority by the national allocation of funding.

At the same time, there are some apparent losers within the investment programme, especially among the small-size municipalities and those with a less-established environmental profile. Many of our respondents witness how difficult it is for those municipalities with limited staff and resources to develop an application that fits the national requirements for funding. In the first round of grants, a small sum (50,000 SEK) was allocated to small-size municipalities to help towards this end, but they are still behind. Another type of loser can be found among those local groups and movements that engage in solidarity issues and issues related to education and social welfare within the LA21 movement. Due to the emphasis on technical and industrial aspects of environmental improvements, certain groups have been favoured at the expense of others. Even the well established Swedish Society for Conservation of Nature has only been involved in about one-third of all municipalities' design of their first application (SSCN, 1998). In particular, the educational side has been neglected, although much of the restructuring process towards a sustainable society concerns environmental attitudes and behaviour. There was much criticism of this neglect in the first round of allocations from the investment programme, and the second round allocated slightly more money towards information and education. Nevertheless, the requirement that any informational activities must be directly connected to a particular physical investment still remains, and this probably inhibits municipalities from involving a broader range of local interest groups and social movements.

The 19 per cent of the municipalities that were given a share of the investment programme in the first round are very ambivalent about its influence on the preconditions for LA21 work. Only 16 per cent of them say that it has been of great influence, 23 per cent of moderate influence, 31 per cent of slight influence, and as many as 26 per cent claim that it is of no influence at all. Over 60 per cent of all respondents in our survey were still largely unsatisfied with the government's support towards LA21. Moreover, the great majority of municipalities have not been reached by external funding for LA21 (Brundin and Eckerberg, 1999). The picture of a growing gap between pioneers and laggards is confirmed in our interviews. Hence, it seems likely that LA21 and the local investment programme could grow apart in the near future unless the allocation from the national programme is revised to reflect local priorities. There is also a danger that those municipalities that have reduced their efforts in LA21 will also lose out in the competition for national support.

In Stockholm, several of the city councils' LA21 coordinators have now abandoned the idea of applying for national funding towards local investments. They refer to budget restrictions, which prevent investments in a situation where public expenditure exceeds the local tax income. They were required by the municipality of Stockholm to contribute 50 per cent of the cost in order to be included in the Stockholm investment programme. Most Swedish municipalities are currently struggling to make ends meet, and to provide even basic funding to schools, care of the elderly and other municipal tasks. Nevertheless, it has been possible in some municipalities to combine local programmes for energy or environmental improvement technologies with the new national programme. For example, in the municipalities of Hjo and Luleå, the LA21 coordinators are quite satisfied with the connection between LA21 and the activities supported by the investment programme. The LA21 coordinator from Hjo, however, notes that measures to support gender equality and quality of life are not included in the national programme. Likewise, the LA21 coordinator from Luleå emphasises the fact that grass-roots activities are not supported – only physical investments. Other municipalities are critical of the fact that the investment programme is much more bureaucratic than LA21 and requires cooperation between traditional bureaucrats within the municipality and LA21 activists. This may not be so easy to achieve.[5]

Furthermore, the competitive element in receiving funding from the investment programme may create tensions between municipalities and reduce the transparency between municipalities in their contacts with the Ministry of the Environment during the selection procedure. In addition, small-size municipalities may stand lesser chances of financing both in terms of finding enough resources and expertise to develop the application, and in terms of providing the necessary local finance (Parliamentary Auditors, 1999). Our interviews indicate that a wider range of projects might have materialised if the national allocation had been distributed more widely among all municipalities according to size, rather than with this competitive element. The signals from the national level might, by now, have steered the municipalities' applications towards more traditional environmental projects compared with those that would have been developed without nationally set priorities.

Evaluations recently made by the state auditors show that the introduction of this new procedure has not been without problems. In particular, the follow-up of impacts on the environment as well as on the creation of new jobs is severely questioned. Satisfactory control and evaluation mechanisms have not been developed. The decision procedure is criticised for inadequate transparency and too little use of expertise outside the Ministry of the Environment. The various sector agencies have hardly been consulted in this process, and there is also great uncertainty about how the investment programme might skew competition within the environment sector (Swedish National Audit Office, 1999). The traditional division of work between the ministry and the sector agencies is turned on its head, which contradicts the government's aspirations during the 1990s towards a comprehensive system of goal-steering. It becomes difficult to distinguish the government from the administration, which challenges political legitimacy and traditional roles of responsibility. In addition, the principles of decentralisation and local autonomy are broken down by this new procedure (Parliamentary Auditors, 1999). The procedure allows the state to keep itself in the spider's position within the 'web', controlling the dialogue with municipalities (Lundqvist, 2001).

As previously mentioned, the local investment programme was launched to help solve two problems: environmental sustainability, as defined by the 15 national goals, and unemployment. To fulfil two such divergent goals in one programme is probably an impossible task. Those municipalities that have received funding during the first two years have calculated that 11,500 new jobs will be created during the years 1998–2001 through the investment programme. These figures are most likely overestimated, since they have not been checked by the national and regional agencies responsible for labour market policy. On the one hand, it may be noted that the new jobs have largely been created within the building sector and not, for example, within traditionally female-dominated areas, such as health care, schools and care for the elderly, which are also in need of investments. On the other hand, the technical and building sectors are perhaps major examples of areas in which LA21 has not been very successful, and the investment programme could thus contribute to bringing in sustainable-development initiatives in these male-dominated sectors. The gender perspective could be interesting to explore further in future research, especially since it is one of the objectives of the programme.

Similarly, the environmental effects of the investment programme are insecure and poorly calculated. It will be very difficult, if not impossible, to evaluate the extent to which the investment programme has reached its goals (Parliamentary Auditors, 1999). Currently, figures of those in employment are rising in Sweden, as is the case in much of Europe. Perhaps this programme has already fulfilled the purpose of demonstrating political initiative within the new Social Democratic government, and bringing in the support from the Green Party. The conclusion from the state auditors' evaluations and our own interviews is that the national programme has moved the emphasis more towards ecological modernisation within the municipalities' LA21 work, since such activities can more easily be justified as physical investments that create jobs. Many of these projects would probably have been conducted even without national support, since they are in line with a general trend in Sweden of creating incentives for reducing material and energy use within industry, as well as an increased consumer pressure towards green products.

Support from the national level – government, agencies and coordinating institutions – is crucial in order to change development at the local level towards sustainability. Only one out of four municipalities in the survey thought that this support is quite good, while most said it was incomplete or insufficient. According to the survey, the regional associations of local authorities and the Swedish Association of Local Authorities have been the most supportive. About a quarter of the respondents said that the Swedish Environmental Protection Agency and the National Agenda 21 Committee (established in 1995) had been of great assistance. There is a general despair among LA21 coordinators that their work is not followed up through national policies. Also, the lack of funding and personnel within municipalities is pointed out as a major obstacle. About one-fifth of the municipalities have received external funding for their LA21 work. Some of this is channelled through the new investment programme for ecological restructuring. However, as the above discussion has shown, it is unlikely that this programme will reduce the gap between local expectations and national support for the LA21 movement.

LOCAL INITIATIVES: PARTICIPATION AND PLANNING FOR SUSTAINABILITY

This section looks further into the extent to which local planning for sustainability within LA21 has led to greater use of participatory methods. The motives for increasing citizen involvement are discussed and some of the methods that are used within the LA21 work are described. A short background to the current debate on democracy within Sweden, however, is necessary.

No issue has been so extensively discussed within societal planning as citizen participation (Khakee, 1999). The political debate in the 1990s in Sweden has revitalised the issues of representative democracy and public participation through a number of central initiatives. A governmental commission on democracy has recently produced a long list of reports on how Swedish society works in this respect. The Swedish Association of Local Authorities has initiated a special programme on local development and participatory democracy. The campaign 'All of Sweden Should Live', which was introduced in the late 1980s, created favourable conditions for a bottom-up movement to develop the dialogue between citizens and politicians within local society.

These efforts should be seen as a direct response to falling numbers of members in political parties; decreased turnout in national and local elections; growing problems of legitimacy within the political process; and reduced confidence in political leadership among citizens. Increasing citizen participation can thus been seen as a reaction against a declining belief among many citizens that representative democracy can solve societal problems. In a recent series of government commission reports, a variety of new methods are suggested for revitalising democracy within Swedish society (SOU, 2000).[6]

In democratic theory, two main arguments for public participation can be discerned:

- A democratic right for citizens to be involved in the public-policy process.
- Participation can increase efficiency within the policy process and create 'better implementation' (Pennington and Rydin, 2000).

The first argument says that all citizens should have the right to get their voice heard in a functioning democracy. This is a way of increasing legitimacy in the policy process and creating a higher degree of consensus. It can also be justified by the need for empowerment of different societal groups in policy-making; that is a normative argument.

The second argument is based on a desire to improve the achievement of policy goals, to avoid unintended or unwanted effects and to ensure that the costs for goal attainment should not be unreasonably high in relation to the benefits. Participation can then be a way to increase the information on local preconditions and preferences, since the local citizens have access to a range of knowledge about how to succeed in implementation which the local politicians and public officers may not possess themselves. With efficiency in mind, participation can help reduce the level of conflict throughout the implementation process, not only to increase legitimacy but also to counteract any disputes or delays that may create further costs (Pennington and Rydin, 2000).

Within LA21 public participation becomes important in creating consensus about what should be done and how. Participation may be viewed as the only way to take genuine consideration of highly diverse needs, as for example from different societal groups to future generations and even non-human interests such as plants and animals. How this should be done in practice, however, is difficult. For example, who should represent these interests and also find forms for conflict resolution? The understanding of cause and effects of various environmental problems and knowledge about what a sustainable society requires demand strong support from the state and local authorities to educate a broad range of groups (Baker, 1999).

Policy design within LA21 and Sustainable Sweden thus requires both a widened definition of who should be involved and of the distinction between public and private spheres. Many of the greatest challenges concern lifestyles and consumption patterns, which traditionally have been seen as private decisions. A constructive dialogue between many groups in society is needed, not only between experts and political decision-makers. From the 1960s, attempts have been made in all Western societies to increase public participation in environmental policy and physical planning. Repeatedly, it has proved difficult to find methods to involve diverse groups of people. The well educated and well organised tend to establish good contacts with public officers and thereby promote their interests (Pennington and Rydin, 2000). Contrary to the idea of public participation as a way to increase efficiency, it may also delay the planning process and create increased costs both for decision-making and for implementation, at least in the short term. Therefore, in practice, many planning officers are reluctant to involve citizens other than as recipients of information (Khakee, 1999).

In Swedish municipalities, political parties and traditional social movements now leave room for a range of new interest groups, including one-issue groups, 'rescue actions' and youth movements that sometimes favour non-parliamentary methods and work outside the establishment. These new groups have great difficulty in influencing state and local government institutions. Even when attempts are made to bring more people into the planning process, there are many obstacles to creating a two-way communication between citizens and local government representatives. However, LA21 within Swedish municipalities implies a greater emphasis on public participation that might lead to a change in this respect.

As described in the above section, almost all of the municipalities have made efforts to involve a broad range of groups in the LA21 work. The methods used are varied, and sometimes innovative. Over 70 per cent of the local authorities have provided information about LA21 to households in the form of brochures and newsletters, for example. About the same number have arranged exhibitions and market events, and provided information through local newspapers. Additionally, courses, meetings and seminars are frequently used. Many have arranged special forums or meeting places, through which local citizens can contact municipal officers. Workshops devoted to 'visioning' for the future have been used in one out of five municipalities, and consultation conferences have taken place in almost one-third. About one out of four municipalities have employed a special person to give information about Agenda 21. The municipalities' internet home pages are also frequently used to provide information about LA21. On the whole, these figures are quite impressive and show that it is a well-known concept at the local level.[7]

How does this public participation work in practice? Is it mostly one-way information from the municipality to the local citizens about what has been decided, like previous procedures for public participation in municipal planning (Khakee, 1999), or does it involve new elements of participatory democracy? In an attempt to answer this, examples are selected from the interviews we have carried out in nine selected municipalities, which range from large to small, and some of which have received funding from the investment programme. They represent a rough cross-section of the total picture. The examples are taken from those activities that involve two-way communication between local administration and citizens, rather than more general information campaigns and gatherings, even if the latter may be effective for educational purposes and in raising the level of consciousness within the local society. Thus, all of the municipalities studied have used a variety of one-way communication methods, but it is the citizens' involvement in the decision-making that we examine in more detail here.

Consultation groups have been created for LA21 in four (Gotland, Nacka, Uppsala and Luleå) of the nine municipalities studied. They represent new approaches to public participation, aimed at soliciting ideas from local citizens rather than just informing them. It may be noted that these are all middle-size units, and that two of them (Gotland and Luleå) are also 'eco-municipalities', which means that they have joined the network of about 50 municipalities in Sweden who are trying to achieve more ecologically friendly activities.

In the rural municipality of Gotland, an island in the Baltic Sea, an environment council was created in the early 1990s as a network for various NGOs, environmental groups and representatives from all local political parties to discuss environmental policy issues. It should be mentioned that Gotland has chosen to use the eco-municipality concept, rather than LA21, to label local environment-and-development activities. There were already ongoing grass-roots initiatives before the Earth Summit that could be built upon and strengthened through the international movement. The municipality decided to combine the eco-municipality concept with a local action plan for LA21 and to use the environment council as a way to consult with the local citizens. When the LA21 plan was developed, many of the ideas emanated from about one year's interaction with local business, building enterprises, households and interest groups. During this process, weekly reports about Agenda 21 were published in the local newspapers according to 12 different themes. The local educational associations were also involved in this work. The proposals were then discussed within the environment council before the final document was adopted. More recently, however, the interest for environmental issues has declined and the local newspapers are no longer as active.

In Nacka, one of Stockholm's city-councils, a similar environment council was formed in 1995 on the initiative of the municipal environment board, and various organisations, individuals and firms were invited to work on different themes. The local politicians chose not to participate, but to wait for ideas from the council. But the suggestions that came from the council were found to be in conflict with those of the politicians. Old antagonisms and party cleavages surfaced and created a sharp contrast between the council and the politicians. The result was that no LA21 was adopted. Nevertheless, in the local planning processes, citizens have become involved in the design of certain residential areas. One area concerned the creation of ecologically adapted housing, while another affected the creation of a wetland area in connection to a housing area. Both these activities were regarded as part of the LA21. However, enthusiasm for LA21 in Nacka is now decreasing. The environment board has been dismantled; the municipal budget is strained and the LA21 coordinator has resigned.

The university town of Uppsala put considerable effort into involving citizens in the process of developing its LA21 plan. At the initiative of the municipal council, it formed citizen consultation groups to cover issues such as traffic, industry and consumption. Municipal officers participated, as did representatives from NGOs and interested individuals. The bottom-up perspective had already been prevalent in the start-up of LA21 work in 1994. The consultation groups worked hard for over a year and produced many investigative reports and proposals. The traffic group was particularly constructive. In some of the groups, conflicts surfaced when the proposals were presented to the politicians. Even if the politicians felt responsible for what had been suggested, they could not share all the suggestions. Eleven reports were published from the consultation groups and circulated for review, and the LA21 plan was developed from this work. However, it is unclear how Uppsala will continue and implement this plan. The previous municipal LA21 secretariat has recently been abolished. Many of the posts for 'environmental ambassadors', who were employed on a temporary basis to inform citizens about LA21, have now ceased. Instead, LA21 is to become integrated into all the municipal sectors.

As in Uppsala, the northern industrial town of Luleå elaborated its LA21 plan following extensive participation. They combined employment measures in the form of environmental guides, who would answer questions about LA21 and inform citizens through round-table discussions on what should be included in the work. Invitations were sent out to all citizens to participate in these discussions over seven different issues, which had been identified by the municipal environmental section. About 200 local citizens participated in the round-table discussions, which were conducted in early 1997 after a series of public presentations. Special efforts were made to make the round-table groups as diverse as possible in relation to gender, age, education and profession. The results of the seven groups were presented to the environmental section, which then finalised the LA21. The plan was also discussed within the municipality's different sectors during several days of internal education.

Later, Luleå also developed its own sustainability indicators as a way to measure progress and channel information back to the local citizens about what had been achieved. They were formulated in a two-way process between the municipal officers and the local inhabitants. A total of 80 potential indicators were developed during a new series of round-table discussions. These were reduced to 30 by the municipal environmental section and then presented to the public. A local referendum was held, in which 700 people participated, to select those ten indicators that would best reflect local concerns. The purpose of this process was to create broader acceptance and understanding of the indicators within the local community. Nevertheless, similar to the previous municipalities, Luleå also reports less interest in LA21 and environmental work. Environment seems to be less in fashion among local business as compared with the mid-1990s.

General experience from our municipalities, which has also been noted in previous studies, is that the message of sustainable development must be as simple as possible. Many LA21 coordinators report difficulties in generating public interest concerning complex environmental problems or overall municipal planning. It is much easier to create interest in questions related to the immediate neighbourhood than those related to, for example, transboundary environmental problems. It is also difficult to maintain interest among local citizens over long periods. There tends to be a wave of inspiration within the local community that can easily erode, especially when the benefits from engaging are either insecure or may show up only after a very long time. Thus, in many of the municipalities studied, even where great efforts were made to create conditions for participatory democracy, the results are often discouraging in terms of maintaining this interest.

It must be emphasised that the new relations between local administrations and civil society, which are developing from LA21, can be described as a process of trial-and-error. It appears that many municipalities have placed too much confidence in traditional information strategies to reach the local citizens. Research shows that information materials provided by mailings to households are seldom read, except by those who are already convinced (Bennulf, 1996). Likewise, new environmental teams tend to engage previously motivated people, rather than those who need to change their attitudes towards the environment. It is therefore important to use those organisations that already exist, and that the citizens trust and enjoy being members of. In many municipalities, including those that we have studied, attempts have been made to involve a large number of local organisations in the information strategies, rather than creating new channels. For example, sports clubs, tenants' associations and the church have shown their interest in participating in local environmental work. This is probably a promising strategy for establishing LA21 within the local society.

THE FUTURE: PROBLEMS AND PROSPECTS

The above analysis shows substantial differences between national and local understanding of sustainable development. In the investment programme, which is supposed to connect to LA21, certain measures are supported at the expense of others. Moreover, it combines the two goals of environmental protection and eco-efficiency with the creation of new jobs. This means that it does not cover the criteria that we have developed to distinguish LA21 from pure 'environmental initiatives' (Lafferty and Eckerberg, 1998). In other words, the investment programme is launched to 'conserve nature and/or improve and redress the environment', which represents a narrow, more technical and more 'natural-science' type of perspective (ibid).

The criteria for support from the investment programme do not indicate that the investments should address underlying political and economic pressures; connect to global impacts, solidarity and justice; achieve cross-sectoral integration of environment-and-development concerns; or address local problems within a broader ecological and regional framework or an expanded time frame. The only criterion in the investment programme that coincide with our criteria for LA21 is the objective to increase community involvement. However, with the investment programme, the participation of local industry and NGOs is required to ensure successful implementation rather than to promote participatory democracy. Efficiency is emphasised at the expense of the democratic goal.

There is a built-in paradox within the investment programme related to efficiency. With the creation of a new institutional procedure for deciding which projects should be winners in the competition for the 6.77 billion SEK, expertise within the various agencies is not used. Moreover, a strategy for measuring the attainment of policy goals is yet to be seen. If such a strategy does not exist, there is no way that the programme can be evaluated. Perhaps it will go the same way as the 'Recycling Billion Programme' – the billion Swedish kroner that disappeared![8] This is hardly a way of achieving efficiency and legitimising further support for a Sustainable Sweden among voters.

According to theories of collective action and social capital, the state should try to play the role of a facilitator rather than a controller. If the state takes over most of the decisions related to LA21, there would be few incentives for local groups and citizens to take part. Instead, they would wait for the state, or the local authority, to solve the problems for them. Also, there would be few reasons for local citizens to build-up local structures and networks for collaboration, creation of trust and internal control mechanisms. Therefore, the state should be careful not to push for ready-made solutions in terms of institutional arrangements and norms of behaviour. Local citizens should themselves be stimulated to develop the rules, norms and organisations within the local community to solve the problems.

In this respect, the local investment programme is counterproductive. It provides a strict framework for how investments towards ecological sustainability should be perceived and organised. Since it involves such massive financial benefits to poor local authorities, which are struggling to make ends meet, the state programme can hardly be seen as an objective facilitator. The programme clearly steers local activities towards certain objectives, rather than facilitating local priorities and initiatives. When those initiatives and priorities coincide with the investment programme, all is fine. However, there is reason to believe that many municipalities have changed their priorities according to what could be supported from the national level. The core idea of LA21, building on local concerns, is thus challenged.

According to our findings, the investment programme can play at least three different roles in relation to LA21. First, as we can see from many municipalities, it can spur LA21 efforts and play a supportive role to local initiatives for sustainable development. In this case, there is a mutual dependency between the two that leads to positive outcomes in both processes.

Second, there are signs that it can take over LA21, thus moving initiatives and implementation of environment-and-development work from the LA21 coordinators and their partners to other formations at the local level, notably within the more technical and industrial sectors. In this case, national priorities could override local concerns within LA21 and the coordination function would be tilted towards national government rather than local authorities.

The third option is the continuation of LA21 initiatives regardless of the investment programme. In several of the municipalities studied, the implementation of LA21 seems to be entering a new phase of increased integration. In this situation, the local level may be able to continue its LA21 work even if national support is not provided. However, there are signs of shrinking resources in some of these municipalities. It is difficult, therefore, to say whether this merging of LA21 into the daily work can succeed without some kind of national government back-up in terms of goal-setting or special resources.

There is no doubt that LA21 has contributed to a revitalisation of democratic methods in relation to environment-and-development policy. Many, but not all, municipalities have introduced new participatory approaches in planning for sustainable development, but the majority can be characterised as one-way information and education rather than two-way communication and active partnerships. Moreover, several municipalities that have tried to involve their citizens in planning have had great difficulty in sustaining this engagement.

It is clear that the gap between pioneer and laggard municipalities is increasing. The investment programme seems to encourage such differentiation rather than help those municipalities that have few staff and resources to manage comprehensive LA21 programmes. More support to municipalities that lag behind might be required if sustainable-development goals are to be attained in Sweden, as in the case of similar recent redistributions of local tax revenues from richer municipalities to those in greatest need. The growing gap between Swedish municipalities in relation to their environment-and-development work is perhaps as challenging as are the growing social cleavages within Sweden and the increasing municipal budget deficits, leading to a dismantling of public welfare. In other words, the 'success story' may be viewed from at least two sides.

The four modes of LA21 involvement in Sweden are summarised in Box 1.1.

Box 1.1 Four modes of LA21 involvement in Sweden

- Consultation groups have been created for LA21 in four municipalities: Gotland, Nacka, Uppsala and Luleå. The groups aim at soliciting ideas from local citizens, rather than just informing them.
- In the municipality of Gotland, an environmental council was created in the early 1990s as a network for various NGOs, environmental groups and representatives from all local political parties to discuss environmental policy issues. The municipality consulted with the local citizens to adopt an LA21 plan. The proposals were then discussed within the environmental council before the final document was adopted.
- In one of Stockholm's city councils, Nacka, a similar environmental council was formed in 1995, with various organisations, individuals and firms invited to work on different thematic areas. The local politicians chose not to participate, but to wait for ideas from the council. Old antagonisms and party cleavages surfaced and created a sharp contrast between the council and the politicians. The result here was that no LA21 was adopted.
- The university town of Uppsala put considerable effort into involving citizens in the process of developing its LA21 plan. At the initiative of the municipal council, it formed citizen consultation groups for ten issue areas. Municipal officers participated, as did representatives from NGOs and interested individuals. Eleven reports were published from the consultation groups and circulated for review, and the LA21 plan was developed out of this work. At the moment, however, it is unclear as to whether Uppsala will continue and implement this plan.
- As in Uppsala, the northern industrial town of Luleå elaborated its LA21 plan from extensive participatory methods. They combined employment measures in the form of environmental guides, who would answer questions about LA21 and inform citizens through round-table discussions on what should be included in the LA21 work. The results of the seven groups were then presented to the environmental section of the muncipal administration, which then finalised the LA21 on the basis of this work. Subsequently Luleå has developed its own sustainability indicators as a way of measuring progress and channelling information back to the local citizens as to what has been achieved.

Notes

1 The research is supported by the Ministry of the Environment. The transcripts from our 34 interviews of LA21 coordinators, local politicians, and individual 'firebrands'(high-profile local leaders) have been used to answer some of the questions in this chapter.

2 'Ecologically sustainable development' is the term used by the Social Democrats as the national response to 'sustainable development', thus placing special emphasis on the ecological dimension of the concept (see also Eckerberg, 2000).
3 The Delegation for Sustainable Development was abolished after the 1998 elections, when all the five ministers were replaced or moved to new positions.
4 The same approach has been used with 'Kunskapslyftet', a national programme towards adult education. However, it is the first time that ministerial ruling has been applied within the environment sector.
5 This information is derived from interviews in nine municipalities.
6 The government commission has published a total of 32 small booklets and 13 research volumes on the current status and development of democracy in Sweden. It has also produced an interactive home page www.demokratitorget.gov.se/.
7 A survey carried out in 1996 by the Swedish National Bureau of Statistics revealed that 40 per cent of the population had heard of LA21 and 20 per cent knew of at least one ongoing project (but only 3 per cent were themselves engaged in an LA21 project).
8 The Swedish National Audit Office, report 1999:28. This programme was launched by the government through the Ministry of the Environment in 1996 towards investments within waste management, refurbishing, and water and sewage. It contained three objectives, which are very similar to the local investment programme: environmental improvement, use of new technology or methods and creation of new jobs.

REFERENCES

Baker, S (1999) 'What is Required to Achieve a Sustainable Society? The view from political science', paper presented at the conference Towards a Sustainable Society in the New Millennium, Umeå School of the Environment, 10–12 June 1999, Umeå

Bennulf, M (1996) 'Det Gröna Handlingsutrymmet' (The Green Area of Discretion) in Holmberg, S and Weibull, L (eds) *Mitt i Nittiotalet (In the Mid 1990s)*, SOM report no 16, University of Gothenburg, The SOM Institute, Gothenburg

Brundin, P and Eckerberg, K (1999) *Agenda 21 i Svenska Kommuner: En Enkätundersökning (National Survey of LA21 in Swedish municipalities)*, Kommentus Förlag, Stockholm

Eckerberg, K (2000) 'Sweden: Progression despite recession' in Lafferty, M W and Meadowcroft, J (eds) *Bringing Rio Home*, Oxford University Press, Oxford

Eckerberg, K and Forsberg, B (1995) 'Agenda 21 i Svenska Kommuner: Några utvecklingsvägar' (Agenda 21 in Swedish Municipalities: Some development paths), *Alternativ Framtid*, no 3, Universitetsförlaget, Oslo, pp18–27

Eckerberg, K and Forsberg, B (1998) 'Implementing Agenda 21 in Local Government: The Swedish experience', *Local Environment*, vol 3(3), pp333–347

Eckerberg, K and Brundin, P (2000) *Lokal Agenda 21: En Studie av Tio Svenska Kommuner (Local Agenda 21: A Study of Ten Swedish Municipalities)*, Kommentus Förlag, Stockholm

Eckerberg, K, Coenen, F and Lafferty, W M (1999) 'The Status of LA21 in Europe: A comparative overview' in Lafferty, W M (ed) *Implementing LA21 in Europe: New Initiatives for Sustainable Communities*, ProSus, Olso

Eriksson, O (1996) *Bygg om Sverige till Bärkraft! (Rebuild Sweden to Sustainability!)*, ABFs Idé och Faktabibliotek, ABF, Stockholm

Forsberg, B (1999) *Lokal Agenda 21 vid Millennieskiftet: Ekonomism och Socioekologism som Världsbilder i Rörelse (Local Agenda 21 at the turn of the Millennium: Economism and Socioecologism as World Views in Motion)*, research report X, Department of Political Science, Umeå University, Umeå

Government Bill, 1997/98:1 *Budgetpropositionen (The National Budget)*, Parliamentary Record, Stockholm

Khakee, A (1999) *Demokratin i Samhällsplaneringen (Democracy in Societal Planning)*, Government Commission on Democracy (1999) 'Medborgarnas erfarenheter', research vol V, SOU 1999:113, Ministry of Interior Affairs, Stockholm

Lafferty, W and Eckerberg, K (eds) (1998) *From Earth Summit to Local Agenda 21: Working towards Sustainable Development*, Earthscan, London

Lundqvist, L (2001) 'Implementation from Above: The ecology of Sweden's new environmental governance', Department of Political Science, University of Gothenburg, manuscript submitted to *Governance*

Ministry of Environment (1997) *Agenda 21 in Sweden. National Report. From Environmental Protection to Sustainable Development*, National Committee for Agenda 21, Stockholm, English version of 'Five Years after Rio: Results and future' SOU 1997:105 (also available at www.agenda21.se)

Parliamentary Auditors (1999) *Statligt Stöd till Lokala Investeringsprogram för en Ekologiskt Hållbar Utveckling (State Support to Local Investment Programmes for an Ecologically Sustainable Development)*, Report 1998/99:8, Riksdagens Revisorer, Stockholm

Pennington, M and Rydin, Y (2000) 'Public Participation and Local Environmental Planning: The collective action problem and the potential of "social capital"', *Local Environment*, vol 5(2), pp153–169

Rskr (1998/99) *Hållbara Sverige (Sustainable Sweden), Monitoring and Further Measures towards an Ecological Sustainable Development*, government communication, Rskr 1998/99:5, Parliamentary Record, Stockholm

Rskr (1996/97) *Ekologisk Hållbarhet (Ecological Sustainability)*, government communication, Rskr 1996/97:13, Parliamentary Record, Stockholm

SOU (1997) *Agenda 21 i Sverige: Fem år efter Rio, Resultat och Framtid (Agenda 21 in Sweden: Five Years after Rio, Results and Future)*, final report of the National Agenda 21 Committee, SOU 1997:105, Ministry of Environment, Stockholm

SOU 2000:1 *En Uthållig Demokrati. Politik för Folkstyrelse på 2000-talet (A Sustainable Democracy. Politics for Democracy in the 21st Century)*, Demokratiutredningens slutbetänkande (Final report of the Government Commission on Democracy), Ministry of Justice, Stockholm

SSCN (1998) *Konsten att Använda 5,4 miljarder. En Kritisk Granskning av Stödet till de Lokala Investeringsprogrammen för Hållbar Utveckling (The Art of Spending 5.4 Billion. A Critical Analysis of the Local Investment Programme for Sustainable Development)*, report 9423/98, Swedish Society for Conservation of Nature, Stockholm

Swedish National Audit Office (1999) *De Lokala Investeringsprogrammen i Praktiken: En Uppföljning av Kommunernas Arbete (The Local Investment Programme in Practice: A Follow-up of the Municipalities' Work)*, report 1999:37, Riksrevisionsverket, Stockholm

2. Finland
In search of new implementation patterns

Anita Niemi-Iilahti

INTRODUCTION

In the implementation of sustainable development, citizens are expected to contribute to administration through active participation in the formation of a local action programme. The idea of LA21 involves a conscious attempt to combine a top-down implementation and a bottom-up mobilisation of local actors. Thus, of particular interest is how citizen participation in the implementation process is promoted and whether the process enables the emergence of policy innovations. Are there new patterns of interaction between government and citizens? Are there new forms of action that cross the traditional institutional boundaries? This chapter presents an evaluation of the status of LA21 in Finland, discusses some explanatory factors, sums up the most distinctive Finnish experiences, and concludes with some more general lessons learned for future implementation of complex policies presupposing citizen involvement. The data consist of government documents, research reports, interviews and questionnaires and more in-depth case studies of local implementation processes.

THE STATUS OF LA21 IN FINLAND AT THE BEGINNING OF THE 21ST CENTURY

In the Finnish interpretation of the Earth Summit documents, the municipalities are seen as core actors in promoting sustainability (UNCED, 1993). In 1999, 63 per cent of Finnish municipalities had initiated the LA21 process. Of the remaining 37 per cent, 23 per cent were going to start the process in the near future, whereas 14 per cent had no plans. In more than 90 per cent of those municipalities that have initiated the process, a political decision was taken on LA21 (AFLRA, 1999a).

According to the Association of Finnish Local and Regional Authorities (AFLRA, 1999b), LA21 has become:

> *'one of the most important tools at the disposal of municipalities to achieve sustainability ... and has brought about more emphasis on global awareness, social sustainability and partnership in the communities'.*

What kind of evidence do we find to support this statement? There is great variation in the Finnish LA21 processes. The timing, the activities, the initiator, the main actors and the implementation models vary between municipalities. Following the typology of Rogers and Shoemaker (1971), there are 'early birds', 'adopters' and 'laggards' among the municipalities. In the early 1990s, there were a small number of very active 'eco-communities', but the actual drawing up of LA21 action programmes progressed slowly. A breaking point, in the sense that LA21 had advanced from being a curiosity to a more common municipal activity, was reached in 1998, when a majority of municipalities had started LA21 processes. Processes first got under way in the larger towns, whereas the smaller municipalities – often in cooperative networks – became more involved towards the end of 1996. Nearly all the cities and larger towns had started the LA21 process by 1999. Further, the bigger the municipality, the more measures are in evidence. But, there are also some very small municipalities that display a special interest and activity in implementing LA21.

An exceptional 'best case' of LA21 in Finland is the region of Åland, located in the archipelago of the south-western coast. In Åland, the initiative was taken in 1994 by a local environmental NGO. An agenda office, financed by the provincial government and the capital of the province, contributes to the activities of the local groups with training courses, exhibitions, campaigns and newsletters. The office also works directly with individuals, as well as with trade and industrial organisations. Since most of the municipalities have less than 1000 inhabitants and scarce resources, the question is what households and individuals can do, rather than what municipalities can do. In a short time a wide network of contacts, the mass media included, has been developed.

There are several factors that explain the success story of Åland. Firstly, the inhabitants of the Åland islands depend on the tourist industry as the main source of their livelihood and the islands are ecologically sensitive. Thus, the blooming of blue algae experienced in the late 1980s in the waters off Åland functioned as an alarm signal. Secondly, in small homogeneous, insular communities it is easier to adopt a genuine grassroots perspective in practice. Thirdly, the proximity of Sweden, in a region where the official language is Swedish, also helps to adopt good examples from across the border. Further, there is here, as in many other cases in Finland, one particularly dedicated individual – a 'firebrand' – who devotes considerable time and leadership efforts to the cause. Most of the problems faced by LA21 actors in Åland have occurred with the provincial and capital organisations – the big organisations. To build a common understanding of the importance of the process and to convince the organisations to give the process enough time to achieve results has proved laborious (Åland, 1996).

In general, the emphasis of Finnish LA21 policy includes the greening of local economy; the development of survival strategies of rural areas; the involvement of municipal personnel; changing consumer patterns in purchasing; working with problems of climate change; and involving citizens in land-use planning (AFLRA, 1996). The forms of action include both the traditional implementation of environmental policy and more integrative, cross-sectoral approaches of sustainable development. Both internal work within the municipal organisation (European Eco-Management and Audit Scheme (EMAS) training) and more external activities, such as citizen forums, newsletters, training and study groups, future workshops and campaign days, are present.

The initiative is often taken by the municipal environmental officials, in some cases by citizens or NGOs, but seldom by local politicians. A municipality's international contacts have in some cases given a push to the process. The profile of NGOs in mobilising LA21 processes was low in the early 1990s. Finnish Nature Conservation started its first activities in promoting LA21 processes as late as 1996. The Swedish-speaking sister organisation, Nature and the Environment, is operating on a more limited geographical area, but has been very actively engaged in the establishment and management of LA21 processes. The Finnish Friends of the Earth is a newcomer on the scene, but is active in making known the civic viewpoints of sustainable development. Since 1997, there has also been a campaign entitled 'Finland 21', which is a joint sustainable-development action programme of several NGOs.

AFLRA has also been active in spreading information on LA21 and preparing the programme's fieldwork. It operates mainly as a 'facilitator', organising training events and producing and distributing information. Since the early 1990s, the association has spurred municipalities into taking action towards local sustainable development. In the background, the influence of the UN and ICLEI can also be traced. The local authorities in Finland were invited to strengthen their LA21 activities through a pilot project launched in 1992 by AFLRA together with the Ministry of the Environment and the Ministry of the Interior. The aim of the project (with 14 municipalities) was to find means of promoting sustainable development locally and to obtain information on local solutions (AFLRA, 1994a and 1994b). The project was clearly effective and Finnish LA21 pioneers are to be found among these 14 municipalities. In 1997, AFLRA launched a second project, this time involving 60 municipalities.

AFLRA also promotes and coordinates the municipal climate protection campaign. Climate change is one of the 'top ten' issues in LA21 processes, mostly in larger towns and cities (AFLRA, 1999b). AFLRA has, throughout the 1990s, been the most active national organisation in transferring the notion of sustainable development to a local policy strategy, whereas the National Commission on Sustainable Development has paid little attention at the local level. Rather late, in 1997, a special local section for sustainable development was formed by the commission. Since then, the section has served to provide inspiration and ideas for municipalities and others, and has drawn attention to indicators used on different levels of governance. AFLRA has also contributed to the process of demonstrating greater measurable progress. In building capacity for LA21 implementation in Finland, AFLRA has focused on LA21, whereas the government's contribution has been in strengthening the normative and administrative basis for sustainable development.

It is difficult to evaluate how far the Finnish municipalities have progressed on the road towards a sustainable society. Surveys made on the progress of LA21 in Finland give an overview of the situation (Kettunen, 1998; AFLRA, 1998 and 1999a; Grönholm and Joas, 1999). They show that a majority of the municipalities have started processes, and that most of them have made a political decision, but the surveys also reveal that the awareness of the content is still rather weak. The main obstacles to the implementation of LA21 are negative attitudes (38 per cent), economic constraints (37 per cent), lack of information (17 per cent) and administrative reasons (8 per cent). There are various reasons for negative attitudes. Information on sustainable development and LA21 is abundant in publications, newsletters and on the internet, but the core content, the meaning of the words, is not clear. The concepts used are often too abstract and thus difficult to translate into everyday action. Additionally, because the agenda concept is used in its English form, it raises connotations, in the Finnish context, with the EU concepts of Agenda 2000 and Natura 2000. These again raise negative reactions among those critical towards the EU in general. In addition, certain groups of people do not like to be labelled as 'greens', particularly in the countryside.

Activities related to LA21 processes in Finland seem to be closely connected to the degree of general environmental awareness at the local level (Kettunen, 1998). Relatively large urban municipalities have a professional environmental administration with full-time, highly educated and numerous personnel. The initiatives in LA21 activities often come from these officials who bring the issue to the political agenda. Small- and medium-sized rural municipalities, on the other hand, usually have a mixed type of administration with part-time technical personnel with relatively low levels of education. Another factor affecting the implementation of LA21 in the municipalities is the political climate concerning the environment. In some municipalities, spontaneous local environmental activity can be found, while in other, mostly rural communities, almost hostile attitudes towards ecological aspects are dominant (Konttinen and Litmanen, 1996; Sairinen, 1994).

The capacity of the Finnish public administration in implementing the goals of sustainability has increased remarkably during the 1990s. Professional environmental knowledge is now available at different levels of government. There are new tools available for increasing environmental awareness and changing attitudes. The performance of public administration has also improved through decentralisation and deregulation. The fact that successful implementation of a policy requires an appropriate capacity of local public administration (Pressman and Wildavsky, 1973; Goggin et al, 1990) has been well heeded. The Finnish implementation of LA21 is a combination of direct and indirect efforts taken by various actors (Table 2.1).

The capacity of the different actors is, in addition, affected by the prevailing economic conditions. Finland's GNP decreased during four successive years in the first half of the 1990s. Although this exceptional

Table 2.1 *Actors, strategies and initiatives in LA21 implementation*

Actor	*Strategy*	*Initiative*
National and regional government (the State)	*Indirect* Systematic transformation of supra-national policy into national commitments creating a solid basis for local processes	Acts, plans, programmes, publications with guidelines and recommendations; subsidies (marginal); organisational development
Local government (municipalities)	*Direct* Active local government officials making LA21 a local political issue; local council takes a decision to start an LA21	Addressing LA21 to local councils' political agendas; diffusion of knowledge; writing LA21 programmes
Interest organisation: AFLRA	*Direct and indirect* Actively spurring municipalities to take action; backing up LA21 processes	Projects; production and diffusion of knowledge and recommendations; information, education, research reports, handbooks
NGOs	*Direct and indirect* activating citizens taking LA21 initiatives	Campaigns and seminars; publications

situation changed in the mid-1990s, and was followed by continual growth, the cutback policy introduced in the early 1990s has had a weakening impact on the municipalities' resources in general and in the field of local environmental policy in particular. Short-term solutions targeted at rapid economic recovery have led to a reduction in the number of environmental officials (Niemi-Iilahti, 1998). Thus, some of the policy reforms aiming to improve the capacity of public administration in implementing sustainable development at local level have not had the desired effect.

THE NATIONAL GOVERNMENT'S ROLE IN THE IMPLEMENTATION OF A GLOBAL POLICY

Efforts taken by the Finnish government to promote the implementation of sustainable development at the local level mainly consist of the production and distribution of information and organisational development. The government's first response to the global policy can be traced to its report 'Sustainable Development and Finland' (published by the Ministry of the Environment in 1990). In 1993, the government presented the basic national goals and measures for sustainable development to the Finnish Parliament in the report 'Charting Finland's Future Options' (cited in MoE, 1994). The National Commission on Sustainable Development, established in 1993 and chaired by the Prime Minister, has had an important role in transforming the notion of sustainable development to a national policy strategy. At the beginning of 1997, after the Commission's initiative, the major actors (for example, the Central Commercial Union, the Central Union of Agricultural Producers and the Union of Finnish Entrepreneurs) also began to prepare their own action plans for sustainable development.

An indirect factor in building administrative capacity for the implementation of LA21 was the reform of environmental administration in 1995. At the national level, administrative duties were the responsibility of the Ministry of the Environment, and research-and-development duties came under the National Environment Institute. At the regional level, environment centres with comprehensive functions were established. The former dual structure in the regional environmental administration was simplified to two administrative bodies. The environment offices of county administration and the water and environment districts were combined into a single regional environment centre in each of the 11 regions (see Box 2.1). The establishment of regional centres resulted in 'environment houses' – regional headquarters for the environment – with the previously scattered functions now also physically located (in most cases) in one building. The reform supports municipalities in their efforts to integrate

Box 2.1 Regional environment centres in Finland

- In 1995 each of the 11 regions in Finland established a regional environment centre.
- The centres have a wide range of environmental functions, varying from traditional environmental protection, use and management of water resource, to the promotion of environmental awareness.
- The centres are highly involved with LA21 implementation in Finland. Since 1998, they have organised joint seminars for municipalities, and so as to meet the objectives and responsibilities of LA21, all centres have appointed LA21 contact persons.
- Focal tasks for the centres are the gathering and compiling of information, environmental education and network building related to regional environmental challenges.
- Information on the state of the environment is compiled to provide a basis for LA21 programmes. Through their websites they also provide information and offer numerous links to other sources of information.
- The centres promote and take initiatives to enhance environmental education in schools. They also arrange theme days, seminars and training courses related to Agenda 21, targeting local politicians and officials, LA21 contact persons and citizens.
- The centres take part in networking by building LA21 learning networks for schools, creating joint programmes on sustainable development for groups of municipalities, and producing LA21 manuals to support the work in their respective regions. Centres from the southern part of Finland have also worked together with Estonian counties on environmental issues and LA21 activities in a vital cross-border context.

environmental concerns into other policy areas. The centres are responsible for environmental protection, land use and nature conservation including buildings, the establishment and care of nature preservation areas, landscape protection and biodiversity, and protection of endangered species, as well as for the use and management of water resources. Further, they are also responsible for monitoring and assessment of the environment, and for the promotion of environmental awareness.

Towards the end of the 1990s, regional environment centres have increased their involvement with LA21 work in Finland. In 1998, as earmarked funding was available for LA21-activities in the state budget, regional environment centres organised joint seminars for municipalities. To meet the objectives and responsibilities, all centres have appointed LA21 contact persons. The centres compile information on the status of the environment, making substantial data available to LA21 programmes.

Centres provide general and also sometimes LA21-specific information through their websites, offering numerous links to other sources of information. About a third of the centres have monitored the state of programmes and activities in the region through questionnaires to the municipalities. Some have disseminated the results to local authorities in published reports. A few of the centres publish a bulletin or a newsletter on the advancement of LA21 in the region.

Environmental education is another focal point of the work of regional environment centres. The centres take initiatives to enhance environmental education in schools. Many have organised thematic days, seminars and training related to Agenda 21. The target groups of these events have included local politicians and officials, LA21 contact persons and citizens. The centres also build LA21 learning networks for schools, create joint programmes on sustainable development of groups of municipalities, and produce manuals to support the work in their prospective regions. Centres cooperate with the regional councils, which are set up by the municipalities as authorities for regional development. They also take part in cross-border cooperation, such as the so-called '3+3 project' where two centres and three regional councils from southern Finland work together with three Estonian counties in land use, environmental education and LA21 activities of municipalities.

The Ministry of the Environment formulates environmental policies and makes decisions such as the Finnish action programme for sustainable development, 'Environment Programme 2005' (MoE, 1995), which aims at integrating environmental aspects into other policy areas. The programme forms the basis for the ministry's cooperation with the other actors in environmental policy. The duties of the Finnish Environment Institute include the promotion of sustainable development by monitoring and assessing its implementation. The ministry and the Finnish Environment Institute have stressed the importance of the production of information on the environment, and have thereby tried to increase both governmental and average citizen awareness of the LA21 goals. All chapters of the UNCED plan of action, including Chapter 28 on local government, were translated into Finnish in 1993. The aim was to encourage discussion on sustainable development as well as to increase the opportunities for citizens, organisations and authorities to promote the policy. The concept of sustainable development was introduced to the legislature step by step – to the Building Act in 1990, the Local Government Act in 1995 and the Nature Protection Act in 1996. Likewise, the environmental impact assessment (EIA) procedure has, since 1994, increased the possibilities of citizens, organisations and experts to influence matters by expressing opinions on the sufficiency of plans and accounts. The legislation pays broad attention to sustainable development, the need for democratic planning and increased citizen participation. However, any explicit LA21 legislation does not exist.

A recent important effort to link the policy of sustainability to existing societal functions was made in June 1998, when the Council of State in Finland adopted The Finnish Government's Programme for Sustainable Development (MoE, 1998). Although the programme is general in nature, it includes concrete proposals for action, such as the certification of forests and the assessment of the climatic impacts of different energy policy scenarios. In ecological land-use planning it emphasises the need for more collaboration of local authorities in the regions, and the need to strengthen the interaction between citizens and local authorities. Thus, both the global dimension and the participatory aspect are given a more specific normative dimension by the authorities.

The reformed Land Use and Building Act, enacted in January 2000, offers a new forum for local democracy in planning issues. A participation and assessment plan is drawn up at the beginning of the planning work and the participation of citizens in the initiation phase is promoted by making the planning process public from the outset. This includes a chance for citizens to participate in both the preparations of the plans and in the assessment of their impacts in cooperation with a large number of experts. Implementation itself will lead to a policy change, since making assessments of environmental impacts was previously undertaken mainly by experts.

In Finland, all the major actors within the institutional setting – the state government at the central and regional levels, local self-government, local and regional authorities and NGOs – are participating in the implementation process. Since no single actor can do the job alone, cooperation is vital. Additionally, there must be sufficient convergence of objectives and interests to make it possible to reach a 'win-win' situation (Kooiman, 1993). This is probably one of the major challenges, since the interests and priorities of the different actors do not always coincide.

THE MUNICIPALITIES' DILEMMA: HOW TO TAKE ACTION?

Implementing LA21 deviates radically from traditional implementation processes where the policy goals and instruments are defined in advance. What to do and how to do it is in this case left to the local actors. Moreover, there are no formal sanctions for those municipalities who do not comply with the goals set at the Earth Summit. Thus, there is room for varying interpretations of LA21, ranging from doing nothing to doing something in either a traditional or new way.

The role of the municipalities is central in the Finnish political system. They provide welfare services and allow for citizens' participation. The impact of citizens on their own self-governing community is strongly protected by the Constitution. The two main tasks of the municipalities are 'to promote the welfare of their citizens and sustainable development' (Local Government Act, 1995). The most important services provided are education, social welfare, health care, planning of land use and maintenance of the technical infrastructure. Municipalities also have a major role in the national economy, since two-thirds of public expenditure and public employees are municipal. There is thus an opportunity and a responsibility for local authorities to integrate ecological aspects into all sectors. The correspondence with Chapter 28 is obvious because:

> *'so many of the problems and solutions being addressed by Agenda 21 have their roots in local activities, the participation and co-operation of local authorities will be a determining factor in fulfilling its objectives...'*

The municipalities are obliged to supervise and promote environmental protection at the local level. The most important environmental issues at the end of the 1980s and the beginning of the 1990s were those concerning waste management, air and water protection, noise control and nature protection. The period since the Earth Summit has added land use, transport, energy, citizens' attitudes and environmental education to the list. This poses clear challenges for cooperation between the social, ecological and economic subsystems. The municipalities choose different solutions in organising their environmental administration. In every third municipality there is an environmental board; in other municipalities environmental duties rest with the technical board, the building board, the health board, or some other administrative body (Kettunen, 1998).

Several reforms have been made concerning central–local relations during the last two decades in Finland. The main features in the modernisation process are decentralisation and the delegation of authority and decision-making to the local level, as well as the deregulation of administrative processes in general (Naschold, 1995; Pollit et al, 1997). New lines of policy implementation stress the importance of increasing local self-steering and are thus clearly consistent with the principle of subsidiarity. The primary goal of public management reforms has been to increase efficiency and effectiveness in the public sector. The ideas of 'new public management' have been applied in public management reforms aiming to improve the public sector's productivity and performance, and are most clearly visible in the adoption of 'management by results'. Participation in the local elections in Finland used to be high. In the 1960s and 1970s the turnout was near 80 per cent; in the 1980s it gradually came down to 70 per cent; and in the latest local election in 1996, it was as low as 61 per cent. There is an evident call for new channels of citizen participation, since the channels of the traditional representative democracy seem to be losing their meaning. Thus, successful LA21 processes might serve as patterns for citizen participation in general.

The local implementation models of LA21 in Finland vary due to timing, activities, the main actors and the implementation, as shown in surveys made by AFLRA (1998 and 1999a) and Grönholm and Joas (1998). The surveys are mostly based on the views given by one or two respondents (environmental officials, municipal managers) in each municipality. They give an overview of the situation and show that LA21 processes began first in the larger towns – rural municipalities only became involved towards the end of 1996. The surveys also reveal some of the obstacles to the implementation of LA21. Negative attitudes, economic constraints, lack of information and administrative reasons were obstacles often mentioned by respondents. The type of implementation varies from traditional bureaucratic and professional procedures to more market- or citizen-oriented approaches, and from single-actor approaches to more cooperative efforts. They reflect the different implementation patterns used by municipalities in general in the quest for the 'perfect' way of managing the tasks (Rothstein, 1991; Peters, 1996). The surveys also show that municipal environmental officials, the AFLRA, and in some cases the NGO, Nature and the Environment, are the main actors taking the initiative on LA21.

FOUR CASE STUDIES: HOW AND WHY DO LA21 PROCESSES ADVANCE?

The surveys made on LA21 progress in Finland describe how many municipalities are involved, the main actors and the obstacles for progress. In order to learn more of how the LA21 processes advance, and how citizen participation is promoted, several in-depth studies that apply case methodology were conducted (Niemi-Iilahti, 1999; Niemi-Iilahti and Vehkala, 1999; Vehkala, 1998). A multiple-case design (Yin, 1994) was used to obtain a holistic interpretation of the complex phenomena of LA21, and to identify meaningful characteristics of the implementation process. Four cases were selected. Each case serves a specific purpose within the overall scope of analysing LA21 implementation in Finland. The cases present different types of municipalities and implementation models (Table 2.2).

Multiple sources of evidence were used in the data collection conducted during 1997–1999. Each case includes questionnaires to local council members and officials, interviews with key persons (politicians, officials and NGO representatives), and document analysis.

Case A is the city of Helsinki and relies on the city's administrative capacity and a steering group of politicians. The city joined the

Table 2.2 *Implementation models in urban and rural municipalities*

Model	*Urban*	*Rural*
Traditional public administration	*Case A* Large city The city's 'environment centre' serves as 'driving force' and projects are initiated by citizen organisations Farsighted process and comprehensive interpretation of LA21	*Case C* Four cooperating municipalities Environmental officials are the 'driving force' 'engine' with a project by AFLRA Intensive progress at the outset – strong risk of dying out once the project is concluded
'New' models	*Case B* Medium-sized city Use of outside consultants and municipal task force Incremental process and limited interpretation of LA21	*Case D* Ten cooperating municipalities A project led by an NGO Ecologically oriented events, interest drying out in most municipalities after the project

'Sustainable Communities' project conducted by AFLRA in 1992. Active environmental officials played a key role. In 1994, the city signed the Aalborg Charter. In 1997, the city council made a decision to prepare an LA21 plan of action and a task force was appointed. In 1998 and 1999, citizens were involved in the process in terms of citizens' forums and theme groups. Financial resources were also made available for use by citizens. A local agenda for Helsinki is to be adopted in 2001. The LA21 process in Helsinki has advanced smoothly – and professionally. The work is a continuation of the city's cross-sectoral environmental work. The case has triggered considerable exchange of opinions between citizens and civil servants. The input of the citizens is included in the draft of the LA21 action programme.

Case B, the city of Vaasa, has hired consultants who are steered by a group of leading local officials. The city participated in the LA21 project conducted by AFLRA in 1992–93, when the focus was on waste management. In 1994, the board of a local open college initiated an environmental education project, and suggested that the city should aim at being an 'ecocity'. In 1995, the city council adopted sustainable development as one of the main principles for future development, and two open colleges arranged study groups for citizens. In 1996, an external consultant prepared a proposition for further sustainable development, and in 1997 the city council decided to start an LA21 process. A task group was set up and a new consultant hired. In 1998, two citizens' forums were organised, one for students and the other for residents in a specific area. In 1999, the project was cut back to internal work within the municipal organisation. However, in September 1999, the board of the environment made a decision that the city should still sign the Aalborg Charter. In this case, the implementation of LA21 advanced more as a separate project rather than as a holistic process. LA21 now has low political status and there is no consultation between citizens and the administration.

Case C consists of four municipalities which participated in the LA21 project conducted by AFLRA in 1997–98. The initiative was taken by civil servants in 1996. In 1997, the local authorities of the four municipalities decided to start LA21 work, and the four municipal councils signed a common declaration on LA21 and hired a coordinator. They all participated in an AFLRA project in 1997–98. The environmental officials acted as the core group in the implementation process, organising citizens' forums and columns in local newspapers to promote the process. Several efforts were taken to increase the awareness of the members of the city councils as well as that of the citizens. Since 1999, the municipalities have relied on their own administration. Cooperation between the four municipalities continues, although they no longer have a coordinator. Two of the councils have approved an LA21 action plan. In the initial phase, citizens were interested and active, but when the AFLRA project was finished the interest seemed to decline.

In case D, which consists of ten municipalities in a rural coastal region, the initiatives of citizen organisations in 1996 led to local authorities starting LA21 planning in 1997. The planning was organised as a project conducted by Nature and the Environment. A project coordinator worked with the help of a steering group to spread information and organise education on LA21 in the region. Seminars, courses and exhibitions were organised and a newsletter was published. Events with specified target groups and concrete action drew much attention, whereas some of the more general events had to be cancelled due to lack of interest. The project lasted for a little less than two years. Cooperation between the ten municipalities was loose during the project. The parallel implementation of the Natura 2000 by the EU raised several conflicts of interest and had a weakening effect on the results of the project. At the end of the project, interest is low in the majority of the ten municipalities. However, in a couple of the municipalities the process is continuing actively.

Common problems in all of these cases are passive citizens, negative and undermining attitudes of some civil servants, the abstract concept of sustainable development, and the slow progress made. These issues surfaced from interviews and questionnaires used in all cases. The questionnaire aimed at getting information on the success of increasing the awareness of LA21, the level of commitment in the local community, and the level of citizen participation. Concerning information dissemination, awareness of the content of LA21 and the respondents' views on the commitment of local officials and politicians, cases A and C were more successful than the other two. Although all the cases show that citizen participation is given a high priority, the level of participation experienced is generally low. Only in case A is it viewed as somewhat active. The most active citizens in LA21 processes are those who are known to participate in other types of voluntary activity, too.

The process in case A reflects the problems of an urban community: large size, inhabitants unfamiliar with each other, many kinds of industries and related interests, a high-consumption lifestyle, and conflict between the interests of the environment and other involved parties. The growth in population, construction and traffic continuously forces administration to monitor the state of the environment. The attitude towards LA21 varies among the key decision-makers. A small group knows it very well and works actively for it. The city's top leaders have committed themselves visibly. But in other quarters, lack of knowledge and commitment is obvious. To many, LA21 is a secondary matter, in some extreme cases even something negative. Most feel that the effort is important and stress its role as a channel of influence for the inhabitants, but at the same time they do not believe that citizens really want to participate.

In most cases, the methods used in implementing LA21 were copied from LA21 activities in other municipalities. The diffusion of ideas and forms of action seem to be very effective. Forum is the most usual 'new' way of spreading information and spurring discussion, as well as action. In case A, the truly innovative element is the high ambition to combine professional knowledge with citizens' experience. The professionals designed the work programme, and the citizens were invited to participate. The results of the work were presented to different branches of administration in the city. Administration had to react to the ideas and give a response to the citizens at a forum. Although citizens were involved only after the goals had been set, this was a new way of proceeding in local planning.

IMPLEMENTATION OF LA21 IN FINLAND: SUMMARY AND CHALLENGES

The loosely formulated global policy has, in Finland, resulted in a variety of implementation models and forms of action. The national government's role in promoting LA21 implementation is as an intermediary, the emphasis having been on transformation of the supra-national policy of sustainable development into national commitments and creating a solid basis for voluntary processes arising from the local level. The main actors in the actual LA21 work are local governments and the AFLRA, and in some cases environmental NGOs. AFLRA has consistently acted on transferring knowledge and instigating LA21 processes. At the local level, the main initiators have been active environmental officials who have tried to accommodate LA21 to political agendas since the early 1990s.

The strength of Finnish local authorities in implementing sustainable development is considerable. Local self-government, based on local democracy, the municipalities' economic power and the responsibility to take care of a wide variety of functions, forms an arena for taking action for LA21. The most evident constraints are not of constitutional origin, but instead limitations related to the political values predominant in the country. The choices made by local decision-makers are of great significance.

The production and distribution of information has been intensive and comprehensive. Information is used to influence people through the transfer of knowledge, communication of reasoned arguments and persuasion. As mentioned before, there are various reasons for negative attitudes. Information on sustainable development and LA21 is abundant in publications, newsletters and the internet, but the core content and the meaning of the words are not clear. The concepts used are often too abstract and thus difficult to translate into everyday action. This is experienced by both municipal politicians and officials, as well as by citizens. The concept of sustainable development seems to have a plethora of possible meanings.

LA21 processes are in a phase of transition. The first steps towards the goals set by Agenda 21 have been taken. In the best cases, citizens have been involved in the process in a new way, although their number is limited and the opportunities for civic participation could be further improved. Knowledge has been transmitted, and the dialogue between environmental and other professionals in the administration and citizens has started. The administration emphasises global ecological issues, whereas the citizens' main interests lie in developing participatory processes and improving the local neighbourhood. There are now grounds for continued negotiations between the local partners. Local politicians are still in the background, but there are some signs of growing interest in LA21 among them too. Naturally, there is always the danger of the process coming to an end once the contribution of the citizens has been documented. A feeling that the process has been completed gradually creeps in.

A significant feature of activities since the Earth Summit is that hardly any new economic resources have been allocated to environmental functions. The existing staff has new duties – but no new resources. This again affects the attitudes. Another obstacle is the lack of cooperation between the municipal administrative bodies, along with an overall weak commitment from local politicians. A prominent feature in some municipalities is, however, that new cooperation models within the local government administration and between local authorities and other organisations or citizen groups have been created. Ambitious pilot projects in the spheres of land use, traffic and schools have been initiated.

The management styles and economic resources of the municipalities vary considerably. Accordingly, LA21 processes show great variation concerning their local background, the starting and financing of the processes, as well as the forms of action and participation. Although serious attempts are made to fulfil the LA21 criteria, the actual implementation is weakened by the slow change of attitudes, lack of resources, and also competing projects such as Natura 2000. The reorganisation of environmental administrations has promoted integration at the local level and thus LA21 implementation, whereas the increased discretion of power at the local level both promotes and hinders the implementation. In connection with economic pressure, the lack of clarity in the LA21 goals has had a negative effect. An economically sustainable development is an avowed goal, but in practice there is an evident risk that the economic aspect is being separated from the ecological and social aspects of sustainability. On the other hand, some local communities have been successful in discovering new and more flexible local implementation models. The biggest challenge in the 21st century will still be promotion of broader citizen involvement.

LA21 processes have to be anchored in everyday decision-making. Political decision-making should give the process the emphasis that it requires. The requirement is hard to achieve, however, since both 'sustainable development' and 'local agenda' are relatively imprecise terms. We cannot tell what a sustainable society will be like in the future and what makes economic, political and social structures sustainable. But we do have knowledge about what is unsustainable development and how to avoid it. Environmental professionals have this knowledge, but it has not yet reached the policy-makers and citizens to a sufficient degree. Functioning systems that combine professional administration, political decision-making and civic participation are the real challenge of the 21st century.

LA21 is not yet at the centre of political decision-making, but there are clear signs of advancement. Concerning the content of LA21 policy, the perspective of sustainable development is present in different sectors. Concerning the process, citizen empowerment is emerging and there are signs of a new administrative culture. The need to share tasks and responsibilities has gradually given birth to new ways of action characterised by different types of co-management, co-steering and partnership. However, the relation between direct and representative democracy raises questions. There are increasing signs that, in the future, citizens, politicians and professionals will be developing new types of citizens' forums and other similar arenas. A forum where the members of a local community can occasionally review the state of local sustainable development, exchange opinions and suggest new ideas is needed. The new Land Use and Building Act in Finland will be a good testing arena for combining citizen participation and political decision-making. Functioning systems of civic participation are a prerequisite for community-wide learning processes and sustainable development. The contribution of citizens to planning and implementation is a key factor for the process to continue.

REFERENCES

AFLRA (1994a) *Kestävän Kehityksen Käsikirja Kunnille (Handbook for Municipalities on Sustainable Development)*, Suomen Kuntaliitto, Helsinki

AFLRA (1994b) *Kunnat Kestävää Kehitystä Etsimässä (Municipalities in Search of Sustainable Development)*, Suomen Kuntaliitto, Helsinki

AFLRA (1998) *Kestävän Kehityksen Pullonkaulat Kunnissa (The Obstacles for LA21 Programmes)*, Paikallinen Agenda 21 – projektin julkaisu, Suomen Kuntaliitto, Helsinki

AFLRA (1999a) *Paikallisagenda Suomessa 1999 (LA21 in Finland 1999)*, Suomen Kuntaliitto, Helsinki

AFLRA (1999b) *Local Agenda 21 in Finland*. The Association of Finnish Local and Regional Authorities, Helsinki

Åland (1996) *Åland för Hållbar Utveckling (Åland Toward Sustainability)*, Agenda 21 på Åland, Mariehamn

Association of Finnish Local Authorities (1996) *Learning New Skills*, Association of Finnish Local Authorities, Helsinki

Goggin, M L, Bowman, A O'M, Lester, J P and O'Toole, L J Jr (1990) *Implementation Theory and Practice: Toward a Third Generation*, Scott, Foresman/Little, Brown Higher Education, Glenview, Illinois and London, England

Grönholm, B and Joas, M (1999) *Local Environmental Activities Within and Across Borders*, Åbo Akademi University, Department of Public Administration, Union of the Baltic Cities, Åbo

Kettunen, A (1998) *Kunnat ja Ympäristökonfliktit (Municipalities and Environmental Conflicts)*, Åbo Akademi/Suomen Kuntaliitto, Helsinki

Kooiman, J (ed) (1993) *Modern Governance: New Government–society Interactions*, Sage Publications, London

Konttinen, E and Litmanen, T (eds) (1996) *Ekokuntia ja Ökykuntia: Tutkimuksia Ympäristöhallinnan Erilaisuudesta (Ecological Municipalities and Their Opposites: Studies on the Differences in Local Environmental Governance)*, Yhteiskuntatieteiden, valtio-opin ja filosofian julkaisuja 6, Jyväskylän yliopisto, Jyväskylä

Local Government Act (1995) Kuntalaki 365/95 (Finnish Local Government Act)

MoE (1994) *Implementation of Agenda 21 in Finland (1994)*, Ministry of the Environment, Helsinki

MoE (1995) *Environment Programme 2005*, Ministry of the Environment, Helsinki

MoE (1998) *Finnish Government Programme for Sustainable Development*, Council of State Decision-in-principle on the Promotion of Ecological Sustainability. The Finnish Environment 254, Ministry of the Environment, Helsinki

Naschold, F (1995) *The Modernization of the Public Sector in Europe: A Comparative Perspective on the Scandinavian Experience*, Labour Policy Studies 93, Ministry of Labour, Helsinki

Niemi-Iilahti, A (1998) 'Finland: Working with LA21 under conditions of economic uncertainty' in Lafferty, W M and Eckerberg, K (eds) *From Earth Summit to Local Forum: Studies of Local Agenda 21 in Europe*, ProSus, Oslo

Niemi-Iilahti, A (1999) *Kansalaisten ja Hallinnon Vuorovaikutus. Helsingin Paikallisagendaprosessin Arviointia (Interaction Between Citizens and the Administration. Evaluation of LA21 in Helsinki)*, Tutkimuksia 11, Helsingin kaupungin tietokeskus, Helsinki

Niemi-Iilahti, A and Vehkala, M-M (1999) *Utvärdering av Projektet Österbottens Agenda (Evaluation of the Ostrobothnian Agenda 21 Project)*, Vaasan yliopiston julkaisuja, Selvityksiä ja raportteja 40, Vaasan yliopisto, Vaasa

Peters, B G (1996) *The Future Governing: Four Emerging Models*, University Press of Kansas, Kansas

Pressman, J and Wildavsky, A (1973) *Implementation. How Great Expectations in Washington are Dashed in Oakland*, University of California Press, Berkeley

Pollitt, C, Hanncy, S, Packwood, T, Rothwell, S and Roberts, S (1997) *Trajectories and Options: An International Perspective on the Implementation of Finnish Public Management Reforms*, Ministry of Finance, Helsinki

Rogers, E H and Shoemaker, F F (1971) *Communication and Innovations. A Cross-cultural Approach*, The Free Press, New York

Rothstein, B (1991) 'Demokrati, Förvaltning och Legitimitet' in Rothstein (ed) *Politik som Organisation: Förvaltningspolitikens Grundproblem*, SNS Förlag, Stockholm

Sairinen, R (1994) *Ympäristökonfliktit Kuntien Suunnittelussa ja Päätöksenteossa*, Suomen Kuntaliitto, Helsinki

UNCED (1993) *YK:n ympäristö- ja kehityskonferenssi Rio de Janeiro 3–14 June 1992 (The UN Conference on Environment and Development)*, Ministry of the Environment, Helsinki

Vehkala, M-M (1998) 'Riosta Keski-Suomeen. Illuusio kuntalaisten osallistumisesta (From Rio to Central Finland. An illusion of citizen participation)', *Kunnallistieteellinen Aikakauskirja*, vol 26(4), pp337–347

Yin, R K (1994) *Case Studies: Design and Methods*, Sage, California

3. Denmark
The participatory and consensus-seeking approach of the Danish LA21

Jesper Holm and Mercy Wambui Kamara

Introduction

In Denmark, national and local efforts have, by and large, been successful in implementing LA21. Three-quarters of the 275 municipalities and 14 counties have an LA21 consisting of local action-plans, activities and projects.[1] LA21 has focused on and enhanced local green activism and networking, while raising public awareness of local environmental problems and adequate responses. The process of implementation has been top-down, with innovative campaigning by the Ministry of the Environment and Energy (MEE) in cooperation with local authorities' associations. They have advanced a 'hands-on-practical-issues' LA21 regime that has been characterised by appeals for greater public involvement and participation – after being initially prepared by local authorities' programmes and planning. For the most part, Danish LA21 activities have been characterised by 'exterior *add-on* activities' to existing local environmental, social and business policies (see Holm, in Lafferty, 1999). Therefore LA21 programmes and activities in general only appeal to citizens, NGOs and public institutions to voluntarily participate in local practical arrangements, debates and policies. Conventional regulatory activities on issuing permits, nature preservation and environmental infrastructures have been neglected. Business organisations, unions, private enterprises and farms, for example, have rarely been involved, if at all, in LA21 activities. We have accordingly criticised the Danish LA21 strategy for having a narrow consultation approach and being soft- and easy-target oriented, lacking innovative policies for sustainable production (Holm, in Lafferty, 1999).

Here we shall seek to turn our observation on its head and explore whether the dominating storyline of Danish LA21 has actually been successful in generating new modes of public participation or cooperation and by this approach also new policy content. Are there signs of a new cultural–politics paradigm of shared responsibility and cooperation that may, in time, supplement or merge with the more conventional environmental policy paradigm (see Lafferty, 1999)?

First we look at the background of the 'deliberative democracy' policy style of Danish LA21 implementation. Of importance for this style, and for the subsidiarity question, we focus on the development of an experimental bottom-up culture. Also of importance here is the institutional implementation process of LA21, consisting of new cross-sectoral alliances, networks and initiatives among Danish government and associations of local authorities. Secondly, general LA21 developments are analysed in order to identify what kind of participatory efforts on what subjects have taken place. The status of the LA21 products is described to find whether new signs of shifts in environmental policy paradigms have occurred. Third, we turn to a more in-depth study of the pioneering municipality of Albertslund, in order to look more closely at the relationship between forms of public participation and new environmental policy paradigms under very favourable conditions.

BACKGROUND

Local experiments and community innovation

The culture of Danish policy is, in general, characterised by the tradition of a decentralised public administration, which also applies in the legislation of spatial planning and public administration of environmental policy relevant to LA21. With this comes the consensus-seeking approach, together with the Danish civic tradition (the so-called 'people's enlightenment tradition' dating from the turn of the 19th century) that has, to a large extent, influenced the policy processes of social interest groups (Læssøe, 1990). In areas such as environmental policy and spatial planning, practices based on consultation with interest groups have been commonplace. This Danish element of public, corporate and NGO consultation that implies relative openness in all areas of environmental policies is an important principle in the Danish Environmental Act and in the Spatial Planning Act. The policy culture[2] has come to provide a favourable infrastructure for the deliberative and stakeholder-democracy implementation style of the Earth Summit's appeal for LA21.

During the late 1980s, Danish environmental policy came to adopt a twofold path partly due to criticism of lax enforcement of acts and rules and partly due to a new worldwide approach to environmental problems (Andersen, 1999). On the one hand, environmental policy came to focus on cleaner technology options, pollution prevention and cradle-to-grave perspectives instead of a more general carrying-capacity approach. On the other hand, environmental policy came to promote active involvement of various stakeholders in designing and implementing pollution prevention in manufacturing, farming and transport. In other words, environmental policy turned 'eco-modernistic', 'interactive' and 'de-formalised' (Holm, in Lafferty, 1999). This development gradually introduced local authorities to the challenge of relating environmental problems to underlying economic and technological causalities, and integrating corporate partners into new interactive regulatory approaches – all important LA21 features and themes. However, local authorities have, until recently, failed in the firm implementation and enforcement of this new regulatory paradigm (Mortensen, 2000). Accordingly, by the mid-1980s, local authorities faced considerable pressure from the government and green NGOs.

One opportunity for the local authorities in this situation turned out to be a new 'practical activism' among NGOs and green entrepreneurs in many residential areas. Local politicians and employees from public institutions began to show interest in supporting combined social and green practical initiatives. This activism included mobilising clients and citizens in making renewable energy utilities; developing energy-saving measures; renewing urban areas with ecology projects; and reducing the amount of traffic (Læssøe, 1993). The municipalities and the government thus found an open door, within the eco-modernism, win-win approach, for gaining legitimacy by enhancing a shared-responsibility regime with green activists and entrepreneurs as a target group.

The Ministry of the Environment's 1988 campaign, *Our Common Future*, inspired by the Brundtland Report, was the first pre-LA21 policy initiative from the government that encouraged citizens and NGOs to join practical activities as part of a general environmental regulatory effort. With a fund for new projects for local authorities and citizen groups, over 600 projects were supported up to 1992. New political entrepreneur/practitioner identities were stabilised, and new cross-sectoral and public–private experiments were initiated. The campaign was meant to be a learning process for local authorities, by generating experiments and revealing options and hindrances for a bottom-up strategy (Læssøe, 2000). The campaign also wound up with a review of the four-year municipal and county planning documents where more qualitative targets were stipulated for the environment, transport and energy.

Similarly, following the government's action plan for 'Environment and Development' in 1988, the MEE initiated a 'Green Municipality' (*Grøn Kommune*) scheme. This scheme, which was scheduled between 1988 and 1992, created experiments within the local public sectors in order to assess the institutional obstacles to the new paradigm and to experiment with new and less costly environmental innovations. Nine municipalities were subsidised to join the various green projects that included educating children on environment matters, nature conservation and developing a cleaner technology option.

The experiences from these new practical, experimental initiatives influenced the MEE to form a strategy for sustainable development through local, spatial master planning. Thus, in 1992, the national planning document, a framework for regional and municipal spatial planning ('Denmark Heading for Year 2018'), made a plea for Denmark to become an environmental pioneer and to be a front-runner in sustainability issues (MEE, 1992). For many municipalities and counties, this document signalled a move towards more profound environmental concerns and activism within the areas of spatial planning and urban development. As a result of the planning document, and partly due to linking up to the Organisation for Economic Co-operation and Development (OECD) project on *Sustainable Cities*, 11 municipalities were funded to find new ways of realising the document's goal of a cleaner Denmark. From 1996 to 1997, the OECD project municipalities came to be partners with the MEE in developing LA21 ideas for information campaigns (Noah, 1997).

As is clear, these preceding and yet dispersed environmental activities inspired a number of publicly launched initiatives in practice. The initiatives and networks formed an important basis for the subsequent initiation of LA21 projects in the municipalities. Of most importance is that the experiments revealed a new path in environmental policy, where supporting bottom-up approaches formed new visions for local development and social mobilisation. New partners were found for a number of environmental areas that were not under the rules of environmental acts and regulations. They formed the basis for a change towards including citizens, NGOs and authorities in more comprehensive and constructive efforts to rebuild cities and infrastructure. Resource accounting, quality of city life and environmental goods became a positive focus, instead of protecting the environment through restrictions on activities (interview, Jørgensen, 1999).

LA21 activities and initiatives from the Danish government and association of local authorities

Following the Earth Summit, the Danish government took two years before it initiated the implementation of the mandate on LA21. In the autumn of 1994, the Ministry of the Environment (and Energy (MEE) since 1994) assigned two academics the responsibility of initiating LA21 campaigns among the municipalities and counties. They were placed in the department of national spatial planning and have been very active in working directly with the municipalities (interview, Møller, 1999; *Megafonen*, 1998). There have been no efforts to include others in LA21 activities – not even the departments for industry, agriculture, cleaner products or pesticides.

The MEE has, since the initiation, adapted a collaborative regime with relevant interest groups, the National Association of Local Authorities (KL) and the Association of County Councils (*Amtsrådsforeningen i Danmark* (AF)). A network of active municipalities has functioned as the ministry's access to local authorities when information and other types of campaign have been launched. MEE, KL and AF requested local authorities to start (voluntarily) using five terms of reference as guidelines for their planning processes. In summary, the local authorities were to initiate:

1 cross-sectoral and holistic efforts;
2 active public participation;
3 a cradle-to-grave perspective;
4 global concern; and
5 a long time-span perspective.

These terms of reference have become a crucial point for many local authorities in the Danish top-down implementation process of LA21 (MEE, 1995 and 1997a; Newsletter, nos 1–18, MEE 1995–1998; KL/MEE, 1998). For our purpose, the interpretation of the second term of reference is of special interest:

> '*...sustainable development will require thorough changes of society – from basic infrastructure to households...Within regional and municipal master spatial-planning procedures, public hearings are common [and mandatory]. But the aim is to go beyond simple hearings...it is also an aim to involve citizens in order to elevate the role of the municipalities from being authorities to becoming supervisors and partners.*' (MEE, 1995)

At approximately the same time, the MEE published a 30-page introductory booklet ('Local Agenda 21: An introduction for counties and municipalities') for local authorities and other interested organisations (MEE, 1998). According to the booklet, LA21 activities were to promote consumption reduction and pollution reduction, while at the same time improving the general quality of life. Three levels of intervention were proposed:

1 An LA21 strategy was to be integrated in spatial planning documents.
2 Sector action plans or internal initiatives such as green accounting or purchasing were to be stipulated.
3 LA21 projects were to be initiated.

In the same way, the booklet gave some advice on how to organise cross-sectoral initiatives and how to form new links for active citizen groups. It also proposed LA21 projects that could be of interest to Danish industry.

In 1994, the MEE adopted the ideas from *Our Common Future*. It also established a financial aid scheme, The Green Fund: an initiative that turned out to be a key resource for over 100 local, full-time employed Green Guides that became green catalysts within similar LA21 processes (Vejledning, 1997; Gramm-Hansen, 1998). Furthermore, the Green Fund funded urban ecology projects, green information campaigns, international environmental collaborations among NGOs, adult training, the greening of institutions, and cross-sectorally related projects. In 1996, The Green Fund was supplemented by a parliamentary programme, Pool for Green Jobs, which finances green-job initiatives and efforts that seem to have a competitive advantage on the market. Such projects have included green tourism, ecological clothing and environmental management systems for SMEs (Vejledning, 1998).

A number of networking activities, information campaigns and booklets from MEE, courses and LA21 forums have been giving advice on how to organise cross-sectoral initiatives and how to form new links to active participating citizen groups on new issues, such as transport and energy consumption (MEE, 1997a and 1997b). There has, however, been little focus on how to apply the guidelines to agricultural, transport and housing sectors, or within traditional environmental regulation fields. Accordingly, there has developed a lack of collaboration with NGOs, industries, trade unions, labour or farmers' organisations, except for two initiatives fostered by the MEE and Denmark's largest environmental NGO, Danmark's Naturfredningsforening (DN) (KL, 1998; MEE, 1999b). NGOs have, on their part, been reluctant to follow up on the Earth Summit concerning LA21 as a policy issue (with one exception: CIBU, 1994). Thus, DN (DN, 1998a) has only recently become seriously involved with committees in all municipalities, changing their negligent attitude towards LA21 in 1996–97. Similarly, very few local trade unions have been involved in LA21[3] and generally, even though MEE has financed a number of activities, campaigns and projects (under the Green Fund and the Pool for Green Jobs), there lacks a visible commitment for a united front for LA21.

The government also launched an initiative in September 1999 to develop a national Agenda 21 strategy for the period until the forthcoming Earth Summit in 2002, which will partially include efforts to coordinate and back-up local and regional initiatives from the MEE and other ministries (MEE, 1999c). This initiative was met through the coordination of several grass-roots initiatives, creating a bottom-up process for Denmark's 'declaration on Agenda 21' (www.danmarksdeklarationen21.dk). In addition, in February 2000 it was enacted that it is mandatory for all municipalities and counties during their four-year period of governance to make a formal statement regarding their strategy for sustainable development, according to the five LA21 terms of reference. The statement has to include figures or initiatives on pollution prevention, biodiversity, consultation with citizens and manufacturers, and initiatives for the enhancement of environmental policy integration into a number of sectors (Lov L176, 2000).

The outcome of these two steps of further formalisation and aggregation is yet to be seen. Denmark will, however, definitely see more governmental political focus on Agenda 21, and LA21 free-riders will have to give greater consideration to the process.

Summing up the storyline of the Danish government's LA21 strategy is very much a continuation of a consensus-seeking, bottom-up, and practical-involvement approach from the experimental period of the mid-1980s. The aim has been to create opportunities for new practical initiatives, where lay people and green professionals can cooperate with local authorities on issues that are resource-oriented and with a visionary content, but within a local context. The interesting new approach from the Danish LA21 is that the previous bottom-up policy support of practical activism is not only met but also initiated by a top-down approach, for example, in spatial and strategic planning approaches launched from MEE, KL and AF, and subsequently adopted by the local authorities. It is unique that the bottom-up and top-down approaches seem to fit so well with each other in actual LA21 policy. Shared responsibility has definitely formed a beneficial environment for mutual learning and involvement of many actors. Whereas NGOs were originally active in promoting local and global linkages before and during the Earth Summit (CIBU, 1995), they were largely absent until December 1999 in linking up with developing world problems. Business innovation towards sustainable production and consumption is not yet a central issue, but there are signs that such changes are on the way.

PROFILES, PARTICIPATION AND NEW POLICY PARADIGMS

General LA21 developments

Several surveys have been carried out to evaluate the implementation of LA21 in Denmark and to use it for political campaigns, adjustment of implementation strategies and status reporting to the United Nations Commission on Sustainable Development (UNCSD). In December 1995, a first survey of the early starters evaluated how 20 municipalities and two counties, all labelled 'green', were executing LA21 activities (AKF, 1996). The survey showed that half of the supposedly active authorities had not progressed further than expressing a political commitment, whereas one-third were about to embark upon such a process (interview,

Poulsen, 1999). In addition, the study showed that the majority of the municipalities used the mandatory, spatial planning system's strategic part and the formalised hearing procedure to introduce LA21 to the public. It is rather common that this procedure for public hearing is used for discussions on general developments, but it has become primarily a tool for *post facto* hearings (Braun and Lauesen, 1997).

An external survey of LA21 activities among the municipalities was carried out in 1998 for DN. In DN's evaluation, four criteria were used to categorise the municipalities:

1 Existence of a green enterprise.
2 Existence of a manager and supporter of green lifestyles.
3 Existence of a forum for ensuring citizen participation.
4 The development of major sustainable development patterns (DN, 1998).

With a response rate of half of the municipalities, only three municipalities were categorised as green, that is, as working towards sustainable development (by scoring above average in at least three out of the four criteria). According to the survey, 123 municipalities could not be categorised as working for sustainable development. With reference to the question of consulting the public, the survey showed that, in general, most of the authorities (60 per cent) used LA21 as a forum – not for consultation or participation, but for new ways of informing the public on environmental infrastructure issues (field studies, visiting waste water treatment plants and incineration utilities, for example). On the other hand, the number of municipalities that have established new dialogue groups or public forums has been low, although this number has risen from 19 in 1996 to 44 in 1998. The number of municipalities in which authorities have established working groups that also included lay people has nearly doubled from 30 to 63 during this period. The survey also showed that the same municipalities claimed that they (economically) supported citizen initiatives, while holding public meetings to expand the agenda of environmental issues (DN, 1998).

In 1999, DN carried out a follow-up survey of counties, where only Storstrøm County was classified as a green county, with positive scores on more than two-thirds of the criteria (DN, 1999). Six other counties (of Denmark's 14) were reported to be on track. With reference to public participation, the survey showed that there was very limited public participation at the county level. For example, only two counties had involved citizens in the drawing up of their respective LA21 plans, whereas four counties had not gone further than to endorse public participation in regional planning. However, most of the counties stated that they were planning to promote public participation in the planning and design of the forthcoming county action plan document for the year 2001 (DN, 1999). This is, however, what they have been obliged to do by law since 1976.

The MEE conducted its own survey between 1996 and 1997 (together with KL), claiming that over 50 per cent of Danish local authorities were engaged in LA21 activities, highlighting the success of the national LA21 campaign (MEE, 1997a) – a slightly different conclusion from the one reached by DN. Better still, in December 1998, the MEE carried out another survey that maintained that approximately 70 per cent of Danish municipalities were engaged in LA21 activities (MEE, 1999a). And, with reference to public participation, the survey agreed with the DN conclusion that, between 1996 and 1998, the number of municipalities that started to consult with citizens through LA21 increased from 70 to 96. Out of these, 48 municipalities have initiated consultations, while 62 have organised citizen forums. Fifty per cent of the active LA21 municipalities answered that, in general, they have initiated their LA21 activities without initial public consultation. With a top-down LA21 policy, many of the municipalities may have actively supported and financed bottom-up citizen initiatives, as the level of support has doubled amongst the LA21 active municipalities.

Individual activism in LA21 activities is another case in point. For example, MEE's survey claimed that green individuals initiated 33 per cent of all LA21 activities, followed by green organisations with 24 per cent, citizen groups with 14 per cent, while local housing groups scored just 7 per cent. However, children, youth, business managers, labour unions and researchers have been inactive (MEE, 1999a).

In evaluating the scope and nature of involvement, surveys show that the municipal activities have predominantly been in-house measures, profiling the municipality as a green enterprise or a manager and supporter of green services or products. Table 3.1, however, shows that the use of structural sustainability-oriented policy instruments for consumption and manufacturing has been limited.

Table 3.1 *Structural sustainability-oriented policy instruments for consumption and manufacturing*

Means and methods	*Percentage of LA21-active municipalities*
Energy management in public institutions	49
Environmental management in public institutions	29
Green accounting in public institutions	38
Green accounting for the whole municipality	13
EIA of decisions	7
Sustainability indicators	6
Green purchasing	33
Ecological food in public institutions	30

Source: MEE, 1999

Table 3.2 *Policies and initiatives under LA21*

LA21 activities	*Percentage of LA21-active municipalities that have put these types of activities into practice*
Health and quality of life	39
Sustainable housing/siting*	25
Lowering air emissions	24
Renewable energy and cutting consumption*	37
Forest regeneration	20
Sustaining agriculture*	12
Enhancing biodiversity	11
Protection of oceans*	23
Protection of watersheds and drinking water	48
Protection of water courses, lakes, ponds	32
Cutting use of chemicals and toxic waste*	35
Solid waste and waste water	32
Greening business technology/development*	21
Greening tourism*	11
Education and awareness raising*	38

Source: MEE, 1999
* Not covered by conventional, local environmental policy

On the other hand, Table 3.2 indicates that a considerable number of LA21 projects and activities have covered sustainability policy issues that were disregarded by the local conventional environmental policy.

It is not clear from the survey whether the non-asterisked items in Table 3.2 go beyond conventional regulation. Danish LA21 activities seem to have overlooked global environmental issues such as climate change and ozone-layer problems, while giving priority to local problems such as drinking-water pollution.

Among the group of municipalities and counties that have been classified as best cases, 62 per cent were early starters and scored above average on the more deliberate use of the LA21 concept; experimenting with new forms of dialogue; cross-municipality cooperation; and giving importance to sustainability issues. Thus, the best cases that have had a high score on LA21 methods and content also happen to be the ones that have experimented more with new ways of public involvement and participation.

Best cases

If we turn to some of the best cases (Newsletter, MEE, 1995–1998), the general impression from the survey remains. They have a far more integrated approach, covering substantial efforts to integrate both production, manufacturing and green lifestyles. Among these we find cases where the ideas from the Earth Summit were adopted so as to expand or reorient their already existing environmental activities under an LA21 banner. For example, the county of Storstrøm, which participated in the Summit, had in 1989 started a Green County Project with the purpose of promoting sustainable development in the county (Storstrøms Amts Miljøavis, 1996). And between 1991 and 1994, the county focused its attention on environmental activities that promoted cleaner technology options together with environmentally sound housekeeping. This project later continued as an LA21 project, while expanding in scope and variety. Thanks to the local green council, the organisation has 17 members from NGOs, industry, agriculture, labour and youth, for example. In the same way, the green council has established six working groups that have involved local experts and laymen in developing ideas and concrete projects. Issues of concern have ranged from sustainable agriculture, green tourism, cleaner technology, environmentally sound housekeeping to environmental training. Other diverse LA21 activities include international activities in the county that have promoted and inspired its own ideas. For example, the county has organised an environmental training course for employees in Riga, Latvia. In the same way, the county not only launched an environmental campus in 1992 – being active in the ICLEI Conference, while participating in many UN projects – but also continued to use developing-world experts as training consultants in its environmental activities.

The pioneering municipalities of Albertslund (see the following section), Silkeborg, Herning and Horsens, and the county of Vejle, are the most well-known best cases as well as the early starters. In these municipalities, it has been argued that LA21 activities have not only improved the local environment, but, more generally, that they have served as a prototype for new policy measures or goals (Newsletter, MEE, 1995–1998). This is exemplified by the green purchasing and climate projects in Albertslund; the comprehensive water-related environmental accounting and management plans in Silkeborg; and the green networks of environmental managers among industries in Vejle and Herning, which have all made significant improvements to the local environment (interview, Husmer, 1999). These pioneers have shown that it is possible to start cross-sectoral and alternative environmental projects that may go beyond conventional environmental regulation, while providing new legitimacy for local governance. Whereas the global environmental focus that was emphasised at the Earth Summit has encouraged local actors among these best cases to give pressing local environmental problems an international profile, it has also helped to address these issues in a more substantive local way. In the same way, LA21 has provided a hospitable infrastructure for promoting and strengthening environmental focus under a joint strategy or purpose. A new political platform has gradually emerged for promoting the integration of LA21 issues within the municipalities' administration.

It should be underlined here that the best LA21 cases were not only the municipalities or counties that substituted pre-Earth Summit environmental initiatives with LA21. 'Generic' LA21 cases were also inspired by the KL/AF/MEE campaigns. The municipalities of Stenløse, Køge and Haslev are cases in point. Here, prior to the Earth Summit, public participation in environmental matters or green associations from below were unheard of (interviews, Poulsen, Gelardi, 1999). However, inspired by the above LA21 campaigns, together with enthusiastic contributions of new, young and enthusiastic staff in the planning and environment offices, new activities, new ways of organising and new issues developed. In 1997 and 1998, Haslev adopted an environmental action plan and a traffic action plan – plans that motivated the municipality to initiate LA21 activities (Haslev Kommune, 1998; DN, 1998). Though the comprehensive action plan for the environment was formulated and planned from above, there was an all-inclusive public hearing that gave the local public an opportunity to come up with innovative comments and suggestions (interview, Buch Madsen, 1999). This meeting also prepared the general public for active participation in the preparation of a local traffic plan and other LA21 activities. During the preparation and formulation of an environmental action plan, members of other sectors were involved while coming up with substantial and precise targets that were stipulated in the plan, for example, the reduction of energy consumption, waste reduction, improvement of green areas, enhanced pollution prevention, dialogue with farmers and industry, resource consumption, waste-water treatment, soil contamination and noise. Specific responsibilities, timetables and projects have been worked out for each sector and, annually, the sectoral departments report back to the politicians and to the coordinating planning department.

Though the 1997 traffic plan had some top-down stipulated goals, after a comprehensive monitoring, resources were disbursed to local groups together with the freedom to find solutions and priorities within these restricted target areas. 1998 saw the launch of traffic projects covering mainly security issues, with the exception of one project, which deals with public transport problems. Together with this, a citizen board has been set up. The board oversees the disbursement of funds to support LA21 projects or groups, including ecology projects, health and nutrition projects, the greening of housing areas and car-pooling. Most notably, in Harslev, LA21 activities are exceptional in the sense that the municipality has appointed LA21 staff in its planning and development department while all sector departments have particular persons who have the responsibility of overseeing the environmental action plan as well as LA21 activities.

Whether LA21 cases were generic or add-on, the integration of LA21 concepts seems to foster new forms of shared responsibility, thereby finding new issues beyond environmental protection. However, if we were to examine how new participatory activities in LA21 may provide an infrastructure for developing and promoting new environmental initiatives, we need to map the cases more closely. Accordingly, the following pages will explore LA21 initiatives of the pioneering municipality of Albertslund. The favourable conditions in Albertslund for democratic participation and environmental concern provide an opportunity to analyse more clearly what can actually be achieved.

A PIONEERING MUNICIPALITY IN LOCAL AGENDA 21 ACTIVITIES: THE CASE OF ALBERTSLUND

The Albertslund Municipality, situated in the western suburb of Copenhagen, is a new town that was founded in the 1960s. It has approximately 30,000 inhabitants and 60 per cent of the municipality consists of state forest and different types of municipal green areas. The state forests cover 900 hectares, and in an open valley with a stream there are four municipal nature parks. The municipality, which is made up of small villages with common electricity and water supplies, originally comprised four villages in an agricultural area that has now become a state forest (AK, 1997b).

Due to its social-democratic political orientation, the municipality has, since the 1970s, attracted a certain kind of resident, a good number of whom happen to be environmentally conscious. Issues of environmental protection can be traced back to the 1970s, since which time there have always been people in the municipality who have been engaged, voluntarily, in such matters. Similarly, as a result of its recent establishment, there is a general feeling of combined ownership and responsibility in all common matters, including environmental issues. As a result, people in the area have developed strong interests in methods and plans for improving the local environment. This strong political will and dedication to environment protection is depicted by the results of a recent survey. It showed that 94 per cent of the local residents were willing to pay an extra 1000 kroner in tax on top of the conventional tax (60 per cent), provided the money was to be used exclusively to improve the environment in the municipality (AK, 1997b).

Environmental protection issues have received strong political support and engagement from Albertslund's local citizens since the 1970s. Environmental campaigns can be traced back to 1971, when local citizens first took voluntary initiatives to develop plans and methods for improving the local environment. This environmental activism together with the tradition of citizen participation in all local policy matters has provided the foundation for the implementation of the Earth Summit mandate for an LA21. In fact, following the Summit, and even before the mandate had received moral or political back-up from the national government, local citizens started to pressurise local politicians to initiate an LA21 for the municipality (AK, 1997b).

Public participation and local organisations

Principally, in the municipality's policy-making processes, we can identify two broad types of public participation (see Box 3.1). On the one hand, the binding direct involvement of grass-roots organisations contributes to the policy process, operating within structures overseen by elected or appointed officials. On the other hand, the non-binding direct involvement of citizens contributes towards the deliberative processes, the outcome of which is mediated by an administrative or legislative body. These include stipulated periods for public comment, open meetings and some citizen–advisory commissions. This non-binding direct involvement allows Albertslund's citizens to express their preferences and increase their involvement in policy deliberations beyond reliance on their local government representatives. The public hearings and periods for commentary also allow local citizens to provide input into the policy-making processes (http ref 8). In the municipality's planning exercises, there has been a greater potential for compromise while also providing an opportunity for more detailed expression of public preferences – which in turn allows for more information to enter the process. It is through these broad types of public participation in all local policy matters, including LA21 activities, that all interested and affected groups or persons express and define their targets, while also contributing useful information to the decision-making process (cf. AK, 1997c; 1997e).

This culture of public participation and influence is clearly expressed by the numerous grass-roots organisations that are found in the municipality, and not least the interaction and cooperation between them. These are, for example, a user group, an agenda centre, and a green network organisation, not to mention the various local nature organisations. The user group through which each village is represented was formed in 1980. It has 79 members who represent landowners associations, local boards and 'residents tribunals'. The group expresses its opinion on all matters of environmental significance before they are presented to the municipal council. It also discusses relevant local budgets and accounts, while reinforcing local dialogue between citizens, local administration and politicians. All political decisions in the municipality must be aired in the user group. It has real influence over all political decisions and the local authority has never ignored any of its suggestions. All matters of local residential interest are presented to the group before they are forwarded to

Box 3.1 New participatory approaches in Albertslund

Two main, broad types of public participation have been developed in and through the policy-making process of the municipality of Albertslund: a binding direct involvement of grass-roots organisations, and a non-binding direct involvement of citizens, where the outcome is mediated by an administrative or legislative body.

1 Binding direct involvement of grass-roots organisations

Through cooperation between various grass-roots and interest-group organisations such as a user group, an agenda centre, and a green network organisation.

- In the user group each village in Albertslund is represented. It has 79 members who represent landowner associations, local boards and residents tribunals. All matters of local residential interest are presented to the group before they are forwarded to the municipal council for final decision. The group has significant influence over all political decisions, as exemplified by the fact that the local authority has never ignored any of its suggestions.
- The Albertslund agenda centre is an independent institution with its own board. Its primary task is to carry out LA21 plans with each individual housing area, while also conducting specific demonstration projects. The centre aims to encourage local residential areas to address environmental issues in their local neighbourhoods.
- The green network came into being when the Albertslund agenda centre, Albertslund School of Ecology and Culture and Albertslund Municipality merged. The network's main responsibility is to ensure that information and ideas that are derived from various LA21 activities are communicated to all local grass-roots organisations, citizen groups and administrative departments in the municipality.

2 Non-binding citizen involvement

- Consists of stipulated procedures for soliciting public comment, open meetings and some citizen advisory commissions.
- Allows Albertslund's citizens to express their preferences and increase involvement in policy deliberations.

the municipal council for final decision (AK, 1997b; http ref 8; interviews, Ramskov, Markussen, 1999).

The Agenda Centre Albertslund was formed in 1996, and is an independent institution with its own board. It is financed by the user group, and its primary task is to carry out LA21 plans with each individual housing area while also carrying out specific demonstration projects. One example of these projects is an organic garden project; another is the solar-cells project that is promoting the use of solar energy as an alternative source of energy for the municipality. The centre, which has a limited number of employed staff and some volunteers, aims to encourage local residential areas to address environmental issues in their local neighbourhoods. In 1995, the centre and the Albertslund School of Ecology and Culture, together with Albertslund Municipality, joined together to form a green network to ensure that information and ideas that are derived from various LA21 activities are communicated to all local grass-roots organisations (AK, 1997e; http ref 7; interviews, Markussen, Ramskov, 1999).

LA21 history, processes and activities

In 1992, at the suggestion of the user group, the municipality set out to define its 'environmental space' in order to establish a basis for LA21 objectives. To date, the municipality has managed to estimate its approximate environmental space for CO_2 and groundwater, but more work is being carried out to obtain a more detailed definition of this concept and also to quantify the parameters for SO_2, NO_2 and waste, for example. Similarly, by 1993, the municipality had drawn up its local green accounts, which quantified its over-consumption of energy and resources. These data assisted the local authority in estimating the resulting environmental load from this measured consumption. The data also made it possible for the municipality to spell out its LA21 objectives more effectively, stimulating wider public discussions while inspiring local consumers to reduce resource consumption. With this, Albertslund became the first municipality in Denmark to effect a system of green accounting (AK, 1997c).

In 1993, following initiatives and pressure from local citizens – who in return received support from the local authority – the municipality set out to plan its LA21 initiatives. General involvement of citizens, the business community, associations and other interest groups in the planning, development review and revision of LA21 plans were encouraged (http ref 6). According to the local authority, sustainability cannot be achieved without greater participation of all its citizens. Therefore all interested or affected groups or persons were invited to express and define their targets and were also encouraged to take part in ensuring that these targets were achieved.

It was not until 1994 that an LA21 for the municipality was stipulated. Albertslund was to become a 'sustainable city', where resource and energy consumption were to fit the municipality's environmental space. All local activities were to preserve, strengthen and develop the municipality's natural environment. With the help of the environmental-space concept and the quantified green accounts, the municipality's technical and environment department – together with other interested local NGOs – drafted nature, water supply, waste, CO_2 and environmental action plans (AK, 1997a, 1997b and 1997e; http ref 1).

The draft plans were submitted to the politicians, who gave comments on the documents, and then in turn submitted them to the user group, which provided further suggestions. From here, between 1995 and 1997, the technical and environment department, in cooperation with the user group and other local grass-roots organisations, scheduled a series of public meetings and discussions. All interested or affected local citizens were invited for comments and suggestions to allow input into the formulation of LA21 goals towards a sustainable city. The town mayor, the chairperson of the local environmental council and other local politicians attended the hearing sessions to show their political will and support for these LA21 exercises. After the public hearings, the technical and environment department drew up the final drafts that included the information obtained at the public hearings. The drafts were then submitted to local politicians who, after commenting, submitted the final drafts to the user group for suggestions, before submission to the municipal council for final endorsement (AK, 1997b and 1997c).

These public exercises have provided useful data and more information in the formulation of the respective LA21 plans, while local grass-roots organisations have been active in the planning, formulation and implementation of the plans. As an example of the latter, in the development and review of the nature plan, the nature organisations voluntarily helped in the collection of raw data. For example, they measured and counted plants and animal species in the locality and these data formed the bulk of the technical report. Together with this, the nature organisations came up with proposals for the structure and development of a comprehensive nature plan (AK, 1997e and 1998).

LA21 goals and means

In the various LA21 plans that were to make Albertslund Municipality a sustainable city in the 21st century, the municipality came up with some intermediate and long-term goals. Among the intermediate goals were the reduction of CO_2, SO_2 and NO_2 emissions by 40 per cent, and the reduction in the consumption of groundwater by 35 per cent, both by 2000. For waste management, the municipality was to reduce the volume of waste production considerably by the year 2000. More waste was to be managed through recycling and 50 per cent of green kitchen waste was to be recycled from the source or at the local areas by 2000, while land filling was to be reduced. Together with this, the commitment of local citizens to LA21 activities was to be encouraged, so that by 1997 20 per cent of the local residential areas were to have worked out a sub-municipal LA21 (http refs 1, 2, 3, 5).

For the long-term goals, the municipality was to reduce CO_2, SO_2 and NO_2 emissions by 80 per cent, and the consumption of groundwater by 70 per cent, both by 2005. The municipality was also to reduce the volume of waste production by 2010. A major part of waste management was to be through recycling, with land-filling minimised and 75 per cent of green kitchen waste being handled at the source or the local areas by 2010. By 2010, all local residential areas were to have drawn up a sub-municipal LA21 (http refs 1, 2, 3, 5).

Due to an overall lack of economic, judicial and legal support from the central government, the municipality came to depend on voluntary and structural approaches to environmental protection in order to realise the stipulated goals. Examples of the voluntary self-regulation approaches include value–chain demands (customer or supplier requirements of environmentally friendly products), and self-augmented degrees of governmental incentives (such as public recognition through awards or public disclosure of offenders in the local newspaper). With a structural approach to environmental protection, the municipality initiated public awareness activities (such as green fairs and green flag campaigns for schools) that were hoped to change behaviour and attitudes towards environmental problems (http ref 4).

With the help of the user group and the green network, the municipality is carrying out discussion campaigns about environmentally correct behaviour – discussions that are often based on the green accounts data. The campaigns are meant to raise public interest and awareness of LA21 activities in the municipality and the environmental burden that is incurred by increased consumption. Similarly, these campaigns are hoped to inspire local citizens to change their consumer attitudes and habits, while restructuring their everyday lifestyle in order to reduce the consumption of energy and other resources (http refs 1, 2, 3 and 5).

Since 1996, together with a total ban on the use of pesticides on the municipality's own property and green areas, all day-care and public institutions have been purchasing organic food and environmentally friendly office materials. The municipality planned, by the end of 1999, to introduce organic food to all public schools, old people's homes and public canteens, for example. The local authority's main objective is to raise public awareness, while encouraging local citizens to treat their natural surroundings in accordance with ecological principles (interviews, Ramskov, Markussen, 1999).

Conferences about the various action plans have also raised public awareness about environmental correctness and LA21 activities. These exercises are arranged to give local citizens and interested organisations an opportunity to participate in various LA21 activities. They are also arranged to increase public awareness of LA21 plans and their status of development. Environmental forums are held by the municipality to spread information and exchange experiences amongst local citizens. Together with disseminating information through the local newspapers and local newsletters, the municipality arranges citizen meetings and door-to-door delivery of leaflets, which have become the most popular and effective measures that are used to persuade local citizens to participate in LA21 activities (http refs 1, 2, 3 and 5).

Impacts

Since 1992, Albertslund municipality has set out to make it a sustainable city in the 21st century. Due to a lack of economic, judicial and legal support from the central government, the municipality has adopted voluntary self-regulation and structural approaches to environmental protection as tools for realising its LA21 goals. Similarly, in the spirit of its tradition of dialogue and cooperation between the administration, citizens and politicians, the municipality has adopted a non-binding, direct public involvement and a binding, direct policy-making. This exercise has allowed greater citizen input into the LA21 policy-making process. It is, therefore, interesting to see whether these approaches to environmental protection will produce more environmentally sustainable results than has been possible through the traditional command-and-control regulation, or through market-based instruments (AK, 1997a and 1997b).

According to the municipality itself, it has, since 1996, witnessed positive developments that are now bearing fruit. For example, 1997 saw a reduction of 26 per cent in the emissions of CO_2, 43 per cent of SO_2 and 23 per cent of NO_2. Similarly, the 1997 green accounts showed that groundwater consumption had been reduced by 21 per cent, while the consumption of pesticides had been reduced dramatically by 91 per cent. Almost everyone in the municipality knows what an LA21 is, and not least, what the current LA21 plans and developments are. By 1997, 20 per cent of the villages in the municipality had also initiated their own sub-municipal LA21 initiatives. Though these 'soft' policy approaches may have made headway in contributing to this progress, it is not clear whether the LA21's exercises are solely responsible or whether its activities in combination with the more conventional regulatory approaches are responsible. Though the success of these activities is apparent, without economic, judicial and legal support from the central government in the future, these policy approaches may not be sufficient to alleviate environmental problems that extend beyond firms or individual self-interest (AK, 1997a and b).

The LA21 public comment and hearing exercises in Albertslund have facilitated the free flow of information from the local public to the municipal administration. This is largely because the exercises have provided an opportunity for more detailed expression of preferences. On the other hand the grass-roots organisations have not only given technical assistance and substantial contributions to the planning process, but have also contributed to promoting an increased public interest and awareness of LA21 activities and environmental matters. These LA21 exercises have not only influenced general attitudes towards the environment and generated better dialogue between the citizens, stakeholders and the authority, but also have increased a more specific awareness and understanding of LA21 activities in their own right.

Since the 1970s, local people have initiated informal LA21 activities that in return have received political back-up and support from the local government. Therefore, what the LA21 mandate facilitated was the opportunity for active local citizens and politicians to formalise and institutionalise the activities that were already in place. This has given local citizens and politicians an opportunity to relate their local environmental problems, initiatives or activities to national and global issues or discourses. This is exemplified by the adoption of the environmental-space concept and the green accounts that made it possible for the municipality to spell out its environmental objectives and results more effectively while relating them to global discussions.

CONCLUSION

The Danish tradition of a decentralised public administration and the consensus-seeking approach together with a tradition of popular enlightenment provide a favourable basis for the implementation of LA21. In the same way, the local government's tradition, characterised by public participation in local planning together with a local environmental policy of integrated pollution-control measures, has prepared local authorities for the implementation of the Earth Summit LA21 mandate. In addition, the multi-partisan tradition that incorporates plural interest groups in the design and implementation of local policies, together with a comprehensive number of local green 'do-it-yourself' experiments, has made it relatively easier for LA21 officials to initiate LA21 projects with a considerable degree of public interest.

In this chapter we have claimed that although public participation and public involvement are old issues in Denmark, LA21 activities have nevertheless contributed to a better integration of lay people's opinions in local environmental policies. For example, through LA21 activities, several local authorities have started to involve the local public in the agenda-setting part of the policy process. And increasingly the lay public has come to be a key actor in the problem-definition phase of the agenda-setting, while also stipulating targets and priorities and participating in the search for visible, socially and locally desirable solutions. Similarly, national and local governments have started to disburse human and economic resources for the purposes of enhancing public interest and public participation in LA21 activities. The process is still in a relatively early stage, however, since the majority of municipalities in Denmark have not yet started a consultation process with their citizens on LA21.

Although Denmark is known for its relatively robust participatory methods, traditionally this has mainly been at the national level and characterised by formal and rigid rules where professionals and administrators set the criteria for discussions and future plans. However, new and young entrepreneurs who are more flexible are more eager to arrange LA21 participatory activities in an informal way. Nevertheless, LA21 is at an early stage. With reference to public participation, most of the authorities (40–60 per cent) have used LA21 more in the expert–lay tradition as a forum for 'schooling' citizens. That is, LA21 programmes and activities have only promoted true, shared responsibility and cooperation regimes amongst local citizens and local authorities in the best cases. The change in participatory modes has not affected any of the counties, with the exception of Storstrøm. We may, therefore, hypothesise that this has to do with the greater distance between the authorities and the citizens at this level of government, and a lack of common, cultural, political identity.

When it comes to the question of policy content, a significant change is traceable in the deliberate greening of public administrative units, purchasing and servicing, as well as in efforts for greening lifestyles. Whereas new structural measures for sustainability are not generally apparent with LA21 in Denmark, a few new environmental subjects within LA21 projects represent a transformation from traditional environmental protection towards sustainability issues. LA21 is turning the municipalities into green enterprises, supporters of green lifestyle and a forum for ensuring citizen participation. These are targets that do not occur in traditional environmental policy. These LA21 initiatives have only been exterior 'add-ons' to existing local environmental, social and business policies, and not cross-sectoral sustainability policies. This may also have been successful for the shaping of new discursive alliances from below, as bureaucratic and corporate interests were not threatened. However, the recent developments in some of the municipalities with industries as LA21 targets point to a future situation where these two approaches to environmental regulation may merge. LA21 is not making the municipalities and counties develop major sustainable patterns of manufacturing and consumption. The global dimension, the cradle-to-grave perspective and the long time-span perspective are absent. This is, on the one hand, an effect from the consensus-seeking policy style of Danish LA21 in general, but also stems from a deliberate avoidance of undermining existing environmental regulation.

A third question is about how the vertical and horizontal organisational structures have developed and influenced the process. Here central politicians and the MEE have been innovative in advancing a horizontal networking strategy for the top-down promotion of LA21 in Denmark. This seems to have resulted in new kinds of catalysing approaches (Læssøe, 2000); for example, the appointment of LA21 officials or green guides, not as administrative staff but as semi-public/private consultants, with a responsibility for mobilising citizens, initiating debates and establishing socio-environmental activities. Networking is another case in point. Through contact persons, informal and formal networks, and other collaborative national or regional LA21 activities, LA21 officials and interested citizens have been given the opportunity to exchange ideas and share experiences.

Among some observers, the national Agenda 21 strategy that is gradually emerging (ultimo 2000) is hoped to give a new impetus to LA21. Others find that the recent obligation to report on LA21 initiatives and strategies in the Master Spatial Plan will encourage further development. We feel that LA21 in Denmark today has achieved such a level of recognition and development that it is time to leave the consensus style and address the real conflicts of interest that must occur when radical transformations are to take place. Our explorative study of some of the best cases reveals that the options and resources in instruments, organisational structures and involved actors are actually in place for a more effective turn towards local sustainability. Thus, it seems to be a lack of political will, perhaps from the lack of public support, that is the major hindrance in Denmark to developing LA21 into a more powerful instrument for change. In Haslev and in Albertslund, we have seen how the more conventional political, economic and technological approaches to environmental regulation are being supplemented by more cultural and everyday-life dimensions. Here citizens' moral and cultural rationalities come to play a new and important role. This has facilitated the greening of a considerable number of local projects, not least with respect to social relations. The best cases that have had a high score on LA21 methods and content also happen to be the ones that have experimented more with new ways of public involvement and participation. In other words, we can conclude that pleas for politicians to address the real targets and develop new policy instruments are not realistic if not embedded in a new and broader public discourse for change.

Although a new participatory regime has occurred while stimulating a new type of local democracy that is beyond normal public consultation practices, key environmental problems and rigid bureaucratic regimes have generally not been affected (although this is visible in some of the best cases). The front-runners may encourage municipalities with similar favourable conditions concerning citizens and culture. But it remains an open question whether the more reluctant and less democracy- and environment-oriented municipalities may not still have to be pressed by more traditional legal measures.

NOTES

1 Between 1992 and 1994, only a few pioneering groups (between two and ten, at any one time) were active in LA21 activities. However, since 1994, the figures have increased (1995: 80 groups; 1996: 140; 1997: 190; and 1998: 200).

2 The Danish Constitutional Act, enacted in 1849, came to guarantee autonomous municipal governance, which gave full authority to the municipalities (kommuner) and counties (amter) to rule under legally defined areas under the supervision of the Ministry of Internal Affairs.

3 The Danish National Trade Organisation (LO) published a pamphlet on trade unions and LA21, but with no further initiatives for LA21 activities. Local trade unions have been taking part in LA21 activities in Køge, Kalundborg Silkeborg and Albertslund.

REFERENCES

AKF (1996) AKF Nyt, no 3, August 1996

Albertslund Kommune (AK) (1997a) *Grønt Regnskab 1997*, Kommunale Bygninger, Albertslund

AK (1997b) *Naturplan* (tekstdel), Albertslund Kommune, Albertslund

AK (1997c) *Naturplan* (tekstdel), Forslag, Albertslund

AK (1997d) *Grønt Regnskab 1997*, Boliger/Erhverv, Albertslund

AK (1997e) *Agenda 21, 1997 Status*, Albertslund Kommune, Albertslund

AK (1998) *Naturplan* (høringssvar), Albertslund Kommune, Albertslund

Andersen, M S (1999) 'Denmark: The shadow of the green majority' in Andersen, M S (ed) *European Environmental Policy*, Manchester University Press, Manchester

Braun, T and Lauesen, J E (1997) *Dialog over Ligusterhækken?* Roskilde University, Institutf for Miljø, Teknologi og Samfund, Roskilde

CIBU Centre for International Sustainable Development (1994) *Lokal Agenda 21; Lokale Handlingsplaner for en Bæredygtig Udvikling – Idékatalog for Lokale Grupper og Aktive*, CIBU, Copenhagen

CIBU (1995) *Det er Madsen der Tæller*, CIBU, Copenhagen

Danmarks Naturfredningsforening og Friluftsrådet (DN) (1998a) *Det Bæredygtige Samfund, Idéhæfte om Agenda 21 i Danmark*, DN, Copenhagen

DN (1998b) *Grønne Realiteter i Kommunerne 1996–98*, DN, Copenhagen

DN (1999) *Grønne Facts – Om Amternes Indsats for en Bæredygtig Udvikling DN–Kontakt* 1/98, Copenhagen

Gramm-Hansen, K (1998) *Evaluering af Den Grønne Fond*, Hovedrapport, Statens Byggeforsknings Institut, Hoersholm

Haslev Kommune (1998) *Miljøhandlingsplan for Haslev Kommune, Januar 1998, Agenda 21 i Haslev Kommune, Februar 1998*, Haslev Kommune, Haslev

http ref 1: Agenda 21 for Albertslund www.mem.dk/lpa/landsplan/agenda21/database.htm

http ref 2: Sænkning af CO_2 emission fra fjernvarmen i Albertslund www.mem.dk/lpa/landsplan/agenda21/database.htm
http ref 3: Grønt regnskab til boligområderne i Albertslund www.mem.dk/lpa/landsplan/agenda21/database.htm
http ref 4: Indkøbsmesse i Albertslund www.mem.dk/lpa/landsplan/agenda21/database.htm
http ref 5: Opgørelse af det økologiske råderum for grundvand i Albertslund www.mem.dk/lpa/landsplan/agenda21/database.htm
http ref 6: Erhvervslivets Miljøforum i Albertslund www.mem.dk/lpa/landsplan/agenda21/database.htm
http ref 7: Kulturøkologisk Forening i Albertslund www.mem.dk/lpa/landsplan/agenda21/database.htm
http ref 8: Albertslund Kommunes Brugergruppe www.mem.dk/lpa/landsplan/agenda21/database.htm
Kommunernes Landsforening (KL) (1998) *En Fælles Sag*, Kommunernes Landsforening, Dansk Industri mfl, Copenhagen
KL/MEE (1998) *Lokal Agenda 21 – Startpakke til Kommuner*, Kommunernes Landsforening and Miljø- og Energiminsteriet, Copenhagen
Lafferty, W M (ed)(1999) *Implementing LA21 in Europe*, ProSus, Oslo
Lov L176 (2000) *Lov om Aendring af Lov om Planlægning* (1997–98), Lovforslag nr L176, Folketinget 1997–98
Læssøe, J (1990) 'The Making of the New Environmentalism in Denmark' in Jamison, A et al (eds) *The Making of the New Environmental Consciousness*, Edinburgh University Press, Edinburgh
Læssøe, J (1993) *Folkeoplysning om Bæredygtig Udvikling i Danmark*, Tværfagligt Center DTH, Lyngby
Læssøe, J (2000) 'Folkelig Deltagelse i Bæredygtig Udvikling' in *Dansk Naturpolitik i Bæredygtighedens Perspektiv*, Naturrådets temarapport nr 2, Copenhagen
ME (1992) *Danmark på vej mod år 2018,* Miljøministeriet, Copenhagen
MEE (1995) *En Introduktion til Kommuner og Amter*, Miljø- og Energiminsteriet, Kommunernes Landsforening & Amtsrådsforeningen, Copenhagen
MEE (1995–1998) 'Lokal Agenda 21', *Nyhedsbrev* (Newsletter), nos 1–20, Miljø og energiministeriet, Copenhagen (www.mem.dk/lpa/landsplan/Agenda21/nyhedsbrev/)
MEE (1997a) *Lokal Agenda 21 – Dansk Status ved Årsskiftet 1996–97*, Miljø- og Energiministeriet, Landsplanafdelingen, Kommunernes Landsforening, Copenhagen
MEE (1997b) *Tværsektorielt Samarbejde,* Miljø- og Energiministeriet, Landsplanafdelingen, Copenhagen
MEE (1998) *Gode Råd og Konkrete Eksempler, Idékatalog*, Miljø- og Energiministeriet, Landsplanafdelingen, Copenhagen
MEE (1999a) *LA21– Dansk Status ved Årsskiftet 98–99*, Miljø- og Energiministeriet, Landsplanafdelingen, Copenhagen
MEE (1999b) *Nye Partnerskaber, Konferencemateriale, 1999, Den Grønne Fond*, Miljø- og Energiministeriet, Copenhagen
MEE (1999c) *Natur- og Miljøpolitisk Redegørelse,* Miljø- og Energiministeriet, Copenhagen

Megafonen (1998) Ministerial monthly review, June issue.
Mortensen J P (2000) *Regulering af Miljøforbedringer, Integration af Kredsløbstankegang*, PhD-Rapportserien, no 6, May 2000, Dept of Environment, Technology and Social Studies, Roskilde University, Roskilde
Noah (1997) 'Miljøsk', *Tidsskrift om Miljø og Samfund. Tema: Lokal Agenda 21*, vol 10, November 1997
Storstrøms Amts Miljøavis (1996) *Tæt på Projekt Grønt Amt*, Storstrøms Amts, Storstrøm
Vejledning (1997) *Vejledning om Den Grønne Fond*, Miljø- og Energiministeriet, Pjece
Vejledning (1998) *Vejledning om Den Grønne Jobpulje*, Miljø- og Energiministeriet, Pjece

USEFUL WEBSITES

www.mem.dk/lpa/landsplan/agenda21/ (Miljø & Energi Ministeriet, Landsplanafdelingen, Lokal Agenda 21, homepage)
www.mem.dk/lpa/landsplan/agenda21/english/ministry.htm (Ministry of the Environment and Energy, Spatial Planning Department, Local Agenda 21 in Denmark, English language homepage)

INTERVIEWS

Bodil Bruun, Green Families, Roskilde
Dorthe Røtzler Møller, Landsplanafdelingen i Miljøministeriet
Johannes Poulsen, Kommunernes Landsforening
Kirsten Ramskov, Danmarks Naturfredningsforening
Lis Husmer, Danmarks Naturfredningsforening
Michael Svane Jørgensen, Center for Experimental Urban Ecology, Roskilde
Povl Markussen, Albertslund Kommune
Pia Buch Madsen, Haslev Kommune
Jan Poulsen, Stenløse Kommune
Pia Gelardi, Køge Kommune

4. Norway
Local Agenda 21 as a means of interpreting and achieving sustainable production and consumption

Carlo Aall

Introduction

In this chapter the results from the high profile, government-funded project Sustainable Local Communities (SLC) are presented. The project involved seven pilot municipalities and ran from 1996 to 1999. The results from the project have been a major influence in establishing what LA21 means in practice in the Norwegian context. This has also been stressed by the Norwegian Pollution Control Authority (NPCA) in its final report for the project (NPCA, 1999). At the same time, it is a fact that the SLC project was issued directly as a result of Norway's strong focus on sustainable production and consumption within the United Nations Commission on Sustainable Development (UNCSD). This is reflected in the first of the two overall objectives of the project: the project should contribute to establishing the concept of sustainable production and consumption (NPCA, 1996). In this way there is an important political link between Chapters 4 (Consumption Patterns) and 28 (Local Authorities) of Agenda 21 in Norwegian environmental politics.

However, the SLC project is also somewhat special in the way it focuses on obstacles, and not only prospects, which often seems to be the case in projects of this kind. The second of the two overall objectives of the SLC project states that it 'should 'identify obstacles and necessary means to overcome the obstacles on the local and national level of governance' (NPCA, 1996). Being an important part of the specific 'storyline' of introducing and implementing LA21 in Norway, the experiences gained from the SLC project are used to address the following two questions:

1 How can LA21 be used as an instrument to interpret and introduce policy issues into municipal environmental policymaking?
2 What are the key problems and prospects of implementing LA21 in Norway?

The chapter begins by giving a short presentation of how LA21 has been introduced into the political process in Norway, and then, by using experiences gained from the SLC project, discusses how the concept of sustainable production and consumption has been interpreted at the local level of governance in Norway. In the last part of the chapter, the issue of implementation is addressed, discussing lessons learned from the SLC project on the problems and prospects of implementing LA21 in Norway.

The chapter is based on two projects, both done in cooperation with the Western Norway Research Institute and ProSus for NPCA: a national survey on the status of LA21 in Norway (Lafferty et al, 1998) and an evaluation of the SLC project (Aall et al, 1998). In the survey, a questionnaire with 33 questions was sent to all municipalities, with an 88 per cent response rate. The evaluation was carried out as a case study along methodical lines suggested by Yin (1984) and Vedung (1997). Data were gathered through analysis of relevant documents produced by NPCA and the seven participating municipalities. This was followed up by telephone interviews of project leaders of most of the sub-projects; semi-structured, in-depth interviews – on location – of project leaders of nine selected sub-projects believed to be of special interest; and a group interview of the seven project leaders in each of the participating municipalities.

THE INTRODUCTION OF LA21 IN NORWAY: FROM 'ADAPTOR' TO 'INNOVATOR'

Though Norway is usually considered a pioneer with respect to the Earth Summit and sustainable development, analyses have shown that this was definitely not the case with respect to LA21 (Armann et al, 1995; Sverdrup, 1998; Lafferty et al, 1998) (see Box 4.1). In an eight-country study of LA21 implementation in Europe presented at the Rio+5 Summit in New York in 1997, Norway and Finland were described as 'adaptors', with Sweden, the United Kingdom and the Netherlands denoted as 'pioneers', and Germany, Ireland and Austria as 'late-comers' (Lafferty and Eckerberg, 1998). In a strictly formal sense, Norwegian municipalities had clearly done very little by the end of 1996 to comply with the recommendations of Chapter 28 in Agenda 21. At that time, only one Norwegian municipality (Sogndal) had submitted a document that might qualify as an LA21 plan, and only a handful of other municipalities had started planning processes (Lafferty et al, 1998).

BOX 4.1 THE INERTIA OF EXISTING REFORMS IN NORWAY

- LA21 got off to a very slow start in Norway. It was mainly a question of not being willing to recognise the value-added aspect of the LA21 challenge.
- At the time of the Earth Summit, Norway was in the middle of a major reform entitled environmental policy in the municipality (EIM). This created a form of achievement barrier.
- Due to intensive lobbying by environmental and research organisations, the position became reversed with the White Paper no 58 (1996–97) on environmental policy for a sustainable development. Here LA21 is included as one of four main target areas, with LA21 to replace EIM as the new programmatic heading for municipal environmental policy.
- LA21 is to be understood primarily as a planning process, to be gradually conducted as part of the mandatory municipal planning authorised in the Planning Act.
- A separate strategic unit for facilitating LA21 activities was set up in 1997 located within the planning department of MoE. Earmarked government allocations also allowed NALRA to set up a parallel LA21 unit, thus following up the close and positive cooperation on the EIM reform.
- The strategy of the MoE is to give priority to LA21-relevant activities, but is also intended to draw up a framework for interaction between other ministries and external participants; to establish both a national and regional network; and to facilitate communications between the municipalities and the MoE.
- Central government funds have been used to establish a network of regional nodes in most counties (the administrative level above the municipality). A national competence network and an official LA21 internet page have also been set up, and a separate LA21 journal is published quarterly through the joint efforts of MoE and NALRA.

For various reasons, the Norwegian government remained extremely passive in implementing Chapter 28 after the Earth Summit. It was mainly a question of not being willing to recognise the value-added aspect of the LA21 challenge (Lafferty and Eckerberg, 1998; Lafferty et al, 1998). The reason for this lack of compliance is to be found in the history of local and regional environmental policy in Norway. At the time of the Earth Summit, Norway was in the middle of a major reform entitled Environmental Policy in the Municipality (EIM), and thus the timing for introducing a new – and to some extent competing – concept seemed poor (Malvik, 1997; Aall, 1998; Sverdrup, 1998). EIM was introduced in 1988 as a joint programme by the Ministry of the Environment (MoE) and Norwegian Association of Local and Regional Authorities (NALRA) involving 91 out of a total of 435 municipalities. This initiative can only partly be related to the national follow-up of the Brundtland Report. The idea of such a programme – and a corresponding reform – was launched two years before the submission of the Brundtland Report, in a public enquiry on outdoor recreation policy in 1985 (MoE, 1985). The programme was designed to test new administrative and political models for the organisation of municipal environmental policy (Jansen, 1991). The national authorities financed the appointment of a municipal environmental officer, while the pilot municipalities committed themselves to developing an environment-and-natural-resource plan.

The EIM programme was followed up in 1991 by a corresponding reform through the parliamentary White Paper no 34 on municipal environmental policy (MoE, 1991), so that in 1992 all municipalities with more than 3000 inhabitants were offered state financing of an environmental officer. For smaller municipalities, the offer was limited to a part-time position. The arrangement with earmarked allocations terminated on 31 December 1996. At the end of this reform period in municipal environmental policy in Norway, nearly 90 per cent of all municipalities had a permanent or temporary post as an environmental officer and 70 per cent of all municipalities had adopted separate environmental plans or declared that such planning had been launched (Lafferty et al, 1998).

An important milestone in the introduction of LA21 into municipal environmental policy in Norway was the decisive Fredrikstad Conference held in February 1998. More than 700 participants from 150 municipalities took part, discussing in depth the launching of LA21 in Norway. During this conference the Fredrikstad Declaration was adopted, which can be viewed as a Norwegian version of the Aalborg Charter. The Fredrikstad Declaration states a moral obligation to support the goal of sustainable development and signals the will to start LA21 processes (see Box 4.2). By the end of 1999, nearly 40 per cent of Norwegian municipalities and all but one county had signed the declaration.[1] However, by the end of 1996 only 6.6 per cent (29) of Norwegian municipalities reported that they had actually started LA21 processes (Lafferty et al, 1998). These figures increased to 17 per cent (75) by the end of 1998 (Mathiassen, 1998). No exact figures for 1999 are available, but impressions gained from newspaper clippings collected systematically from the main Norwegian newspapers indicate a steady increase in LA21 activities. The number of registered clippings has increased from around 75 in 1996 to around 850 in 1999.[2]

The intermediate level of government in Norway – the county – has also taken up Agenda 21. At the annual national conference for counties in 1996, a suggestion was presented for them to initiate specific regional Agenda 21 processes.[3] The counties of Nordland and Akershus immediately picked up the idea. Soon other counties followed, and today at least five counties have resolved regional Agenda 21 plans or declare that such

BOX 4.2 THE FREDRIKSTAD DECLARATION

I We are:

Local authorities, regional authorities and organisations that wish to ensure that local communities in Norway contribute to sustainable development, and who therefore endorse this declaration.

II Our objectives:

a Sustainable development to secure quality of life and a means of existence now and for future generations.

b To ensure that activities in our communities are environmentally sustainable at both the local and global levels. We aim, therefore, to reduce consumption of resources and environmental pollution.

III Our point of departure:

a The call by the UN Earth Summit held in Rio in 1992 for local authorities to mobilise residents, organisations and businesses through local action-plans for sustainable development (Local Agenda 21).

b Local authorities must take responsibility for involving residents in this programme, and ensure active participation, shared responsibility and collective decision-making.

c Local communities can play a key role in making sustainable development a reality. Questions concerning development and the environment are best dealt with by involving those who will be directly affected.

d The Rio challenge can also help to revitalise local democracy in Norway.

IV Our aims:

a To mobilise residents, organisations, businesses and employees to play an active part in Local Agenda 21 activities by setting up suitable forums and networks.

b To establish the principle that action for sustainable development is the responsibility of all sectors in society.

c To ensure that a long-term, systematic approach, aiming for continuous improvement, is the hallmark of all sustainable development projects.

d To establish local plans, regional plans and other regulatory and advisory documents as binding commitments and practical instruments for achieving sustainable development.

e To monitor sustainable development projects in local communities, eg, by employing environmental indicators.

f To work for open dialogue between local authorities, regional authorities and central government bodies, and concerted action by them, to ensure synergy between local, regional and national interests.

V Our priority tasks:

- a Raising the awareness of the need to consider environmental factors in all consumption and production activities.
- b Spelling out the implications of the ecocycle for our local communities.
- c Making more efficient use of energy, and switching from fossil fuels to alternative, renewable energy sources.
- d Establishing local development patterns, particularly in towns and built-up areas, which reduce land and car use.
- e Ensuring that resources are managed locally in a way that safeguards biological diversity and provides a basis for vibrant communities.
- f Highlighting the connection between, health, environment and well-being.
- g Finding ways of organising our own municipal operations so that we take a lead in reducing consumption of resources and environmental pollution.
- h Placing environmental action in a global context by working in conjunction with representatives of other countries and cultures.
- i Preserving our cultural heritage and natural landscape as an integral part of our identity and environment.

VI Our petition:

- a That other communities endorse this declaration during 1998.
- b That central government bodies work with us on this basis.
- c That a meeting of all parties take place in the year 2000 to report on the action being taken in our local communities, and to consider whether this declaration should be revised.

planning has been launched. These initiatives are of the more innovative activities related to new strategies for sustainable development in Norway, and Norway appears to be an international leader in terms of developing and introducing the concept of regional Agenda 21 into environmental policy-making (Aall, 1998; Haukvik; 1998, Lafferty, 1998).

The government's formal starting point of what seems to be a transition from the EIM reform period to an LA21 period of municipal environmental policy in Norway, is to be found in White Paper no 58 on environmental policy for a sustainable development (MoE, 1997). In this, LA21 is included as one of four main target areas, and the government states that LA21 is to replace EIM as the new 'heading' for municipal environmental policy. The other three areas are protection of biological diversity, reduction of greenhouse gas emissions, and initiatives to limit emissions of environmentally harmful chemicals. It is further stated that LA21 is to be understood primarily as a planning process, and that such planning should be conducted as part of the mandatory municipal planning authorised in the Planning Act (MoE, 1997). A separate strategic unit for facilitating LA21 activities was set up in 1997 located within the planning department of MoE, consisting today of four full-time positions. Earmarked government allocations also allowed NALRA to set up a parallel LA21 unit with three positions, thus following up the very close cooperation stemming from the start of the EIM programme in 1988. In the autumn and winter of 1997–98, the MoE followed up the White Paper by developing a national LA21 strategy in cooperation with NALRA. The strategy has been presented in several revised versions, with the current version dated April 1999.[4] The strategy deals primarily with giving priority to so-called LA21-relevant activities in the MoE and the environmental directorates, but is also intended to draw up a framework for interaction between other ministries and external participants. Three main initiatives are proposed to put LA21 high on the political agenda in as many municipalities and counties as possible:

1 To establish a regional network and provide national funds to finance regional LA21 coordinators.
2 To establish a national network for the dissemination of competence to municipalities and counties.
3 To communicate input from the municipalities to the MoE and other ministries as to needs for coordination of national framework conditions and management signals affecting municipal policies for a sustainable development. (MoE, 1999)

Currently a regional network is in place with a full-time LA21-coordinator in almost every county. A national competence network and an official LA21 internet page[5] are also in place, and a journal named *Local Agenda 21* is published quarterly through the joint efforts of MoE and NALRA. A manual describing a detailed set of criteria for evaluating LA21-processes and results has been published (Bjørnæs and Lafferty, 1999), and a number of other sector-oriented manuals, for example on transportation, climate policy and energy policy, are in the process of being produced. A number of research and development projects have started, focusing on different aspects of LA21-implementation; the SLC project being the major effort in regard to its focus on the issue of identifying obstacles and necessary means to overcome them at the local and national level of governance. However, as we will see in the concluding section, the paradox of growing expectations regarding LA21, combined with little or no action when it comes to producing a national Agenda 21, becomes more and more striking in Norway. There is no cross-ministerial body or any other kind of Agenda 21 body set up to coordinate national policy on sustainable development; no reference to a national Agenda 21 in existing national policy documents; and no political debate on the need to develop a specific national Agenda 21.

TOWARDS STANDARDS FOR LA21 IN NORWAY: THE SUSTAINABLE LOCAL COMMUNITIES PROJECT

The SLC project (see Box 4.3) comprised seven pilot municipalities (Table 4.1), conducting approximately 100 sub-projects of various size and character (Aall et al, 1998). The NPCA financed the project with a total budget of 15m NOK (1.8m Euro) in support of the activities in the municipalities.

There are several reasons for focusing on this project when writing about LA21 in Norway. Although the project started as a sustainable consumption and production project, the project design stated that it contains, 'for all practical reasons, those elements that characterise LA21' (NPCA, 1996). By the end of the project, an LA21 perspective had gained total dominance compared to a sustainable consumption and production perspective. The results from the project have been strongly promoted by

BOX 4.3 THE SUSTAINABLE LOCAL COMMUNITIES PROJECT

- The NPCA financed the SLC project with a total budget of 15m NOK (1.8m Euro) in support of the activities in the municipalities.
- Seven pilot municipalities conducted approximately 100 sub-projects of various sizes and types.
- The project started as a sustainable consumption and production project, but the project design stated that the SLC project contains, for all practical reasons, those elements that characterise LA21.
- The municipalities focused in most cases on non-controversial and positive themes, thus enabling them to sell the project and the new concepts of LA21 and sustainable production and consumption.
- Most of the sub-projects were add-on activities, not just a renaming of traditional municipal environmental policy. This was most apparent organisationally, where the sub-projects to a large degree involved new partnerships among local stakeholders and households.
- The SLC project also signalled a new, softer policy approach in a Norwegian context, with a greater emphasis on highlighting information and positive policy measures, and focusing strongly on changing people's attitudes.
- Experiences from the project illustrate that there is a need to shift the focus towards the underlying causes of the environmental problems; that is towards obstacles of a more fundamental and structural character.
- The project also revealed a clear over-emphasis on local responsibility. Without stronger integration in a National Agenda 21, the potential for LA21 achieving its goals is very limited.

Table 4.1 *Municipalities participating in the Sustainable Local Communities project*

Municipality	*Population*	*Type of municipality**
Fredrikstad	66,000	Large city; central, mixed service industry and manufacturing municipality
Hurum	8000	Central, mixed service industry and manufacturing municipality
Kristiansand	70,000	Large city; central service industry municipality
Stavanger	104,000	Large city; central, mixed service industry and manufacturing municipality
Flora	11,000	Less central, mixed service industry and manufacturing municipality
Røros	5400	Less central, mixed service industry and manufacturing municipality
Steigen	3100	Mixed agriculture and manufacturing municipality

* Based on categories established by Statistics Norway (SSB, 1994)

NPCA and the Ministry of the Environment as a possible standard for how LA21 can be done in practice by Norwegian municipalities (NPCA, 1999). Further, the project provides a source of solid information on obstacles to local implementation of sustainable development generally, and to some extent the specific task of implementing LA21; and it also provides good information on sustainable production and consumption issues that are relevant to the LA21 discourse. Lastly, it seems right to characterise the issue of sustainable production and consumption as a dominant feature of the content of LA21, and a decisive indicator for distinguishing LA21 from other local environmental initiatives (Aall et al, 1998). This specific policy area inevitably raises the issue of social justice, thereby focusing on the core issue of both the Brundtland Report and Agenda 21 (Lafferty and Langhelle, 1999).

INTERPRETING SUSTAINABLE PRODUCTION AND CONSUMPTION LOCALLY

Agenda 21 links the concepts of sustainable development and sustainable production and consumption in the following way:

> *'To achieve sustainable development and a higher quality of life for all people, States should reduce and eliminate unsustainable patterns of production and consumption and*

> *promote appropriate demographic policies'* (Agenda 21, Basis for Action, emphasis added)

It is clear from the context that the focus is on end-use consumption by the consumer (individuals and households), and not on the total resource use by society. This represents, to some extent, a new perspective on environmental policy. The Agenda 21 document does not, however, form any basis for defining more clearly what is meant by production and consumption patterns. Does this apply to changes in the volume or merely the composition of production and consumption, and whose consumption should be changed, if any (Aall et al, 1998)?

At the first UNCSD meeting after the Earth Summit, the former Norwegian Minister of the Environment, Mr Thorbjørn Berntsen, suggested putting sustainable consumption higher on the agenda. At the same time he said that Norway could undertake to organise a preliminary meeting on this subject. His invitation was accepted and thus the first international conference (The Oslo-I Conference) on sustainable consumption, with top-level political participation, was staged in Oslo between 19 and 20 January 1994. Just prior to this conference, the Norwegian Labour government had introduced its long-term economic programme for the period 1994–97, which included a goal of doubling the volume of consumption per inhabitant by the year 2030. During the opening session, Mr Berntsen made a statement referring to the Norwegian long-term economic programme, which quickly secured the conference considerable attention in the media:

> *'One thing is crystal clear: The goal of doubling the volume of consumption in Norway by the year 2030 is absurd. If India were to emulate us, the world would collapse. We Norwegians must realise that there is no room for further growth in prosperity. The problem is that, regardless of how environmentally friendly Norwegian industry becomes and how environmentally correct our products become, any growth in the Northern Hemisphere will have a negative impact on the global distribution policy.'* (as quoted in the major Norwegian newspaper, *Aftenposten*, 19 January 1994)

What is radical in Mr Berntsen's statement is that he emphasises that making production processes more efficient and changing the pattern of consumption is not sufficient for attaining sustainable consumption, at least not if we also take into consideration a fair distribution between the industrialised and developing countries. The conference, however, agreed on a working definition of sustainable consumption with no direct reference to the volume of consumption or the distributive perspective:

> *'Sustainable consumption means providing services and products which cover basic needs and improve the quality of life, while minimising the use of natural resources and toxic materials, as well as emissions of wastes and pollutants throughout the life-cycle of the service or the product, without jeopardising the needs of future generations'* (MoE, 1994)

It eventually turned out that Norway would host five out of the first six international conferences held on this subject. The first two were especially important. In February 1995 the first conference was followed up by the ministerial-level Oslo roundtable conference on sustainable production and consumption. The objective was to make a draft plan for UNCSD. The draft working plan was later endorsed in UNCSD, and the subject has subsequently been a key target-area for commission. After the UN special session in the summer of 1997, sustainable production and consumption was listed as one of two subjects to be monitored during the next five-year period by UNCSD.

The initiative for sustainable local communities issued directly as a part of the Norwegian follow-up of its own initiative within UNCSD, trying to place the issue of sustainable consumption and production higher on the international political agenda. However, the SLC project also had to match ongoing domestic environmental political processes. One year after the launching of the SLC, a new government White Paper on environmental policy was presented (MoE, 1997). Together with identifying LA21 as one of four main target areas, the White Paper makes a distinction between three perspectives on sustainable development:

1. An ecological perspective.
2. A welfare perspective concerning global justice.
3. A generational perspective.

However, in the introduction to the White Paper, a decisive reservation is made whereby the government states that it mainly aims to 'clarify and elaborate the *ecological* perspective' (MoE, 1997, author's emphasis). The more ambitious perspectives linked to the distributional aspects of sustainable development gain less attention.

Nevertheless, the White Paper takes up the issues of changing both the composition and level of consumption. In Chapter 2, entitled 'Driving forces and framework conditions', there are a number of references to the need for reducing the volume of consumption. On the one hand, a technologically optimistic view is presented, where it is still seen as possible to achieve sustainable development by changing the content of economic growth through increased resource efficiency and changing the patterns of consumption (MoE, 1997). On the other hand, the White Paper points in the direction that a technologically optimistic strategy is perhaps not sufficient (MoE, 1997). But when the White Paper moves further towards a concrete discussion on policy measures, we are back again at a traditional technological and growth perspective. Typically, the introduction to Chapter 3 is entitled 'Changes in production and consumption patterns'.

We find an alternative unofficial perspective on sustainable production and consumption in the SLC project. In the overall design for the SLC project outlined by NPCA, a number of significant statements on the concept of sustainable production and consumption are put forward, the most important being that 'both *composition* and *level* of consumption and production *of the rich countries* must be assessed' (NPCA, 1996, author's emphasis). Here we return to the perspective of Mr Berntsen at the opening of the first Oslo Conference, focusing on changing both the composition and level of consumption. This was also the overall perspective presented to the municipalities that applied to participate in the SLC project.

The initial main purpose of the project was to develop municipal perspectives on sustainable production and consumption (NPCA, 1995). However, to find the political roots of the concept of sustainable production and consumption in municipal policy-making, we must return to an important resolution made by the NALRA congress in 1991, one year before the Earth Summit and three years before the Oslo-I Conference:

> *'The high consumption and economic growth in the West are incompatible with sustainable development and an equitable global distribution of the world's resources. Our pattern of consumption is an important factor in this context. Local authorities must lead the way in an active effort to promote consumption patterns that are compatible with natural resources and ecological carrying capacity...The Congress calls on local politicians to make an active contribution towards a more equitable redistribution of purchasing power and towards a pattern of consumption and lifestyle which safeguards the environment and supply of natural resources for future generations.'* (NALRA, 1993)

Even though NALRA uses the notion 'pattern of consumption', there is a clear link made between criticism of economic growth and the distributional perspectives on sustainable development, directing the focus thereby towards the question of volume of consumption.

Our informants admit that in most cases they had deliberately focused on non-controversial and positive themes in the SLC project, thus enabling them to sell the project and the new concepts of LA21 and sustainable production and consumption. However, a number of the informants emphasise the necessity of something they describe as a 'quantum leap' in environmental policy, expressing the hope that the time will soon be ripe for bringing up the controversial aspects of sustainable development. Thus we find that quite a few of the sub-projects were dealing with the issue of energy and how to reduce consumption of energy, rather than just shifting to more environmentally friendly energy sources. Some of the projects also focused on the links between reducing energy use and mobility, hence taking up one of the most controversial aspects of environmental policy (Høyer, 1997).

A case in point is the municipality of Stavanger, where a sub-project was given political backing to apply stringent environmental criteria in the development of a new housing estate planned for 1000 households. One of the main points in the sub-project is that the residents commit themselves to choosing water-borne heat by means of a heat pump, using the fjord as the source of energy. This is a major shift in Norwegian energy policy, considering that 75 per cent of energy use in Norwegian households is hydroelectricity. Another point refers to transportation. According to the municipality, the current road system is not sufficient to take the increased transport load resulting from the new housing estate. By combining certain restrictions on the use of private cars and a planned development of bicycles and buses, the municipality hopes to keep the use of private cars at an acceptable level, thus avoiding the need to construct new roads. The municipality also hopes to reduce the transport of waste by stimulating a high degree of composting in every household. For this reason a requirement is included to provide areas for local composting in the building plan as well as making space for garden compost facilities. There have been many pilot projects for constructing single, environmentally friendly houses in Norway, but this is the first case of a large-scale effort (Aall et al, 1998).

Another case in point when it comes to focusing on the controversial aspects of sustainable consumption and production deals with the issue of environmental impact by tourism-related transportation. The United Nations Educational, Scientific and Cultural Organisation (UNESCO) defines Røros, with its old wooden houses in the mining part of the town, as a world heritage cultural monument, and tourism is a vital industry. According to White Paper no 14 on tourism (MoE, 1986), Røros is included as one of six major attractions in the national tourism plan of Norway. The question of energy use and emissions from transportation has only been focused on to a minor degree by the tourism industry. Instead, the focus has been on typical local environmental and aesthetic problems (Høyer, 2000). Nevertheless, in cooperation with the local tourism industry, the municipality of Røros had set a goal of reducing environmental impacts of tourism-related transportation to and within Røros, while still maintaining the values of the tourism industry.

As expected, the municipality met with serious obstacles. Lack of information and marketing for travellers regarding the options of going by train or bus instead of plane or private car; lack of local alternatives to the use of private cars; lack of national promotion of public transportation; increased mobility among tourists; and a desire for shorter stays at each destination, are all examples of obstacles experienced by the municipality (Aall et al, 1998). An attempt to market Røros as an environmentally friendly destination by a European tour operator, with transport distance to the destination as a decisive criterion when putting together a green tourism product, came to nothing. The tour operator pointed out that Røros was too far away from their client groups to justify the inclusion of the town as a green destination, despite the fact that the stay and activities at the destination appear to be environmentally friendly. The environmental gain of an environmentally friendly stay in Røros, then, does not outweigh the environmental cost of travelling to and from Røros (Jäggi, 1998). Therefore, the consequence for Røros may be to reduce tourism from more distant countries, concentrating on national and neighbouring markets in the Nordic countries. However, it remains to be seen whether such a strategy will be put into action, or if the municipality will have to give up its ambitious attempts to reduce the environmental impact of tourism-related transportation to Røros.

The history of how the concept of sustainable production and consumption has been interpreted – from the Earth Summit down to the local level of governance – and attempts to introduce the concept into national and local politics in Norway, show that it is of vital importance how we understand the appeal to change the pattern of consumption. If this is understood exclusively as a question of changing the composition of consumption, rather than recognising the significance of reducing the volume of consumption as well, the result will be different initiatives and policy measures. Furthermore, the experiences from the SLC project illustrate a dimension of the level of society (Figure 4.1). At the one extreme, we find cases with an exclusive concentration on proximate and individual-oriented obstacles, whereas at the opposite end of the continuum, the attention is directed towards structurally conditioned obstacles at higher levels of governance and responsibility. The above example of attempts to reduce environmental impacts from tourism-related transportation in Røros might serve as a case in point of the latter. However, current focus on sustainable production and consumption in Norway – as well as in most industrialised countries – seems to be on the role of the individual in influencing the composition of consumption. Experiences gained from the SLC project indicate that there is still a lot to be done within such a confined perspective on sustainable development. If, however, one wants to make what our informants describe as a 'quantum leap', there is a need to shift the focus towards obstacles of a more fundamental and structural character. Also it seems difficult to retain the distributional perspectives on the goal of sustainable development without accepting the need for reducing the level of consumption. Examples from the SLC project

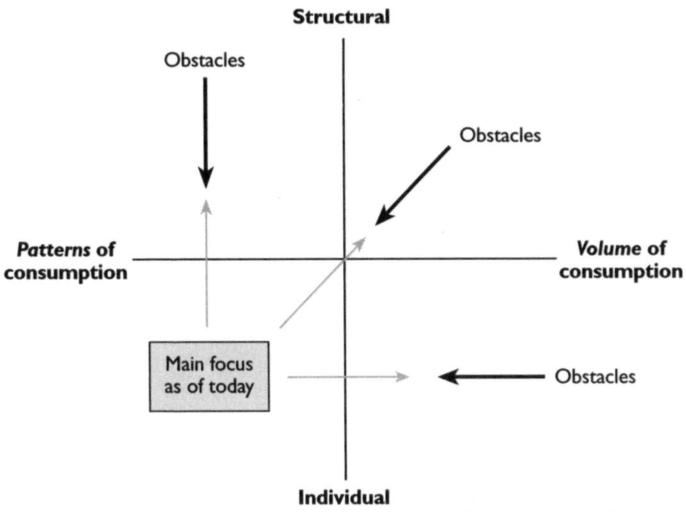

Figure 4.1 *Main challenges in extending perspectives on sustainable production and consumption*

indicate a willingness among the project municipalities to go beyond a technologically optimistic approach towards the concept of sustainable production and consumption. However, as is shown in the following section, such attempts launched as LA21 initiatives of varying types often face serious obstacles – obstacles that in most cases are very difficult to handle solely by the municipalities.

OBSTACLES TO SUSTAINABLE CONSUMPTION AND PRODUCTION EXPERIENCED BY THE MUNICIPALITIES

The starting point for the evaluation of the SLC project was the project's own intuitive understanding of an obstacle as something the persons in charge of a sub-project experienced as difficult and problematic in the realisation of the project goals. However, as a first step in the direction of a more systematic understanding, a scheme of five different obstacle levels was developed (Aall et al, 1998):

1 Individual obstacles linked to people's attitudes and behaviour;
2 Local obstacles linked to local clashes of interests;
3 Municipal obstacles linked to municipal politics and implementation of local policy measures;

4 National obstacles linked to national politics and implementation of national policy measures; and
5 Global obstacles linked to supra-national and international premises (EU and General Agreement on Tariffs and Trade (GATT) regulations, for example).

Furthermore, obstacles were categorised on the basis of differences in degrees of conflict based on Thompson's (1970) distinction between clear and diffuse goals and policy measures, with the first category of obstacles to be called trivial. In principle there is agreement on goals, the policy measures are known, and there is agreement as to the use of policy measures. The second category is a situation with diffuse policy measures; that is, when there is disagreement as to the effect of a given policy measure or when there is political disagreement as to the type or strength of the policy measure required. Obstacles linked to diffuse goals – that is, when there is either a political disagreement, or when there are other reasons why there are no clearly defined goals – lead to the highest level of conflict. In total we then end up with 15 categories of obstacles, taking into consideration both the level and degree of conflict.

Our analysis of obstacles as experienced by the municipalities suggests two general findings (see Figure 4.2):

1 There is a clear connection between obstacle level and the degree of conflict: the higher the level, the more problematic for the municipalities.
2 Larger metropolitan municipalities tend to experience less serious conflict over obstacles than small and peripheral municipalities.

We identified three main groups of obstacles experienced by the municipalities:

1 Trivial obstacles at the individual and local level.
2 Medium-level conflicts, linked to the use of policy measures at the municipal level.
3 High-level conflicts linked to national or international framework conditions.

About 70 per cent of the cases, where the municipalities experience strong conflicts, were linked to the national or global level of obstacles, whereas 85 per cent of the trivial obstacles were linked to the individual or local level of obstacles (Aall et al, 1998). Our informants expressed the view that the municipalities would like to do more in establishing sustainable production and consumption, and somewhat flippantly we might characterise these attitudes as 'the municipalities dare – but are not allowed'.

Our informants pointed out that internationalisation and its ensuing guidelines are perhaps the most important obstacles. At the same time, they pointed out that national policy – without regard to EU and other types of internationalisation – also produces important obstacles. As a concrete case in point, many of the municipalities referred to the weak Norwegian energy tax policy as an important obstacle. With a more ambitious energy tax policy, according to many of our informants, more sustainable transportation and energy systems would emerge locally at a much faster rate. However, obstacles in municipal policy as well as among local players are important as well. Many municipalities referred to the considerable task involved in changing people's attitudes towards private car use as a challenge that would be hard to meet. All of the project municipalities had some kind of green family sub-project. In most cases it seemed relatively easy to encourage people to do home composting and buy green-label products, but to make them leave their cars at home often seemed very difficult. Deep-rooted attitudes in the municipal organisation were also mentioned, and it was asserted to be just as hard to change attitudes in the municipal administration and among local politicians as among the general public.

To some extent we found a centre–periphery dimension with regard to both the level of obstacles and the degree of conflicts experienced by the municipalities. The smaller and peripheral municipalities seemed more willing to choose controversial themes for their sub-projects, hence experiencing a higher level of conflict. We found that 50 per cent of the identified obstacles in the small and peripheral municipalities of Steigen and Røros could be classified as high level of conflict, with 30–45 per cent relating to the international or national level. At the opposite end of the scale we find the city municipalities of Fredrikstad and Kristiansand, where 60–70 per cent of the identified obstacles could be classified as trivial, linked to individual, local and municipal levels (Aall et al, 1998).

Vedung (1997) offers a possible explanation for these findings. He distinguishes between pilot activities as social experiment and implementation strategy, whereby in the latter the pilot activity is used merely as a policy measure to realise previously set goals. The large and central municipalities were also those with a more sophisticated and long-living environmental management system. In these municipalities we found indications that they had used the SLC project as a strategy for implementing an already known environmental policy derived from existing municipal environmental plans. Conversely, we found that the environmentally immature municipalities of Steigen and Røros, with a less sophisticated, less developed and younger environmental management system, seemed to use the SLC project to develop a genuinely new environmental policy to a much higher degree (Figure 4.2).

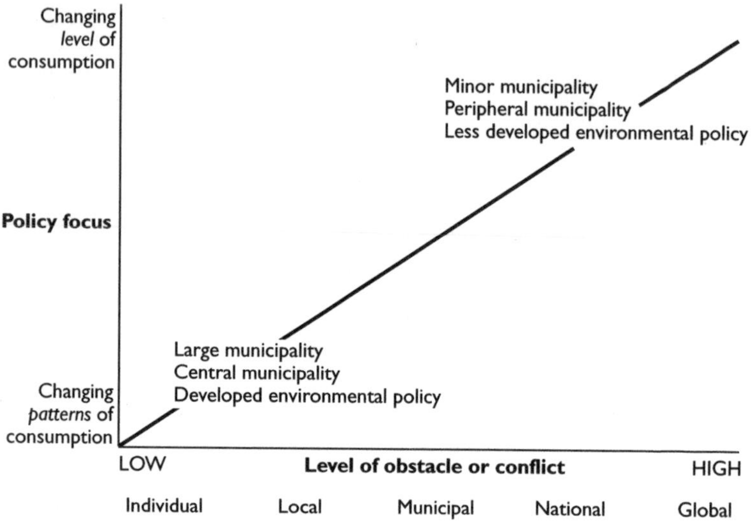

Source: Aall et al, 1998

Figure 4.2 *Relation between policy focus and level of obstacle or conflict*

PROSPECTS AND PROBLEMS OF LA21 IN NORWAY

What is so special about LA21 is the specific link between the international and local, involving the responsibility of local authorities in trying to achieve global policy goals, combined with a strong focus on community involvement. Chapter 28 in Agenda 21 thus introduces three important and, in many ways, new dimensions in municipal environmental policy-making (Aall, 2000):

1 The global–local relationship: the substantive issue of how global environmental problems are manifested locally, and the new role of local authority as implementers of global policy goals in addition to national and local policy goals.
2 The local–global relationship: the substantive issue of how local action interacts with global environmental problems, and the procedural issue of how local municipalities start to participate as international participants in environmental policy-making.
3 The local–local relationship: the idea of bringing both average citizens and groups, particularly NGOs, business and labour unions, into the planning and implementation process with respect to environment and development issues.

These aspects – or at least the first two – relate to the more general process of globalisation seen within all aspects of society. What is clear, however, is that there is a fundamental contradiction in the globalisation process between, on the one hand, progress towards a global, interdependent community and, on the other, the quest for national and local autonomy and distinctive identity. Some are even using the term 'glocalisation' to embrace both sets of trends. Hempel (1996) and Crowley (1998) describe the term as a development of power away from nation-states up towards supra-national – and down towards regional and local levels of governance – in response to global changes in ecology and the political economy. Crowley (1998) states that 'globalism evokes borderlessness and the rise of strategic, global alliances and markets against the decline of traditional notions of state sovereignty that will see state-centralism under increasing attack into the twenty-first century'. Hempel and Crowley argue that political institutions will become increasingly 'glocal' in character, reflecting the global and grass-roots implications of an ecological crisis and an economy straining to expand world markets. This development raises issues of how to redefine local environmental governance, how to fund it and how to negotiate environmental policy flows, essentially from the global to the local level, given the institutional and fiscal hurdles in between. It also raises the need for enhanced and new ways of community participation and local democratisation.

Previous assessments of the EIM reform in Norway concluded by stating that 'local management bodies...can (hardly) function as activators in the work with more superior, global environment problems', given that studies of the municipalities had shown that 'the municipalities give priority to issues which lead to visible local gains' (Naustdalslid, 1994). A long-standing tradition of community involvement in local planning processes in Norway further leads to the following White Paper statement on how Norway is to follow up the commitments from the Earth Summit: 'The Norwegian system of local master-planning is in accord with the recommendations of Agenda 21' (MoE, 1992). These studies and assessments were, however, carried out prior to LA21 entering the political agenda in Norway. Signs of a new policy style seem to have been developing during the late 1990s at the local level of governance in Norway, as LA21 picked up elements from all three of the above mentioned new dimensions in municipal environmental policy-making (Aall, 1997 and 2000).

Returning to the SLC project and the pilot municipalities, we first of all found that most of the sub-projects deserved to be characterised as add-on activities, not just as a renaming of traditional municipal environmental policy. The sub-projects differed from a traditional municipal environmental policy, first and foremost, when it came to the policy process involving new policy partners (Aall et al, 1998). The municipalities pointed at the rate of cooperation with local business and households as an important and genuine new type of process under the LA21 heading.

To a certain extent this applies to cooperation with NGOs as well. The SLC project also signalled a new, softer policy approach in a Norwegian context by highlighting information and positive policy measures, and focusing strongly on changing people's attitudes. We found less emphasis on the role of the municipality as a controlling and public-planning institution, and more emphasis on the role of a green model, giving priority to setting one's own house in order before interacting directly with local business and households.

Thus, such a change represents a new course in the direction of a more continental 'soft-policy' model, putting more weight on specific sub-projects and less weight on general participation in planning processes. Several municipalities indicated that they consider these changes decisive in their further work with LA21. If this is the case, it represents a marked change in Norwegian municipal environmental policy. Since the late 1980s, both MoE and NALRA have made efforts to strengthen municipal environmental planning and local environmental policy. If such a change replaces the existing model, this may lead to a weakening of municipal environmental policy. If, on the other hand, this becomes a supplement, the change of direction expressed by the municipalities may strengthen local environmental policy.

The SLC project, and other projects and local initiatives, show growing examples of ambitious and genuinely global-oriented LA21 processes in both substantive and procedural matters. The SLC project was in itself part of an international policy-making process, being part of Norway's attempt to give the issue of sustainable consumption and production higher priority within the UNCSD process. Many of the project municipalities have also taken part in international activities set up by ICLEI and others, such as taking part in or arranging international environment conferences, signing charters like the Aalborg Charter and establishing twinning with developing world municipalities. Most of this has happened with direct reference to LA21 (Aall, 2000). We also find examples from Stavanger and Røros of municipalities taking up issues like energy, transportation and climate policy linked to a specific global context in their LA21 activities. Another notable example is from the city of Kristiansand, which produced the first local climate action-plan in Norway in 1998; a plan which also superceded any national climate action-plan in Norway. In this case, the municipality took upon itself the responsibility of following up the Norwegian target from the Kyoto protocol: a maximum of one per cent increase of greenhouse-gas emissions by 2008–12 as compared to 1990 emissions. With no further action, Norway's greenhouse-gas emissions will probably increase by 23 per cent by 2012 compared to 1990. However, the first national climate action-plan, presented at the same time as that of Kristiansand, could only count for a 9 per cent reduction in the stipulated 23 per cent increase, leaving an approximate 13 per cent reduction still to be addressed in the next national action-plan. Even more ambitious, in a Norwegian context, is the city of Bergen, which has twice adopted a council resolution of a 20 per cent reduction in CO_2 emissions by the year 2005 compared to 1991 emissions (Lundli et al, 1999).

However, as long as LA21 does not have any real support in the form of a National Agenda 21, its potential as an instrument of interpreting and introducing sustainable development into serious politics will be limited. Experiences from the SLC project illustrate how municipalities have been left to themselves to sort out the difficulties and problems of sustainable development within the framework of LA21 processes. The effect is a paradox in which the lack of policy coordination at the national level is being transferred downwards by prescribing stronger coordination at the lower level (Naustdalslid, 1994, Langhelle, 2000). Nevertheless, even though we do not have a specific National Agenda 21 in Norway with a potential to help the municipalities sort out the national obstacles, national government has officially recognised this paradox. One of two main goals for the SLC project was namely to identify obstacles and necessary means to overcome them at both the local and national level of governance. Such an ambition is also mentioned in the national LA21 strategy document presented by MoE and NALRA (MoE, 1998).

It still remains to be seen, however, whether information on national obstacles, communicated upwards from the municipalities, will result in national policy changes overcoming the same obstacles. In 2001 the government plans to present a White Paper on sustainable cities, whereas no plans are known for a specific National Agenda 21 in Norway. Due to the possibility of little or no action at the national level of governance regarding the need for a National Agenda 21, the municipalities are left to address the national and global obstacles of sustainable development by participating directly in international political processes or, as in the SLC project, to continue to identify and communicate the nature of national and global obstacles whenever such obstacles appear in local policy-making.

NOTES

1 See www.agenda21.no/magasin/magasin.htm.
2 See www.prosus.no/la21/barometer98.html.
3 A presentation made at the annual national conference for counties in 1996 by Karl G Høyer from the Western Norway Research Institute.
4 See http://odin.dep.no/md/la21/strategi.html.
5 www.agenda21.no.

REFERENCES

Aall, C (1997) *Summary Overview of the Eco-municipality Programme, 1989–96*. (In Norwegian with English summary), VF-report 2/97, Western Norway Research Institute, Sogndal, Norway

Aall, C (1998) 'Norway: Confronting the inertia of existing reforms' in Lafferty, W and Eckerberg, K (eds) *From Earth Summit to Local Forum: Studies of Local Agenda in Europe*, Earthscan, London

Aall, C (2000) *When is Change Change? Local Government on its Way to Sustainability?* (Partly in Norwegian, with six English articles), Doctoral thesis at the Department of Development and Planning, University of Aalborg, Denmark

Aall, C, Lafferty, W and Bjørnæs, T (1998) *Hindrances in Achieving a Sustainable Production and Consumption Locally* (in Norwegian with English summary), Western Norway Research Institute, Sogndal, Norway

Armann, K, Hille, J and Kasin, O (1995) *Local Agenda 21: Norwegian Municipal Environmental Policy after Rio* (in Norwegian), Project Alternative Future and The Ideabank, Oslo

Bjørnæs, T and Lafferty, W (1999) *Implementation of Local Agenda 21 in Norway*, Report to the Ministry of Environment (in Norwegian), The Ministry of Environment, Oslo

Crowley, K (1998) '"Glocalisation" and Ecological Modernity: Challenges for local environmental governance in Australia', *Local Environment*, vol 3(1), pp91–97

Haukvik, L (1998) 'Regional Agenda 21. The Agenda 21 policy of the counties' (in Norwegian), *Journal for a Sustainable Society*, vol 2/98, pp75–78

Hempel, L C (1996) *Environmental Governance: The Global Challenge*, Island Press, Washington, DC

Høyer, K G (1997) 'Sustainable Development' in Brune, D, Chapman, D and Gwynne, M (eds) *The Global Environment*, VCH Publ, Weinheim, pp1185–1208

Høyer, K G (2000) 'Sustainable Tourism – or Sustainable Mobility?' *Journal of Sustainable Tourism*, vol 8(2), pp147-161

Jäggi, S (1998) *Project 'Destination Røros – environmentally friendly'* (in Norwegian), Report to the municipality of Røros, June 1998

Jansen, A (1991) *Reform and Results: An Evaluation of the Pilot-project on Environment in the Municipalities* (in Norwegian), The Norwegian Research Council, Oslo

Lafferty, W (1998) 'Local and Regional Agenda 21: A politically viable path to sustainable development'. Paper presented at the Graz Symposium on 'Regions – Cornerstones for Sustainable Development', Graz, Austria, October 28–30, 1998

Lafferty, W and Eckerberg, K (eds) (1998) *From Earth Summit to Local Forum: Studies of Local Agenda in Europe*, Earthscan, London

Lafferty, W and Langhelle, O (eds) (1999) *Towards Sustainable Development: The Goals of Development – and the Conditions of Sustainability*, Macmillan, London

Lafferty, W, Aall, C and Seippel, Ø (1998) *From Environmental Protection to Sustainable Development in Norwegian Municipalities* (in Norwegian), ProSus Report 2/98, ProSus, Oslo

Langhelle, O (2000) 'Norway: The "institutionalization" of sustainable development' in Lafferty, M W and Meadowcroft, J (eds) (2000) *Implementing Sustainable Development: Strategies and Initiatives in High-Consumption Societies*, Oxford University Press, Oxford

Lundli, H E, Groven, K and Aall, C (1999) *Local Climate Policy: International and Norwegian Experiences* (in Norwegian with English summary), VF-rapport 4/99, Western Norway Research Institute, Sogndal, Norway

Malvik, I V (1997) *Think Globally and Act Locally: Agenda 21 – From International Agreement to Practical Implementation* (in Norwegian), SMU Report 4/97, Centre for Environment and Development, University of Trondheim, Trondheim

Mathiassen, E (1998) *Light Spots and Black Holes. Follow-up of LA21 by Norwegian Municipalities* (in Norwegian), The Future in Our Hands, Oslo

MoE (1985) *Outdoor Recreation Life. An Enquiry from the Ministry of Environment* (in Norwegian), The Norwegian Ministry of the Environment, Oslo

MoE (1986) *Government White Paper on Tourism* (in Norwegian), The Norwegian Ministry of the Environment, Oslo

MoE (1991) *Government White Paper on Municipal Environmental Policy* (in Norwegian), The Norwegian Ministry of the Environment, Oslo

MoE (1992) *On Norway's Follow-up on the UN Conference on Environment and Development in Rio de Janeiro* (in Norwegian), White Paper no 13 (1992–93), The Norwegian Ministry of the the Environment, Oslo

MoE (1994) *Symposium: Sustainable Consumption: 19–20 January 1994, Oslo, Norway* (in Norwegian), The Norwegian Ministry of Environment, Oslo

MoE (1997) *Environmental Policy for a Sustainable Development* (in Norwegian), White Paper no 58 (1996–97), The Norwegian Ministry of the Environment, Oslo

MoE (1998) *Local Agenda 21 Strategy Note* (in Norwegian) The Norwegian Ministry of the Environment, Oslo

NALRA (1993) *Think Globally – Act Locally. Priorities for Environmental Protection at the Local Level*, The Norwegian Association of Local and Regional Authorities, Oslo

Naustadslid, J (1994) 'Environmental Problems, the State and the Municipalities' in Naustdalslid, J and Hovik, S (eds) *Local Environmental Policy* (in Norwegian), Tano, Oslo

NPCA (1995) *Sustainable Production and Consumption* (in Norwegian), Report from a pre-project, The Norwegian Pollution Control Authority, Oslo

NPCA (1996) *Sustainable Local Communities – Project Plan*, The Norwegian Pollution Control Authority, Oslo

NPCA (1999) *Putting Ideas into Practice*, The Norwegian Pollution Control Authority, Oslo

SSB (1994) *Standard Classification of Municipalities 1994*, Official Statistics of Norway

Sverdrup, L (1998) 'Local Agenda 21 in Norway' in O'Riordan, T and Voisey, H (eds) *The Transition to Sustainability: The Politics of Agenda 21 in Europe*, Earthscan, London

Thompson, D F (1970) *The Democratic Citizen: Social Science and Democratic Theory in the Twentieth Century*, Cambridge University Press, Cambridge, UK

Vedung, E (1997) *Public Policy and Program Evaluation*, Transaction Publishers, London

Yin, R (1984) *Case Study Research. Design and methods*, Sage Publications, London, New Delhi

5. The United Kingdom
Mainstreaming, mutating or expiring?

Chris Church and Stephen Young [1]

THE NATIONAL STATUS

A profile of LA21 in the UK: Process, policy and product[2]

The UK LA21 process emerged from the Earth Summit with a lack of clarity and even as an object of confusion, but also as an idea whose time had come. The idea that local authorities should take an active role in developing a local strategy for the environment was a recent but not altogether new one. The first local authority environmental audit had been done by Kirklees Council in 1988 with the support of Friends of the Earth UK, and the upsurge of public concern about environmental issues at this time (due primarily to issues such as the ozone layer and global warming) led to many others producing environmental plans. They were supported in this by the Friends of the Earth *Environmental Charter for Local Government* (FoE, 1990) and by the Environment City programme run by the Royal Society for Nature Conservation, which worked in six cities to produce integrated action plans.

Before the Earth Summit there had been little political support for such initiatives, so that when the Local Government Management Board (LGMB) started to promote the idea of LA21 there was a receptive audience of about 50 'early adopter' local councils. This was the first wave of activity. The LGMB played a crucial support role as there was little support elsewhere (Young, 1997a). Some NGOs (see below) were keen to help but under-resourced, and central government took a long time to recognise the value of the initiative.

This initial lack of financial support or a clear government-supported launch, coupled with a lack of enthusiasm from some environmental NGOs, was influential in what came after. LA21 sidled on to the stage with little in the way of media interest. Another problem was the lack of any clear marketing strategy. While the LGMB encouraged local authorities to launch these processes, there was initially little in the way of material to help staff, who were keen to see it happen, sell the new idea to sceptical senior staff, elected members, and local media.

In June 1997 the UN General Assembly Special Session (UNGASS), widely known as 'Earth Summit +5', took place just after the Labour Party's victory at the general election, and the new government went to New York, along with local government representatives, hoping to be seen as taking a leading role on sustainable development. The prime minister stated that he wanted to see every UK local authority have an LA21 by the year 2000. This was later clarified as completion by 15 December 2000 (LGMB, 1999).

In January 1998 the government gave its strongest lead when the deputy prime minister spoke to a conference of local authority chief executives to launch a joint guidance document, *Sustainable Local Communities for the 21st Century* (DETR, 1998b). The document sought to spell out how and why local councils should produce an LA21. It drew heavily from earlier LGMB work and was criticised by some community groups for its 'top-down' nature. But it did, together with Labour's interest in environmental issues (Young, 2000), encourage a further wave of interest in LA21 amongst the third or so of all councils that had so far ignored the issue (LGMB, 1999).

LA21 and environmental action

From the beginning, there was a lack of clarity about the purpose of LA21. This is not surprising, as it is a fundamentally new approach to local development with no established procedures; nor is it a statutory duty. The original aim, as expressed in Agenda 21, was a local plan for sustainable development that would focus on the key issues in the document, including poverty, health, and livelihoods as well as environmental issues. However, LA21 came at a time when many UK councils were starting to consider their environmental responsibilities. It was seen as a direct development out of this, and most work was, and remains, in the hands of local authority environmental coordinators.

While LA21 was seen as a way for local councils to focus on sustainability, it was also influenced from the start by the key phrase in Chapter 28 of Agenda 21, calling on local authorities to 'consult with their communities'. This has had a major impact on LA21 in the UK. The early-adopters (those who started LA21 programmes in 1993–95) were often those where strong local NGOs had been actively involved in the Earth Summit process. United Nations Association UK (UNA UK) had run some 30 meetings around the UK before the summit, and in many places voluntary groups were committed to 'bring Rio home'.

Certain features of LA21 have become widespread, notably some form of internal environmental management and the use of topic-specific working groups as a way of enabling involvement of local activists. A typical LA21 might have six to eight such groups on topics including waste, energy, transport, natural environment, pollution, health and social issues. These working groups would be asked to produce a chapter for the final LA21 action plan, and often lacked a clear role after such a plan was produced. A limited survey in 1998 suggested that groups where there was primarily a need for implementation work, such as waste or energy, lost support much faster than those where there was more to talk about and less consensus, such as health or the economy.

Despite such fluctuating support, there is no doubt that since 1992 the map of environmental activity in the UK has been transformed by the arrival of local authorities as more proactive participants. There are at least four areas where surveys (LGMB and others) show there has been clear progress:

- Waste: national targets for waste minimisation and recycling have been set by government, and councils are tracked on their progress towards these goals. Some have already achieved the main initial target of 25 per cent of waste being recycled.
- Energy: with the government taking a lead on the Kyoto process, many councils have set their own targets, and programmes to meet those targets. Many have linked this to fuel poverty – an operational link between environment and exclusion.
- Biodiversity: while the call for biodiversity action plans initially met with scepticism, many authorities are now working effectively in this field.
- Transport: this has become the most contentious environmental issue in the UK. The government has called for all local authorities to develop local transport plans, and many have active and imaginative programmes to cut car use, linked through the 'TravelWise' and 'Don't Choke Britain' campaigns.

One other common issue has been the lack of support. The LGMB produced a great deal of written material, but could offer little in the way of advice. This led to something of a consultancy boom, with both NGOs and established consultancies seeking to provide guidance on how LA21s should develop. This provided much-needed advice, but it is open to question how far it may have led to authorities avoiding the more difficult or innovative areas of sustainability. Consultants were asked to advise within specific briefs and were keen to demonstrate achievement and to play to their own strengths. Environmental consultancies were also often badly placed to advise on community participation.

When the LGMB was restructured in 1998, the Improvement and Development Agency for local government (IDeA) emerged (founded in April 1999). A year later there was further rationalisation. The Sustainable Development Unit, which provided support for LA21, was incorporated into the Best Practice Unit, and specific support for LA21 ceased in July 2000.

The broadening agenda

The late 1990s saw a growing appreciation of the need to develop the agenda beyond predominantly environmental issues. LA21 and sustainable development are rooted in the inter-connectedness of issues. They require the integration of programmes for different sectors, so that the aims and impacts of transport or employment policies need to be assessed against environmental, social and economic criteria. In Britain this integrated approach to policy-making is referred to as holistic or cross-sectoral. Labour ministers use the phrase 'joined-up thinking' (Social Exclusion Unit, 1998; Young, 2000). A 1995 report (Church, 1995) had argued that housing, health, poverty and economic development were higher concerns for many councils than LA21, but they had only been integrated into LA21 to a very limited extent. Crime and social exclusion were scarcely addressed. University of Westminster survey work for the LGMB (Tuxworth and Thomas, 1996; Morris and Hams, 1997) shows only limited success in this field.

The British approach to LA21 has been handicapped by institutional and historical factors. Within local authorities, departments are organised sector by sector. LA21 requires complex inter-departmental thinking. But narrow compartmentalised approaches have often prevailed. Policies for housing or social services, for example, have been developed with little regard for connections to other issues. This has been seen as a problem since the reorganisation of local government in the mid-1970s (Stoker, 1991), but attempts to deal with it by corporate planning, decentralisation, political leadership and powerful executive departments have had little impact. This helps explain why so much LA21 work has been done on a sector-by-sector basis, and why the record in Britain is so patchy (Audit Commission, 1997; Buckingham-Hatfield and Percy, 1999; Wilkinson and Appelbee, 1999). In developing cross-sectoral approaches, LA21 officers have often faced negative attitudes and institutional problems.

The area where social and environmental concerns have come together most effectively is perhaps public health. Links between a bad environment and bad health have been recognised for a century or more. UK bodies such as the Chartered Institute of Environmental Health working on this have promoted work on sustainability to their members, some of whom have been running LA21 programmes. There does not appear to have been any assessment of whether or how far an environmental health LA21 differs from one led by planners. While there was some friction locally between these departments, the increasing merging into larger environmental services sections has lessened this, and the Labour government's initiatives on health action zones and local environment and health action plans have also opened the way for more cross-sectoral working (WHO, 1997; Lloyd, 1999).

The essence of LA21 in the UK is its variety. By the end of the 1990s several different approaches were in evidence:

- Some early LA21s were running out of steam and becoming marginalised; in some cases local participants were becoming sceptical about what had been achieved (in Hounslow the LA21 strategy document was publicly burnt by its supporters because the council was no longer taking it seriously);
- Late starters were looking for blueprint programmes they could adopt;
- Growing numbers of councils were getting environmental management programmes into place;
- A small number were promoting integrated cross-sectoral approaches, and, encouraged by voluntary organisations, adopting the broader agenda;
- A smaller number were working LA21 priorities into budgets and council-wide programmes.

Evaluation

Some sources have made over-optimistic claims for LA21 and the new localism (Marvin and Guy, 1997). Others have seen local authority involvement in sustainability as a 'superficial veneer' (Selman, 1998). We have argued above that the dominant feature of the UK case is the variety of approaches. Published LA21 reports vary from wish lists to complex and ambitious documents. After the Earth Summit, LA21s were envisaged as adequately resourced strategies designed to tackle the range of local economic, environmental and social issues (Lafferty and Eckerberg, 1997). Judged against these criteria, between 60 and 81 can make a real claim to be viable LA21s in the UK. There is a long trail of other documents. Many relate just to environmental management, while others have been marginalised. Evans and Percy conclude that 'very few' councils are pursuing LA21 'at the levels envisaged by the authors of the LA21 document in the pre-Rio PrepCom (preparatory) meetings' (1999).

However, the LA21 process has had wider impacts, although it is difficult to assess how much of the effect is due to LA21, NGO campaigning, increased interest from the government, or other factors. LA21 has certainly helped promote environmental awareness amongst the public, and has helped promote campaigns that have begun outside LA21. The

'Don't Choke Britain' campaign was launched by a few local authorities and came to involve over 230. Much of the later support came through LA21 programmes, but the first steps did not involve it.

LA21 has also changed professionals' perceptions. Many planners, frustrated with traditional statutory consultation processes, have found in the non-statutory LA21 a way to explore other methods of participation; while others have been astonished to find audiences of 200 or more turning up for LA21 launches and looking to discuss both large- and small-scale planning matters. Similarly, local economic professionals have adopted new approaches to draw green ideas into their work. Gibbs et al (1998) suggest there are up to 16 types of local authority approaches to greening the local economy.

Lastly, LA21 has attracted new support and resources into council work. Many councils have worked hard to bring local business views into LA21. Some large businesses, aware of their role as major local employers, have become active, and LA21 launches have taken place at conference centres linked to car factories, airlines, and chemical plants. Reasons for involving business have varied from a simple desire to do the right thing (seeing businesses as a key part of the local community), through a desire to gain extra financial support through sponsorship, to an openly expressed desire to counteract the influence of environmental groups in the process. This last point illustrates how much work sustainability practitioners have to do.

Evaluating the LA21 process

LA21 has promoted interest in the need to monitor progress. The first major national programme to develop within the LA21 framework was on the use of indicators. Following a UNA seminar in January 1993, the LGMB set up a programme to work with ten cities. This work produced a list of 95 indicators, many drawn from programmes elsewhere, and the pilot projects were asked to make a balanced selection from the main list. In the event, only seven indicators were chosen by more than seven of the ten cities, many were adapted and 45 new ones were developed within the authorities (LGMB, 1995). Most of the pilot projects lacked clear objectives when they made their selection, so indicators were chosen partly on grounds that included ease of access to information, rather than on the basis of information that would inform a subsequent plan of action. Despite some setbacks, many authorities have further developed this work, including some pioneering approaches such as Lancashire's Green Audit 2.

Such work was given a major boost in 1999 with the publication of a core set of national indicators as part of the government's sustainability strategy (DETR, 1999c). Work is ongoing, through a central–local government partnership, as to how these can best be linked to local activity.

The ultimate purpose of this work must be to evaluate LA21 itself. How far has it actually been a success, and what does the word mean in this case? In early 1997, some NGO agencies supported the '3 Ps' model (Church, 1997):

- *Process:* Has the process of consultation been designed so as to ensure that all stakeholders had a genuine opportunity to take part and have an input?
- *Product:* Are things actually happening in the locality as a result of the LA21 process?
- *Policies:* Are the policies of local authorities and other affected bodies changing as a result of the LA21 process in ways that support moves towards sustainable development?

Other researchers (for example, Selman, 1998) have worked on similar models, and ways to quantify activity in these fields have been discussed. One common problem has been the resources needed to objectively assess such diverse processes. Self-assessment has been discussed, and tele-guided self-assessment is at the core of the Local Authorities Self Assessment of Local Agenda (LASALA) project, a new multi-partner initiative of the International Council for Local Environmental Initiatives (ICLEI). However, a first meeting of UK local authorities to consider assessment felt that self-assessment would be of limited value. There is also the question of how other stake-holders might be involved – no NGOs were invited to that meeting.

Reasons that explain the overall profile

The fundamental point is that from the Earth Summit to the 1997 Summit, LA21 remained non-statutory and thus optional for councils. Even after the prime minister's speech, many authorities are still doing little or nothing. The situation was made worse by the lack of support from central government, and the limited resources available to LGMB. LA21 is also a dynamic, innovative process, and it is a common feature of such processes to throw up areas of tension and dispute. There are four areas where such tensions are evident:

1. Participation versus representation.
2. Campaigning against versus working for.
3. Conflict versus consensus.
4. Environmental management versus community empowerment.

Participation versus representation

With any interest in participation comes concern from those in authority about real – or imagined – loss of power (Abbott, 1996). This is particularly relevant in LA21, since those in power are elected through representative local elections. Some advocates of participation are critical of local government, seeing it as bureaucratic and inefficient (and unwilling to take on the radical agendas often proposed by such advocates), and argue that, on democratic grounds, people should be involved more frequently in decision-making than just through local elections (Commission for Local Democracy, 1995; Stewart, 1995; Mason, 1999). On their part, some elected local councillors have adopted the attitude that, 'I know what my community wants, so there's no need for all this consultation'. Their critique of LA21 programmes is that activists from unrepresentative groups are using it as a way to gain influence.

The general tension here is revealed as being between competing models of democracy – representative and participatory (Buckingham-Hatfield and Percy, 1999). It will not be resolved easily: neither side is entirely wrong. The most positive approaches are developing where each viewpoint has acknowledged the other and has agreed on the need to link these different processes in a well-defined and transparent manner. The continuing and growing interest in different forms of democratic involvement between elections has begun to address this problem.

Campaigning against versus working for

Most environmental activity over the last 30 years can be seen as campaigning against existing or proposed processes, be it road-building, nuclear power, or the destruction of natural habitats. Yet the solutions-based approach inherent in sustainable development means that groups may sit round discussion tables with organisations that they historically opposed, notably local councils.

This led some policy-centred NGOs to be initially suspicious of the LA21 process, fearing that local branches might be co-opted. Other more radical organisations tended to dismiss the process as a compromise-riddled talking-shop. This is unfortunate since it has often meant that local activists with a grasp of national policy issues have not been sufficiently involved and have missed opportunities to feed in firm policy targets. Similar tensions can be seen on the social side, where anti-poverty or disability action groups have often found themselves having to convince conservation groups of the relevance of their concerns, as well as having to deal with service providers such as local councils.

This shift from campaigning against to working for was completely new for many groups. It involves trusting other partners, building social capital (see below), and commitment over time. Even business partners often find it hard to sustain a commitment through the months of working-group meetings necessary to produce the LA21 plan. While groups put their energies into this positive approach, there is always the possibility that another part of the council would suddenly appear to be undermining the LA21 initiative. Manchester's support for a second runway at the airport is an example of this problem. Groups involved in LA21 scurried back into campaigning mode.

Conflict versus consensus

The basic principles of LA21 call on councils to achieve a consensus with their community. This has led to an increased interest in consensus and mediation from many local councils, backed up by active promotion by the LGMB. On the other hand, many NGOs and community networks remain sceptical about consensus, seeing it as compromise by another name. Some flawed or inconclusive exercises provide evidence to support this view. Jobs versus green spaces or wildlife was the commonest example. The desire to integrate economic and environmental priorities has often foundered on the suspicions of business and economic-development professionals that environmentalists are still anti-business, and that LA21 is first and foremost an environmental process.

It must also be stressed that a number of councils have deliberately set the framework for consensus-building exercises in ways which have meant that areas of conflict have been concealed rather than openly discussed and resolved. As conceived at the Earth Summit and presented in much of the LGMB's literature, the LA21 process challenges 'the culture and practices of a council, and can be seen to threaten the status quo' (LGMB, 1999). In some cases senior members and officers set out to keep control over all that LA21 begins to open up. Often this only becomes clear over time when LA21 proposals are not integrated into statutory documents like land-use plans, or into budgets. This sometimes happens where two departments within the council are in conflict – and departmentalism wins out over joined-up thinking.

Environmental management versus community empowerment

Many of the frustrations that have emerged during LA21 work can be traced to community activists who subscribed to Agenda 21, only to find that their councils were more interested in waste reduction or internal environmental management. This reflects the earlier point about LA21 often leading to more detailed unintegrated programmes, and councils focusing on internal environmental management. LA21 is often limited by a lack of resources and expertise. Waste management and energy efficiency, for example, have become increasingly technical fields, and it has been difficult for under-resourced staff to provide useful information and advice to businesses who may still be sceptical about the need to take any action at all. In some places the enthusiasm of local groups means that the LA21 process is dominated by local environmental agendas and the broader agenda is ignored. This led to one health professional suggesting in 1996 that LA21 had been 'hijacked by environmentalists'.

This should be the most easily resolvable problem. Much of it relates to a lack of communication, and few would dispute the need for councils to put their own house in order. But this is perhaps a symptom of the problem at the root of many such participative exercises: Who is in charge and what do they want to achieve?

Central–local relations and broader contextual factors

The discussion of the factors that explain why LA21 worked out as it did in the UK has focused on what might best be termed the operational reasons. But these were all conditioned by the way that the key concepts – community, sustainable development, and participation – were contested. Competing understandings of sustainable development have been especially significant. Language itself has been a barrier. This helps explain why LA21 has inaugurated different processes producing such a variety of products.

More conceptually, the UK LA21 experience fits Downs' issue-emergence-cycle model (Downs, 1973). Growing environmental concerns lead to discussion of how to use LA21 to promote sustainable development. In theory LA21 offers a viable approach – but in practice the process of building consensus and then implementing the strategy proves too difficult. This parallels the experience of other major cross-sectoral policy initiatives in UK local government during the last 20 years. Programmes designed to tackle differing forms of inner-city deprivation, for example, appeared coherent in theory, but were beset by implementation problems.

In the background there are the effects of central–local relations on individual councils. The last 25 years have revealed two distinct central strategies (Stoker, 1991; Stoker and Young, 1993; Rhodes, 1999). First, as typified by regulations put in place by Margaret Thatcher's government in the 1980s, all councils have to respond when changes are compulsory – as with financial controls and new statutory obligations. An example from the 1990s is the changed approach to land-use planning with regard to brownfield sites and out-of-town development. These, and related changes, will have a slow, but unavoidable cumulative impact over time (DETR, 1998a and 1999b).

In the 1990s, governments often adopted a weaker, persuasive approach. This also applied to many LA21-related initiatives. Ministers increasingly relied on voluntary targets as, for example, with recycling; legislation with powers that might be used; advisory and best-practice documents; and financial incentive packages for councils. These were backed up by ministerial speeches urging councils to change. In practice, councils can respond in a token way to this strategy. What ministers propose is optional, not compulsory. Often it is difficult for councils to fund such non-statutory initiatives. The language of consensus-building and partnership at the heart of LA21 also meant that ministers did not want to force initiatives on councils. Transport provides a good example of this process. During 1998–99 ministers urged councils to adopt the policies it was pursuing ahead of its legislation – but few responded.

Central government can clearly stop councils from doing things, but ministers find it harder to get them to adopt new ideas. The Audit Commission concluded that many councils were 'failing to take an effective corporate approach and could stand accused of paying only lip service to the environmental agenda' (1997).

The culture of compartmentalism makes it more difficult to promote initiatives. Few councils used their LA21 framework to integrate the range of documents they were being instructed to produce: for example, land-use plans and strategies covering such diverse topics as air quality, biodiversity, 'best value', transport, economic development and crime. Ministers aim to tackle a lack of joined-up thinking via the broader agenda of modernising local government (DETR, 1998a and 1999b), but this had a limited impact during the 1997–2000 period.

THE OVERALL GOAL OF CONSULTING WITH THE COMMUNITY

The influence of NGOs

The UK has a strong and diverse voluntary sector, broadly composed of issue-focused NGOs operating mainly at the national level with some local branches; and location-focused community-based organisations (CBOs) operating at the local level. The different approaches and responses to LA21 initiatives by these two sets of groups are central to any assessment of its impact. The NGOs played an influential role in two senses. They supplemented the LGMB's promotional role – holding conferences, working with groups, health authorities, councils, and publishing explanatory material. The second role arose from their being – unlike LGMB – free of any formal link to the government. They were thus able to be much more critical of low-key, compartmentalised approaches, and of central government's limited role – as over indicators and the broadening of the agenda to cover social issues.

The lack of any formal process of marketing LA21 as a government-backed initiative has been noted above. This resulted in approaches to community-based groups coming from their local authorities as the process developed, while NGO involvement at first depended very much on that organisation's level of interest in the Earth Summit process. There was little immediate follow-up to this. The UNA ran events prior to the Summit and developed the NGO network into the United Nations Environment and Development UK Committee (UNED-UK), and set up the Sustainable Communities Project, which was the first national NGO initiative to encourage LA21 activity.

UNA set up a 'flagship' system and worked with the three local authorities of Gloucestershire, Vale Royal and Bedford for a year and supplied support to others. A general lack of resources meant, however, that little further development took place. Alongside the New Economics Foundation (NEF), they worked with councils on the LGMB Indicators programme (LGMB, 1995) and this in turn led to NEF's further involvement both on indicators and on participation. WWF also developed its own consultancy programmes, along with a Business Agenda 21 programme based around specific councils. This attempted to facilitate the involvement of small businesses in LA21 activity, and in at least one case led to a successful self-sustaining business offering consultancy and advice. But such isolated good practice is still a long way from becoming standard.

The LGMB recognised its obligation to work with other sectors and set up a national LA21 steering group, which involved various environmental NGOs, notably WWF and the Women's Environment Network, as well as others such as the National Federation of Women's Institutes.

The common problem faced by all these NGOs has been a lack of development funding, alongside a perception of local government as a source of funding. This meant that they increasingly competed as consultants, which may have limited their ability to take forward the policy agenda. WWF especially took on this work, and their community education department became active in setting up some pilot projects, offering training and running seminars.

Other environmental NGOs were more reserved. Those involved in urban and rural planning issues – including the Town and Country Planning Association (TCPA) and Campaign for the Protection of Rural England (CPRE) – were concerned as to how this voluntary initiative would cut across statutory planning processes, notably unitary development plans and green-belt issues. Others, notably Friends of the Earth, were at first disturbed by the new idea. They saw the potential for members of their large local-groups network to end up in compromise situations, and were also justifiably concerned that many of their groups would leap enthusiastically into this work, leaving less time and resources for what they saw as their core work of campaigning to change central government policies. This position was not tenable: increasing local group involvement led to calls for support from the national office, and to help with briefing materials and training. Friends of the Earth groups have often been important at a local level in LA21s, since they are well-briefed on issues such as transport and energy, often more so than LA21 staff.

Wildlife and conservation networks also saw this as an opportunity. The wildlife trusts already had involvement through their 'Environment City' programme, and the lessons learned from this work were widely disseminated (Wood, 1995). Others, such as the British Trust for Conservation Volunteers (BTCV) and Groundwork, encouraged local involvement, although nationally they took some years to find a clear niche in the process.

More recently, Friends of the Earth have made links between local and national sustainability. On the launch of their 'Barriers to Sustainability' report (CAG Consultants, 1998), they suggested that there was a green gap between national rhetoric on sustainable development and what happens in practice. They also viewed a lack of political will at the national level as a key reason why little progress had been made. The report suggested that the lack of local-authority power is a major obstacle, and an accompanying press release called for green tax reform and for local sustainable development to become an 'over-riding statutory duty for local government and other devolved bodies such as Regional Development Agencies'. LA21 networks were one of several sources of pressure that led to sustainable development being added to the Agencies' terms of reference.

All these groups were clearly from the environment side, but the broadening of the agenda in the late 1990s (as discussed above) brought other groups in. The Poverty Alliance was one of the first social bodies to take an interest, while the Community Development Foundation became actively involved in 1995 and has since been a leading player in policy-level work on sustainability and urban regeneration (Chanan et al, 1999), and on public participation and developing the Sustainable Communities Agencies Network.

The energy of the NGO networks in Britain was clearly demonstrated at Earth Summit II. Some 50 local networks fed their ideas into the UK Citizens Report (UNED-UK, 1997) which was launched at the UN event. It highlighted how far the vanguard of the local sustainability movement had moved. The priorities that emerged were, in order:

- Citizenship and participation.
- Poverty and exclusion.
- Transport.
- Energy.
- Sustainable consumption and production.
- Global development, aid and trade.
- Valuing the whole community.

The crucial role played by NGOs and CBOs in the UK is summarised in Box 5.1.

Box 5.1 A crucial role for NGOs in the UK

- The UK boasts a strong and diverse voluntary sector, broadly composed of issue-focused NGOs operating mainly at the national level with some local branches, along with more locally focused CBOs.
- NGOs played a vital role in the early phases of LA21 implementation. They have supplemented the promotional role of LGMB – holding conferences, working with groups, health authorities, councils, and publishing explanatory material.
- NGO involvement at first depended very much on an NGO's level of interest in the Earth Summit process. The UNA ran pre-Summit events, developed the NGO network into UNED-UK, and set up the sustainable communities project, which, in early 1993, became the first national NGO initiative to encourage LA21 activity.
- The LGMB recognised their obligation to work with other sectors and set up a national LA21 steering group, which involved various environmental NGOs over the years.
- Friends of the Earth UK were at first sceptical of the new idea, but have come to play a vital role in developing LA21s, given their strong competency in areas such as transport and energy. More recently, they have made links between local and national sustainability, particularly within the context of their report on barriers to sustainability.
- Other groups like wildlife trusts, WWF and various wildlife and conservation networks have also played a central role in the LA21 work in the UK. The energy of the NGO networks was clearly demonstrated at Earth Summit II, where some 50 local networks fed their ideas into the UK citizens' report.

Getting the processes right: Participation and involvement in LA21

As the 1997 'Citizens Report' shows, public involvement has probably been the central issue throughout LA21 in the UK. Indeed, it was this aspect of LA21 that the UK became best known for in Western Europe. In the mid-1990s a great deal of energy and imagination went into developing ways of promoting participation (Stoker, 1996). Examples include environment forums, neighbourhood LA21s, and visioning exercises. The best experiences of community involvement in LA21 managed to establish different stakeholder groups as equal partners with local councils, thus countering the critics who saw local government as remote and unresponsive.

More recently, further democratic initiatives have been assessed in the context of LA21, for example, citizen juries and community planning. The

Democracy Network of the Local Government Association (LGA) has been working for some time on the prospect of 'E-democracy'. Many of the innovative tools under development have been used by LA21, and it has been suggested by Christie (1999) that LA21 practitioners should be happy to stand back and not insist on taking credit for their own innovations.

Participation on its own does not ensure change. The differences between the traditional consultation used in most statutory planning processes, and effective participation, where local people help shape and manage the process and thus become empowered, have been shown very clearly. A general lack of resources, of guidance, and of an understanding of the 'art of the possible', have led numerous LA21s, especially those where there has been a relatively hands-off approach from council managers, to produce 'vision programmes' that are never likely to be funded or implemented. While these may have been useful and inspiring exercises, it is in these areas where disillusion with the process has been most obvious.

Many local networks admit that they have failed to build an alliance that represents a genuine cross-section of the community. Specific areas of concern have been the under-involvement of black and ethnic minority communities, poorer communities, and youth and the aged (Buckingham-Hadfield and Percy, 1999). The lack of involvement of such groups is a common failing of participative processes that have developed with little forward planning or policy (Taylor, 1995). But there is still a great deal more to do. Research (CDF, 1999) shows that there is still a dearth of good practice in involving disadvantaged and black and ethnic minority communities in LA21. The Community Development Foundation (CDF) survey shows that a number of LA21 programmes that are hailed as good practice appear to have very questionable practice on the issue of ethnic minority involvement.

Much of the debate about moving from tokenistic consultation to more serious attempts at empowerment has been taking place amongst LA21 enthusiasts. Many organisations specialising in work on participation – as with housing or problems of social exclusion – have not seen LA21 as a priority, and some LA21 enthusiasts have been slow to learn from what has been done in other sectors. The slow but increasing involvement of social-sector groups approaching these issues has helped move things forward.

It is also true that few of the innovatory approaches were developed within LA21. Usually, they have come from other social development programmes where there is much more experience and history of participative working – as in housing and health. Lessons were learned from participation exercises in regeneration areas that have linked economic, environmental and social issues, thus embracing the broadened agenda and cross-sectoral approaches. In many places LA21 has acted as an arena for experimenting with newer approaches to participation and empowerment. LA21 has certainly started to bring participation on environmental and sustainability issues into line with good practice in other spheres, occasionally taking it further.

Building a new way forward

Given the somewhat erratic impact of community involvement and the attempts at consensus-building across whole local authorities, it is perhaps not surprising that it is at the level of specific sustainable development projects run by NGOs and CBOs where success is most obvious.

Many of these emerging projects have their roots in the environment. Examples include farmers' markets, furniture and white-goods refurbishment and reuse, and other recycling schemes. One of the most successful policy sectors in the UK has been biodiversity. Local branches of the wildlife trusts and other conservation and amenity organisations have been active in promoting butterfly gardens, nature reserves, tree-planting, green corridors and other projects. They are often linked to schools.

Other projects set out to link environmental and social concerns, often in areas of urban disadvantage. The best regeneration and 'health-action-zone' projects, with clear deliverables and outputs, are likely to develop as models of good practice for sustainability in the next few years. In remote rural areas too, similar projects have emerged. The Duthchas projects in North Sutherland (as commented in the *West Highland Free Press*, 2000) or the Islay Development Company are EU-backed pilot projects that are implementing integrated rural development showing excellent sustainability practice.

NGOs and councils working together have in some places also been effective at developing projects that link environmental, social and economic issues and draw in the broader agenda. Urban regeneration and rural development programmes have shown how such projects can emerge alongside training programmes and business support. Agenda 21 is in places self-contradictory, calling for full employment while also recognising that what is needed is sustainable livelihoods rather than simply jobs. The idea of livelihoods that include voluntary work alongside paid employment is not a new one, and such schemes had been in the UK for several years before the arrival of LA21. Many of their advocates saw LA21 as a natural partner and sought to use this new focus as a way to substantially increase their outreach.

Local authorities have been ambivalent at best on such innovation. A few have given staff responsibilities for Local Exchange Trading Systems (LETS), but there has only been limited take-up, despite an increasing body of work to suggest that such schemes, if set up in an appropriate way, can be of real value in tackling exclusion. Many councils have been more actively involved in promoting credit unions. The role of LA21 has been to open the door to such ideas, but it will be up to those specialising in this work to take it forward. LA21 has also opened up discussions on sustainable local economies, an effort that has been taken forward by groups such as Forum for the Future and books such as *Factor Four* (von Weizsäcker et al, 1998), but so far these programmes have had little overall effect on local council economic development plans.

Towards sustainable communities

The idea of integrating these approaches is an attractive one, and the phrase sustainable communities is increasingly used and is claimed by projects ranging from 'eco-villages' in rural Wales to those based around tower blocks in depressed urban areas. Detailed study shows that some of these embrace the environmental, social and economic dimensions (Young, 1997; Wilkinson and Applebee, 1998). The UK government's sustainable development strategy, 'A Better Quality of Life', included a section with this title, and the DETR recently invited NGOs in the sustainable communities agencies network to produce 'A Blueprint for a Sustainable Community'.

One of the most interesting emergent ideas is that of a social economy with growing numbers of projects operating on a not-for-profit basis between the public and private sectors (Young, 1997; Wilkinson and Appelbee, 1999). Thus, in Liverpool, what appeared to be a few isolated projects in the early 1990s, were, by the end of the decade, trading with each other, generating further social economy activity, and getting the council to develop EU-funded programmes. The social economy could grow into providing one part of the transition to sustainable development. It is also part of a wider phenomenon of the 1990s whereby local government has started to evolve into an expanded system of local 'governance'. This involves using complex sets of public, private and voluntary, not-for-profit organisations to deliver services and run projects (Rhodes, 1997).

However, one of the problems with these projects is the difficulty in evaluating them. It is comparatively easy to measure the hard, tangible outputs like people completing training schemes. But it is much harder to assess the more intangible benefits, and the wider outcomes – like rebuilding community pride. The lack of any identification by residents with their neighbourhood is seen as one reason for vandalism and local environmental degradation.

Third-sector[3] projects also contribute to the attempts to identify indicators that help evaluate the contributions of local communities and councils' perceptions of them. Few of the LGMB's indicators were used beyond those relating to voter turn-out in elections and membership of voluntary organisations. The best work on evaluating community activity is perhaps that done by the Scottish Community Development Centre and the University of Glasgow. Their work on monitoring and evaluation of community development in Northern Ireland (Barr et al, 1996) provides an example of how local indicators can be developed to link core principles and local needs.

These projects are emerging largely because of committed activists. Often they grow out of frustration and disappointment with the lack of sustained impact typical of LA21 processes. Sometimes there are tensions with local councils – as over LETS. On other occasions there are significant inputs from committed officers. This activity is not LA21 as originally envisaged, but it has provided an influential framework and a new forum for exploring these ideas. It has opened the door to a wider understanding of the links between the social, economic and environmental aspects of local sustainability. It has been significant in facilitating cross-sectoral thinking and a wider understanding of the broader agenda. It is at the level of CBO projects like these that this has found expression. Further, these projects do promote empowerment. Local people are designing projects that relate to their needs – as they, and not bureaucrats, perceive them. In this sense they are sometimes, at the level of the village and urban neighbourhood, building consensus and fulfilling the community involvement aim as set out at the Earth Summit.

Developing social capital and strengthening civil society?

Third-sector activity is increasingly important in the wider political context because its growth represents evidence of an increasing number of councils accepting the need to empower communities at the level of the village and urban neighbourhood. Even though Taylor (1996) and others have argued the case over the last 25 years, the need to promote empowerment in the context of LA21, as distinct from consultation, was resisted by the majority of councils during the 1990s. By the end of the decade, however, increasing numbers were prepared to concede the principle and to start to apply it at neighbourhood level.

It is important to link LA21 to the development of social capital and civil society. This relates to perceptions of what constitutes community and civil society, and links to the government's vision of a 'third way' in a rather different way from that endorsed by the modernisers. Civil Society is a phrase that has been widely adopted by NGOs working on Agenda 21, as a way of encapsulating the multi-sectoral approach inherent in that document. A commonly accepted definition would be that civil society can be seen as that sector that is related to both the state and the market, but that has a core of activity that is not accountable to either, an independence of the state that the third way seems not to recognise.

Building social capital is fundamentally about building trust (Putnam, 1993; Maloney et al, 1999; Chanan, 1999). The attempts by NGOs to move from campaigning against to working for, and to build consensus, are significant in this context. The process of building social capital, of building confidence and trust between citizens and institutions is extremely relevant to councils in the UK (Commission for Local Democracy, 1995; Stewart, 1995; Wilkinson and Appelbee, 1999). They have long been subject to a lack of trust from citizens, reflected in the negative media coverage of local government and lower voter turn-out in elections. The government has also recognised the importance of this issue. The sustainable development strategy section on building sustainable communities stressed the importance of building community pride. Much work done through LA21 processes relates directly to building social capital, even if those doing it would not recognise the phrase.

CONCLUSION

The LA21 programme in the UK is undergoing major changes, with the result that the national government has initiated a programme on modernising local government. The government has proposed various specific measures in this field, for example 'best value' in the provision of local services to replace compulsory competitive tendering. This became law in April 2000 (Wilkinson and Appelbee, 1999). The Queen's Speech in November 1999 also proposed a new process of community planning. This is being presented as 'mainstreaming LA21'.

Some argue that this, along with the decline in Local Government Improvement and Development Agency support, is the end of LA21, or that, at the very least, it represents a loss of faith in the process and is likely to send a negative message to LA21 initiatives across the UK. Optimists such as Christie (1999) argue, on the other hand, that 'there is a deep affinity between LA21 and the aims of the modernisation project of New Labour to revitalise democracy and achieve more "joined-up" policy making'. His idea that LA21 should 'dissolve into the bloodstream of local governance' runs the risk of seeing hard and perhaps unpopular decisions that need to be taken on environmental issues pushed into the background. Senior local authority figures involved in LA21 have already been accused by activists of feeding the UK a diet of 'Sustainability Lite' and any further retreat into the rhetoric of modernisation is likely to fuel scepticism and leave completed LA21 action plans gathering dust. The danger is that, if the end result is merely best value programmes that reflect a few environmental criteria, much of LA21 will have been in vain.

It may be optimistic to call LA21 'one of the most striking advances in progressive politics over the last decade' (Christie, 1999), but there is no doubt that tens of thousands of people have taken part in a process that has developed both their environmental awareness and their perceptions of how such issues are related to broader social issues. In the best cases there has been capacity- and confidence-building, and the creation of new local structures that seem certain to be self-sustaining.

If LA21 is to be absorbed into the mainstream, it is hard to predict whether it will be diluted beyond having any effect; whether it will act as a stimulant to aid the revival of local democracy; or whether it will even help to transform structures and create new ones. This is now a live debate for practitioners, and much will depend on what strength the new community planning initiative is given by the government. It may become a duty for local government (so that they have to take it forward), or it may merely be a power (they can do it if they wish).

Whatever happens, the dichotomy between influencing the national policy agenda and building stronger and more sustainable communities will continue. Several key developments lie ahead. The EU community action programme for local sustainability will reinforce this work and has clearly been influenced by lessons learnt in the UK and elsewhere. Revised planning guidelines are imminent. The government has also been working on the amount of detail to go into two key documents – the urban white paper and the rural white paper. A stronger focus on the neighbourhood level has, for example, been flagged up for the urban paper. All these developments have significant implications for the future of LA21, and for the mainstreaming of sustainable development.

LA21 has opened up new ways of working, locally, nationally and even globally. What is less clear is how far it has helped deliver the key objectives of Agenda 21. In retrospect, this activity will probably be remembered not primarily for LA21 as such, but for two other things.

Firstly, many councils began to understand joined-up thinking in new, more sophisticated ways. This is a necessary prelude to a clearer appreciation of how to promote the broadened agenda and of the need to get sustainable development into budgets and statutory documents. Here Britain is catching up with what is routinely done in many European countries.

Secondly, LA21 has created new opportunities for NGOs and local groups to be more involved in discussions, not just about council policies, but about integrated approaches at neighbourhood level. While there have been disappointments, there has probably been a net gain in terms of building trust and social capital which will bear dividends during the next decade with the further development of the social economy. Certainly one of the main lessons that the UK experience has to offer is an increased understanding of the processes of establishing and sustaining, or simply working with, social-economy organisations.

NOTES

1 This chapter draws from research conducted as part of an Economic and Social Research Council research programme – 'Cities: Competitiveness and Cohesion' (Award No L 130251052).

2 The analysis here relates mainly to England and Wales. However, the same trends are discernible in Scotland (Scottish Office, 1998), and become evident later in Northern Ireland.

3 The third sector is otherwise known as the voluntary or independent sector.

REFERENCES

Abbott, J (1996) *Sharing the City*, Earthscan, London

Audit Commission (1997) *It's a Small World: Local Government's Role as a Steward of the Environment*, Audit Commission, London

Barr, A, Hashagen, S and Purcell, R (1996) *Monitoring and Evaluation of Community Development in Northern Ireland*, DHSS Voluntary Activity Unit

Buckingham-Hatfield, S and Percy, S (1999) *Constructing Environmental Agendas*, Routledge, London

CAG Consultants (1998) *Barriers to Sustainability*, Friends of the Earth, London

CDF (1999) *Down to Earth: Report of a National Conference on Environmental Action and Sustainable Development in a Multi-cultural Society*, Community Development Foundation, London

Chanan, G, West, A, Garratt, C and Humm, J (1999) *Regeneration and Sustainable Communities*, Community Development Foundation, London

Church, C (1995) *Towards Local Sustainability*, UNED-UK, London

Church, C (1997) *The Local Agenda 21 Process in the UK: Lessons for Policy and Practice in Stakeholder Participation: The Challenge of Environmental Management in Urban areas*, Ashgate Publishing, London

Church, C (1998) 'A Survey of LA21 work on Health, Poverty and Global–local Linkages', *Connections* (UNED-UK newsletter), no 1, 1999

Church, C, Cade, A and Grant, A (1998) *An Environment for Everyone: Poverty, Exclusion and Environmental Action*, Community Development Foundation (CDF), London

Christie, I (1999) 'LA21 and Modernising Local Government', *EG – Local Environment News*, October 1999

Commission for Local Democracy (1995) *Taking Charge: The Rebirth of Local Democracy*, Municipal Journal Books, London

DETR (1998a) *Modern Local Government: In Touch With the People*, The Stationery Office, London

DETR (1998b) *Sustainable Local Communities for the 21st Century: Why and How to Prepare a Local Agenda 21 Strategy*, DETR, Cm 4014, The Stationery Office, London

DETR (1998c) *Planning for Sustainable Development: Towards Best Practice*, Department of the Environment, Transport and the Regions, London

DETR (1999a) *Modernising Planning: A Progress Report*, Department of the Environment, Transport and the Regions, London

DETR (1999b) *Local Leadership, Local Choice*, Cm 4298, The Stationery Office, London

DETR (1999c) *A Better Quality of Life: A Strategy for Sustainable Development in the UK*, Cm 4345, The Stationery Office, London

Downs, A (1973) 'Up and Down with Ecology' in Bains, J (ed) *Environmental Decay*, Little Brown, Boston

FoE (1990) 'The Environmental Charter for Local Government: Practical recommendations', Friends of the Earth UK, London

Gibbs, D, Longhurst, J and Braithwaite, C (1998) 'Struggling with Sustainability: Weak and strong interpretations of sustainable development within local authority policy', *Environment and Planning*, vol 30

Lloyd, D (1999) *Growing Places for Life: Healthy Living Initiatives which Combine Agenda 21 and Health 21*, Pioneer Health Centre, London

Lancashire County Council (1997) *Lancashire's Green Audit 2*, LCC, Preston

LGMB (1995) *Sustainability Indicators Research Project Report*, Local Government Management Board, London

LGMB (1999) *Sustainable Local Communities*, Local Government Management Board, London

Maloney, W, Smith, G and Stoker, G (1999) *Social Capital and Urban Governance: Civic Engagement in Birmingham and Glasgow*, Paper given to American Political Science Association

Marvin, S and Guy, S (1997) 'Creating Myths Rather Than Sustainability: The transition fallacies of the new localism', *Local Environment*, vol 2(3)

Mason, M (1999) *Environmental Democracy*, Earthscan, London

Morris, J and Hams, T (1997) *Local Agenda 21 in the UK: The First Five Years*, LGMB, London

Power, A (1997) *Estates on the Edge*, Macmillan, London

Putnam, R (1993) *Making Democracy Work*, Princeton University Press, Princeton

Rhodes, R A W (1997) *Understanding Governance: Policy Networks, Governance, Reflexivity and Accountability*, Open University Press, Buckingham

Rhodes, R A W (1999) *Control and Power in Central–Local Relations*, Ashgate, Aldershot

Scottish Office (1998) *Changed Days: Local Agenda 21 in Scotland*, Scottish Office, Edinburgh

Selman, P (1998) 'A Real Local Agenda?' *Town and Country Planning*, January 1998

Selman, P (1998) 'Local Agenda 21: Substance or spin?' *Journal of Environmental Planning and Management*, vol 41(5), pp533–553

Selman, P (1999) *A Sideways look at Local Agenda 21*, Paper delivered to Murdoch University, Australia

Social Exclusion Unit (1998) *Bringing Britain Together: A National Strategy for Neighbourhood Renewal*, Cm 4045, The Stationery Office, London

Stewart, J (1995) *Innovation in Democratic Practice*, INLOGOV, Birmingham

Stoker, G (1991) *The Politics of Local Government*, 2nd edition, Macmillan, London

Stoker, G (1996) *Local Political Participation: A Review Paper*, Rowntree Trust, York

Stoker, G and Young, S C (1993) *Cities in the 1990s*, Longman, Harlow
Taylor, M (1995) *Unleashing the Potential*, Joseph Rowntree Foundation, York
Tuxworth, B and Thomas, E (1996) *Local Agenda 21 Survey 1996*, LGMB, London
UNED-UK (1997) *The UK Citizens Report: Keeping our Side of the Bargain*, United Nations Environment and Development UK Committee, London
Weizsäcker, E von, Lovins, A B and Lovins, L H (1998) *Factor Four: Doubling Wealth, Halving Resource Use*, Earthscan, London
Wilkinson, D and Appelbee, E (1999) *Implementing Holistic Government: Joined-up Action on the Ground*, Policy Press and DEMOS, Bristol
Wood, C (1995) *Stepping Stones II,* Wildlife Trusts, Lincoln
WHO (1997) *Sustainable Development and Health: Concepts, Principles and Framework for Action*, World Health Organization, Copenhagen
Young, S C (1997a) 'The UK: A mirage beyond the participation hurdle?' in Lafferty, W M and Eckerberg, K (eds) *From Earth Summit to Local Agenda 21*, Earthscan, London
Young, S (1997b) 'Community-based Partnerships and Sustainable Development' in Baker, S, Kousis, M, Richardson, D and Young, S C (eds) *The Politics of Sustainable Development*, Routledge, London, pp217–236
Young, S (1999) 'Slowing down on LA21 – or Pausing before Accelerating?' in Lafferty, W M (ed) *Implementing LA21 in Europe*, ProSus, Oslo
Young, S C (2000) 'Labour and the Environment' in Coates, D and Lawlor, P (eds) *New Labour into Power*, Manchester University Press, Manchester, pp149–168

6. Ireland
Starting late: Building institutional capacity on the reform of sub-national governance?

Gerard Mullally

INTRODUCTION

LA21 in Ireland, when compared with the broader European experience, has had a relatively late start and provoked a limited response from local authorities. Recent developments at the national and sub-national level of governance suggest, however, that a gradual institutionalising process is taking place. The more visible hallmarks of LA21, such as the production of a local Agenda 21 plan or instances of democratic reform, are still little in evidence, yet county and city development plans are increasingly distinguished by a rhetorical appeal to sustainable development and a specific identification with LA21 in their texts. Equally, consultation and consensus-building exercises on environment and development are still very limited and tend to relate to existing models of environmental policy rather than LA21 per se. That said, the institutional landscape governing environment and development has changed significantly when compared with the situation that obtained in Ireland prior to the Earth Summit. The question is, to what extent has the Earth Summit or, more importantly, Chapter 28 of Agenda 21 actually played a role in effecting this change?

In order to address this question, we have to understand what is different and significant about Local Agenda 21.

> *'If LA21 is to be understood as anything resembling "environmental policy", the idea will quickly deteriorate into a catch-all category with little potential for either evaluation or cross-national comparison and analysis.'* (Lafferty, 1999)

The first challenge, then, is describing the actual implementation of LA21 in Ireland. In addition to describing the implementation, however, we are also faced with the challenge of analysing and explaining the particular Irish 'story'. Why has LA21 been approached primarily as a problem of building institutional capacity for the governance of issues related to environment and development? Why have community consultation and consensus-building been so limited in the Irish case?

Sibeon (1996) has defined governance as the management of networks in the sense of a negotiable and interactive process of steering, rather than top-down management from a central position of power. He calls for a methodological approach to the study of governance that includes an investigation of actors' 'forms of thought'. Sibeon argues that 'in order for something to be manageable it must first be knowable'. Therefore, as an initiative originating outside of the Irish context, it is crucially important to explore its interpretation and introduction into the political process. A particular focus is therefore called for on how policy-makers at the national level and key actors at the regional and local levels have interpreted and responded to LA21.

The Irish story begins with a brief assessment of progress on LA21 measured against the 'substantive criteria' developed within the SUSCOM project. To understand the particular circumstances of the implementation of LA21 in Ireland, attention is then focused on the existing and dynamically evolving institutional landscape in respect to environment and development. The late response by Irish local authorities is placed against the backdrop of the dependence of local government on central government; of the dependence of Ireland on the EU, and on the changing nature of national environmental policy. This institutional profile then provides a baseline against which we can establish how and where Agenda 21 has contributed to the elaboration of existing structures, routines and norms, or to innovation regarding environment and development. In addition, however, it also allows a discussion of how LA21 has been interpreted by highlighting existing understanding of environment and development issues and asks if the initiative has provoked change. The focus turns therefore to the interpretation of and response to LA21 by national and local government.[1] There are, however, individual cases where, despite the general picture, LA21 can be shown to be making an impact on the practices underpinning local governance in Ireland. Two cases in particular stand out, one because it extends existing models of consultation by local authorities with their communities, the other because it suggests that LA21 has the potential to stimulate corporate, rather than fragmented, responses to environment and development issues.

The national status: A late start and limited response?

Given the fact that LA21 represents an externally generated initiative, it is useful to begin by reflecting on one of the principal objectives of Chapter 28 of Agenda 21.

> *'By 1996, most local authorities should have undertaken a consultative process with their populations and achieved a consensus on "a Local Agenda 21" for the community.'* (Lafferty, 1999)

In the Irish case, the first notable response to Chapter 28 was contained in central government guidelines on 'Local Authorities and Sustainable Development: Guidelines on Local Agenda 21' in 1995. There is no evidence that Irish local authorities, either individually or collectively, had any antecedent role in the genesis of LA21 or an active interest in the period immediately following the Earth Summit. The guidelines provided the first indication of central government's intent and created a focus for the first phase of limited practical engagement with LA21. At this stage, although the guidelines were careful to be suggestive rather than prescriptive, a number of key institutional features were signalled pre-figuring the principal institutional arrangements identified in the national strategy for the implementation of Agenda 21: *Sustainable Development: A Strategy for Ireland* (DoE, 1997). Although the guidelines were quite wide-ranging, they clearly identify the level at which LA21 should be addressed:

> *'For the purposes of Local Agenda 21, the pivotal role should be taken at a county/county borough level, where there is a major concentration of functions, responsibilities and capabilities which will be central to implementing sustainable development.'* (DoE, 1995)

The principal emphases of the guidelines centred on: the greening of local government; a coordinating and facilitative role for regional authorities; and, indications that consultation and consensus-building in the context of LA21 required movement beyond existing legislative provision for public consultation regarding environment and development issues. The stated intention of central government was, by issuing the guidelines prior to the preparation of the national strategy, that some degree of synchronisation could be achieved between the local and national levels. In any event, neither the national strategy nor the anticipated response from local authorities had materialised. However, while the deadline passed by largely unobserved, the emphases outlined have remained central to subsequent innovations surrounding LA21. The key point here is that, even in the initial interventions by central government in 1995, LA21 was placed firmly in the larger strategic context of the national framework for the implementation of Agenda 21.

Measuring the actual extent of LA21 in Ireland has consistently proved to be a precarious activity. The 22 local authorities reported by ICLEI to be involved in LA21 would appear to encompass instances of both active engagement and authorities that are beginning to consider the implications of the initiative. The SUSCOM research indicates that Ireland belongs to the group of European countries where less than 20 per cent of local authorities have responded to LA21 (Lafferty, 1999). We can, however, present a slightly differentiated picture, since the timing and the extent of responses by Irish local authorities can be grouped into three phases following key interventions by central government. It must be clearly acknowledged, however, that no local authority in Ireland is substantially beyond the first stage outlined in the Aalborg Charter; that is, the recognition of existing planning and financial frameworks as well as other plans and programmes (Lafferty, 1999).

The first phase follows the launch of the LA21 guidelines at a national Agenda 21 conference in Dublin in 1995. The main local authorities mobilising in this phase were Cork County Council, Dublin Corporation, Dun Laoghaire Rathdown and Louth County Council. These local authorities are now the most advanced in terms of training, developing an interim LA21 plan, and integrating LA21 into existing plans, policies and activities. Many of the local authorities in this phase have created inter-departmental or corporate LA21 steering committees. The local authorities that started in the first phase have experimented with new forms of consultation and consensus-building directly in response to LA21. The systematic and exhaustive public consultation envisaged in the Aalborg stage model, however, has proved to be the greatest challenge for Irish local authorities.

The second phase began with the publication of *Sustainable Development: A Strategy for Ireland* in 1997, which requested that all local authorities complete an LA21 for their areas by 1998. Approximately 16 local authorities initiated LA21 activities in the period beginning with the publication of the national strategy in 1997 to mid-1998. The activities of these local authorities are principally related to the completion of a local state of the environment report, internal or external auditing of city and county development plans for sustainable development and LA21 criteria, and addressing or highlighting the need for education and training for staff. The majority of local authorities mobilising in this phase have not yet engaged in any public consultation in relation to LA21. Many of these local authorities do have public consultation procedures in the context of existing environmental policy obligations, for example waste management strategies, and argue that these either help to build a constituency for LA21 or that the informal influence of LA21 has induced them to take these procedures more seriously.

The third phase brings us from mid-1998 to the present, when central government realised that the 1998 deadline was unrealistic and suggested the formation of the national Local Agenda 21 network. Not all of the 14 local authorities in this phase could be described as mobilising. The responses to LA21 range from displacing responsibility up to the regional level, to the adoption of a wait and see attitude, or in a handful of cases dismissing it as an impediment to execution of their functional remit. Many of the local authorities in this case are waiting for the newly formed national LA21 network to devise a methodology for implementation which they can then transpose to their areas.

LA21 is beginning to have an effect in terms of moving some local authorities beyond traditional environmental protection. Many of the local authorities in Ireland have projects or initiatives that are aimed at moving towards sustainability, but these generally tend to focus on environment–economy integration, and are driven by the availability of EU funds. Local authorities are, however, relating local issues to wider global impacts. Climate change and biodiversity are, for example, being addressed on a project basis through collaboration with programmes like the Global Action Programme (GAP) and the creation of habitats to support diverse forms of flora and fauna. The issues of global solidarity and justice, however, do not normally fall within the horizon of these types of actions. One of the most visible obstacles to LA21, in the Irish case, is the absence of a systematic approach to increasing community involvement. Issues like cross-sectoral integration, and working within broader ecological and regional frameworks, are beginning to be addressed through county and city development plans. Many local authorities have made a specific identification with the Earth Summit and Agenda 21 either by passing a resolution, endorsing an interim LA21 report, or, as is the case for an increasing number of local authorities, including it as a specific reference in their spatial development plans. Measured rigorously against the SUSCOM criteria, LA21 would still appear to be at the early stages of development. Even allowing for the very real possibility of intransigence by local authorities in the face of a morally rather than legally binding initiative, LA21 was faced with definite structural and institutional impediments in the Irish case. Despite the limited response by Irish local authorities thus far, LA21 has formed part of a larger institution-building process to create the capacity to address the governance and implementation of sustainable development.

THE DIFFICULTIES FACING A GLOBAL–LOCAL REFORM IN IRELAND

The problem of mobilising local authorities

Local government in Ireland principally consists of 34 major local authorities (29 county councils and five county borough councils) operating under the coordination and supervision of the Department of the Environment (now the Department of Environment and Local Government). Local authorities derive their power and function from legislation with a consequent regard to the policies and objectives of central government rather than from any constitutionally mandated powers (Dooney and O'Toole, 1998). The system of local government employs a managerial system introduced in 1929 and divides the functions of local government into executive and reserved functions. The executive functions refer to the power of the city or county manager to control local authority staff, the preparation of budgets and control of expenditure. The elected councillors have power over general policy, which is reserved for collective judgement – for example, the development plan. The limited capacity that local authorities have for autonomous action has meant that local authorities have generally waited for direction from national government regarding LA21.

There have recently been some important developments reforming local government in Ireland that are significant for LA21. In July 1999, the 20th amendment to the Irish constitution recognised the role of local government in Ireland for the first time. This marks a significant development in the history of local government in Ireland, but it also reflects a larger process of reform at the level of sub-national government. The reform programme – Better Local Government – has been covered in some detail in earlier reports (Lafferty, 1999). The main implication of this reform, however, is that it seeks to embed the national experience of social partnership at the local level of governance. The instrument designed to effect this development is the creation of strategic policy committees, which bring the elected and administrative dimensions of local government together with local interest groups and voluntary associations in order to assist with policy formulation within the competencies of local authorities. *Better Local Government* (DoE, 1996) and *Sustainable Development: A Strategy for Ireland* (DoE, 1997) both identify this mechanism as a vehicle for consultation and consensus-building for LA21.

The European horizon of LA21

The relative autonomy of Irish local authorities to respond to LA21 is limited by the fact that the initiative is embedded within a national system of governance and environmental protection that is dynamically evolving at the same time that the authorities are charged with the implementation of the initiative. In this system, local authorities have been largely passive recipients of policy directions formed in the general context of EU/national relations. They are neither structurally equipped nor actively encouraged to mobilise with respect to initiatives beyond the limited scope of their statutory function. This limits the potential for global–local reform to the functional horizon of existing legal obligations. The impacts of EU regional and environmental policy in Ireland are significant because they are contributing to the transformation of the institutional landscape for environment and development issues and more generally the context in which local authorities are to play a role in implementing Agenda 21.

The LA21 guidelines for local authorities issued in 1995 envisaged that regional authorities would take an active role in facilitating 'coherence and co-ordination between the activities of their constituent local authorities' (DoE, 1995). The difficulty is that the system of sub-national governance in which regional authorities could play such a role had not sufficiently evolved by the 1996 deadline for the initiation of LA21 processes. Since Ireland was classified as an 'Objective 1' region within the EU system, national government effectively became the regional authority for the purpose of structural funds. Irish local authorities are therefore not permitted to apply directly to Brussels for structural funds. However, the change in EU regional policy after the 1988 reform did add an additional tier to government with the formation of eight regional authorities in 1994. Generally speaking, the regional authorities provide a focus for regionally based coordination; between different areas and sectors, between local and other public authorities and agencies, and in the provision of services. One of the principal difficulties surrounding the regional tier of government is that it is seen to act primarily as a functional mechanism for drawing down European funds. This has become problematic, as the strength of the Irish economy has effected a transition in the regional status of the country for the purpose of structural funds. The European Commission (EC) has demanded that sub-national governance become substantive rather than illusory. Arguably, part of the process of meeting this demand is the rhetorical and practical 'retrofit' of regional authorities as key players in coordinating LA21.

Recently, the regional authorities have begun to play a more active role in coordinating and facilitating LA21 through their participation in a national LA21 officers network. In July 1999, an additional layer was added to regional government with the establishment of two new regional assemblies. These assemblies reflect changes in the regional status of

Ireland within the EU, post-1999. The Border, Midlands and Western Regional Assembly establishes a single administrative structure for those areas retaining Objective 1 status, while the Southern and Eastern Regional Assembly represents the rest of the country, which has Objective 1 in transition status from 1999. In some respects the assemblies will mirror the responsibilities of the eight existing regional authorities that will remain in place. Although the assemblies have no additional functions concerning LA21, they are responsible for 'sustainability proofing' (quality control) of the regional development plans for the two new supra-regions under the National Development Plan (2000–06). The National Development Plan will involve an investment of approximately IR£41 million of public, EU and private funds.

Regional policy is not the only relevant horizon for LA21 in Ireland. The EU now exerts the most important and effective influence on Irish environmental policy and politics (McGowen, 1999). McGowen argues, however, that the objectives of environmental law in EU member states are determined by Brussels, and the mechanisms through which these objectives are reached are determined nationally. Local authorities play a crucial though dependent role in this relationship. By European standards, Irish local government has a very limited range of functions but these primarily relate to the physical environment through planning and development, and environmental management and control. While these functions are, of course, important for the implementation of LA21, they primarily relate to the implementation of national environmental policy, which reflects the emphases of EU environmental action programmes. The legitimacy of Irish local authorities in performing these functions came under serious public scrutiny in the late 1980s and early 1990s, both in relation to their own environmental impacts and their statutory role as regulator. The early 1990s were characterised by a period of intense institutional innovation in respect to environment and development issues largely driven by EU programmes. One of the principal developments arising out of this was the transfer of many regulatory and enforcement powers to the Environmental Protection Agency.

From environmental to sustainable development policy?

The first coherent expression of Irish environmental policy did not emerge until the publication of the Department of the Environment's first *Environmental Action Programme* in 1990 (DoE, 1990). The key commitments of the policy programme were sustainable development as advocated by the World Commission on Environment and Development, the precautionary principle and the integration of environmental considerations into all policy areas. The programme was primarily concerned with conventional command and control regulation of the media for pollution (air, inland waters and the marine environment) and regulating the effects of economic sectors on the environment (agriculture, industry, forestry). It also reflected an increasing orientation towards global problems, for example protecting the ozone layer and climate change, and the creation of new institutions like the Irish Environmental Protection Agency. Moreover, it tentatively embraced the integration of environmental protection and economic growth by highlighting the benefits of clean technology, environment-friendly industry and the positive growth potential of the environmental technology sector (DoE, 1990).

In 1997, this policy was subsumed within the framework of 'Sustainable Development: A Strategy for Ireland' which placed the environment steadfastly within a new rhetorical frame of reference. The main focus of the strategy is on the measures required to place the major economic sectors in Irish society on a path towards sustainable development. Pepper (1999) argues that 'the presumptions underlying the official approach to sustainable development in Ireland are, as they are in the wider EU, clearly those of ecological modernisation theory'. Jansen et al (1998) have recently argued that ever since the publication of 'Our Common Future' there has been a necessary correspondence between the greening of the market economy and the greening of government. In both of these processes of ecological modernisation the problem of integration into the existing logic of the respective institutions is important. The greening of government process provides us with an access point to the implementation of LA21 in Ireland, since the national sustainable development strategy creates a new institutional framework linking national, regional and local government in the implementation of Agenda 21. This includes the establishment of a national sustainable development council, now the National Sustainable Development Partnership (Comhar); a regional approach to sustainable development; the ascription of a pivotal role to local authorities through LA21; and the establishment of the Environmental Partnership Fund as a mechanism for partnership at the local level.

PROMPTING INNOVATION OR ADAPTING EXISTING REFORMS?

Transformations in the Irish institutional landscape since the early 1990s have simultaneously provided an opportunity and a constraint for the implementation of LA21. There is no doubt that the systems of subnational governance and environmental protection in the early 1990s were insufficient to adequately respond to Agenda 21 and particularly Chapter 28. From the initiation of the first Environmental Action Programme in 1990 to the launch of the national sustainable Development Strategy in

1997, environmental policy has, through a series of iterations, shifted to a more comprehensive embrace of ecological programmes and initiatives. Pepper (1999), drawing on the national development plan (1994–99), the blueprint for Irish regional development, argues that government's general approach to sustainable development values the environment 'not for intrinsic value or broader social value but because of perceived economic advantage'. In this light, many of the institutional changes can be interpreted as modernising and adapting the instruments of governance to address an economic imperative (Taylor, 1998). Brundtland and Agenda 21 have, however, established that sustainability principles must also include, alongside environmental protection and enhancement, elements of social justice both now and in the future (Pepper, 1999).

The impetus deriving from Agenda 21, and specifically Chapter 28, on the other hand, has had the effect of adapting and extending existing models of social coordination towards an embrace of wider implications of sustainable development. At the national level, the mechanism of social partnership has evolved and progressively extended its scope and franchise since 1987. The formation of the national economic and social forum in 1994 included sustainable development as a substantive concern and extended representation to specific environmental organisations. The reform of local government has localised the national model through the formation of strategic policy committees, and Comhar has engaged Agenda 21 in extended social partnership.

INTERPRETING LOCAL AGENDA 21

LA21 as a problem of integration and coordination with national priorities

The implementation of LA21 has clearly been viewed by central government as an integral part of a more complex negotiation between national development priorities and fulfilling Ireland's obligations to implement a national Agenda 21 plan. The publication of the plan in 1997 clearly outlined the larger strategic and institutional parameters for the implementation of Chapter 28. Meanwhile, the emphasis has moved to the creation of mechanisms for the coordination and integration of the response to Agenda 21 across the various levels of governance. Comhar was established in 1999 to advance the national agenda for sustainable development, to evaluate progress, to assist in devising suitable mechanisms and advising on their implementation, and to contribute to the formation of a national consensus (Comhar, 1999). The membership of Comhar is drawn from the state and public sectors, the economic sector, environmental NGOs, social and community NGOs, and the academic sector. Comhar's first work programme has identified four key priority areas to be pursued by working groups in the period from 1999 to 2002. The group working on local sustainability, public participation and education' has been allocated the responsibility for 'guidance on the pursuit of sustainable development within reformed Local Government structures, issues related to Local Agenda 21 and other forms of community action for sustainability' (Comhar, 1999). This is significant for a number of reasons. Firstly, it creates a national partnership for sustainable development that can help to embed LA21 within a larger national framework. Secondly, it can help to establish a more comprehensive picture of the extent and nature of LA21 and local sustainability initiatives in Ireland. Thirdly, it can help to provide guidance and support for local authorities to move LA21 into the community more systematically than before.

By mid-1998, when it had become apparent that LA21 was not being implemented, central government suggested that each local authority designate an LA21 officer. The LA21 officers coordinate with other local authorities in their region with the cooperation of the regional authority, and each region is represented in a national network. The LA21 officers provide a focal point for contact with the general public and access for communication across the various levels of government. One of the effects of the network has been the capacity for regional cooperation, and it has set up a working group to generate its own guidelines for the implementation of LA21. This is important because the original guidelines issued by central government were viewed as being handed down without any consultation with the local authorities. The network provides a link between local communities, their broader regional context and the national partnership for sustainability.

The formation of county and city development boards represents a move to integrate the local development and local government systems in Ireland. In its initial report, the Interdepartmental Task Force on the Integration of Local Government and Local Development Systems (1998) highlighted the existing overlaps in the activities of local government, the state agencies and local development agencies, and identified the need for integration. The development boards will be drawn from the local government sector, the local development sector (for example LEADER II and community groups), state agencies and social partners. Their function is to design a strategy for economic, social and cultural development. The fact that these boards are broadly focused on a strategic approach to local development and are to be supported in each case through the creation of a broadly based community forum suggests that this would be an ideal vehicle for a community-wide approach to LA21. The report of the task force stressed that local strategies should be developed in the context of the national strategies in key areas of public policy, including sustainable development. This is being reinforced since the directors of the new boards are being informed to include LA21 in their activities. The difficulty at present is that the integration of environmental concerns is assumed, but there is no explicit mention of LA21 and the UNCED process in official documentation.

A problem of reform, subsidiarity and consultation

For Irish local authorities, LA21 is generally defined as a process to implement sustainable development at the local level, in which public participation is seen as both a functional and normative goal. Beyond this primary level of consensus, however, lie a number of intersecting strategies for the framing and interpretation of LA21. Throughout Ireland, local authorities have tended to view LA21 as part of a larger process of ecological, structural and regional reform of sub-national government. This, however, is as far as the consensus has stretched, since LA21 has been fundamentally bound-up with differing interpretations of the nature and priorities of the reform process, the proper level at which action should be taken and the type of consultation that LA21 entails.

The dominant understanding of LA21 among local authorities has been a greening of local government, which has been contingent on the more general process of local government reform. In some cases this has been seen holistically at an organisational level, but it most frequently reflects a rationale that community participation would not take place unless local authorities amended their own practices first. In a closely related interpretation, a number of local authorities have viewed LA21 as instrumental in achieving funding from Europe, and was particularly prominent among local authorities in counties that remained eligible for Objective One status, after 1999.

In a minority of cases, however, LA21 has been seen as adding value to these more general processes. In these cases, LA21 is seen as enhancing democratisation and reform. This 'framing strategy' (setting interpretive boundaries) tends to be employed where individuals have become invested and informed about LA21, but where their local authority has not yet seriously engaged with the process. A final, less frequent but nevertheless significant, strategy has been to view LA21 as extending existing understandings of sustainable development beyond an environment and economy core. In this understanding LA21 is seen as enhancing existing reform processes and emphasising the social dimensions of sustainable development. This interpretation was a subordinate understanding in many cases, but was elaborated by those local authorities that had engaged in the first phase of LA21 mobilisation in 1995.

The general lack of response by local authorities has been interpreted as a typical example of the issue of a proper division of power and responsibility between the three levels of government: local, regional and national. There are two competing strategies reflecting this interpretation.

The first is the delegation of responsibility downwards from the centre and is invariably identified as a barrier to the implementation of LA21. This strategy characterises the implementation of LA21 as a story of top-down failure, wherein central government has failed to provide adequate direction, resources and political pressure to facilitate implementation. This tends to be a widespread understanding among local authorities regardless of the phase in which they mobilised. A distinctive variation can be linked, however, to local authorities that have only recently begun to address LA21, who argue that they are unable to act because of the failure of regional government to provide training and models for implementation for their constituent local authorities. In some cases this failure reinterprets the regional authorities' mandate for the coordination of LA21 as a responsibility for implementation. The second though less frequent interpretation is that the natural relationship implicit in the implementation process is bottom-up. In other words, supra-ordinate authorities should only exercise such powers that add value to the actions of local authorities to implement LA21.

The goal of achieving a community-wide 'consensus' for LA21 has been universally identified as a barrier to implementing the initiative. Community consultation has been generally confined to explaining the inhibiting nature of the structure, capacity and culture of the institutions of the Irish State. The dominant interpretation has been the lack of consultation related to the institutional dependence of local on national government, and this has reflected the structural and constitutional location of local government in the Irish State. It is linked to an interpretation of LA21 as a story of top-down failure. The wider implications of LA21 as a consensual process are seen as hindered by the late response of the Irish government; the lack of political interest at the national level; and a failure by central government to consult with local authorities on the original guidelines for LA21. Local authorities are therefore unable to engage in consultative processes with their communities because of their dependence on central government, which many local authorities argue is motivated by an unwillingness to devolve power downwards.

A second though closely related device is institutional incapacity. Local authorities are seen as being unable to address the consultative dimension of LA21 because of the scale of ongoing reforms imposed by central government. Many of the LA21 officers using this device attribute the consultation barrier to the lack of human resource development and insufficient corporate commitment to the mechanism of partnership.

A third principal rhetorical device was used to highlight the residual difficulties in the institutional culture of local government in Ireland. Unlike the problem of institutional incapacity, which it was argued could be remedied through corporate adjustment, changing the institutional culture of local authorities was seen as a much more fundamental and difficult challenge.

Interpreting LA21 as 'planning and democratic reforms'

In many cases, Irish local authorities have set aside the short-term objective of having a separate LA21 plan, opting instead for spatial development planning as a vehicle for LA21. Many of the respondents questioned have argued that it is the ideal model for LA21 since it acts as a focus for the integration of economic, social and environmental development through land-use planning. At the moment, this represents the modification of an existing instrument by:

- auditing development plans for sustainability and LA21 criteria; and
- including a specific reference to the Earth Summit and LA21.

The question of democratic reform remains, since no local authority has addressed public consultation on LA21. Local authorities have identified this as an institutional problem. This analysis, as we have seen, is linked to questions of subsidiarity, but also to the lack of sufficient norms, structures and routines at the local level to support community consultation. There is, however, a related question – how is consultation understood? The dominant interpretation has been that no consultation can take place in advance of greening local authorities or beyond existing statutory provisions for public participation. A second interpretation is that LA21 requires consultation through information. In practical terms, local authorities have used existing community networks or school programmes financed through the environmental partnership fund as a means of informing the public about aspects of sustainable development. The third interpretation is that the process should involve consultation through partnership. Although closely related to the previous interpretation, this has a more clearly defined institutional base through the strategic policy committee system of local authorities. The fourth interpretation is consultation through targeting major stakeholders. In this case, major stakeholders are to be targeted with a view to identifying priorities with the intent of establishing more formal relationships. The final interpretation is consultation through deliberation. This is the least prominent but most innovative interpretation, where a few local authorities (for example, Cork County, Dublin City and Louth County) that responded to LA21 in 1995 are experimenting with new forms of dialogue with their communities (Lafferty, 1999).

Democratic experimentation and institutional mobilisation: Two cases of 'good practice'

Cork County: LA21 as an experiment in discursive democracy?

> *'Cork County covers an area of 7454 square kilometres and has a population of 282,790 and its coastline stretches for 1094 kilometres. As the largest county in Ireland and supporting an immense industrial and agricultural industry, the breadth of its environmental protection needs are extensive.'* (Cork County Council, 1998)

Satisfying these needs has proved to be a difficult task and the 1980s and early 1990s were marked by a protracted period of environment and development conflicts. In the mid-1990s, Cork County Council set about trying to redress the situation by changing its own environmental practices. Prior to the launch of the LA21 guidelines in 1995, the council had been involved in the planning and environment group of the EuroSyNet Inter-Regional Co-operation Project under the European Union's RECITE programme. Although the project focused on environmental audit models for local authorities, an ancillary effect was that the council became aware of models of LA21 employed in the UK, particularly the idea of an environmental forum.

The principal responsibility for coordinating LA21 within Cork County Council rests with the council's LA21 committee, a cross-departmental team that was established in June 1996 'to ensure that Agenda 21 principles are implemented in Cork County through the direct involvement of the council' (Cork County Council, 1998). A draft LA21 plan was prepared by the Agenda 21 committee and published in September 1998. Although the draft LA21 does not set out targets, it does assess the sustainability of existing actions. The distinguishing development to date, however, has been the creation of the Cork Environmental Forum that is identified with LA21. The relationship between the council and the forum is mediated through interaction between the LA21 committee and the environmental forum steering committee that includes members of the plenary and council officials. A number of thematic working groups (for example, landscape, water and waste) have been established in relation to the plenary work on specific project areas within LA21. The initial composition of the forum included representatives from the council, the agricultural sector, business and industry, environmental groups and community organisations. Recently, one of the major environmental groups has withdrawn, arguing that the forum was primarily a means of containing conflict rather than creating an opportunity for dialogue and progress on LA21. The initial goals of the forum were established unilaterally by the council. They were to:

- satisfy the local features of the Earth Summit Agenda 21 and the EU's Fifth Environmental Action Programme;
- support sustainable development, which will produce good quality jobs in a good quality environment;
- provide a forum for all parties with an interest in the environment to engage in debate on current environmental issues against measurable environmental performance indicators and to focus such debate on the future rather than what has happened in the past;
- promote Cork as an unpolluted and environmentally aware area; and
- raise the general level of environmental awareness among the people of Cork.

In effect, the capacity of the forum to act as a mechanism for consultation was constrained because it was precluded from uncovering the underlying causes of the environmental impacts of past developments. From 1995 to 1998 the forum was therefore largely ineffective as a vehicle for LA21 (Broderick, 1999). However, the situation has changed and the forum is slowly beginning to function with small but significant effects. In 1998, it received a grant of IR£5,000 from the environmental partnership fund to create a database of all the voluntary and community groups engaged in sustainable development activities in the region and to continue its operation. Through a series of subsequent debates, the forum has redefined its goals to:

- satisfy the local features of the Earth Summit Agenda 21 and the EU's Fifth Environmental Action Programme;
- support sustainable development which achieves a good quality of life in a good quality environment;
- provide a forum for all parties with an interest in the environment to engage in debate on current environmental issues and seek agreement on ways of resolving them;
- stimulate and sustain the level of active environmental awareness, concern and care among the people of Cork; and
- participate in local, national and international Local Agenda 21 networks.

In redefining the goals of the forum, the participants have established a collectively agreed platform for moving forward with concrete projects for making a contribution to LA21. The forum has decided to operate with a consensus model, with reports or decisions including a qualified account of the opposition. One of the issues that became obvious to the forum in the process of evaluating its procedures was that while the round-table model was useful, it was by its nature limited in size. The forum has now begun a process of reaching outwards to community groups and upwards to Comhar in an attempt to optimise the potential for maximum horizontal and vertical integration of efforts towards sustainable development.

Although the initial experience of the forum was one of procedural wrangling, the process of reconstitution has been an interesting one. On one level, a normative learning process has occurred as existing institutional tools have been reoriented to encompass an extended notion of consultation as deliberation. In this case, more traditional environmental concerns like waste management or spatial development plans are opened up to deliberation. New institutional rules are emerging which structure the context of communication and decision-making for LA21. On the other hand, there is an ongoing learning process where environmental understandings are gradually being reframed in the broader conceptual understanding of sustainable development and the implementation horizon of LA21.

Despite the avowedly local nature of the process, there is a practical recognition of the wider context. The forum recognises, for example, that sustainable development is not something that can be delivered solely at national level, but that it requires input and effort at all levels of government and society. In debates within the forum, this learning process has focused on the interaction between global issues and local action. For example, the working group on landscape has highlighted contradictions in the practices of the council in managing the hedgerows, which contribute substantially to the biodiversity of the rural environment. Interaction through the forum has prompted the council to counterbalance their legal obligations to ensure the proper management of hedgerows with information leaflets directed at contractors and emphasising strategies to avoid excessive damage. Although the forum and the council have not achieved complete agreement on this particular issue, it is an important illustration of how LA21 is connecting a local context with a global issue in a social-learning process. In terms of change towards sustainable development, we can only see hints of progress in the types of areas and issues previously mentioned. One of the key features of the Cork case is that, although there are weak links in the decision-making procedures of the council, there is a forum in which the existing horizons of policy implementation can be broadened (Lafferty, 1996).

Dun Laoghaire Rathdown County: Corporate mobilisation for LA21

Dun Laoghaire Rathdown County Council is one of the youngest local authorities in Ireland. It is the product of the reorganisation of Dublin County Council in 1994 in which three new administrative areas were created. The launch of the guidelines for local authorities in 1995 was the catalyst. The county manager at the time set the agenda for the council by immediately establishing a cross-departmental, multidisciplinary LA21 team. The establishment of the team in itself represents a qualitative shift in the practice of local authorities, since departments normally work in isolation from one another.

The manager recommended the adoption of the Aalborg Charter in March 1996. The adoption of the charter had the effect of creating an internal constituency for LA21 among the elected representatives in the council who endorsed the LA21 interim report in April 1996. The emphasis of the report was, according to the LA21 officer, 'excessively environmental'. However, it has evolved through participation in the European sustainable cities and towns campaign. Following the endorsement of the report by the elected representatives, three principal actions have been given priority: an internal environmental housekeeping review, advancing the agenda within the council and interaction with the wider community.

The environmental housekeeping review basically amounts to modifying the internal practices of the organisation in relation to energy usage, green purchasing and internal waste management. Perhaps the most interesting aspect of the process is that all of the council's employees were asked for suggestions for internal improvement through a questionnaire. The county development plan has been a critical focus in terms of specifically binding the council to sustainable development through LA21. The county manager used the opportunity of the review of the county development plan to write a position paper linking the principles of sustainable development to the instrument of the development plan.

The strategy for advancing LA21 within the council is particularly interesting since, in addition to the activities of the LA21 team, it also aims to create an internal 'corporate' identification with LA21. Initially this proceeded through internal seminars introducing the idea and implications of LA21 to the staff and elected representatives. There are plans, however, to put a formal structure in place for LA21, which seeks to transpose the collective learning of the LA21 team into organisational learning for the entire council. This involves a suggested framework that would oversee the implementation of LA21 through a steering group made up of the county manager and the senior heads of departments, with the existing LA21 team acting as a coordinating focus for implementation. The strategic intent of this structure is to give LA21 a legitimacy and impetus from the top down.

Although the designation of an LA21 officer has undoubtedly advanced the process within some local authorities, one of the principal weaknesses in the system is that it represents an additional aspect of top-down administration. One of the ways in which Dun Laoghaire Rathdown has attempted to overcome this is by building up a core of volunteers

Box 6.1 Experiments in democratic and institutional mobilisation in Ireland

Cork County as an experiment in 'discursive democracy'

- The distinguishing characteristic of LA21 in Cork has been the creation of the Cork Environmental Forum. The forum has since its inception been explicitly identified with LA21.
- The Cork County Council has its own LA21 committee that drafted an LA21 plan in 1998. The relationship between the council and the forum is mediated through interaction between the LA21 committee and the environmental forum steering committee. The latter includes members of the plenary and council officials.
- The initial composition of the forum included representatives from the council, the agricultural sector, business and industry, environmental groups and community organisations.
- The forum has decided to operate with a consensus model, with reports or decisions incorporating oppositional perspectives.
- After a slow beginning, the forum has now begun a process of networking outwards to community groups and upwards to Comhar.
- A learning process has occurred in the forum as existing institutional tools have been expanded to encompass an extended notion of consultation as deliberation. Environmental issues are gradually being reframed within a broader conceptual understanding of sustainable development and the implementation of LA21.

Corporate mobilisation for LA21 in Dun Laoghaire Rathdown County

- The county manager has here taken an initiative for LA21 in the council by establishing a cross-departmental, multi-disciplinary LA21 team. The establishment of the team represents in itself a qualitative shift in the practice of local authorities, since departments normally work in isolation from one another.
- The strategy for advancing LA21 within the council focuses on creating a corporate identification with LA21. Internally, the role of the county manager has been axial in establishing LA21 as a corporate rather than a departmental priority. Initially this proceeded through internal seminars introducing the idea and implications of LA21 to the staff and elected representatives.
- There are plans to integrate such a corporate identification into a more formal structure to succeed LA21, where the aim is to transpose the collective learning of the LA21 team into organisational learning for the entire council. Such plans involve establishing a steering group made up of the county manager and the senior heads of departments, with the existing LA21 team acting as a coordinating focus for implementation.

- The mechanism of the cross-departmental LA21 team has allowed the council to consider the implications of LA21, most importantly what it means for the organisation itself. The attempt to embed this learning in the organisation through training and the evolution of formal structures indicates a long-term transformational commitment to LA21.

through internal seminars to provide communities with information on LA21. It is also extending existing public consultation with community groups to create a constituency for LA21. However, more expansive mechanisms for inclusion have eluded the efforts of the county council. In particular, the idea of a forum, while desirable from a council perspective, found little purchase among the local community. Although the idea of an LA21 forum has not been abandoned, the LA21 officer argues that it will have to be built up by building from an existing base of community associations and groups. The strategic policy committee is seen as an integral part of a strategy of moving LA21 into the community. The council is also working in partnership with other agencies through the county strategy board in order to compile a guide for the county. Through this process the council is considering the implications of all national directives and initiatives, including Agenda 21, for their activities. This partnership is providing the LA21 officer with a platform to extend the reach of Agenda 21 beyond the immediate confines of the local authority.

The case of Dun Laoghaire Rathdown illustrates the scale of change that LA21 implies for Irish local authorities and therefore the importance of systematically building a constituency both internally and externally for the initiative. Internally, the role of the county manager has been axial in establishing LA21 as a corporate rather than a departmental priority. The mechanism of the cross-departmental team has allowed the council to consider what LA21 means, but more importantly what it means for the organisation. The attempt to embed this learning in the organisation through training and the evolution of formal structures indicates a long-term commitment to LA21. The Aalborg Charter has been instrumental in binding the council to the implementation of the initiative, and has provided a mechanism whereby environment and development issues are being reconsidered in the framework of sustainable development. The experience of community consultation has shown that the creation of an LA21 forum is not immediately transferable across different types of local-community settings, nor is it a panacea for public engagement in the process. While this may function as a new normative reference point for some local authorities, the question of community consultation has to be addressed by building a constituency for change through existing social networks and mechanisms of social coordination in a purposeful, goal-directed strategic approach.

Conclusion

Although the actual implementation of LA21 is still in the very early stages, its unfolding institutional impact cannot be dismissed as inconsequential to environment and development issues in Ireland. The implementation story reveals a complex relationship between the path of a global–local reform like LA21, contextual institutional dependencies, and prevailing narratives about environment and development interrelationships. Behind the immediate inertia towards LA21 among local authorities – who often interpret it as part of an innovation overload facing sub-national government – lies a deeper structural barrier. The constitutional structure of central–local authority patterns underwrites the heavily dependent relationship between local and national government. This is compounded by the dependent relationship of Ireland within the EU. Although both of these relationships are currently in transition, they partially explain the barriers to autonomous mobilisation by many local authorities. Paradoxically, this dual dependency has resulted in a situation where LA21 may become more robustly institutionalised than in other contexts where there have been more specific attempts at implementation.

Central government has interpreted LA21 as part of an integrated response to the implementation of the national Agenda 21 strategy. As we have seen, there has been substantial institutional adaptation and innovation laying the foundation for the integration of Agenda 21 at all levels of governance. Mechanisms like Comhar and the LA21 officer network are creating conditions where implementation can be adapted to embed the initiative in local governance. Beyond the current unwillingness of some local authorities to engage with LA21, and the challenge of community consultation it invokes, lies the more fundamental problem of how LA21 is understood and how this is related to the evolving institutional landscape.

The actual implementation of LA21 depends on many factors, not least the challenge of moving beyond its interpretation as being just another environmental initiative. The LA21 officer network can provide a mechanism for reconsidering environment and development relations and linking these to concrete actions (for example embedding LA21 in county and city development planning), or by providing an external stimulus for organisational change (for example, by encouraging local authorities to create formal structures for LA21).

The democratic potential of the initiative remains ambiguous in the Irish context. For many local authorities the challenge of community consultation is seen as a barrier rather than an opportunity for implementation. The precise nature of what consultation might entail is quite diverse and frequently errs on the side of caution. In the larger national context it varies between interpretations of subsidiarity that enhance regional and local authority for its own sake, and sharing authority with non-governmental participants. The actual implementation of LA21 remains limited, but the institutional changes outlined suggest that there is significant potential for progress. It remains to be seen whether the coalescence of political and social legitimacy that the initiative now requires can be mobilised to progress towards sustainability.

NOTES

1 The analysis is based on 35 telephone interviews conducted in July 1999. This includes 29 semi-structured interviews with LA21 officers, three interviews with responsible officials at regional authority level and three supplementary background interviews at the Department of Environment and Local Government and the Institute of Public Administration. The interviews were supplemented, where available, with relevant documentation from interim LA21 plans, reports, policy statements and references in city and county development plans.

REFERENCES

Broderick, S (ed) (1999) *Community Participation in Partnership: Our Common Future?* Proceedings of a conference held by Cork Environmental Alliance, 19–20 February, Cork Environmental Alliance, Cork

Comhar – The National Sustainable Development Partnership (1999) Work Programme 1999–2002, 25 May, Dublin

Cork County Council (1998) *Draft Local Agenda 21 Plan: A Discussion Document*, Cork County Hall

DoE (1990) *An Environmental Action Programme*, Department of the Environment, Dublin

DoE (1995) *Local Authorities and Sustainable Development: Guidelines on Local Agenda 21*, Department of the Environment, Dublin

DoE (1996) *Better Local Government: A Programme for Change*, Department of the Environment, Dublin

DoE (1997) *Sustainable Development: A Strategy for Ireland*, Government Publications Sales Office/ Department of the Environment, Dublin

Dooney, S and O'Toole, J (1998) *Irish Government Today*, Gill & Macmillan, Dublin

Dun Laoghaire Rathdown County Council (1996) *Local Agenda 21 Interim Report*, April 1996

Government of Ireland (1997) *Report of the Joint Committee on Sustainable Development*, The Stationery Office, Dublin

Government of Ireland (1999) *Ireland: National Development Plan, 2000–2006*, The Stationery Office, Dublin

Interdepartmental Task Force on the Integration of Local Government and Local Development Systems (1998) *Preparing the Ground: Guidelines for the Progress for Strategy Groups to County Development Boards*, Department of Environment and Local Government, Dublin

Jansen, A-I, Osland, O and Hanf, K (1998) 'Environmental Challenges and Institutional Changes: An interpretation of the development of environmental policy in Western Europe' in Hanf, K and Jansen, A-I (eds) *Governance and Environment in Western Europe: Politics, Policy and Administration*, Longman, Harlow, pp277–322

Lafferty, W M (1996) 'The Politics of Sustainable Development: From global norms to national implementation', *Environmental Politics*, vol 5(2), pp185–208

Lafferty, W M and Eckerberg, K (eds) (1998) *From Earth Summit to Local Agenda 21: Working Towards Sustainable Development*, Earthscan, London

Lafferty, W M (1999) *Implementing LA21 in Europe: New Initiatives for Sustainable Communities*, ProSus, Oslo

McGowan, L (1999) 'Environmental Policy' in Collins, N (ed.) *Political Issues in Ireland Today*, Manchester University Press, Manchester, pp163–176

Pepper, D (1999) 'Ecological Modernisation or the "Ideal Model" of Sustainable Development? Questions Prompted at Europe's Periphery', *Environmental Politics*, vol 8(4), pp1–34

Sibeon, R (1996) *Sociology and Public Policy: The New Sociology of Public Policy*, Tudor Business Publishing Ltd., Merseyside

Taylor, G (1998) 'Conserving the Emerald Tiger: The politics of environmental regulation in Ireland', *Environmental Politics*, vol 7(4), pp53–74

7. The Netherlands
Probing the essence of LA21 as a value-added approach to sustainable development and local democracy

Frans Coenen

INTRODUCTION

In a recent national workshop (March 1999) in The Netherlands on the future of Local Agenda 21 (LA21) it was concluded that the body of ideas behind LA21 was widely supported by the directly involved key actors at the national level for its implementation – the Ministry of the Environment (VROM), the Association of Dutch Municipalities (VNG) and the NGO umbrella organisation, the National Committee on International Cooperation and Sustainable Development (NCDO).[1] Elsewhere, the body of ideas is considered vague and the implementation is a subject of discussion by many municipalities (ERM, 1999b). The discussion is largely about the added value of LA21 to already existing initiatives in the area of local sustainable policies and changes in local democracy.

In an earlier national report (Coenen, 1998a), the Dutch situation for the implementation of LA21 was characterised as very fertile because the baseline conditions looked very promising. Dutch municipalities were well ahead with environmental policy; sustainable development had become a political issue; and experiences with participation in environmental policy had been gained. These baseline conditions looked promising at that stage because they were in line with key characteristics of an LA21 identified within the SUSCOM project as a set of criteria to distinguish LA21 from older, already existing activities. For example, Dutch municipalities were already working on a more focused policy for achieving cross-sectoral integration and improving efforts to increase community involvement.

This chapter argues that, in the process of interpretation of LA21, key actors in The Netherlands neglected another key identifying characteristic, namely a specific identification with the Earth Summit and Agenda

21. The national 'storyline' for the Dutch case – the interpretation by key actors that LA21 was an initiative with only a limited added value to existing initiatives in Dutch political culture – explains for a large part the current state of affairs. This has to be seen in the context of The Netherlands as an advanced country in environmental policy and sustainable development, which on the one hand creates excellent baseline conditions for implementing LA21, but at the same time places heavy burdens on the interpretation of LA21 as a new and worthwhile initiative.

The chapter is divided into two parts. The first gives a general overview of the status of LA21 implementation in The Netherlands. The second part asks the question: How far can the current state of affairs and future development of LA21 in The Netherlands be explained on the basis of storylines as to the added value of LA21, which can be identified in three Dutch discourses on: local democracy; the self-responsibility of local authorities for sustainable development; and innovations in local governance?

THE STATUS OF IMPLEMENTATION OF LA21 IN THE NETHERLANDS

This overview is based on surveys (Brijer, 1997), self-reports of the municipalities within the framework of the grants scheme for the development of municipal environmental policy (VOGM) (Inspectorate, 1997; Coenen, Seinstra and Teunissen; 1999), interviews with 15 'best case' municipalities (CSTM, 1998) and policy documents from about 25 municipalities.

The state of affairs of LA21 in The Netherlands is closely linked to the so-called VOGM funding. In 1996 the national government introduced a financial measure which provided municipalities with an incentive to work on an LA21. LA21 was a so-called task of choice in the supplementary contribution scheme for the VOGM, run by the VROM. Municipalities could receive extra funding for four policy priorities out of a list of nine, of which LA21 was one. Over 140 municipalities chose LA21 as one of their four action areas, and about 30 municipalities voluntarily chose to draw up an LA21 separate from the funding scheme. The environment inspectorate (the national environmental inspection and enforcement agency) audits the implementation of municipalities' environmental policy each year. During the auditing process of VOGM funding the progress of LA21 was monitored.

The introduction to this chapter referred to the three key actors at the national level: the VROM, the VNG and the NCDO. In this national commission, about 50 NGOs from all sectors of society participated to stimulate the debate on sustainable development at the national level. Within the NCDO all important NGOs are represented. Other major organisations are of course the municipalities themselves and in some cases regional inter-municipal networks who work together on LA21 (the environment inspectorate, consultancy firms and the Ministry of Foreign Affairs).

Numbers of LA21 initiatives can be confusing in The Netherlands because during the VOGM period (1996–98), through division of the municipalities, the total number went down from over 600 to about 540. The figures over the last year are based on reports from 545 municipalities and 16 Amsterdam city districts.

On the basis of the inspectorate survey (1999), about 80 per cent of the municipalities that chose LA21 as a VOGM task had a so-called plan of approach, which was a formal requirement for funding. A least 26 municipalities that did not choose LA21 for VOGM funding made, or were making, an LA21 'plan of approach'.[2]

The municipalities were asked to what extent the following elements were part of their plan (Inspectorate, 1998):

- vision on local sustainable development (63 per cent);
- relation with international solidarity (59 per cent);
- relation with policies within different municipal departments (63 per cent); and
- the shape of the dialogue with citizens, companies and societal organisations (78 per cent).

About 60 per cent of the VOGM municipalities and about 37 other municipalities had made a separate policy document for nature and environment education, which was a closely related task in the VOGM funding.

It is difficult to get a complete picture of the implementation of these plans of approach. At least 57 per cent of the VOGM municipalities and about 22 others reported actual implementation of projects and activities. Within the framework of the VOGM funding, end terms for an adequate level of VOGM implementation were formulated. The inspectorate concluded that 74 per cent of the municipalities reached an adequate level at the beginning of 1998 and 21 per cent would reach this level during 1998. Five per cent of the municipalities could be considered as laggards. Another 26 municipalities that did not choose LA21 within the VOGM were expected to reach an adequate level before or during 1998. On the basis of other studies (Coenen, 1998a; CSTM, 1998; ERM, 1999a; Brijer, 1997), some of the typical characteristics of the Dutch LA21s can be summarised as follows:

- Participation processes are very diverse and range from limited consultation to structural participation platforms.
- In general, LA21s take the form of activity agendas, and visioning processes are limited to a very small part of the municipalities.

- The content of LA21 often concentrates on issues from the surrounding environment, such as animal droppings and litter, or on projects in areas like sustainable building or energy saving.

The typical characteristics have some consequences for LA21 in The Netherlands compared to the SUSCOM criteria for an LA21 (Lafferty and Eckerberg, 1998):

- The integration of ecological, economic and social aspects of sustainability is very limited; LA21 is mainly concerned with the issue of environment.
- The global dimension receives relatively little attention in Dutch LA21s.
- Links with existing decision-making procedures are weak, which often makes LA21 an isolated activity.

In Dutch literature and research, several implementation barriers are identified that can explain these general characteristics. LA21 officers (CSTM, 1998) of front-running municipalities identified several implementation barriers within their municipalities:

- capacity in terms of lack of man-power resources but also in experiences with interactive policy-making;
- a small societal basis for LA21, leading to 'green-ghetto' participation (only traditional green organisations) or a lack of representation (for example, the lack of business involvement);
- disturbed relations with local groups from past experiences and a negative attitude towards the local authority in general;
- lack of support from internal government officials;
- lack of political support and back-up;
- unclear scope and meaning of the LA21 process and its influence on decision-making.

This chapter is not about these classical implementation barriers, although they are very important, but about the views that those involved in the participation processes hold on the position of LA21 in local democracy and local environmental policy. The concluding section considers some of the characteristics of LA21s in The Netherlands resulting from the typical Dutch interpretation.

GOALS AND RESEARCH QUESTIONS

This national report on Dutch experiences with the implementation of LA21 adds to three specific goals of the SUSCOM project. The first knowledge goal follows from LA21 as a particular type of global policy. The understanding of LA21 implementation in The Netherlands must begin with an analysis of the interpretation and introduction of LA21 as a policy initiative into the policy process, given the specific policy context of an advanced country in environmental policy and sustainable development. In this respect, the Dutch national report tries to contribute to theories of policy implementation and the first goal of the project.

Another discourse on local self-responsibility in environmental policy in The Netherlands addresses two other implementation problems and goals, namely central–local relations and the substance of LA21. The dominance of the so-called VOGM funding raises issues on the top-down implementation of LA21 and issues of substance of LA21 within general discussions on local responsibility for environmental policy.

The major knowledge discourse to which this chapter contributes is the discourse on planning and democratic participation. By its very nature, LA21 is a planning and democratisation reform. In the process of interpretation of LA21, the question is not only how it influences existing modes of participation, but also how existing democratisation, planning and administrative reforms influence its interpretation. This leads to the following two research questions.

1. Which storylines on the added value of LA21 can be identified in three Dutch discourses on local democracy, local authority self-responsibility in sustainable development and innovations in local governance?
2. How far can the current state of affairs and future development of LA21 in The Netherlands be explained on the basis of these storylines?

The views held by those in the participating processes follow storylines that interpret the added value of LA21 as, for example, purely an exponent of political renewal or that LA21 is first and foremost about the quality of the immediate surrounding environment. Storylines are narratives on social reality through which elements from many different domains are combined and that provide actors with a set of symbolic references that suggest a common understanding (Hajer, 1995). In this chapter it is argued that the current state of affairs and future development of LA21 can be explained on the basis of the views of participants in the implementation of LA21 and their adherence to certain storylines. Our thesis is that the coalescence of multiple storylines about how LA21 fits into local democracy and local governance in The Netherlands strongly influences the perception and implementation of LA21.

VIEWS OF PARTICIPANTS AS AN IMPLEMENTATION FACTOR

The first generation of implementation research, dealing with the question 'does implementation matter?', has revealed many factors that can hinder policy implementation in general (Lester et al, 1987). One set of factors which determines the course of a policy implementation process is the beliefs held by the participants of that process (Maarse, 1989). According to Scharpf (1978), policy implementation is inevitably the result of interactions among many different actors with separate interests, goals and strategies. In the implementation literature, much attention is given to the appreciative gap between policy-makers and implementing actors on the policy content as a possible failure factor. But, apart from assent to the policy content, the views on the implementation strategy that should be followed will influence implementation (Coenen, 1993; Berman, 1980).

This chapter considers the views held by the different participants in the Dutch LA21 implementation process, and especially their views on the position of LA21 in local democracy and local environmental policy, as a crucial factor that explains the state of affairs of LA21 in The Netherlands. In policy science and public-administration literature we find several methods of approach to analyse policy actors from the perspective of their assumptions, such as policy theories (Hoogerwerf, 1984), belief systems (Sabatier, 1987) and discourse-coalitions (Hajer, 1995).

The choice made here is not simply to present empirical facts about the implementation of LA21 in The Netherlands. This would lead us to obvious success and failure factors such as the capacity of implementing agencies, information and power. Our thesis is that the perceptions surrounding LA21 – and how LA21 fits into local democracy and local governance – influence its implementation in The Netherlands to a far greater degree than the classical implementation barriers.

The importance of the views of the participants as an implementation factor calls for an alternative approach to implementation research. The process of interpretation and meaning given to LA21 is most crucial: interpretation precedes implementation. The beliefs that the participants of the Dutch implementation process hold determine this process. Doubts about the value-added aspect and the confusion of LA21 with other innovations in urban governance have biased the implementation of LA21 in The Netherlands.

We borrow here from discourse analysis an analytical approach to the concept of storylines in order to analyse how LA21 is understood and interpreted and as a possible explanation of LA21 implementation in The Netherlands. Statements made by key actors are illustrated on the basis of official publications, newsletters, speeches, websites, interviews and surveys. Clearly some views are difficult to represent. For instance, local authorities, as a whole, and their LA21 coordinators, local government officers and local politicians can hardly be seen as a homogeneous group (Selman and Parker, 1999). The same difficulties would be encountered by taking the views of citizens or businesses.

INTERPRETATION OF LA21

Rather than focus on the individual views taken by different stakeholders in LA21 implementation in The Netherlands, this section looks at their positions in designated discourses on LA21 in order to see what storylines we can discover regarding the added value of LA21. The scope of the chapter does not allow for a detailed description of statements of the different stakeholders; the portrayal of the different storylines is on a generalized level. Neither is there space to go into detail on the specific contexts for the statements.

Discourse on local democracy and interactive policy-making

By nature, LA21 is a planning and democratisation reform. An essential characteristic of the LA21 initiative is greater efforts to increase community involvement, ie, to bring both average citizens and major stakeholder groups, particularly business and labour unions, into the planning and implementation process with respect to environment and development issues. As a democratisation reform, LA21 is more ambitious than just raising the level of public participation. LA21 and Agenda 21 ask for a new social partnership to reach towards sustainable development. Social partnership has to be understood as key social actors working together in joint efforts on sustainable development. It is about new forms of social learning, whereby key actors seek to resolve potential conflicts through new forms of involvement and cooperation (Lafferty and Eckerberg, 1998).

As a planning reform, Agenda 21 promotes a more communicative approach towards other groups in society. According to Agenda 21, sustainable strategies should be developed through the widest possible participation (UNCED, 1992). It incorporates the idea that sustainable development is not possible without close cooperation with the community. To reach this approach, participation in planning processes is stressed. The roots for such policy-making and planning can be found in the 'communicative approach' to planning and policy-making (ie planning by participation and dialogue among the affected actors). The communicative planning concept states that the problem with planning is not one of knowledge and control, as orthodox planners often assume, but instead, the need for more civic consciousness, motivation, formation of political will and emancipation, for example (van Gunsteren, 1976). The intelligent and responsible participation of many people is seen as indispensable for planning. Exponents of communicative theory in the planning literature (eg, Healy, 1992 and 1996; Fischer and Forrester, 1993) stress this communicative aspect of the process. In this view, public involvement in planning aims to build consensus around appropriate actions and a sense of ownership of the goals of the plan. This is important because it means that third parties will plan their own decisions and actions to fit in with the intended government policy in the plan (Coenen, 1998b).

The interpretation of LA21 in The Netherlands has to be placed within the typical Dutch interpretation of communicative planning. A main feature of Dutch society is its high, consensus-based social structure and a long-standing tradition of government consultation with various social groups. This is expressed in environmental policy-making through the well-known Dutch target-group approach. The political system in The Netherlands is characterised as a paradigm of the consensus model of democracy (Lijphart, 1984; Anderson and Guilory, 1997). This is not only based on the way formal institutions express democratic relations but even more through informal institutions. Widely known is the Dutch economic system, which is based on formal cooperation between employers, employees and government. Through its formal institutions, the Dutch system is relatively well organised along consensual lines (Hendriks, 2001), but it is mostly at the informal level that consultation and compromise dominate the political and administrative culture of dialogue. The philosophy that environmental problems are best solved through consultations with target groups, such as polluters, had already been developed in The Netherlands in the 1980s. This philosophy fits very well with the main feature of Dutch society as a consensus-based social structure with a long-standing tradition of government consultation with various social groups.

At the beginning of the 1980s, the ideas from the Dutch Scientific Advisory Council to the government (WRR) on open planning were very influential in pointing out that the government should leave its administrative-centred position and give more attention to the external dimension of governmental planning (den Hoed et al, 1983). The first (1989) Dutch National Environmental Policy Plan (NEPP) assigns responsibilities to the various target groups, which are comprised of companies and individuals. The Netherlands has chosen the target group approach because the achievement of sustainability is an enormous task that cannot be carried out by a single ministry. In fact, the entire country has been asked to participate in the realisation of this national objective. The NEPP states that sustainable development can only be achieved through partnerships and cooperation between all members of Dutch society. Consequently, the VROM initiated and prepared the first NEPP. Four ministries contributed to its content and four ministers signed it, while provincial and municipal authorities also participated in its development.

The target-group approach is a key element in the implementation of the NEPPs. This means creating a consultative structure encompassing the government and the representatives of these target groups to internalise environmental responsibility. Provincial and local authorities are seen as playing a critical role in encouraging target groups to realise their objectives. The second NEPP (between 1990 and 1994) supports the notion of self-regulation more strongly as this provides target groups such as industry with more room to fulfil their responsibilities. The government is responsible for the formulation of environmental objectives and the target group is responsible for meeting these objectives. Usually these arrangements are laid down in voluntary agreements called covenants and other forms of guidelines incorporating targets.

Together with the more general target-group approach, a specific development in local democracy, so-called political renewal (*bestuurlijke vernieuwing*),[3] is particularly relevant for LA21. The discussion on the value-added perspective of LA21 in The Netherlands has to be placed in the changing institutional context of local democracy. The key motives for political renewal were the low local election turn-out in combination with the disinterest of the voters in municipal polices. This disinterest was shown through voting behaviour, dominated by national issues and national parties, with a relative lack of interest in being involved in local politics (Coenen, 1998a). In particular, the low turn-out at the 1990 local elections (62 per cent) led to many activities in the field of political renewal, and almost 96 per cent of Dutch municipalities took up initiatives under the flag of political and administrative renewal (Gilsing, 1994).

Identifying storylines on local democracy and LA21

We will first try to identify the storylines on the mutual influence between LA21 and developments in local democracy. A national overview by Brijer (1997) shows that the arguments for drawing up an LA21 in The Netherlands are varied. Municipalities often see LA21 as an important issue because it is new, serves a useful purpose, and can support and encourage more involvement in environmental policy implementation. In some cases, municipalities see LA21 as a means of cooperating with other municipalities. In other cases, LA21 is adopted because it complements existing activities such as nature and environmental education programmes (Andringa, 1988).

The choice to become involved with LA21 was, for the majority of the municipalities (except for the pioneers),[4] linked to the VOGM funding. A survey among the 43 largest municipalities that chose LA21 as a VOGM action-point revealed that policy continuation and new possibilities were the main motives for making the choice. Policy continuation means that

LA21 was chosen because it was seen as a logical consequence of an already established policy in the local environmental policy plan or the political programme of the alderman (mayor). This motive is largely connected with the nature and environmental education component of the LA21 VOGM tasks. LA21 was seen as an opportunity to apply innovative environmental policies. Innovation was especially mentioned in the context of dialogue and participation (Coenen, 1998a).

In The Hague, the most well-known Dutch LA21 pioneer, the leading initiator, the alderman for environmental affairs, gave two reasons for launching LA21 in his municipality. The first was to encourage further involvement in environmental policy and its implementation. This argument is closely linked with the general argument for interactive environmental policy-making, in which successful implementation requires the involvement of target-groups. Secondly, the alderman stressed the importance of public participation: 'also from the viewpoint of political renewal, people should have the possibility to influence their immediate surroundings'.[5] This was with reference to the recognised crisis in local democracy during the early 1990s.

The NCDO states that: 'LA21 is a local plan to work jointly on a sustainable municipality. It is a combination of sustainable development and political renewal' (NCDO website). The VNG (1996) writes in its main publication on LA21:

> *'The concepts of LA21 and political renewal have much in common. In both cases it is about renewal in method that is linked with renewal in content. As far as general goals and methods are concerned, LA21 and political renewal run parallel.'*

As a first aspect of the surplus value of LA21, the VNG (1996) sees:

> *'the explicit attention given to the way policy is formulated, namely in dialogue with citizens, societal organisations and business. The surplus value of LA21 lies in reaching relatively inaccessible target-groups like consumers, neighbourhood inhabitants and small- and medium-size businesses.'*

The VNG (1996) states, as an aim of the LA21 dialogue:

> *'... the enhancement of the support for policy by connecting with the initiatives, needs and possibilities of the target-groups; ... the use of knowledge and ideas from society; ... finding possibilities for cooperation in the implementation of policy.'*

National government also states in the third national environmental policy plan (NEPP-3, 1998):

> *'The municipality is that layer of government most closely related to the citizens and therefore has a specific responsibility to involve citizens in environmental policy, for instance through the means of an LA21.'*

In the first of three aspects of the surplus value to the local environmental policy, the NEPP-3 (1998) reads: 'There will be explicit attention paid to the dialogue with citizens, societal organisations and business'. In addition, the director of VNG, Dordregter (1994), stated that:

> *'LA21 doesn't mean something really new for The Netherlands. The relation between communication and dialogue, consciousness-raising and support, processes and environmental success don't have to be explained to the municipalities. My thesis: no environmental success without a dialogue.'*

The NCDO states, under the heading of 'Surplus value of LA21', that:

> *'because citizens feel involved in the formulation of LA21 and have their own responsibility, plans for sustainable development take root. Further, the municipality can derive an advantage from the knowledge available within local groups.'*

On the basis of these exemplary statements, we identified the following specific storylines within the discourse on local democracy:

- LA21 is interpreted as closely linked or even an exponent of Dutch political renewal. The argument for LA21 is linked with the need to overcome the crisis in local democracy.
- LA21 is interpreted as a specific local variant of interactive policy-making with target groups. The surplus value of LA21 is seen as creating support for local sustainable policy, which is a basic premise for Dutch interactive policy-making and the target-group approach. Here it is possible to recognise the functional–analytic perspective on participation (Coenen, Huitema and O'Toole, 1998).

Analysing the storylines

To analyse the storyline that LA21 is closely linked or even an exponent of Dutch political renewal, and therefore a solution for current problems in local democracy, it is necessary to go deeper into the aspects of the problem and its possible consequences for LA21. How did aspects of the need to reform local democracy influence the implementation of LA21?

One previously mentioned aspect of the perceived crisis in local democracy is the nationalisation of local elections. Research (Depla and Tops, 1998) shows that:

- only one-fifth of the voters supported a different party at the local level than at the national level;
- national issues determine the party choice of two-thirds of the voters.

Small but significant differences are found on the basis of different parties and the size of municipalities.

A second aspect of the problem concerns modes of participation. One can argue that if voters turn out it is a good indicator for local democracy, because voting is only one form of participation. Research (Denters and Geurts, 1998) shows a large variety of participation in local Dutch governance. Voting is the most common form of participation in The Netherlands (77 per cent), followed by contacts with local administration (31 per cent), addressing letters or complaints (24 per cent) and submitting petitions (23 per cent). For the implementation of LA21, the relatively low level of public discussions or formal consultation at public meetings (16 per cent) is relevant. This position is explained by the high effort this form of participation requires and the perceived low returns by the participants. Closer investigation into the social representation of the different forms of participation, ranks public discussions as the lowest (Denters and Geurts, 1998).

A positive aspect for LA21 could be the relatively favourable political opportunity structure for new social movements in The Netherlands (Kriesi et al, 1992). Research (SCP, 1996) shows that acceptance of political protest has increased considerably over the last ten years. The desire for more say in sub-national government has constantly been between 60 and 70 per cent over the last 20 years (SCP, 1996).

A third aspect is the attitude of the citizens towards local government. Denters and Geurts (1998) performed research of great relevance to LA21. Firstly, their study shows that satisfaction with local services is high. Secondly, the results show that the respondents rated their own power in local politics as low (34 per cent) or very low (41 per cent). Intervening variables were education and gender: more highly educated males rated their political power significantly higher.

A second aspect of the people's perception of power is their confidence in the responsiveness of local authorities. This perceived responsiveness has much to do with an awareness of matters brought to the attention of local authorities and the feeling that the people's concerns were being taken seriously. The confidence in the responsiveness of local authorities is considerably greater than confidence in responsiveness of national government. Intervening variables here are age, size of the municipality and general attitudes towards the authority. Confidence is greater among young people, inhabitants of smaller municipalities and in municipalities with a positive, general opinion of the authority.

A fourth aspect of the crisis in local democracy is the presumed gap between politicians and citizens caused by a decrease in political authority and trust. Politicians find this gap worrisome. But does the problem really exist? Contact with local politicians ranks low as a type of participation (18 per cent), but above public discussion (16 per cent), public actions (15 per cent) and contact with political parties (11 per cent). The amount of direct contact with local politicians is affected by the size of the municipality; the smaller the municipality, the more contacts. In recent years there has been a rise in the number of local parties, which could point to a gap between the existing established political parties and citizens. In general, the support for national politics is crumbling. Party membership has decreased considerably since the 1950s. Political activism has shifted partly to other social movements, for instance Greenpeace. The rise of local political parties could be negative for LA21 if it leads to trivialisation of local politics, with too many inexperienced politicians with limited time horizons (Hendriks, 2000).

To analyse the storyline that LA21 is a specific variation of interactive planning with target-groups, it is essential to consider the relevance of the target-group approach on a local level.

There are relations between the target-group approach and LA21, but there are also limitations to the use of a target group approach at the local level (Coenen, 1998c). Target-groups have a resemblance to the major groups from Agenda 21, but are definitely not the same. Major groups like women or youth would be part of target-groups like consumers. According to the Dutch national environmental planning framework, local authorities should also involve target-groups in their planning, and there are some specific advantages and disadvantages to a target-group approach at the local level. The main thrust of environmental policy is largely determined by the state, but mainly executed by the provinces and municipalities. There will be less need to formulate a common policy at the municipal level, as a national consensus will usually already have been arrived at by the time the municipality is confronted with the problem. At the municipal level there is always tension between what has already been decided by central government and a particular branch of industry (Coenen, 1998c). It is also a question of whether target-groups at the local level have an adequate mode of organisation to address the problem, as is the case at the national level.

Conclusions

An analysis of the views of citizens on local democracy and local government has shed more light on different aspects of the presumed crisis in local democracy and its possible influence on LA21. Some of the results of the views of the citizens have negative implications for LA21, such as the tendency to nationalise local elections, the negative image of public discussion as a means of participation and, most strikingly, the perceived lack of power in local politics. Positive aspects for LA21 are the confidence in the responsiveness of local authorities, the favourable structure for new social movements, and the increasing acceptance of different forms of political protest.

The storyline that a surplus value of LA21 is to create support for local sustainable policy influenced the functional argument for LA21, which is the basic premise for Dutch interactive policy-making. However, it is questionable whether the target-group approach is equally relevant at the local level.

The discourse on local self-responsibility in environmental policy

The second discussion on the value-added perspective of LA21 in The Netherlands has to be placed within the discourse on local self-responsibility in environmental policy. Let us start by looking at the implementation of LA21 in The Netherlands in the context of top-down and bottom-up initiatives in local environmental policy and LA21.

A positive implementation of LA21 presupposes a relatively high degree of local authority. The degree of local autonomy for LA21 action depends on

- the general level of autonomy of local government,
- specific autonomy with regard to the LA21 policy area and legislation, and
- the local capacity for action as measured by resources and competence (Lafferty and Eckerberg, 1998).

The constitutional position of Dutch municipalities is given by the Dutch Constitution (1848) and the Municipalities Act (1851). The Dutch constitutional system is generally labelled as a decentralised unitary state. The unitary nature of this type of state is based on agreement between the three layers of government (central government, provinces and municipalities) and not on central government alone (Pot and Donner, 1977). The tradition of decentralisation and power distribution goes back to the times of the old republic of the Seven United Provinces (1588–1795), which was a highly decentralised federation. The founding father of the Dutch constitution, the liberal statesman Thorbecke, designed the constitutional system as an 'association of mutually restricting bodies designed to work freely together' – a system of circumscribed independence of higher and lower authorities (Pot and Donner, 1977).

Local authorities have a freedom of initiative within the system of inter-administrative relations. They have the constitutional power to deal with matters of local concern as long as the local authorities take account of legislation passed by higher authorities. A large part of local authority activities is covered by legislation within a system of co-government.

Dutch local authorities have relatively limited tax revenues and depend largely on central government for their resources. About half of this central funding is in the form of specific transfer or earmarked funding. The rest of the central funding is in the form of a municipal fund, dependent on criteria such as the number of inhabitants, which is an open-budget system with a budget ceiling.

Environmental policy in The Netherlands has its roots in local policy. City regulation in the Middle Ages already contained environmental rules. From the beginning of the 18th century until the beginning of the 1970s, the Nuisance Act was the most important environmental law. Before the 1970s, it was the municipalities that were mainly responsible for issuing permits and controlling polluters. Alongside the Nuisance Act, the municipalities, especially in the cities, developed environmental policy concerned with environmental hygiene, such as sewage measures, waste treatment and drinking-water protection. With the recognition of the complexity and importance of ecological issues at the end of the 1960s, the environmental tasks of municipalities became more and more a part of national regulation. Specific tasks, like the licensing of larger and more complex industrial installations, were given to the provinces.

The dissatisfaction of national government during the 1980s and 1990s with the way municipalities performed their environmental duties, and particularly the implementation of the Nuisance Act, led to several measures to improve municipal implementation. In the first instance, these were measures to stimulate a more systematic approach to local environmental policy by introducing specific planning instruments: the Public Nuisance Act Implementation Plan (HUP) and Environmental Policy Implementation Plan (MUP). The HUP and MUP funding programmes were not meant, however, to finance the implementation of the new planning instruments.

The implementation of the Nuisance Act was seen as a basic responsibility for municipalities that had to be financed by the municipal fund. There was a basic discourse on responsibility and funding. The viewpoint of the ministry was that local environmental policy was traditionally a municipal task financed on the basis of general funding through the municipal fund. The discussion on who should pay what for local environmental policy was only solved after research showed that municipalities had a severe deficit in funding through the extension of environmental tasks in the 1970s. Starting in 1990, municipalities received earmarked grants from the Programme for Funding of Municipal Environmental Policy (BUGM) to bring their environmental policy to a basic and adequate level. The Programme for Funding of National Environmental Policy (FUN) regulation, introduced in 1991, covered extra funds to help municipalities meet the targets of the NEPP. It was originally intended that after 1995 the funding would no longer be earmarked for environmental purposes, but an evaluation during the funding period raised doubts about the degree to which environmental tasks had really been institutionalised within municipal organisations (Ringeling Committee, 1993). In response to this, the ministry and the association of Dutch municipalities introduced the VOGM scheme mentioned above, the so-called supplementary contribution scheme for developing municipal environmental policy, to strengthen municipal environmental policy. This new earmarked funding, for the years 1996 to 1998, allowed municipalities more freedom to identify their own priorities. The extra funding was a clear incentive for adopting LA21 as one of the so-called tasks of choice. The environment inspectorate, the national environmental inspection and enforcement agency, audited the implementation of municipalities' environmental policy each year.

Identifying storylines on local self-responsibility and LA21

BUGM and FUN funding, and their successor, VOGM funding, had a clear impact on local responsibility for the environment. The discourse on local responsibility for environmental policy is a long-standing discussion between the Ministry of the Environment and the municipalities, and is linked to the general discussion on local autonomy. The choice not to replace BUGM and FUN funding with unspecified general funding, but to have specific earmarked VOGM funding, was an exception in a period when national government tried to reduce the number of specific transfers under decentralising measures. These transfers went down from over 400 different, specific transfers in 1985, to just over 140 in 1995. The discussions centred on the questions of whether municipalities were ready to take responsibility for their own implementation of environmental policy and whether environmental tasks were sufficiently institutionalised in the municipal organisation. A great fear of the ministry and environmental NGOs was that the positive effects of four years of specific funding on local environmental policy would disappear (Ringeling Committee, 1993). The same discussion surfaced during the VOGM period (Coenen, Seinstra and Teunisse, 1999). For LA21, the discussion is especially relevant if local government, without further specific financial incentives, makes the step from traditional local environmental policy to local sustainable policy, integrating sustainable criteria in other policy fields.

In the autumn of 1996, the ministry exchanged views with municipal administrators on a large scale, involving about a quarter of all municipalities on the future of local environmental policy.[6] As a follow-up, a discussion was organised with representatives of several layers and organisations of government, business and NGOs. The aim was to gain an insight into the ambitions of involved organisations concerning local sustainable development and the surrounding environment.

During the period of earmarked funding, the municipalities felt restricted by their own priority-setting on local environmental policy. Priorities were set through earmarked funding and the value-for-money principle. Not surprisingly, in the discussions, the municipalities asked for a new arrangement of responsibilities between government layers in environmental policy, focusing on a balance between freedom (of acting by the municipalities) and commitment (within the limits set by national government).

In a letter to the municipalities, the former minister, De Boer (11 February 1997) stated that municipalities would be given more freedom of choice as to means of achieving goals set by national government. 'Apart from the advantage of more policy freedom for municipalities, this makes municipalities an attractive partner for local actors in cooperation towards sustainable development.'

The view of the then minister, De Boer, on the future position of municipalities in environmental policy and local sustainable development was laid down in the following letter to the municipalities (13 November 1997).

> *'I expect from all local organisations, business and municipalities, that they will jointly give shape to sustainable development on a local level, whereby increasingly more joint local goals on sustainable development will be formulated. These goals should, through deliberation and allocation of joint responsibilities, be concretised into activities of the local partners. The local partners can interact with each other on their activities and responsibilities. Municipalities play an important role in this process as mediators and partners. As I see it, a Local Agenda 21 is a good framework for this process.'*

In the NEPP-3 (1998), LA21 was labelled as the whole set of discussions around immediate surroundings and sustainable issues, and on the formulation of assessable local goals and concrete local actions. This interpretation of LA21 was criticised by the NCDO, which views LA21 as a broader and more long-term process aiming at sustainable development for the whole municipality (personal communication from the NCDO LA21 working group, 1998).

Two storylines appear here. The first is that, due to previous and existing funded activities at the local level, LA21 already exists because municipalities implement local sustainable policy (even though it is not referred to as 'LA21'). As minister De Boer stated in his address to the IULA conference at The Hague in 1995: 'When LA21 was introduced to local authorities in The Netherlands, the first reaction was "Oh…, but we are already doing all that".' The interpretation of LA21 was restricted to its content, a local sustainable strategy. When the director of VNG, Dordregter (1995), stated that 'LA21 doesn't mean something really new for The Netherlands', he was not only referring to processes of communication and dialogue, consciousness-raising and support, but also to the large number of local sustainable initiatives that municipalities were taking in various fields such as energy, sustainable building, planning and traffic, for example.

The NCDO disagrees, however, that local sustainability already exists. At its website, a local sustainability test is available that gives citizens the opportunity to score their municipality on local sustainability. This test caused some dispute between the NCDO and the VNG at the beginning of 1999. The Ministry of Environment is more critical than the VNG and recognises that some municipalities are doing better than others, but still holds the opinion that at least the forerunners are progressing with local sustainability strategies. However, LA21, as local sustainability, is already there, at least in part.

The second storyline is that LA21 should start from broad-based environmental policy directed towards concrete projects on the quality of the immediate surroundings before local sustainable strategies can be implemented. According to the NCDO, VOGM funding had a positive effect on raising attention around LA21 in The Netherlands, but not on its content. Because the VOGM funding was initially environmental funding, it narrowed down LA21 to environmental policy. It was implemented by the municipal environmental department and seen by other departments as an environmental activity (Coenen, 1998a). During the VOGM funding, LA21 was closely linked to environmental information and nature and environment education. In recent fact sheets published by the VNG (1998) on environmental policy, LA21 is only found under the heading of environmental communication and social instruments, together with environmental information and nature and environment education. The VOGM-funding related LA21 to plans of approaches and favoured concrete projects through an LA21 guideline issued by the inspectorate, which has apparently functioned for some municipalities as a pseudo-regulation.

An important point of discussion between the key actors is the balance between the quality of the immediate surroundings (the here and now) and sustainable development (the there and then – referred to as the global aspect and future generations). For the VNG, the balance lies closer to the quality of the immediate surroundings as a precondition for sustainable development. For the NCDO, the balance lies in the opposite direction: namely, that LA21 is about the sustainable future of a municipality. The ministry tries to combine both perspectives in the NEPP-3 (1998).

To summarise, within the discourse on local self-responsibility in environmental policy we have identified two storylines.

1 LA21 is interpreted, at least in part, as already existing in The Netherlands, because municipalities are involved in producing local sustainable policies.
2 LA21 gets a specific interpretation of its substance as an initiative that has at least to strike a balance between the quality of the immediate surroundings and sustainable development.

The discourse on administrative renewal

The discourse on administrative renewal is closely linked to that on political renewal. In the former, the added value of LA21 is doubted because it is seen as just another innovation in urban governance. An important part of these innovations has been directed towards changes in the way politics are run, focusing mainly on the position of citizens in decision-making.

Apart from this search for political renewal, there are processes of administrative renewal where the position of the citizens is secondary to the improvement of the quality of policies and policy-making processes. Important related innovations for LA21 are (Veldboer, 1996):

- social regeneration and major town policies;
- neighbourhood policies;
- visioning processes; and
- innovations in local environmental policy.

LA21 is sometimes labelled as nothing more than one of these innovations, or is in general confused with these innovations.

Social regeneration became more prominent on the national and local political agenda at the end of the 1980s. Social regeneration was a spin-off of the more traditional urban-renewal policies that concentrated on run-down areas with poor infrastructure and social conditions. Since the mid-1990s, local regeneration has pushed forward within the so-called major town policies, which started with specific attention in four, but now involves 25 of the major cities. Major town policy is a combination of social, urban and economic revitalisation and concentrates on run-down urban areas with specific needs. The policy is funded and stimulated by national government on the basis of agreements with the cities. To receive funding the cities have to develop plans and submit these to national government. LA21 is sometimes confused as a specific variant of major town policy, which stresses the living environment.

In recent years, more and more municipalities have started to reorganise parts of municipal policy-making and the municipal organisation along the lines of urban neighbourhoods or districts. The idea was to bring basic services like waste treatment, road and green-area maintenance, and social services closer to the citizens. Sometimes this also involves decentralised decision-making and budgeting, and even structured planning processes with the involvement of neighbourhood or district councils or the general neighbourhood public. LA21 is sometimes organised on the basis of the same neighbourhoods and therefore confused as being just another form of decentralisation of local democracy.

The end of the 20th century was a reason for many Dutch municipalities to start organising visioning processes. Often these processes focus very much on economic and infrastructural development. Sustainable development is secondary and the environment is considered to be the limiting boundary for development. Nevertheless, if these processes are organised with the participation of citizens and local organisations, which they often are, they draw on the same social partners (such as businesses, NGOs and social interest groups) as LA21. Forms of public debates on the future, like scenario workshops, round-table discussions or broad-based public discussions, also resemble LA21 processes.

Recent innovations in environmental policy – for example the City and Environment Project, which developed from discussions on the problematic character of realising environmental objectives in urban areas – result in confusion with LA21. In practice, municipal urban-planning environmental standards were often too rigid and formal application would severely hinder urban development. This becomes even more complicated when applying criteria for compact cities and mobility.

In the city and environment project, 25 municipalities are allowed to experiment with their environmental and physical planning obligations in order to solve these kinds of problems. Another example is the *Modernisering Instrumentarium Geluidhinder* (MIG) project, which stands for 'modernising noise abatement policy instruments'. The ministry has set up this project with an aim to draft revisions to the Noise Abatement Act. The outcome is that municipalities have to make noise plans, with the participation of citizens, that allow them to accept noise levels at one place and find compensation elsewhere. Another example of these innovations is the Soil Remediation Policy Review (*Beleidsvernieuwing Bodemsanering*, or BEVER project).

To sum up, the implementation is hindered by a large number of innovations in local government that touch on certain aspects of LA21. One consequence is that some municipalities adhere to the storyline that they are already implementing LA21 because they are involved in several innovations that resemble LA21 activities. A second consequence is that

LA21 is narrowed down as simply another innovation, with equal importance and status as many others, neglecting thereby its roots in the Earth Summit. Even the Ministry of the Environment has difficulties fitting LA21 into other national and international innovations, such as agendas related to the Habitat-I and Habitat-II conferences (ERM, 1999).

CONCLUSION

In The Netherlands, LA21 has not been a turning point in local policy as in other countries, such as the UK. The current state of affairs and future development of LA21 can be explained on the basis of the views of participants in the implementation of LA21 through their adherence to certain 'storylines'. These storylines explain a number of the typical, general characteristics of the state of affairs of LA21 in The Netherlands. The national storyline for the Dutch case – that the interpretation by key actors of LA21 as an initiative with only a limited added value to existing initiatives in Dutch political culture – explains, to a large extent, the current state of affairs. This has to be seen in the context of The Netherlands as an advanced country in environmental policy and sustainable development (Juffermans, 1995), which on the one hand creates excellent baseline conditions for implementing LA21, but at the same time places heavy burdens on the interpretation of LA21 as a new and worthwhile initiative.

The first question raised in this chapter is: What is the effect on the implementation of LA21 in The Netherlands of these storylines on the added value of LA21 discourses on local democracy, local authority self-responsibility in sustainable development and innovations in local governance?

Within the discourse on local democracy we identified two specific storylines: firstly, that LA21 is interpreted as closely linked to or even an exponent of Dutch political renewal; and secondly, that it is interpreted as a specific local variant of interactive policy-making with target groups.

In the discourse on local self-responsibility in environmental policy we identified two storylines: firstly, that LA21 is at least already partly in existence in The Netherlands because municipalities are involved in producing local sustainable policies; and secondly, that the substance of an LA21 should start by addressing the quality of the immediate surroundings as a precondition for sustainable development. LA21 gets a specific interpretation of its substance as an initiative that has at least to strike a balance between the quality of the immediate surroundings and sustainable development.

Within the discourse on administrative renewal, the storyline is that municipalities are already implementing LA21 because they are often involved in several innovations that resemble LA21 activities.

This brings us to the second question: How far can the current state of affairs and future development of LA21 in The Netherlands be explained on the basis of these storylines?

The storylines have influenced the specific interpretation of LA21 in The Netherlands. This has partly contributed to the implementation of LA21, but has also created obstacles. The discussion regarding the added value of LA21 to already existing initiatives in the area of local sustainable policies and changes in local democracy is largely determined by these storylines.

What does this mean for the more general knowledge goals of the SUSCOM project?

For LA21 as a particular type of global policy, the crucial characteristic to distinguish it from other activities is a specific reference to the Earth Summit. If LA21 is to be understood as simply anything that resembles environmental policy, the idea will quickly deteriorate into a catch-all category with little potential for either evaluation or cross-national comparison and analysis (Lafferty, 1999). In The Netherlands, as part of top-down VOGM implementation of environmental policy, LA21 is interpreted as a national activity. Some municipalities view LA21 as a task they perform for the ministry and not on the basis of the appeal in Chapter 28. The difficulty is that some municipalities start questioning the value-added aspect of doing something they are supposedly already doing under a new name or label. LA21 is identified with the crisis in local democracy and the need for more interactive policy-making, instead of being an important part of the pathway towards sustainable development that asks for collaborative efforts from all societal actors.

The dominance of the VOGM funding also raises issues of central–local relations and the substance of LA21. In the Dutch case, LA21 loses its sustainable development substance through both the top-down, VOGM implementation up to 1998, and the bottom-up interpretation after the VOGM. An aspect of the top-down national implementation was that LA21 became an environmental and isolated activity (Coenen, 1998a). In the following phase of bottom-up implementation, LA21 as a transition process towards sustainable development is seen as too ambitious.

Furthermore, the implementation of LA21 is hindered by a large number of innovations in local government that touch on certain aspects of LA21. One consequence is that some municipalities adhere to the storyline that they are already implementing LA21 because they are involved in several innovations that resemble LA21 activities. A second consequence is that LA21 is narrowed down to simply another innovation, and treated as such, forgetting about its roots at the Earth Summit.

Finally, looking at the discourse between existing modes of democratisation and planning and LA21, local democratisation and administrative reforms have influenced the interpretation of LA21. It is interpreted as closely linked to, or even an exponent of, Dutch political renewal, and the argument for LA21 is linked to the need to overcome the crisis in local democracy. It is also interpreted as a specific local variant of interactive policy-making with target groups. LA21 is presented as a clear example of interactive policy-making, and in this sense becomes an instrument for another goal. It becomes, by its very nature, a democratisation reform. But Agenda 21 sees public participation first and foremost as instrumental in achieving its goals, and not as a means to overcome crises in local democracy. The emphasis on LA21 as a democratic reform suppresses its nature as a potential strategic initiative for change. The influence of LA21 on existing modes of planning has thus been very limited.

We have not yet explained why certain storylines prevail or become dominant in the implementation process. In Hajer's discourse analysis (from which we freely borrow the concept of storylines) a storyline is closely linked to discourse coalitions. A discourse is defined by Hajer (1995) as an ensemble of ideas, concepts and categorisations that are produced, reproduced and transformed in a particular set of practices.

In contrast to everyday speech, a discourse is more than a discussion or a certain way of talking.

> *'Analytically we try to make sense of the regularities and variations in what is being said (or) written and try to understand the social backgrounds and the social effects of specific modes of talking.'* (Hajer, 1995)

Storylines are the discursive 'cement' that keeps discourse coalitions together. Discourse coalitions differ from traditional political coalitions or alliances, since it is the nature of the storyline itself which forms the basis for the coalition, rather than more specific underlying interests.

This chapter is not an attempt to unravel the dominant discourses in LA21 implementation in The Netherlands, nor to demonstrate how alternative interpretations of LA21, within a particular institutional setting, may have produced a specific discourse coalition. However, it is clear from our account that coalitions are formed around these specific interpretations of LA21.

In the first place, the NCDO, VNG and many municipalities seem to adhere to the storyline that LA21 is closely linked or even an exponent of Dutch political renewal. A second discourse-coalition was identified between NCDO, VNG, VROM and municipalities regarding the storyline that a surplus value of LA21 is to create support for local sustainable policy-discourses. Further, the Ministry, VNG and many municipalities seem to adhere to the storyline that LA21 is at least already partly in existence in The Netherlands, because municipalities are involved in producing local sustainable policies.

These coalitions, formed around these specific interpretations of LA21, have strongly influenced specific Dutch interpretations of what an LA21 is.

Some of the storylines, such as LA21 starting with the immediate surroundings as a precondition for sustainable development, acquire an almost ritualistic character in The Netherlands. It is difficult to answer the question: Why do certain storylines prevail? More important, in the long run, seems to be the position of the individual implementing municipality. In the end it is they who bear the responsibility for '*Local* Agenda 21'.

NOTES

1 In this national commission, about 50 NGOs from all sectors of society participated to stimulate the debate on sustainable development at the national level.
2 Many municipalities, especially the larger ones, chose more than the obligatory four out of nine VOGM action points. The voluntarily chosen action points were often shaped the same way as the chosen action points of other municipalities.
3 We prefer the term 'political renewal' for the Dutch *bestuurlijke vernieuwing* in order to distinguish from administrative renewal.
4 The pioneers were the municipalities that started with LA21 before the VOGM funding started. Reasons for being an early starter were an active alderman, local groups or committed civil servants. For this group of about 30 pioneers it was logical to choose LA21 as a VOGM action point (Coenen, 1998a).
5 Interview with alderman Van der Putten, responsible for environmental affairs, 5 June 1997 (Andringa, 1998).
6 Letter to Parliament, 11 February 1997.

REFERENCES

Anderson, C J and Guilory, C A (1997) 'Political Institutions and Satisfaction with Democracy: A cross-national analysis of consensus and majoritarian systems', *American Political Science Review*, vol 91(1), pp66–81
Andringa, J (1998) 'The Influence of Local Agenda 21 on Local Policy and the Quality of Decision-making: The pioneer city of The Hague' in Coenen, F, Huitema, D and O'Toole, L (eds) *Participation and the Quality of Environmental Decision Making*, Kluwer, Dordrecht
Barrett, S and Fudge, C (eds) (1981) *Policy and Action: Essays on the Implementation of Public Policy*, Methuen, London/New York
Berman, P (1980) 'Thinking about Programmed and Adaptive Implementation' in Ingram, H and Mann, D E (eds) *Why Policies Succeed or Fail*, Sage, Beverly Hills
Brijer, S (1997) *Lokale Agenda 21 nader Bekeken. Inventarisatie en Analyse van de Landelijke en de Haagse aanpak van de Lokale Agenda 21. Succes en Faalfactoren*. Municipality of The Hague, The Hague

Coenen, F H J M (1993) 'Verschillende Visies op de Uitvoeringsstrategie: Een faalfactor' (Different Views on the Implementation Strategy: A failure factor) in van Heffen, O and van Twist, M J W (eds) *Beleid en Wetenschap, Hedendaagse Bestuurskundige Beschouwingen*, Samson H D Tjeenk Wikkink, Alphen aan den Rijn
Coenen, F H J M (1998a) 'The Netherlands: Sudsidized seeds in fertile soil' in Lafferty W M and Eckerberg, K (eds) *From Earth Summit to Local Agenda 21: Working Towards Sustainable Development*, Earthscan, London
Coenen, F H J M (1998b) 'Participation in Strategic Green Planning in The Netherlands' in Coenen, F H J M, Huitema, D and O'Toole, L (eds) *Participation and the Quality of Environmental Decision Making*, Kluwer, Dordrecht
Coenen, F H J M (1998c) 'Policy Integration and Public Involvement in the Local Policy Process. Lessons from Local Green Planning in The Netherlands', *European Environment*, vol 8, pp50–57
Coenen, F H J M, Huitema, D and O'Toole, L (1998) *Participation and the Quality of Environmental Decision Making*, Kluwer, Dordrecht
Coenen, F H J M, Seinstra, A and De Teunisse, P (1999) *VOGM en de Ontwikkeling van het Gemeentelijke Milieubeleid*, PricewaterhouseCoopers, Utrecht
CSTM (1998) *LA21 Lust of Last (Lust or Burden)*, CSTM, Enschede
Denters S A H and Geurts P A Th M (eds) (1998) *Lokale Democratie in Nederland, Burgers en Hun Gemeentebestuur*, Coutinho, Bussum
Depla, P and Tops, P (1998) 'De lokale component bij raadsverkiezing/de invloed van de gemeentegrootte' in Denters, S A H and Geurts, P A Th M (eds) *Lokale Democratie in Nederland, Burgers en Hun Gemeentebestuur*, Coutinho, Bussum
Dordregter, P (1994) *Draagvlak voor Gemeentelijk Milieubeleid en Milieu-Draagvlak door Gemeentelijk Beleid*, Inleiding congres vaksectie milieu, juni 1994
ERM (1999a) *Reflectie op het LA21-beleid: Discussienota voor de Bijeenkomst op 17 Maart te Den Haag*, ERM, Utrecht
ERM (1999b) Toekomst van Lokale Agenda 21: Workshop op 17-3-1999 te Den Haag, ERM, Utrecht
Fischer, F and Forrester, J (eds) (1993) *The Communicative Turn in Policy Analysis and Planning*, Duke University Press, Durham
Forrester, J (1980) 'Critical Theory and Planning Practice', *APA-Journal*, vol 46, pp275–285.
Forrester, J (eds) *The Communicative Turn in Policy Analysis and Planning*, Duke University Press, Durham, pp233–253
Gilsing, R (1994) 'Bestuurlijke Vernieuwing in Nederland', *Acta Politica*, vol 1, pp20–21
van Gunsteren, H R (1976) *The Quest for Control. A Critique of the Rational-central-rule Approach in Public Affairs*,Wiley, New York
Hajer, M A (1995) *The Politics of Environmental Discourse. Ecological Modernization and the Policy Process*, Clarendon Press, Oxford
Healy, P (1992) 'Planning through Debate', *Town Planning Review*, vol 63, pp143–162

Healy, P (1996) 'Planning through Debate: The communicative turn in planning theory' in S Campbell and S Fainstein, eds, *Readings in Planning Theory*, Blackwell, Oxford, pp234–57

Hendriks, F (2001) 'The Netherlands: Subnational democracy and institutional innovation' in Loughin J (ed) *Subnational Democracy in the European Union*, Oxford University Press, Oxford

den Hoed, P, Salet, W G M, van der Sluijs, H (1983) *Planning Als Onderneming*, Wetenschappelijke Raad voor het Regeringsbeleid, serie Voorstudies en achtergronden, 's-Gravenhage

Hoogerwerf, A (1984) 'Beleid Berust op Veronderstellingen: De beleidstheorie', *Acta Politica*, 1984 (4), pp493–531

Inspectorate of Environmental Hygiene (1997, 1998, 1999) *Stand van Zaken Gemeentelijk Milieubeleid in 1996/1997/1998 (Status of the Municipal Environmental Policy in Respective Years)*, Inspectiereeks

Juffermans, J (1995) *Sustainable Lifestyles. Strengthening the Global Dimension to Local Agenda 21. A Guide to Good Practice*, Towns & Development, The Hague

Kriesi, H, Koopmans, R, Duyvendak, J W and Guigni, M (1992) 'New Social Movements in Western Europe', *European Journal of Political Research*, vol 22, pp223–246

Lafferty, W M (ed) (1999) *Implementing Local Agenda 21 in Europe: Varieties of Sustainable Community Development*, ProSus, Oslo

Lafferty, W M and Eckerberg, K (eds) (1998) *From Earth Summit to Local Agenda 21: Working Towards Sustainable Development*, Earthscan, London

Lester, J P, Bowman, A, Goggin, M L and O'Toole, L (1987) 'Future Direction for Research in Implementation', *Policy Studies Review*, vol 7(1), pp200–216

Lijphart, A (1984) *Democracies*, Yale, New York

Maarse, J A M (1989) 'De uitvoering van overheidsbeleid' in Hoogerwerf, A (ed) *Overheidsbeleid*, 4e druk, Alphen aan den Rijn

NEPP-3/Ministry for Housing, Spatial Planning and Environment (1998) *NEPP-3 Nationaal milieubeleidsplan 3*, NEPP-3, Den Haag

PDO (1994) Een Lokale Agenda 21, zo werkt dat. Op weg naar een duurzame gemeente, PDO, Utrecht

van der Pot, C W and Donner, A M (1977) *Handboek van het Nederlandse Staatsrecht*, Tjeenk Willink, Zwolle

Ringeling Committee (1993) *Advisory Committee on the Evaluation of the Development of Municipal Environmental Policy, Steps Forward*, Ringeling Committee, Den Haag.

Sabatier, P A (1987) 'Knowledge, Policy-oriented Learning, and Policy Change' *Knowledge: Creation, Diffusion, Utilization*, vol 4, pp649–692

Scharpf, F W (1978) 'Interorganisational Policy Studies: Issues, concepts and perspectives' in Hanf, K and Scharpf, F W (eds) *Interorganisational Policy Making: Limits to Co-ordination and Central Control*, Sage, Beverly Hills

SCP (1996) *Sociaal en Cultureel Rapport 1996*, Sociaal Cultureel Planbureau, Gravenhage

Selman, P and Parker, J (1999) 'Tales of Local Sustainablity', *Local Environment*, vol 4(1), pp47–60

Tops E A (1991) *Lokale Democratie en Bestuurlijke Vernieuwing in Amsterdam,* 's-Gravenhage, Utrecht, Eindhoven, Tilburg, Nijmegen and Zwolle, Delft
UNCED (1992) *Agenda 21*, United Nations Organization, New York
Veldboer, L (1996) *De Inspraak Voorbij. Ervaringen van Burgers en Lokale Bestuurders met Nieuwe Vormen van Overleg*, Instituut voor Publiek en Politiek, Amsterdam
VNG (1996) *Praktijkboek Lokale Agenda 21*, VNG, Den Haag
VNG (1998) Factsheets gemeentelijk milieubeleid, bijlage bij ledenbrief 98/179 RVW/804902.

8. France
LA21: A new tool for sustainable policies?[1]

Corrine Larrue, Cyria Emelianoff, Francesca Di Pietro and Laure Héland

Introduction

From a comparative perspective, France does not appear to be a pioneer in the implementation of sustainable policies at the local level. Such a conclusion was drawn in the first comparative report issued on the implementation of LA21 in 12 countries (Lafferty, 1999).

However, the local French experience of sustainable development appears to be relatively rich and complex. On the one hand, a variety of policies have been developed and implemented by central government since the 1970s at local and regional levels for environmental protection, as well as social and economic development. On the other hand, several local and regional experiments have been initiated since 1982, when some of central government's powers were devolved to local authorities (under decentralisation laws). These local experiments are, however, isolated and difficult to compile, given the highly fragmented pattern of local government (more than 36,000 municipalities). Moreover, from the 1970s, many attempts have been made to reconcile environmental and development issues across the country, mainly within the framework of the local and national planning policy. The Local Agenda 21 (LA21) concept has only recently emerged in France, as noted in a previous state-of-the-art review (Di Pietro and Larrue, 1999): 'In France the implementation of Agenda 21 remains limited both at national and local levels'. LA21 seems to be a top-down initiative responding to international requirements. It still remains external to local processes of sustainable development that are not specifically labelled LA21.

Taking into account this complex situation, this chapter assesses the role played by LA21 as a tool for implementing sustainable policies at the local level. It will:

- characterise the implementation of LA21 in France and assess the quality of the implementation;
- develop some hypotheses concerning the main impacts of this new approach on local policies, starting from a first global analysis of several LA21 projects; and
- present the actual local impact of LA21, on the basis of a more in-depth analysis focusing on three ongoing examples of LA21.

The analysis is based on interviews with key actors at national and local levels, and on the collection of documents. However, an in-depth empirical analysis remains to be done in order to confirm and improve these preliminary results.

THE IMPLEMENTATION OF LA21 IN FRANCE

National and local policies on sustainable development

In France, environmental policy-making really began in 1971 with the creation of the Ministry of the Environment.[2] Environmental policy is mostly state-initiated, meaning that the role of municipalities is to implement national and European legislation concerning water, solid waste, air quality and also nature protection or management. However, municipalities have the scope for initiative in anything that concerns the quality of life, such as clean streets, green areas, landscaping, land use and noise.

From 1985, the Ministry of the Environment has attempted to involve local authorities in the setting up of a more global environmental policy at the local level. Agreements between the ministry and willing local authorities were proposed, sometimes matched with funding, known as environmental charters.[3] Such agreements were signed by about 100 municipal or unitary authorities. From 1992, this policy explicitly referred to the concept of sustainable development and to the Earth Summit.

On the other hand, several attempts have been made in order to reconcile environmental concern and economic development. One of them, which is usually considered a success by the Ministry of the Environment, is the creation of regional natural parks. These parks are managed by intercommunal administrative bodies within which all the territorial authorities concerned (regions, departments, municipalities) are represented. Unlike national parks, regional natural parks are located in rural districts that often include smaller urban areas. Moreover they are often close to urban areas and their task is explicitly to implement sustainable development at the regional level, and to achieve economic development based on the enhancement and protection of the natural and built heritage. Since 1969, more than 30 regional natural parks have been created.

At the same time, local social policies devoted to tackling the social consequences of unemployment, such as degraded suburbs and urban violence, are implemented through contractual agreements signed between local authorities and central government (*Contrats de ville*, ie, Town Contracts). Those agreements do not explicitly refer to sustainable development, even if most of them are partly devoted to improving the quality of life within degraded districts by the redevelopment of derelict land and the rehabilitation of housing, for example.

Lastly, since 1982, the year of the reform that reinforced the powers devolved to decentralised bodies, most local authorities have initiated incentive policies, in order to attract new firms into their municipalities. These policies were based on the setting up of industrial areas, the building of different types of facilities to be used by companies and upon fiscal policies. These local economic policies usually took into account environmental or social concerns.

The recent law about spatial planning and local development[4] explicitly mentions LA21 as a comprehensive framework including agreements between local authorities and central government concerning the environment (environmental charters); social equity (town contracts) and economic development.

In short, one can say that, in France, at the local level, many initiatives have been implemented in the field of environmental protection, as well as in the field of social and economic development. But so far these initiatives have remained fragmented and conducted independently of one another. The challenge of sustainability therefore relies on the introduction of a better connection between these policies.

The implementation of LA21 in France: A top-down initiative

In France, the reaction to the Earth Summit was rather slow in coming. Even if the French commission for sustainable development (*Commission Française du Développement Durable*, CFDD) was created just after the Summit, it was only in 1996 that political and administrative awareness really developed with the organisation of regional and national meetings on sustainable development. These meetings were organised within the framework of the preparation for the Habitat II Conference in June 1996. That same year the CFDD, which, until then, had not been very active, was transferred to the Ministry of the Environment. In 1997, a French strategy for sustainable development was drawn up (CFDD, 1997) and submitted to the UN Commission for Sustainable Development. In this context, setting up LA21s was one of the priorities of the national strategy for sustainable development (CFDD, 1997).

A national initiative of the Ministry of the Environment

The strategy of the Ministry of the Environment in developing the LA21 approach was first to reinforce cooperation between local authorities within the framework of environmental charters, promoting both cooperation between municipalities and between the municipality and the major urban areas or *agglomération*.[5] However, these charters cannot be considered as equivalent to LA21s, given that they only concern environmental issues.

In order to stimulate initiatives, the Ministry of the Environment launched, in July 1997, a call for projects on the ways and means of implementing LA21s intended for local authorities. The programme aimed at:

- introducing local authorities and government agencies to the concept of sustainable development;
- developing the environmental charter programme; and
- publicising the results achieved by those municipalities that had already gone ahead with the implementation of sustainable development.

Amongst the 51 projects submitted, 16 were selected for subsidies[6] by the French Ministry of the Environment and the Ministry of Towns with the collaboration of various other ministries and public agencies, as well as several environmental NGOs (Table 8.1 and Figure 8.1).

The criteria used by the Ministry of the Environment for the selection of these 16 cases were mainly:

- a project showing a willingness to develop a partnership with other actors;
- a cross-disciplinary approach to a local project;
- an integration between economic, environmental and social objectives;
- an innovative approach to a local project based on participation;
- a willingness to reduce social inequities; and
- a willingness to implement concrete sustainable policies.

These criteria in general meet those established by the SUSCOM project for defining LA21 in each country (see the Introduction to this book), except for the specific reference to the Earth Summit (but there is a specific reference to Agenda 21), and for the effort to relate local issues and global impacts in the perspective of global equity.

The projects that have been chosen represented the most interesting ones according to a jury that had been set up for their selection. Some projects gave priority to integration between economic, environmental and social objectives, although others were more active in the

Table 8.1 *Projects receiving funding from central government for LA21 programmes (1997)*

The organising authorities of the LA21 projects	*Issues to be addressed by the LA21*	*Number of inhabitants*	*Municipal environmental plan/Environmental charter/Aalborg Charter*
The Association for the Development of Northern Alsace, Haguenau	Optimisation of the selective collection of ordinary household and professional waste in Northern Alsace	203,000	
Arcueil, Cachan, Fresnes and L'Hay-les-Roses	Establishment of an inter-municipal facility	100,000 (altogether)	Environmental Charter Aalborg Charter (Arcueil)
Athis-Mons	Methods for the elaboration of an LA21	29,000	Municipal environmental plan Environmental charter
Belfort and the Centre of the Mediterranean with Mohammedia (Morocco) and ENDA-Maghreb (NGO)	Exchange of experience on informing citizens and their participation in sustainable development	53,000	Municipal environmental plan
Bouguenais	POLLEN programme, network of fertile towns and Agenda 21	15,000	
Chambéry – the Massif des Bauges and Chartreuse regional natural parks	Concentration of long-term efforts to render the town inhabitable and have the countryside inhabited	55,000	Municipal environmental plan Aalborg Charter
The Dunkirk Urban Community	Housing policy in the perspective of an Agenda 21	210,000	Environmental charter (in project) Aalborg Charter

Faches-Thumesnil	CLOE programme – the Local Operational Environmental Contract	17,000	Aalborg Charter (Lille)
Epernay	Tools for and approach to the setting-up of an LA21	29,000	Environmental charter
Grenoble	Approach for drawing up LA21 in Grenoble – towards a local pact for integrated development in the 21st century	160,000	Environmental charter Aalborg Charter
Grande-Synthe	Elaboration of an Agenda 21	26,500	Municipal environmental plan
Mamoudzou (Mayotte)	Restorative landscaping of cemeteries	32,700	
District of Poitiers	Trades, services and sustainable development	125,000	Environmental charter Aalborg Charter
Rillieux-la-Pape	Definition and establishment of a neighbourhood observer function	32,300	Environmental charter (project)
SIVOM of Rouvroy and Avion	Local development project	45,000	
Saint-Denis and Aubervilliers	Studies of the environment/economy and the environment/ social equity links	158,000	Environmental charter

willingness to implement more specific sustainable policies. But, as far as we can determine, not all of the selected cases met all the above-listed criteria.

This first call for projects was conceived as a tool for the implementation phase, wherein the LA21 procedure would be set up. Given the limited attention paid by these projects to local economic development, a second call for projects was launched by the Ministry of the Environment in February 2000, focusing on the economic dimension of local sustainable development. One may hope that the initiatives selected will lead to the final phase of the Agenda being achieved.

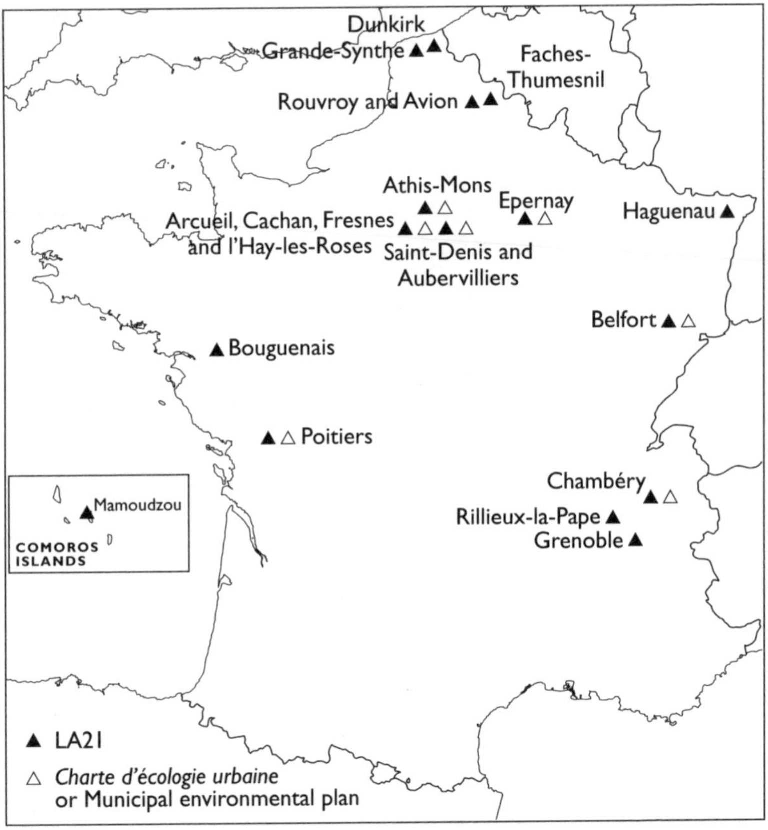

Figure 8.1 *Location of the 16 LA21 projects selected by the Ministry of the Environment*

A more complex reality: Local sustainable development not labelled as LA21

According to the Dossiers et Débats pour le Développement Durable (4d) association,[7] about 40 cities are clearly interested in sustainable development, and 22[8] are drawing up an LA21 (4d, 1999). According to the association, LA21 in France remains 'a voluntary initiative rewarded eventually by a grant; it is not an institutional tool' (4d, 1999).

Some local or regional authorities have begun integrating sustainable development considerations into their policies without grounding it in an explicit LA21 project. Either the municipalities attempt to infuse the principles of sustainable development into the civic services in a trans-sectoral manner (the municipality of Nantes), or they incorporate sustainable development into their existing procedures (the municipality of Strasbourg). In Nantes (in western France), one even encounters the paradoxical situation in which the policy pursued outside the LA21 process corresponds to an ideal of sustainable development better than that of the largely sector-related LA21 itself (which, in effect, is portrayed as a complement to the existing policy, dealing with one-off themes such as cleanliness and animals in the city and noise pollution). Some municipalities have begun developing LA21 independently of governmental support. Such is the case for the city of Valenciennes (in northern France) where the process appears to be relatively advanced. These independent initiatives are sometimes as interesting and innovative – if not more so – than those benefiting from governmental support. In France, the integration of sustainable concerns within local policies is done in several ways.

The 16 LA21 projects selected by the Ministry of the Environment constitute a preliminary sample that has been analysed in the first stage of our work. However, they are not the only LA21 projects and may not therefore be representative of the approaches followed in France as a whole. In order to characterise exhaustively French LA21 initiatives, other cases should also be included in the sample (see Di Pietro and Larrue, 1999). However, they meet most of the common criteria selected in the concerted action for defining LA21 in each country. Moreover, they constitute the only time that LA21 is used as an official policy. The analysis presented below deals therefore exclusively with those approaches to which the Ministry of the Environment is affiliated.

The profile of authorities involved

The main characteristics of the 16 LA21 projects selected by the Ministry of the Environment are as follows:

- Size and type of local authority. In general, the local authorities involved in the LA21 process are urban municipalities of different sizes, in contrast with rural areas, where LA21 seems quite rare. So far only a few larger cities, often regional capitals, have been involved in an LA21 process. The authorities of larger cities tend to be more autonomous than those of smaller cities, which depend more on encouragement from the national level. Two of the selected authorities are large cities, but not regional capitals, the others being medium-sized cities (Table 8.1).
- Initial issues of concern. In many cases, LA21 initiatives were launched in response to specific territorial problems, which triggered action – urban transport and strategic planning of urban mobility, deterioration of urban areas due to the decline of industrial or port activities, industrial pollution prevention, and, nearly everywhere, the

wish to bring nature back into cities by creating lightly managed natural areas. Most of the 16 LA21 projects focused on environmental issues, sometimes together with social issues, as in Rillieux-la-Pape for example, located in the suburb of Lyon, where social housing is important and where neighbourhood departments have been created in order to satisfy local needs. Very few projects deal with economic issues (MATE, 1998). One of them is the town of Eperney, which has oriented its LA21 around support to local business for the integration of environmental quality considerations, and in order to create employment while improving environmental quality. Another example is Dunkirk, where the authorities have been working for many years on the integration of environmental and social concerns within economic development issues.[9]

- Initiation of the process. There are two general situations: either LA21 is inscribed in a pre-existing action in favour of the environment (an environmental charter, for instance), or it is a completely new approach, born of an awareness to sustainable development of some local participants, or due to a mobilisation at the national level undertaken by NGOs. For example, national agencies such as the Agency for the Environment and Energy Control (ADEME) have encouraged local authorities to enter a planning process centred on a specific objective (such as energy saving). Consequently, the local authorities were given the opportunity to receive special funding for a specific project (Amiens, Besançon, Rennes, Rochefort).
- Previous local experience. The 16 LA21 projects selected were undertaken either by the cities that had ratified the Aalborg Charter (Arcueil, Dunkirk and Grenoble) or by cities that were already implementing policies close to sustainable development (in areas such as public transport, urban ecology and economic revitalisation). Among the 16 selected LA21 projects, 11 had previously signed an environmental charter that had represented a first awareness of local participants concerning sustainable development issues (Table 8.1).
- Local issue at stake included in LA21. It is striking to note that almost all the selected local authorities were located in northern and eastern France, from which two hypotheses can be formulated:

1. Border exchanges with countries having already integrated the concept of sustainable development (Germany and Belgium, for example) could have resulted in an earlier awareness of these authorities.
2. Because of the difficulties involved in the economic regeneration of these regions, the initiation of new dynamics of development was absolutely critical. In that context, sustainable development (via LA21) could be perceived as an opportunity to reinitiate a local development process. The Local Agenda falls on fertile

ground, and is not therefore perceived as a top-down requirement but rather as a bottom-up initiative. One should note how this situation differs from the adoption of environmental charters, which were often undertaken by cities already possessing the means to invest in the quality and image of their environment.

Of the 16 cities, seven are small municipalities located at the periphery of larger cities. These municipalities are often, but not always, subject to significant social or environmental problems (unemployment, social segregation, pollution). This observation favours the second hypothesis, that is to say, that sustainable development may be a driving force for the development of communities facing serious development problems.

LA21: A NEW WAY FOR DEVELOPING SUSTAINABLE LOCAL POLICIES?

LA21 initiatives came at a crucial moment when local governments were gaining more and more independence from central administration. Since 1982, a reform has been carried out that reinforces the power devolving on decentralised bodies. It is clear that, in France, the LA21 issue can be linked to decentralisation, which leads us to ask to what extent do the LA21 experiments contribute to the construction of new local sustainable policies?

Our hypotheses are that the launch of LA21 programmes in France introduced three new elements into local policies:

1. The integration of economic, social and environmental aspects, previously managed by local authorities in separate ways and by different departments.
2. The extension and systematisation of public participation.
3. The emergence of more effective levels of local policies.

Another impact would be the development of a new concept of public action, based on public participation, evaluation procedures and the monitoring of actions. Most of the cities presently envisage a reinforcement of their evaluation tools, by means of sustainability indicators or sustainable-development assessments, but the early stage of development of their LA21 process does not yet make it possible to analyse this last point.

We shall now analyse the three possible states of LA21 for local authorities.

An integration of economic, social and environmental aspects

- *Horizontal integration.* Locally, municipalities are confronted with a difficulty arising from the compartmentalised organisation of municipal action. The administrative bodies within local authorities are not used to working together, with the environmental, social and economic domains being particularly uncoordinated. Thus, many cities that have started an LA21 work towards a reorganisation of departmental boundaries or, at least, a better coordination between different departments. This requires information exchange and the joint formulation of projects or actions by several departments. This is clearly the case, for example, in the town of Poitiers. The challenge is to invent a new municipal culture in which an integrated approach can be brought into play.
- *Awareness of local public officers.* Another problem raised is how to make municipal staff and elected representatives aware of sustainable development and how to train them. This is the initial internal work to be undertaken in order to reach a trans-sectoral approach, at a more or less formal level, by the staff responsible for an LA21 project. At Grande-Synthe, this consists of informal discussion, the exchange of viewpoints, information meetings and the building up of working relationships. Poitiers organises training sessions on sustainable development for municipal and district staff. Sometimes this awareness is not achieved, either because there already exists a clear political position in favour of the Agenda, which then becomes a policy keynote, as is the case in Dunkirk, or because the Agenda is still too marginal in city policy, as in Grenoble.

Thus, LA21 is regarded as favourable ground for the working out of a unified vision of development, implemented at municipal level. As pointed out by the previous president of the CFDD, Christian Brodhag, LA21 should be a tool for making different existing sector-related policies such as town contracts and environmental charters consistent.

Public participation

Issues concerning public participation are a central aspect of the LA21 projects. However, given the relatively early stage of development of the approach in France, public participation remains difficult to characterise, but is generally closer to an information process, and usually motivated by electoral reasons. LA21 changes, to some extent, the nature of the problem since public participation must occur at the beginning of the process, not at the end.

- *A need for know-how.* LA21 steering committees bring together representatives of central government, local authorities, associations and experts. However, the inhabitants are not directly associated or represented in these committees. Given that the practice of participation is still experimental in France and that it is often merely considered as public information, we must emphasise that many municipalities are faced with the basic question of how to involve the general public. Some municipalities feel helpless and do not always make the effort to seek the information that is available but rarely circulated. In the field of sustainable development, the local authorities' requests for information and methods are numerous but most of the time not answered. Many questions, especially those that bear on practical achievements, remain unanswered. It is thus necessary for local departments to use public participation methods and tools that are new to them.
- *Different ways of public participation.* Within LA21 processes, public participation is organised through various ways – information campaigns (Arceuil), questionnaires (Grenoble), workshop debates (Athis-Mons and Grenoble), and conferences, training and debate (in most of the cases). The municipality of Faches-Thusmenil has instituted extra-municipal mixed commissions (composed of councillors and of people exterior to the town council, advising on all the town projects and appointed for the duration of the council mandate). The role of this type of public participation is advisory.
- *An uncomfortable position.* Many cities do not feel ready to confront this participation before having produced an initial document, with reflections to be circulated to the public. The fact that the concept of sustainable development remains relatively unknown in France, notably among the public at large, does not allow the local authorities to immediately launch a programme of public participation. This concept remains vague for most participants and there is no consensus on what it covers. At first, the local authorities try to consolidate their own opinion about sustainable development and proceed to generate precise proposals so that the meaning of sustainable development projects becomes clearer before presenting the proposal to the public. This explains why local authorities usually prefer to work on the formulation of LA21 internally first. Some cities that have chosen public participation right from the start, such as Athis-Mons and Grenoble, where the inhabitants have been involved in the drawing up of the agenda through a variety of methods (questionnaires, individual interviews, workshop debates and websites), are currently facing difficulties in continuing to implement this approach. The participation generated is neither sufficiently structured nor constructive enough to allow the preparation of an agenda.

To a large degree, the delay in the development of LA21 in France can be attributed to insufficient communication, information and debate on sustainable development.

Emerging and more effective levels of local policy

LA21 requires a new, integrated approach. Such a new approach should establish bridging structures to coordinate different local and national policies that do not always deal with the same territories.

- *Previous situation.* A national debate is in progress concerning the most appropriate scale for local administration. There is growing dissatisfaction with the existing structure of spatial planning, particularly concerning two administrative levels, the *département* and the municipality, which are accused of not representing a coherent unit regarding the main problems of territorial management (transport, environmental and economic development, for example). The municipality level is especially fragile, given the large number (36,540) of communes, which leads to an extreme fragmentation of local power. However, the municipality is vested with essential powers in spatial planning (drafting of the legally binding *Plan d'Occupation des Sols*),[10] while all the decisions that shape the urban framework and local development are made at higher levels of government.
- *Towards new, enlarged administrative areas.* The LA21 initiative usually involves several municipalities. In larger cities (several hundred thousand inhabitants), the scale is that of the *agglomération* in its various institutional forms, such as the urban community with its extensively shared municipal functions or the looser associations of the city centre and the collection of peripheral municipalities. In the case of smaller cities (several thousand inhabitants), the chosen scale for action is usually the community of municipalities, a new level of inter-municipal cooperation (Arcueil, Chambéry and the municipalities of Northern Alsace). This cooperation does not have the power to modify the administrative structure, but it does encourage intermunicipal action. On the whole, half of LA21 projects are built at a spatially enlarged level, sometimes integrating rural regions (Chambéry, Association for Development of Northern Alsace (ADEAN)). However, these cases of inter-municipality cooperation existed prior to the development of the Agenda, which simply serves to reinforce this level of intervention. The key factor favouring an inter-municipal approach is not so much the development of LA21, as new laws introduced in 2000 to reform the nature of inter-municipal structures, more particularly those defining how to distribute professional taxes across all the municipalities of an urban commu-

nity. Local authorities are attempting to prepare for the changes that will soon be imposed by central government. They are envisaging the orientation of their policies within the framework of the urban area as a whole, while defining LA21 in the municipal framework. Pragmatically, they conceive the agenda as evolutionary, with its starting-point in the existing structure.

In the case of the larger cities, the level of action chosen is not always inter-municipal. Such is the case in Grenoble. The project was initiated by the city's environmental department, and it has not been extended beyond those administrative limits.

To sum up, we wish to emphasise that a broader level of action is not, in general, systematically chosen. If a few local authorities have been proactive and innovative in this domain, most stay within the administrative framework that is most practical for them.

Therefore, one can say that the necessity for an integrated approach and the changes thus implied in the formulation of urban policy are generally well understood by the municipalities, or at least by the officers who lead LA21 work. However, the implementation of this integration is obviously more difficult because the organisation of a municipality still follows sectoral lines.

The second aspect, public participation, is a principle that has also been understood by the cities starting an LA21 process. However, in practice the degree of participation is hesitant, either because local authorities prefer to formulate a preliminary project internally before facing public debate, or because the human and financial resources allocated are insufficient for the organisation of any participation.

Finally, the notion of a new supra-municipal level of public action is most difficult to put into practice because it demands new regulations at the national level. Most local authorities have a pragmatic attitude and promote the Agenda within the existing administrative structures, while only a few institute new cooperative efforts at a broader level.

LA21 PRACTICE: THE CASES OF GRENOBLE, GRANDE-SYNTHE AND DUNKIRK

This initial analysis of the 16 LA21s selected by the Ministry of the Environment is not sufficient to really understand the ability of LA21 to strengthen the implementation of sustainable policies at the local level. A more in-depth study is necessary. Thus we have chosen to illustrate how diverse LA21s have been implemented in France through three cases (see Box 8.1). The first is Grenoble (south-eastern France), which shows an approach of sustainable local policies stemming from environmental

BOX 8.1 DISTINCTIVE APPROACHES TO LA21 IN FRANCE

An environmental approach: The case of Grenoble

- The initiative for developing an LA21 in Grenoble came from the municipal department for the environment and followed an environmental charter. The Agenda was set up by the officer responsible for the environmental department with the help of a private consultancy firm.
- The main purpose in implementing LA21 is to introduce sustainable development concerns into all local policies instead of producing a specific action plan.
- The problem with this approach is that it lacks support from the whole of local government. This is mainly due to two different aspects. Firstly, the project does not benefit from political support because the political majority of the municipality is based on the representation of several parties (including the Green Party), which are going through a period of strong competition. Secondly, various other planning activities are already ongoing and these activities have developed alongside LA21, entering into competition with it.

A pragmatic approach: The Grande-Synthe case

- The LA21 in Grande-Synthe builds on and furthers efforts developed in the municipality's own environmental charter.
- When the renewal of the charter was considered in 1997, the representative of *Gaz de France* convinced the municipality to draw up an LA21 instead. The aim was to enlarge on the more narrow environmental focus outlined by the charter.
- The aims of the approach are raising awareness, training and persuasion, with the aim of including sustainable development in each action and policy of the city, and then in the behaviour of its citizens. The method used to develop sensitivity to sustainable development was based on existing and potential relationships. This approach is pragmatic in so far as all the conditions, particularly the political will necessary to proceed with the action, do not exist in advance.
- The difficulty with the approach is its uncertainty. The municipality gambles that the new ideas will spread and create a new momentum. The choices currently being made lay the groundwork for middle-term decisions, rather than favouring present actions. The future of the Grande-Synthe LA21 undoubtedly depends on the level of political support achieved by the process.

A political approach: The case of Dunkirk

- The direction given by the authorities towards sustainable development here is based on political will. It attempts to include the agenda in the programme for the municipality that schedules all the policies to be implemented during the period 2000–06.
- The head of the supra-local authorities (the *Communauté Urbaine*) is strongly in favour of a clear display of attachment to sustainable development, which has consequently become a political watchword. Sustainable development issues can also be linked to regional level pressure: a green president has governed the region for the last six years, and a Regional Agenda 21 is currently being promoted.
- The Dunkirk approach is, however, top-down. The Environmental department of the supra-local authority has since 1999 been linked to the general secretary's office. Dunkirk's approach is thus drawn up at an upper level rather than at the municipal level. Sustainable development issues are given a strategic perspective, dependent on ongoing political support.
- Dunkirk tends to have a more in-depth approach towards sustainable development than other larger urban areas such as Strasbourg. It tries to develop an approach that is not purely based on the integration of environmental issues. However, this approach runs the risk of confusing economic development with sustainable development.

concerns. The second is the Grande-Synthe case (northern France), which illustrates a pragmatic way of drawing up an LA21. Finally, the Dunkirk case (north-western France) is based on a more political approach. These three cases, based on very different approaches, seem to us to best illustrate the emerging ways followed by local authorities in implementing LA21.

An environmental approach: The Grenoble case

Grenoble is a city of 367,000 inhabitants located in the Alpine mountains, three of which, the Vercors, the Chartreuse and Belledonne, surround the urban area. The city grew after the 1968 winter Olympic games and today is a dynamic city, the economic activity of which is devoted to new technologically-based industry and where important research centres are located.

Environmental issues have been integrated in Grenoble for many years. As a consequence, effective policies have been implemented in the field of transport, such as the creation of a tramways network.

The proposal for developing an LA21 came from the municipal department for the environment, and followed the initial stage of an environmental charter. The Agenda was set up by the officer responsible for the environmental department with the help of a private consultancy firm. The main purpose in implementing LA21 is to introduce sustainable development concerns into all local policies instead of producing a specific action plan. This was to be obtained through three actions:

1 LA21 started with a phase of public policy evaluation, in order to analyse the local situation regarding sustainable development issues.
2 At the same time, a process to consult and involve state representatives, private companies and NGOs (but not the local population, largely due to a lack of means) was initiated. This process of involvement covered six topics: private family economy, local democracy, education on sustainable development, inter-cultural exchanges, enterprises, employment and innovation. However, it failed, and only a few participants attended the five meetings organised.
3 A survey was also completed with a sample of 85,000 inhabitants from Grenoble, in order to prepare an LA21 and to assess the environmental awareness of the population and their knowledge of urban policies. No results from this survey are, however, available.

Generally speaking, the main obstacle to such an approach is that although LA21 is supported by the environmental department and the elected green representatives in the municipal council, it suffers from a lack of support from the whole of local government. The project does not benefit from political support because the political majority of the municipality is based on the representation of several parties (including the Green Party), which are going through a period of rough competition. Moreover, in Grenoble, many planning activities are presently on-going, either voluntarily or as a consequence of new national laws, including a master urban plan, an urban transportation plan and also neighbourhood action plans. These planning activities are developed alongside LA21 (even if the intent of the Department for the Environment was to integrate all of them), and enter into competition with it.

Today, LA21, which is still at the developmental stage, must be strengthened. Thus, internal work regarding the communication process and municipal department mobilisation has recently been initiated. This renewal is based on two different efforts. The first is a series of conferences within which European cities will present their experiences dealing with sustainable development. Secondly, LA21 will focus on the implementation of sustainable development through small practical projects such as the Greening of Local Schools and urban programmes for greater awareness of climate problems and biodiversity.

In Grenoble, LA21 is still in a preliminary phase, trying to overcome political obstacles as well as a lack of awareness, and to create a momentum supported by local representatives.

A pragmatic approach: The Grande-Synthe case

The city of Grande-Synthe is located in the built-up area of Dunkirk (200,000 inhabitants) on the northern coast of France, 20 km from the Belgian border. The city's rate of urban growth has been very rapid, from 1800 in 1962, when the iron and steel industry was established on the waterfront, to 23,300 today. The city has been marked by unemployment and social problems linked to the decline of heavy industry, so that there are now only 4500 employees compared to 12,500 in the 1970s.

The characteristics of the approach

Agenda 21 continues the direction developed in the environmental charter, which had simply taken stock of the actions undertaken by the city in the field of the environment. A lack of cohesion and uncertainty as to the direction to take can be noticed. When the renewal of the environmental charter was considered in 1997, the representative of *Gaz de France*,[11] one of the main partners of the town, convinced the municipality to draw up an LA21 instead. The aim was to enlarge on the strictly environmental problems tackled by the charter.

An inter-departmental mission, responsible for sustainable development, was created in early 1997, its head officer being responsible for the launch of LA21. After working for the authority for 20 years, and recently as head of parks and gardens, he understood the workings of the city departments well. He was given the responsibility, both within the organisation and externally, to raise people's awareness of sustainable development, which included the three following tasks:

1. to determine whether the sustainable development policy was well-founded and what its practical modes of implementation were;
2. to inform, develop the awareness of and mobilise the various local participants; and
3. to get the participants, both among the local authority and the municipality's partners, to identify and formulate the appropriate actions for a sustainable development policy (Ville de Grande-Synthe, 1999).

The LA21 steering committee is now composed of five councillors, five directors or heads of departments, the LA21 manager and the *Gaz de France* representative.

The role devoted to the sustainable development mission illustrates perfectly the situation of local authorities in France when dealing with sustainable development. Their initial task was to develop the awareness of sustainable development, a concept that remains vague and unfamiliar at the local level. In Grande-Synthe, the LA21 manager had the extended task of convincing his colleagues of the relevance of sustainable development. Next, it was a question of mobilising them and inducing them to adapt the concept, so that every officer could draft proposals in his own field. On this basis, parallel action programmes could be conducted while the process evolved.

A method based on relationships

The method used to develop sensitivity to sustainable development was based on existing and potential relationships. The LA21 manager introduced the concept of sustainable development through an initial document drafted with the aid of *Gaz de France*, which represented a preliminary version of the Agenda. Emphasis was on integrated municipal action, making existing initiatives consistent, and on the consensus-building potential of LA21. However, it was, above all, on the basis of individual interactions that the work of raising awareness was advanced by formal meetings with heads of different departments and various informal discussions which attempted to encourage the relevant staff to take over.

The LA21 manager wished to work with the municipal departments, but not all of them are as yet interested in the question of sustainable development. The identification of specific fields of action allowed LA21 to enhance the work of the staff in charge, and they consequently became partners in the LA21 process.

A fairly integrated, but insufficiently participatory approach

The first aim of the awareness regime is to integrate the ecological, social and economic dimensions of local public action. This fundamental characteristic of sustainable development is often cited, but its achievement requires that a majority of the participants understand and subscribe to this position. The difficulty involved when working within the existing structures explains why a majority of the actions proposed in the LA21 framework still fall within the field of the environment. Nevertheless, the LA21 manager is conscious of this bias, which explains Grande-Synthe's choice to continuously work at developing awareness on all three aspects (economic, social and environment).

Concerning public participation, it is surprising that the municipality has not chosen to start working with the general population, even though there exists a strong tradition of public participation. This is linked to the working class ethos and the mobilisation of associations on the subject of the urban reconstruction of Grande-Synthe, particularly in the public town-planning workshops (which in themselves constitute an exception to the normal French administrative culture). In the case of LA21, participation took place internally but the participation of the public is planned only at the second stage. The elements previously presented explain this choice: the municipality does not feel sufficiently secure to initiate a public debate on a theme that it has not yet mastered. One finds the same attitude in other French cities. At the moment, the public is only marginally associated in the initial reflection process, in the context of public workshops on town planning, in which the theme of sustainable development is occasionally addressed.

Lastly, the emergence of new levels of public action is not confirmed at Grande-Synthe. The city knows that a parallel LA21 process is underway at the upper level of the urban *agglomération*, but it does not necessarily agree with all the choices made there. A mutual awareness of the projects being developed exists, but there is no real common work. In France, this situation is fairly characteristic of local authorities that keep up a certain level of rivalry and seek to defend their territory. LA21 projects do not have sufficient weight to change such behaviour.

An action conceived over the long term

The experience of Grande-Synthe has the merit of working on existing structures and of showing that one cannot establish a sustainable development strategy if the various participants do not understand the concept very clearly. The work of the sustainable development mission is therefore necessarily preliminary to the development of a real LA21 in the sense of an action programme. However, the Grande-Synthe LA21 is not conceived as an action programme: it is more of a process in which every municipal department should eventually take part.

This objective is both ambitious and realistic in the sense that no timetable has been fixed. The municipality will take the time necessary to launch its project. In this respect, there are no constraints and therefore no risks. This attitude can be partly explained by the political calendar. The upcoming municipal elections could be expected to modify the composition of the council, hence the moment was not favourable for the launch of an action programme. The LA21 manager wished to base the process on the actions of various departments and to develop his colleagues' awareness for the project to survive a possible change of political orientation. This long-term work is necessary precisely because of the shortness of electoral mandates. The contradiction between these two timescales, the short-term of politics and the long-term of sustainable development, is well known.

For the LA21 manager, the means to commit the partners even more strongly to the sustainable development process, restricting their ability to withdraw, is to establish an advisory board on development and the environment. The 21 members are drawn from six categories: elected representatives (three members), trade union and social institutions (four members), business (three members), the education system (two members), environmental associations (two members) and other associations (seven members). This advisory board has a double role: firstly, it acts as a link between the different types of participants, who should disseminate the concept of sustainable development in their professional fields; secondly, it is the principal sustainable development forum used to exchange ideas and construct the agenda.

An emphasis on demonstrative actions

That the approach is based on raising awareness does not mean that no actions are programmed. An operational aspect is necessary to show that a sustainable development policy can be really implemented, and is not just empty words. The first agenda created in cooperation with *Gaz de France* proposed dozens of small-scale actions, mostly for demonstrative purposes, which are slowly being achieved. The actions chosen were inspired by the recommendations of the national *Comité 21*, which focused on raising awareness and on environmentalism. The municipality wishes to be an initiator in the domain of sustainable development to show how a theory can modify practice. While no large-scale project is planned, Grande-Synthe will be the first municipality in France to institute an experiment in industrial ecology[12] in one of its industrial zones. The existing enterprises are being contacted so that they can consider the idea. It is still at a project stage because such cooperation between the various institutional bodies acting in the economic sphere does not come easily.

A gamble

To a certain degree, Grande-Synthe has gambled that these ideas will spread and create a new momentum. The choices currently being made lay the groundwork for middle-term decisions rather than favouring present actions. In the sustainable development programme (consisting of one person!), the agenda is broadened and given concrete expression at a rhythm depending on the integration of the process by external participants. A young environmental facilitator was to be employed to systematically follow-up the initial relationships established among the members of the municipality. Energy saving, in particular, was to be put on the agenda as a pointer to greater awareness of the sustainable management of resources. However, the further development of the Grande-Synthe LA21 undoubtedly depends on political support.

The city council supports the idea and there is no current major political blockage likely to stop the process. Of course, not all councillors or directors are convinced by the LA21 process, but there is no conflict between the various political forces. The project has not been labelled 'ecologist', as has happened in other municipalities, and which unfortunately often contributes to discredit. Thus, Grande-Synthe founds its political action on raising awareness, training and persuasion, with the aim of including sustainable development in each action and policy of the city, and then in the behaviour of its inhabitants. This approach is pragmatic in so far as all the conditions, particularly the political will necessary to proceed with the action, do not exist. An extensive reflection is devoted to what is at stake in sustainable development, with the aim of creating a series of 'trigger-points' for a wider ownership of the project. In the French context, the interest of this approach does not seem questionable, and owes much to the continual support of the *Gaz de France* representative. His role, as a nationally recognised expert on sustainable development, shows the importance of relationships and personal contacts when putting sustainable development into practice.

A political approach: The case of Dunkirk

Dunkirk is a town located near the Belgian border. It is the third largest French maritime port. The urban area has 200,000 inhabitants (including Grande-Synthe). There have been regeneration problems linked to heavy industry and there is the need to improve the city image.

The approach chosen in Dunkirk is more political than in Grande-Synthe. The direction given by the authorities towards sustainable development is based on political will. It attempts to include the agenda in the '*contrat d'agglomération*',[13] a programme that schedules all the policies to be implemented during the period 2000–06. This contract will attempt to promote sustainable development in all the actions undertaken within the extended urban area. The president of the supra-local authorities (the *Communauté Urbaine*) is strongly in favour of a clear commitment to sustainable development, which has consequently become a political watchword. We must also note that awareness of sustainable development can be linked to regional level pressure: a green president has governed the region for the last six years, and a Regional Agenda 21 is currently promoted.

Dunkirk tends to have a more in-depth approach towards sustainable development than other larger urban areas such as Strasbourg. It tries to develop an approach that is not purely based on the integration of environmental issues. However, this approach runs the risk of blurring the innate conflicts between economic development and sustainable development. If all local policies are to be considered as sustainable policies, then clear arbitration must favour sustainable development objectives. The Dunkirk project is at too early a stage to be able to evaluate whether the objectives of urban sustainable development, such as control of urban sprawl, more sustainable transportation alternatives, pollution reduction, the social composition of the town's neighbourhoods and the participation of the inhabitants, for example, which are set up in the '*contrat d'agglomération*', will be really implemented.

In Dunkirk, environmental concerns have a long history. For many years the city wanted to wipe out its image of an old industrial and polluted city. Efforts for measuring the air pollution level, for introducing waste recycling or developing renewable sources of energy were implemented very early. In 1993, an industrial environmental plan was set up in order to plan a comprehensive policy in this field. It introduced regulations for the setting up of new industries, for water and air pollution abatement, and for landscaping industrial areas. In 1996, the urban community received the European prize for sustainable cities, which crowned their efforts in the field of environmental protection from polluting industries.

Dunkirk then began to set up a sustainable development approach that brings together its social and environmental industrial policies. The *contrat d'agglomération* deals with public health, the regeneration of built-up areas, social housing and economy based on solidarity. In early 1998, in order to draw up such a trans-sectoral approach, the environmental department of the *Communauté Urbaine* (the supra-local authority) began a mission for sustainable development, and since 1999 this department has been linked to the Office of the General Secretary. Sustainable development thus has a strategic perspective, based on political support.

In practical terms, the integration of sustainable development within the *contrat d'agglomération* is based on two elements. On the one hand, the general objectives of the town are assessed against sustainable development criteria, while, on the other, practical actions such as the environmental high quality in social housing projects and wind energy projects are promoted. In order to follow the implementation of the *contrat d'agglomération* in terms of sustainable development, a consultative council for sustainable development was to be set up, composed of state representatives, elected representatives, technicians, NGOs and economic partners.

The approach followed by the urban community of Dunkirk is, therefore, quite different from that of Grande-Synthe because it was drawn up at a higher level of government from the municipal level. Thus, the approach is top-down, whereas it is more horizontal at Grande-Synthe, proceeding via the acceptance of the concept by each participant.

CONCLUSION

The cases of Grenoble, Grande-Synthe and Dunkirk illustrate the variety of situations in France and make it possible to generalise the strengths and weaknesses of the LA21 process in France.

The major weakness resides in the very hesitant character of the initiatives, which benefit from some political publicity but lack practical application. The wavering progress of local authorities can be explained by the low level of information on sustainable development. The way the transmission of this idea works in other European countries, particularly through the research community and local associations, has not yet succeeded in France. This lack of support is one of the main difficulties. Although it exists in front-runner cases, supported locally by key actors (as in Grande-Synthe and Grenoble, for instance), we must recognise that LA21 in France remains an exogenous process, based on ideas that are not familiar to local authorities as a whole. Another weak point is that up to now LA21 initiatives have not succeeded in going beyond the elaboration phase.

A more positive point is the potential for mobilisation around the LA21 theme, supported by central government, or at least by some of its key figures, and by associations that equally possess expertise on sustainable development. This mobilisation could find an opportunity in the ongoing process of decentralisation in French administrative practice. The LA21 process is even likely to make the decentralisation more effective if the elected representatives use the theme as a means to reformulate real local policies in close cooperation with the local population. In this preliminary phase of implementation of LA21 in France, the approaches adopted mostly depend on the viewpoint of the few project leaders (as in the case of Grande-Synthe). As a consequence, the LA21s themselves differ greatly from city to city. Today, it appears that supra-local authorities are more concerned about launching sustainable policies because they are capable of developing strategic approaches. Their greater political willingness to support sustainability themes is, however, not widespread in France today.

The LA21 procedure is currently being incorporated into the national policy on spatial planning. The recent law on spatial planning and local development explicitly mentions LA21 as a comprehensive framework, including agreements between local authorities and central government. According to this law, action programmes set up by local governments in urban areas (*agglomération*) as well as in rural areas (*Pays*) will have to follow Agenda 21 principles. This will undoubtedly increase the number of initiatives and encourage the traditional political system to adapt the process. The choices made by Dunkirk are indicative. This widening of the process requires politicians, local authorities and the public to go through a learning process, which will take some time. One must also expect that, following this initial adoption stage, local sustainable development will be redefined in a way that is not yet easy to foresee.

NOTES

1 This chapter has benefited from an analysis carried out by Karine Deschamps on the implementation of LA21 in France (Deschamps, 1999). The authors wish to thank William Sutherland and Christiane Julien for their help in the English version of this chapter.
2 Which, in 1997, became the Ministry for Spatial Planning and the Environment (MATE).
3 These agreements were first called environmental protocols (1987) and later municipal environment plans (1990). Since 1992 they have been replaced by environmental charters (for rural areas) and urban ecology charters (for urban areas).
4 'Voynet' Law, 1999.
5 *Agglomération*: a group of municipalities located within a given urban area and working together.
6 The amount of the subsidy was very small, ie, about 15,000 euros per project.
7 4d (Dossiers et Débats pour le Développement Durable) is very active in advertising previous European experience in the field of sustainable development and also devotes research to the institutional and scientific gaps preventing the implementation of the Earth Summit commitments. It publishes monthly documentation reviews as well as analyses of previous LA21 experiments in France. It also regularly organises meetings for the public, devoted to the various aspects of sustainable development ('4d Tuesdays'). This association played an important role in the launching of the LA21 process in France. It organised the preparatory meetings for the launching of LA21 projects in Lille, Grenoble, Poitiers, Nantes and Bègles (near Bordeaux).
8 The 16 selected by the Ministry of the Environment (above) and six independent initiatives: Bègles, Le Havre, Mulhouse, Nantes, Romans-sur-Isère and Valencienne.
9 An industrial environmental master plan has therefore been set up, which regulates the location and the setting up of new facilities within the commune. Dunkirk received a European prize for sustainable city in 1996, because of this.
10 Detailed zoning plans.
11 *Gaz de France* is the public utility in charge of gas supply in France. As a member of the *Comité 21* association, it has been involved in the promotion of sustainable development at the national level. Since 1994, this enterprise has been a special partner of Grande-Synthe for the elaboration of its environmental charter through the framework of its 'Ecoville' programme, launched to diversify its services to local authorities and reinforce its environmental image.
12 Industrial ecology is a new organisation of industry where several industries are arranged in an interdependent 'bio-cycle' in which the wastes of one enterprise serve as the raw material for another.
13 The *contrat d'agglomération* was to become operational through the law of July 1999 on spatial planning.

REFERENCES

4d (1999) 'Comments and Complements of the Association 4d to the Draft Paper Entitled *LA21 in France: A New Tool for Sustainable Policies*', SUSCOM Dialogue Conference, 18–21 November, Barcelona

CFDD (1997) *De la Prise de Conscience vers la Mobilisation*, Rapport de la Commission Française du Développement Durable, Paris

Deschamps, K (1999) *L'Agenda 21 Local, un Outil au Service du Développement Durable*, Magistère d'Aménagement, Centre d'Etudes Supérieures d'Aménagement, Université de Tours

Di Pietro, F and Larrue, C (1999) 'France: >From top-down initiative to bottom-up implementation' in Lafferty, W M (ed) *Implementing LA21 in Europe*, ProSus, Oslo

Lafferty, W M (ed) (1999) *Implementing LA21 in Europe*, ProSus, Oslo

Ministère de l'Aménagement du Territoire et de l'Environnement (MATE) (1998) *Dossier de Présentation des Lauréats 'Les Outils et Démarches en vue de la Réalisation d'Agendas 21 locaux'*, Paris

Ville de Grande-Synthe (1999) *Grande-Synthe en Marche vers un Développement Durable. L'Agenda 21 Local*, Ville de Grande-Synthe

9. Austria
From eco-social market economy to LA21

Michael Narodoslawsky and Andrea Grabher

The story of the development of LA21 in Austria is relatively complicated. Austria is the rare case of a country where many of the factors deemed important for early success of LA21 processes were in place, but where the country still ended up being defined as a latecomer. The brief status report that follows this introduction shows that Austria is currently trying to catch up with other countries that are more advanced concerning the implementation of LA21. The chapter aims to explain this development by highlighting the situation in Austria at the time of the Earth Summit (UNCED) in 1992, as well as by providing insight into two particularly interesting case studies.

The progress of LA21 in Austria can be roughly divided into two periods: a long lag-phase in which only a few examples can be recognised, and a turbulent growth phase characterised by the relatively uncoordinated support of municipal LA21 processes by provinces and the national government, as well as by the occurrence of different forms of agendas at different local and regional levels. The chapter will explain the reasons for the lag-phase by discussing the status of the discussion on sustainable development in Austria following the Earth Summit. The first case study, dealing with the city of Graz, exemplifies an exceptional attempt to start an LA21 during this period.

The second case study is characteristic of the exponential growth phase of LA21 implementation that Austria is currently experiencing. It deals with a Regional Agenda 21 in Styria that is not only interesting as a new form that grew out of the concept of LA21, but also from the point of view of how change, namely Austria's accession to the EU, influences the way LA21 is implemented.

The chapter paints a rough picture of a complex situation. The conclusion from the Austrian story of LA21 implementation should provide interesting insights for other cases. The story shows that it is not enough for LA21 to fall on fertile ground, but that LA21 implementation also needs a coherent strategy in order to be successful.

THE STATUS OF LA21 IN AUSTRIA

After a late start, LA21 has finally taken off in Austria. Although there is no comprehensive statistic on the actual number of LA21 processes in communities available at the moment, the estimated proportion of communities that have embarked on an LA21 process may be put at between only 5 and 10 per cent of the approximately 2000 communities in Austria. However, within the last year considerable efforts have been made to increase this number. As a result of these efforts, LA21 has become well known to local administrations. Austria is currently experiencing a rapid growth in the number of communities initiating LA21 processes.

In accordance with the federal political structure of Austria, LA21 implementation varies significantly between the *Bundesländer* (federal provinces). Both the western provinces (Tyrol and to some extent Vorarlberg), as well as the most eastern province of Burgenland, are lagging behind, with the central provinces of Upper Austria, Lower Austria, Vienna, Styria and, to some extent, Carinthia and Salzburg progressing more rapidly.

At the national level the Ministry of the Environment, Youth and Family affairs is responsible for LA21 implementation. By and large this ministry started to act on LA21 implementation only after the United Nations General Assembly Special Session (UNGASS or 'Earth Summit +5') in 1997. As this ministry lacks a strong, direct political and administrative link to communities, its activities concentrated on supporting measures such as commissioning a guideline for LA21 processes (Ministry of the Environment, 1998). This ministry is now preparing an award for best cases of LA21 processes, which is meant to both encourage implementation as well as to gain a comprehensive picture of the status of LA21 in Austria.

The main driving force behind LA21 implementation in Austria is exerted by the federal provinces. This means that there are as many strategies for implementation as there are provinces. Some provinces (Styria and Upper Austria) directly support communities that implement LA21 processes (mostly by providing consultants and information for these processes). Others, like Carinthia, embark on provincial Agendas. Vienna (which is also a province) supports LA21 implementation in some of its boroughs.

One of the more interesting features of LA21 implementation in Austria is the great variety of Regional Agenda 21 approaches. This may be due to both Austria's latecomer status and the richness in formal administrative levels as well as informal cooperative structures in Austria. The accession of Austria to the EU has added to this diverse picture of regions in Austria by introducing the nomenclature of territorial units for statistics (NUTS)[1] III level, which usually does not conform to any existing administrative level. Consequently, we have regional agendas on the level of *Klein Regionen* (a planning unit comprising up to 20, usually small, communities), *Bezirke* (counties, an existing administrative unit directly below the province level) and NUTS III regions (which will be discussed in more detail below).

Besides initiatives from the provinces and national government, NGOs are also joining the efforts to implement LA21s in Austria. Most notable among these activities is the endeavour of the Climate Alliance to foster them in its more than 320 membership municipalities. The Climate Alliance is also important because it consistently includes collaborative ventures between developed and developing countries within LA21 processes.

The general picture of LA21 implementation in Austria is one of rapid and diverse growth. LA21 has, after a long period of neglect that will be explained below, entered the realm of strategic planning in local as well as regional planning. Although there is no substantial support from the federal level in terms of financial subsidies, LA21 is being adopted by various levels of administration as a means of effective planning for a sustainable future. And, although the starting point of many LA21 processes is clearly ecological, many of these processes have matured into long-term development plans.

AN ECO-SOCIAL MARKET ECONOMY

Austria is, in general, a latecomer to LA21 implementation. This is all the more astonishing since Austria perceives itself (and is to some degree also seen from the outside) as a champion of sustainable development. It played a positive and active role in the preparatory phase leading up to the Earth Summit (*Österreichische Bundesregierung*, 1992), and even actively pursued the integration of regional and local aspects into the LA21 document. In order to understand the current situation of LA21 implementation in Austria, it is, therefore, necessary to look back to the time of the Earth Summit and its immediate aftermath.

This retrospection leads directly to the political concept of *Ökosoziale Marktwirtschaft* (eco-social market economy) in which ecological considerations are integrated into a modern economic and social system. At the time of the Earth Summit, Austria could already look back on years of political discussion of this concept introduced by the conservative People's Party (Riegler, 1990). Eco-social market economy totally eclipsed the concept of sustainable development in Austria with the consequence that, to date, in the Austrian political discourse, the German expression for sustainable development (*Nachhaltige Entwicklung*) and *Ökosoziale Marktwirtschaft* are used in a synonymous way. As this concept and its fate is closely related to the implementation of LA21, it is worthwhile to look into its roots, its goals and its consequences for local action for sustainable development and the form and scope of LA21s in Austria.

The concept of eco-social market economy emerged in the mid-1980s from a vivid discussion of the role of agriculture in the quest for environmental stability. In this discussion it became clear that the future of agriculture in the environmentally sensitive alpine regions of Austria is inherently bound to a form of development that takes into account environmental limitations. However, it also became clear that this could not be achieved solely by regulating agricultural activities in order to become more environmentally amenable. Given the already strict environmental regulations in Austria, the small farm sizes and generally unfavourable climatic situation, further restrictions were seen as dangerous to the survival of farms in Austria. In a country dependent on tourism, the erosion of agriculture was not only seen as a threat to farmers but also to the landscape, a vital resource to tourism. Large-scale failure of farms would thus trigger unforeseeable economical and social consequences.

One answer to this challenge was seen in a comprehensive approach to local and regional development that integrated economic, social and ecological goals. From the early 1980s onwards, a number of initiatives at the local level, but almost exclusively targeted towards rural regions, pursued this approach with increasing success. In the national political arena this movement coalesced around Josef Riegler, then minister of agriculture. Riegler, with help from some other young politicians from the conservative People's Party (which was the traditional advocate for farmers and the development of rural areas), formulated the basic concept of eco-social market economy.

Eco-social market economy was radical in its goals, but built on Austria's corporative political system in its means. Superficially, the idea was to integrate an ecological dimension into the framework of a social market economy. The central organising force of future development was still attributed to market forces. However, new boundary conditions based on an ecologically sensible tax system, transparency of environmental costs as well as improved information of consumers were seen as necessary to steer the economy in a more environmentally safe direction.

The main difference to the reality of the corporative Austrian system was in the set of goals laid down in the principles of eco-social market economy. The idea of an eco-social market economy clearly aimed at overcoming an economy centred on the needs of capital, and to enter a development phase based on sufficiency more than on growth. The ecosystem was seen as a limiting factor for economic activity, with the exploitation of resources only possible on the basis of solidarity, both in the national as well as international context.

Another challenge to the Austrian political system (and an important feature of eco-social market economy with regard to LA21 implementation) was the call for further development of democracy to ensure an active involvement of citizens (Riegler and Moser, 1996). Together with confidence in the force of local action, this laid the groundwork for a series of community activities, particularly in rural areas. Many Austrian communities engaged in ambitious programmes effectively based on the principles of sustainable development like many *Dorferneuerungs* (community renewal) processes, emphasising, in particular, the environmental aspect of the concept. For some years after the Earth Summit, these activities had been seen as LA21 processes from the point of view of official Austria, although they usually did not have a clear connection to the UNCED process and lacked important elements of genuine LA21s. Evidence of this was the 1994 country report to the UNCSD (Ministry of the Environment, 1994). In most cases, there was evidence of a comprehensive, strategically oriented approach to the development of the local community, including a broad participatory visioning process concerning economic, social and ecological goals. However, most cases fell short in aspects concerning North-South solidarity, and did not provide for long-term monitoring of progress.

The concept of eco-social market economy was eventually pushed aside on the national level by the discourse on Austria's accession to the EU. However, it had some influence on development strategies of neighbouring countries like Hungary, Slovenia and the Czech Republic that were in the early stages of their transformation from communism to democratic societies, as this concept was dominating the Austrian political discourse. At the same pace as the accession to the EU began to dominate the political discussion in Austria, the concept of eco-social market economy lost its importance and the awareness of the implications of the Earth Summit increased.

Eco-social market economy can be seen, therefore, as both a hindrance and facilitator (at least in the long term) for LA21 implementation in Austria. In the immediate aftermath of the Earth Summit, a concentration on a 'local garden variety' of eco-social market economy prevented widespread implementation of LA21 processes. Only a few pilot cities embarked on LA21s, mostly on the basis of previously existing environmental protection plans, and influenced more by international examples than by national support or strategy. The Graz case study below is an especially characteristic example of an LA21 process in this context.

However, eco-social market economy had a long-lasting, positive influence on the progress of sustainable development in Austria, which can also be seen in the more recently initiated LA21 processes. One consequence is that environmental issues are perceived as interwoven with economic and social development. This leads to interesting integrated approaches like the Regional Agenda 21 in East Styria, which is described in the second case study below. In this regional agenda there is no longer a limited section on environmental improvement. Instead, all economic as well as social strategies have been set up with the clear goal of maintaining a diverse landscape and obtaining a sustainable environmental balance in the region.

THE 'ECOCITY' APPROACH IN GRAZ: A PIONEERING LA21 IN AUSTRIA

LA21 implementation on a larger scale did not 'ignite' until after the UNGASS Conference, especially as far as communities in rural areas (which form the majority of Austria's communities) are involved. Directly after the Earth Summit, only a small number of pioneer communities embarked on LA21 implementation processes. A common denominator of all these cases is that the communities were comparatively big and urban. Usually, the concept of eco-social market economy did not play an important role as a political guideline in these processes. The approach of these pioneering communities was usually oriented towards environmental improvement, with international contacts (for example, via ICLEI) often playing an important role. The LA21 process in Graz is a good example of such a pioneering process in Austria.

Graz is the second largest city in Austria with approximately 250,000 inhabitants. It is located in the south-east, close to the border of Slovenia and Hungary. Graz is surrounded by mountains on three sides, which impede the exchange of air, so that environmental concerns, especially about air quality, led to the first representation of the Green Party in the city council of a major city in Austria in the early 1980s.

Graz has a sound industrial base, with some large companies in the automotive sector. The general economic structure is, however, based on small- and medium-sized companies in a wide range of sectors. Tourism, exploiting a splendid inner city developed over centuries as a centre of relative importance within the Austro-Hungarian Empire, in attractive rural surroundings, is gaining importance. Graz is also the capital of the federal state of Styria, an administrative centre for about one million people.

In 1995 the city council adopted a plan called *Ökostadt 2000* (Ecocity 2000) (List, 1996) (see Box 9.1). This plan was based on work predating the Earth Summit. It set ambitious goals addressing a whole range of environmental problems in the city: air pollution by traffic, industry and households; waste water; hazardous and municipal waste; energy conservation; and also the improvement of nature within the city itself, such as parks and recreational areas. In general, the plan can be rated as an ambitious, comprehensive and implementation-oriented blueprint to achieve environmental sustainability in the city.

The plan also includes a direct reference to Agenda 21. There is, however, no direct reference to Chapter 28 of the Agenda. From the point

BOX 9.1 ECOCITY 2000, GRAZ

- The Ecocity 2000 plan – *Ökostadt 2000* – was adopted by the Graz City Council in 1995.
- The core of the plan is a vision of the environmental quality in the city. The plan sets ambitious environmental goals and has a reference to Agenda 21 – although it has no direct link to Chapter 28.
- It includes features for participation, but is in general based on conventional top-down planning. Highly motivated and competent civil servants in the environmental department have dominated and driven the process.
- A number of innovative approaches have emerged through the plan; in particular the ecoprofit programme. This programme involves business in an attempt to foster the use of cleaner technologies in a wide range of business and service sectors. It has been adopted in a number of other cities throughout Austria as well as in neighbouring countries.
- The approach to evaluation has been the setting up of different working groups that are open to interested parties and NGOs. An 'Öko-team' consisting of independent experts will review a report generated from the working groups.
- The focus on top-down planning has not created a genuine acceptance by the populace, with the plan being seen as mainly an administrative measure. The strong focus on isolated environmental issues has also prevented the plan from reaching its more ambitious goals.
- The Graz administration has recognised the need for broadening the scope of the plan so as to better reflect the ideas from Chapter 28 in Agenda 21. This has led to the establishment of an LA21 coordinator. The new approach aims to integrate social aspects of sustainability and to focus on new ways to strengthen citizens' participation in the planning process.

of view of this plan, the political message of Agenda 21 takes a distant second place to the more specific environmental aspects. Despite this clear focus on environmental protection, Ecocity 2000 included features for participation of citizens, as well as an integrated approach to planning. The plan also included provisions for periodic evaluation of the results, as well as for revising the plan according to the recommendations generated by the evaluation.

At the core of the plan is a vision of the environmental quality of the city. This vision aims at environmental sustainability, with ambitious long-term goals. Around this core plan, a number of measures to achieve these goals have been specified. Implementation and administration of these measures has been largely placed in the hands of the environmental department of the city. This unit of highly motivated and competent officers proved to be essential for the success of the plan. A number of innovative approaches, especially in the field of energy conservation and the dissemination of clean technology, have emerged from this department. In particular, the integration of business via a programme called 'Ecoprofit' (designed to foster the use of cleaner technologies in a wide range of business and service sectors) has gained international interest (Sage, 1998) and has been adopted in a number of other cities throughout Austria as well as in neighbouring countries.

These innovative approaches, as well as the undeniable zeal and success of the department in implementing the measures laid down in the Ecocity 2000 plan, eventually led to international acknowledgement, culminating in the Sustainable Cities Award of 1996.

Ecocity 2000 has been very much driven by a powerful vision, and the development of the vision was dominated by experts. It was not so much based on a specific consultation process with the citizens, as on conventional top-down planning. The department has, however, pursued a vigorous information activity to win over the hearts and minds of the citizens of the city. Although there is a general openness of the environmental department to public grievances, the process of developing the vision for an ecologically sustainable city of Graz fell clearly short of a genuine participation process. As a result, Ecocity 2000 is still regarded by many citizens as an administrative measure. The general level of information in the population about its goals and measures remains at best sketchy, even after five years of successful work along the lines of the plan.

Despite the expert-driven process that generated the plan, the set-up for the evaluation process calls for broader, though still tentative, participation. A so-called *Öko-Team* consisting of independent experts will review a report generated by working groups in the fields of:

- Waste and natural space.
- Traffic and noise.
- Energy and air quality.
- Water, soil quality and reclamation of contaminated sites.

Access to these working groups, which also counsel the environmental department on implementation problems, is more or less open to interested parties and NGOs. The evaluation process, based on the report of the *Öko-Team*, is under way. The main results are that the translation of the original environmental goals into genuine parameters for sustainable development is still an unfulfilled task and that, despite implementation successes, the ambitious goals of the plan have not been achieved.

In general, the following conclusions can be drawn from the ecocity process:

- A relatively young and dedicated team of administrators picked up the challenge of Agenda 21 as a chance to develop a powerful vision for ecological sustainability of a city.
- Political consensus on the plan has helped to keep it alive and to guarantee successful implementation.
- A vision-driven process has led to innovative new approaches in key sectors that have been considerably successful, even beyond the purely ecological focus. This is especially the case with the integration of business in the ecoprofit programme.
- The expert-driven process of developing the vision of the plan did not create genuine acceptance by the populace. The plan is still seen as an administrative measure.
- Despite impressive successes in some sectors, the strong focus on environmental issues prevented the plan from reaching its ambitious goals. Overall, the Ecocity 2000 plan did not achieve environmental sustainability, though progress is clearly visible in several areas.

The Graz administration and city council must be credited with clearly recognising the discrepancy between the relatively narrow focus of Ecocity 2000, and the requirements for a successful LA21 process. In order to overcome these drawbacks, it was decided to establish the position of an LA21 coordinator and to broaden the task, especially to include social aspects of sustainability. This process is now under way. It includes efforts to draw divisions of the city administration concerned with social development into the LA21 process, as well as the development of new ways to strengthen citizens' participation in the planning process. Pilot projects to upgrade city boroughs socially, environmentally and economically (under the so-called URBAN programme) are leading the way towards this new LA21 approach in Graz.

Regional Agenda 21 in Styria: The influence of Austria's accession to the European Union on LA21 implementation

Since the introduction of the Austrian environmental plan (Ministry of the Environment, 1995), and especially since the UNGASS conference in 1997, LA21 has gained considerable interest in Austrian communities. A rising number of communities have started LA21s, often building on existing programmes conceived to improve their environmental situation. Since 1998, a guideline issued by the Ministry of Environment, Youth and Family Affairs (Ministry of the Environment, 1998) helps to standardise the different processes, and has led, in conjunction with initiatives taken by some federal provinces, to a marked increase of LA21 implementation throughout Austria. Although these processes are interesting in many aspects, they usually follow patterns that are well-known and established in other parts of Europe.

Besides these community-based LA21 processes, there are some interesting developments concerning regional agendas currently in the phase of implementation in Austria. There are several reasons why regional agendas are an attractive concept in the Austrian context. Among the most important are:

- Many Austrian communities are relatively small (many with fewer than 2000, some even with less than 500 inhabitants). For these communities many tasks (such as waste management, water supply and waste-water treatment) require cooperation on a regional level. This makes strategic regional planning important.
- Within the Austrian political system there is a certain democratic gap between the provinces and the communities. Although administrative units at the regional level (*Bezirke*) are important in terms of decisions influencing many aspects of life, they lack democratic structures. This makes participatory planning instruments attractive at this level.
- With the accession to the EU, strategic regional planning has become a 'must' in order to obtain money from structural funds. Regional agendas, with their long-term orientation and their comprehensive approach towards development, are especially suited to serve this purpose.

Although all of these factors play a role in the proliferation of regional agendas in Austria, the last point is clearly the most attractive feature of their development in Austria. One case in point is the Regional Agenda 21 for East Styria, which did not exist in a formal administrative way until Austria's accession to the EU. During the course of the accession, Austria defined new regional units in accordance with EU regulations regarding the administration of structural funds. In EU parlance, East Styria is a NUTS III region. This region comprises the south-eastern part of the province of Styria, close to the Hungarian and Slovenian border. It consists of four *Bezirke* (Weiz, Feldbach, Hartberg and Fürstenfeld), and has approximately 300,000 inhabitants. Its western part (the *Bezirk* Weiz) is mainly industrial. Its northern and eastern parts are predominantly oriented towards agriculture.

The provincial government of Styria installed a coordinating agency in the legal form of an association in this region (the EU-regional administration *Oststeiermark*) that was entrusted with the task of supporting applicants to EU structural funds in terms of project formulation and organisation. Although this organisation was not sanctioned as an official administrative unit, it was controlled by a political committee consisting of representatives of the provincial and national parliaments. Neither the regional administration nor, as already mentioned, the *Bezirke* have any elected bodies that could exert democratic control and guidance.

As a matter of fact, European structural funds evolved into a major source for strategic regional development in the Austrian context. The whole region of East Styria falls within Target 2 or Target 5b regional categories and the flow of EU money into the region became considerable. In this situation the need for a strategic development plan for this new regional entity was recognised by the regional administration. It was decided that this plan should be developed in the form of a Regional Agenda 21.

East Styria is a region that is directly concerned with the plan to enlarge the EU, as it borders on two accession countries. This fact had important consequences for the process of implementing a regional agenda. This can already be noticed in the name given to the process. Since the EC initiative that prepares for and accompanies this enlargement process – Agenda 2000 – is seen as a threat to the livelihood of, in particular, small farms (the predominant factor in agriculture in East Styria), it was decided not to use the negatively loaded term of 'agenda'[2] in the name. So, although the process uses the methodology of a LA21, and although documents refer to Agenda 21 and Chapter 28 of the UNCED document, the process was instead christened *Das Entwicklungskonzept Oststeiermark* – DEO (Development Concept East Styria).

Another interesting feature of this process came from the orientation of the administrative agency that implemented this regional agenda process. As the main purpose of the regional administration was the support of regional actors in using European structural funds as a strategic means for development, the process was clearly oriented along the lines of structural, economic and social development within the region. Environmental aspects were seen as generic issues that had to be considered in all working groups concerned with planning the development of the region, and were not assigned to a separate group.

During the planning process, the fact that all *Bezirke* had already devised their own strategic development plans (*Bezirksleitbilder*) had to be taken into account. These plans, which had their origin in an initiative of the provincial government, had been created in participatory processes within the *Bezirke* along similar ideas but with no direct connection to the Agenda 21 document. Below the *Bezirke* some communities already had implemented LA21 plans, including a pioneering one in the city of Weiz. All these processes had to be integrated into the development of DEO. This gave the process of creating DEO a distinct quality, as it was clear from the outset that this regional agenda had to create a new strategic concept for the development of the whole region that would build on existing plans but address topics of importance at the level of the larger region on its way into the uncharted waters of an enlarged EU. This enlargement would radically alter the situation of the region, propelling it from the borders into a central position of the common Europe of the 21st century.

Besides the existing plans and LA21s, additional ideas on the future of the region were collected. This was done through in-depth interviews in the region, as well as through a contest in regional schools where pupils were asked to write down their vision for the region for the year 2025.

On the basis of this material, four working groups were installed that dealt with the following issues:

1 Agriculture, landscape and tourism.
2 Economy and jobs.
3 Education, regional culture, identity and social issues.
4 Energy, infrastructure, mobility and telecommunication.

Access to these working groups was essentially open to regional participation. An information campaign to inform the general public on the activities leading to DEO accompanied their work.

The result of the consultation process was a future accord (*Zukunftsvertrag*) that was signed by the political committee controlling the regional administration. This accord was designed as a means to bind the work of the administration, as well as the political representatives of the region, to the results of the regional agenda process. It contained development projects grouped around eight main tasks:

1 *Improvement of the economic attraction of the region.* This includes the initiation of a regional cluster of ecological economic activities like eco-technologies, technologies for renewable energies, and the construction of ecologically oriented housing. These are industries that are already strong in the region. In addition, the development of new industrial parks (again oriented around ecologically relevant topics) and of regional spatial planning for industrial sites is part of this task.
2 *Regional marketing.* This includes marketing in tourism as well as agricultural products designed to preserve both the finely structured landscape and the small-scale agriculture that is supporting it.
3 *Use of renewable regional resources.* This includes initiatives to implement technologies and knowledge dissemination in a broad range of topics ranging from solar architecture and bio-energy to wind energy and related issues.
4 *Applied research and development.* This includes the initiation of new, as well as the linking of existing research institutions concerned with problems relevant to the region such as use of agricultural products (grass, hemp and wood, for example).
5 *New information and communication technologies.* This task includes the development of information and communication networks adapted to the needs of a rural area.

6 *Spatial planning and settlement structure of the region.* In a rural area with an extremely dispersed settlement structure like East Styria, the provision of public services, especially transportation, is difficult. This task addresses programmes concerning regional public transportation.
7 *Structural change and its consequences on jobs.* This task addresses projects concerning qualification of the regional workforce as well as the provision of regional capital for key investments.
8 *The learning region.* Under this heading initiatives concerning the establishment of new educational programmes and institutions as well as cultural activities reinforcing regional identification are summarised.

With the implementation of DEO now under way, the following aspects of this process seem especially interesting:

- DEO constitutes a Regional Agenda 21 process, which was initiated in a region that was created by requirements of the EU structural funds.
- The process clearly improved the visibility of this new regional level within the broader area, and heightened identification with a region that had no historical roots.
- The integration of existing strategic plans, as well as existing LA21 processes, was a positive element in the establishment of the regional agenda, which succeeded in building on this foundation, and addressed problems that could not be approached at the lower levels of administration.
- The consultation with citizens and the participatory planning process instigated by the regional agenda clearly improved acceptance of the regional administration itself as well as the implementation of strategic programmes in a region whose *raison d'être* is the support of European structural funds.
- The integration of environmental aspects as generic topics into other development issues seems to work well. DEO includes a number of measures towards this end, although there was no separate group working on this topic.

Conclusion

The Austrian situation is, in a number of ways, relevant to the general problems of LA21 implementation and may therefore be relevant in other countries. The following paragraphs summarise the most interesting lessons to be learned from Austrian experiences with LA21 implementation.

Interrelation between international and local level

Austria has had a difficult start with LA21 implementation. Part of the problem lay in the timing of the Earth Summit, as it coincided with an ongoing national political discourse about sustainable development around the concept of eco-social market economy. This discourse even made Austria an active supporter of the idea of local and regional sustainable development in the preparation of the Summit (*Österreichische Bundesregierung*, 1992). Eco-social market economy set in motion 'LA21-like' initiatives in many – particularly rural – communities that otherwise paid almost no attention to the results of the Earth Summit, to Agenda 21 and to the necessity for LA21 implementation. This situation contributed to the late starter image of Austria concerning LA21 implementation. However, it also contributed to the relatively favourable baseline from which an increasing number of Austrian communities could begin their LA21 implementation.

Although the Earth Summit did not ignite LA21 implementation in Austria, the UNGASS conference five years later did. By this time the discussion on eco-social market economy had more or less subsided in Austria. During the course of the preparation for UNGASS, it was realised, particularly at the national level, that Austria had stalled in LA21 implementation, and had also lost its relatively advanced position in implementing sustainable development in general. It was only after UNGASS that the responsibility for implementing LA21 was taken seriously. This is a clear example of how international prestige can lead to action at the national level.

Together with the influence of UNGASS, Austria's accession to the EU has also promoted implementation of LA21. The influence of the EU has, in particular, supported regional agendas, as regional cooperation became a necessary feature of applying European structural funds. Again, the East Styrian DEO is an interesting case in point.

A general feature of Austrian LA21 cases (as compared to those in other countries) is the relatively weak emphasis on international cooperation with developing countries. This is still very much the area of activity for NGOs, such as the Climate Alliance.

LA21 and the relation between different administrative levels

The national level did not spring into action concerning LA21 implementation until after the UNGASS conference. Even then, the initiative to induce communities to start LA21 processes came more from the provincial than from the national and municipal governments.

LA21 processes are perceived by communities as strategic planning instruments. In those cases where communities (or other regional entities) have seriously embarked on LA21 processes, the results have been comprehensive plans that include ecological, economic and social aspects. The East Styrian regional agenda is a case in point. These results from LA21 processes are often more advanced than provincial or national efforts to implement sustainable development. The comprehensive plans that are developed on the local or regional level often meet administrative units at higher levels that are usually more fragmented into sectoral responsibilities. It is clear that this does not help the implementation of LA21 plans.

One further interesting aspect of the Austrian case (also exemplified in the DEO case) is the emergence of a new centre. The EU, especially with respect to the implementation of sustainable regional development and LA21, plays a significant role in Austria. Structural funds act as an incentive to create long-term regional plans and to cooperate regionally. In some cases, this leads directly to regional agendas. The DEO case shows that the influence of the EU can even function to create new regions.

From environmental protection to sustainable development

Immediately after the Earth Summit, only a few communities started LA21 processes. The Ecocity 2000 process in Graz is a good example of these pioneering initiatives, which were started mainly in larger cities. This initiative was clearly driven by the need to improve the urban ecological situation and concentrated mainly on environmental aspects. The Graz example highlights the top-down approach of such processes, which still require some additional effort in terms of participation and integration of social and economic aspects in LA21 implementation.

One of the interesting features of this case, however, is the successful integration of industry into a cleaner production scheme. The Ecoprofit project constructed a new partnership between administration and industry with the goal to reduce environmental pressures in the most efficient way. This project had a lasting impact on the way companies have come to view ecological challenges, as well as on their relationship with environmental protection at the community level of public administration. Ecoprofit has developed into a success story for export, gradually being integrated into LA21 processes in Austria as well as in neighbouring countries including the Czech Republic, Slovakia and Germany.

Regional agendas as a means for improvement of participation in planning

As a latecomer to LA21 implementation, Austria also experimented with regional agendas. One common denominator of these processes is the need to combine forces across the narrow limits of often very small communities in order to take advantage of European structural funds. At the core of this trend one can identify the smallness of many Austrian communities as a driving force. Communities with less than 1000 inhabitants simply cannot handle comprehensive strategic planning challenges. They lack the expertise, the money and most often the administrative capacity to solve ecological problems such as waste management, water supply and treatment, but also economic problems like job creation and a more effective appeal to investors. In this situation it seems clear that higher, regional levels of administration will exercise planning and implementation powers more effectively, thereby promoting sustainable development in a more comprehensive way.

The example of DEO shows that such regional agendas are a powerful tool in bringing democratic elements into administrative levels that are either newly created or do not have democratic bodies (like the *Bezirke*). Although there is no final verdict on these processes, they are generally successful in integrating environmental concerns into development plans, and creating a positive attitude vis-à-vis the strategic role of EU structural funds.

The DEO in East Styria has also proven that Regional Agenda 21 processes are an interesting means to allocate planning power at levels that can effectively deal with the challenges of sustainable development. The important aspect of Regional Agenda 21 processes in this respect is that although decisions are delegated from communities upward, the processes guarantee the participation of stakeholders. Thus Agenda 21 processes are not only seen as a means to empower citizens and bring the level of decision-making as close as possible to the citizen; they may also be seen as processes to allocate power at the most efficient level, while avoiding the drawbacks of conventional delegation to higher levels, namely the loss of influence on the decision and responsibility for implementation by the citizen.

The case of DEO demonstrates that LA21 can play a significant role in integrating new elements into the political process in Austria. Based on a visioning process in a new regional context, a future accord has been adopted that is binding for political representatives as well as key stakeholders in the region. The future will tell us how resilient this accord proves to be in the face of real-world implementation of the ambitious plan.

Box 9.2 Regional Agenda 21 in East Styria

- Austria's accession to the EU resulted in the creation of East Styria as a new formal administrative region. During the course of accession Austria defined new regional units in accordance with EU provisions for administration of structural funds.
- The need for a strategic development plan for this new regional entity was recognised by the official regional administration. It was decided that the plan should be developed in the form of a Regional Agenda 21 (subsequently christened *Das Entwicklungskonzept Oststeiermark*).
- Using European structural funds as a strategic means for development, the process has been structured along the lines of structural, economical and social development within the region. Environmental aspects were seen as horizontal: generic issues that had to be considered in all working groups concerned with planning the development of the region, and were not assigned to a separate group.
- The Regional Agenda 21 built on existing plans from the different municipalities or *Bezirke*, but it created a new strategic concept for the development of the whole region. Generation of additional ideas on the future of the region was done via in-depth interviews with important participants in the region, as well as through a contest in regional schools where pupils were asked to write down their visions for the region for the year 2025. On the basis of this material, four working groups were installed.
- The result of the consultation through these working groups was a future accord (*Zukunftsvertrag*) that was signed by the political committee controlling the regional administration. This accord was designed as a means to bind the work of the administration, as well as the political representatives of the region, to the results of the regional agenda process. It contained concrete development projects grouped around eight main tasks.
- The implementation of the Regional Agenda 21 is currently underway. The process has so far been a success. It has improved the visibility of the new regional level within the broader area, and heightened identification with a region that has no historical roots. The regional agenda succeeded in building a new foundation, and addressed problems that could not be approached at the lower levels of administration. The introduction of generic topics into other development areas also seems to work well.

LA21 and subsidiarity

With its many layers of administration, the Austrian case is certainly rich in lessons relevant to the topic of subsidiarity. One interesting aspect emerging from the Austrian case is a new type of layering of relations between different levels. A case in point has been the active role of Austrian provinces in supporting and initiating LA21 processes at the community level. Although there is no direct hierarchical connection between provinces and the UN, the provincial level picked up the task of supporting these processes much more vigorously than the national level, which has a more direct responsibility to do so. One explanation for this is that the provinces have direct contact with the communities, something that the national administrative level lacks. In a way, LA21 has created a link between provinces and the international community of states, surpassing the national level.

A similar phenomenon can be seen from the DEO case, where LA21 can be seen as linking different levels (in this case the European and the regional level) directly, and surpassing intermediate levels (the national as well as the provincial level in this case). Although these phenomena can also be detected outside LA21 implementation, this new kind of 'parallel subsidiarity' is an important feature in Austrian cases.

NOTES

1 The nomenclature of territorial units for statistics (NUTS), established by Eurostat, provides a single uniform breakdown of territorial units. NUTS subdivides each member state into a hierarchy of increasingly smaller administrative areas:
   - NUTS I regions cover, for example, the *Länder* in Germany, *zones d'etudes et d'aménagement du territoire* (ZEAT) in France, *régions* in Belgium.
   - NUTS II regions cover, for example, the *régions* in France, *comunidades autónomas* in Spain, *regioni* in Italy, *provincies* in the Netherlands.
   - NUTS III regions cover, for example, the *Kreise* in Germany, *départements* in France, *nomoi* in Greece, *maakunnat* in Finland, *län* in Sweden.

2 The term 'Agenda' in both Local Agenda 21 and in Agenda 2000 leads to constant confusion. Many regional participants misinterpreted LA21 as part of the Agenda 2000. As the latter is generally seen as the cause for painful restructuring of the economy in border regions, especially concerning agriculture, it has a definitely negative ring for the citizenry of these regions.

References

List, D (1996) 'Lokale Agenda 21 Graz: Ökostadt 2000', in *Globaler Konsens: Lokale Umsetzung, Auf dem Weg zu einer Lokalen Agenda 21*, Vienna

Ministry of the Environment (1994) *Report to the 2nd Session of the CSD*, Ministry of the Environment, Vienna

Ministry of the Environment (1995) *National Environmental Plan*, Ministry of the Environment, Vienna

Ministry of the Environment (1998) *Leitfaden zur Umsetzung der Local Agenda 21 in Österreich*, Ministry of the Environment, Vienna

Österreichische Bundesregierung (1992) *Nationalbericht an UNCED*, Österreichische Bundesregierung, Vienna

Riegler, J (1990) *Antworten auf die Zukunft*, Verlag Adolf Hozhausen's Nfg, Vienna

Riegler, J and Moser, A (1996) *Ökosoziale Marktwirtschaft: Denken und Handeln in Kreisläufen*, Leopold Stocker Verlag, Graz

Sage, J (1998) *Regional Cleaner Production Projects and Ecoconsulting in Austria: Example ECOPROFIT*, Summer course 'Cleaner Production on the Design, Establishment and Maintenance of Regional and City-based Sustainable Production Programmes', Institute of Chemical Engineering, TU–Graz

10. Italy
Converging pathways between central and local levels of government?[1]

Emiliano Ramieri, Jane Wallace-Jones and Rodolfo Lewanski

INTRODUCTION

LA21 in Italy has had a slow start (Ramieri and Fiorentini, 1999) but is, nevertheless, becoming an increasingly widespread concept and practice. The period 1992–95 is characterised by very limited activity in terms of LA21 implementation. The first relevant initiatives actually started in the second half of the decade, and the most promising developments are to be found only at the end of the 1990s. Perhaps even more noteworthy in the Italian case is the fact that the LA21 implementation process can be seen to have followed two parallel pathways: on the one hand, at the central level of government, on the other, at the local and regional level. These two separate processes have started to converge only in recent times through seeking and finding opportunities for cooperation.

The pathways are distinct in that one comprises the emergence of isolated LA21 processes at the local level (followed more recently by the formation of the Italian 'LA21 coordination network') while the other involves the planning and materialisation of projects and instruments aimed at the promotion and support of LA21 from the central level. It is not only the nature of the activities that makes these two pathways different. In fact, these activities differ in terms of how visible they have been. LA21-related initiatives began at both the central and local levels in 1996. However, those taking place at the central level have only recently entered the LA21 arena in a tangible manner.

This chapter firstly offers a description of the development of LA21 in Italy, both at the central and local levels of government. Subsequently, it examines the role of governmental relations, distinguishing between vertical ones among different levels of government and horizontal ones, as factors that account, to some extent, for such development in Italy. The former refers to those relationships formed initially between regions, provinces and municipalities, and more recently between the central and the local levels, and the latter refers to relationships emerging in the form of partnerships and international and national networks.

The chapter concludes with snapshot and dynamic perspectives of LA21 in Italy and the specific lessons to be drawn from the national experience. The examination of the above-mentioned factors highlights the recent contact made between the two previously parallel pathways and the points of convergence, thus suggesting a more symbiotic relationship between the two levels in the near future. The very nature of some of the recent plans and projects unfolding at the central level gives no indication of government intentions to wrest control of the LA21 activities from the coordination network, but rather, to leave well alone and provide some of the much needed implementation tools. The central level may also gain in that, in pursuing a policy of LA21 promotion and support, it does not need to establish communications with each of the involved or potential administrations, but can instead take advantage of existing communications provided by the network and of its role as spokesman.

LA21 AND SUSTAINABLE DEVELOPMENT IN ITALY

The central level

The Italian Ministry of the Environment (MoE) was instituted in 1986,[2] considerably later than in other developed countries. Although it was not starting from scratch, its activity up until the early 1990s was, to a large extent, absorbed by the need to try to catch up with the policy capacity of other similarly developed Western nations, by completing the legislation, obtaining and spending adequate financial resources and by developing an administrative structure. Therefore in the same period in which the term sustainable development officially entered policy circles, the MoE was engaged in defining national environmental policy. While other countries more advanced in the development of domestic environmental policy were starting to deal with environmental issues through a more advanced strategic approach in which attempts were made to integrate it with economic policies, Italy was still engaged in tackling basic environmental protection.

The first two national reports on the state of the environment, were published respectively in 1989 and 1992 (Ministero dell'Ambiente, 1989 and 1992). Published before the Earth Summit,[3] both make brief reference to the Bruntland Report (WCED, 1987), quoted as being of 'exceptional importance' (Ministero dell'Ambiente, 1989), and to the concept of sustainable development. At that time the concept was already in use in the political arena: A group of politicians and Members of Parliament (largely greens, but also others) had promoted the 'Centre for a Sustainable Future' in 1991, before the Earth Summit, which contributed to the dissemination of the concept. By and large, however, the idea remained confined to a small circle of ecological experts and activists, and was not even particularly central to the concerns of the environmental movement, let alone the policy-makers.

The first official national response to Italy's obligations ensuing from the Earth Summit was the approval of a national plan for sustainable development for the implementation of Agenda 21 by the Inter-ministerial Committee for Economic Planning (CIPE), in 1993.[4] A coordinating committee in charge of evaluating the plan's implementation was also set up shortly thereafter. Although the plan has its strong technical points, it has been ineffective in terms of results in relation to national strategies for sustainable development. Moreover, it totally failed to address the local dimension of Agenda 21 as put forward in Chapter 28.

During this period, the institutional capacity of central government in the environmental policy field was being gradually upgraded, not only through a strengthening of the MoE itself in terms of power and resources controlled by it, but also thanks to the creation of new technical agencies, such as the National Environmental Agency (ANPA) in 1994 and some Regional Environmental Agencies (ARPAs), or through the transformation of the tasks of previously existing agencies, as in the case of the National Body for New Technologies, the Environment and Energy (ENEA).

After a period during which very little happened at the central level, 1996 represents an important year in terms of activity relating to urban sustainability and LA21. In November, the MoE created the working group on sustainable cities, following the suggestions that emerged during a relevant conference in Rome organised by Ambiente Italia[5] and DGXI (now the Environment Directorate-General) of the EC that seems to have played an important role in attracting the attention of the minister to the issue of LA21. The working group was composed of representatives of the principal Italian NGOs committed to the promotion of local sustainability initiatives and of the MoE itself. It met between the end of 1996 and mid-1997, and was officially dissolved at the end of its mandate in September 1998 (Berrini, 1999), producing a document containing suggestions of measures that the MoE could undertake. Over the following years, on the basis of this, the MoE started important initiatives concerning LA21 which, however, only became visible at the end of 1998.

In 1997, the Italian Senate passed a formal resolution that bound the government to adopt measures in favour of sustainability in accordance with the renewed commitments made at the Earth Summit +5 in 1997.

Box 10.1 Strong national guidance in Italy

- In 1993, CIPE followed up the Earth Summit by the approval of a national plan for sustainable development for the implementation of Agenda 21. This plan did not address the local dimension of Agenda 21 as put forward in Chapter 28.
- At the same time, the institutional capacity of central government in the environmental policy field was being gradually upgraded. The Ministry of the Environment was strengthened in terms of new capacities and resources; new technical agencies such as the ANPA and new regional agencies (ARPAs) were created.
- In 1996, the MoE initiated a working group on sustainable cities with an LA21 dimension. Over the following years, on the basis of the group's document, the MoE took several important initiatives for LA21 diffusion and support, which only become apparent at the end of 1998.
- In 1997, the updating of the national plan for sustainable development was started. Pertinent to LA21 is the fact that the new plan, which considers the five traditional sectors (tourism, industry, agriculture, energy and infrastructure) dealt with in the 1993 version, will also specifically address the urban and local dimensions of sustainability.
- A strategic move in this respect is the new programme for the protection of the environment, Agenda 21 for urban areas: pilot initiatives in medium-sized cities. This programme aims to test local implementation of the national plan for sustainable development through LA21 initiatives. At the end of 1999 about a dozen projects for local sustainability were selected for funding through this programme.
- Among the other activities promoted by the working group on sustainable cities, the MoE has awarded the first sustainable cities for children prize in 1998. This represents an indirect stimulus to LA21 diffusion since one of the criteria for the prize is the adoption of an LA21 process.
- ANPA has also recently (1998–99) promoted LA21-related initiatives. Most noteworthy are: the publication of a manual for LA21 implementation, which contains methodology suited to cities of different sizes; the creation of a monitoring effort for local good practice; and the organisation of a series of seminars on LA21 for the professional training of officers working in the new regional agencies.
- ENEA is also involved in a number of LA21 activities.

Act no 344/1997, which was approved shortly after, defines provisions for the development and improvement of interventions and employment related to the environment and sustainability. Of special interest here are the provisions aiming to promote urban sustainability (Article 2) and to allocate funds for the definition and the implementation of the new programme for the protection of the environment[6] (Article 7). This programme, which was recently formulated and approved by the MoE,[7] defines interventions relating to six strategic areas, amongst which is that of instruments for sustainable development, aiming to promote those projects which support sustainable development and play an important role in sustaining all the other interventions foreseen by the programme. The first project concerns the updating of the national plan for sustainable development.

The MoE is analysing, with the technical support of ENEA,[8] the previous national plan for sustainable development's state of implementation and identifying actions in order to update it. A first preliminary version of the plan was to be ready by the summer of 2000 and then submitted for the approval of the CIPE[9] sustainable development commission (Soprano, 1999). The time schedule for completing the plan is uncertain because it depends on internal reorganisation of the MoE, which foresees the creation of a new department on sustainable development. This will bring together all issues of sustainability that are, at the moment, dispersed among various other departments.

Pertinent to LA21 is the fact that the new plan, which considers the five traditional sectors (tourism, industry, agriculture, energy and infrastructure) dealt with in the 1993 version, will also specifically address the urban and local dimensions of sustainability (Soprano, 1999) as themes transversal to these sectors. Thus its goal is to overcome a major limitation of the previous version – the lack of involvement of local authorities – and to include, for the first time, local actions for sustainable development such as LA21.

The new programme for the protection of the environment provides for the project entitled 'Agenda 21 for Urban Areas: Pilot Initiatives in Medium-sized Cities', which aims to test local implementation of the national plan for sustainable development through LA21 initiatives. This project will involve and stimulate the smaller municipalities that normally lack information on LA21, specifically, a small group of cities with less than 50,000 inhabitants to be selected by the MoE (Marzi, 1999). At present, the MoE and ENEA are defining the detailed contents of the project and the criteria for the selection of the cities.

At the end of 1999, some projects for local sustainability were selected to be funded through the new programme for the protection of the environment. These include about a dozen projects that are either LA21 initiatives or energy-environment plans to be defined through a process involving public participation.

Among the other activities promoted by the working group on sustainable cities, the MoE[10] awarded the first Sustainable Cities for Children Prize in 1998 (Ministero dell'Ambiente, 1998). In addition, the MoE established the Prize for Sustainable Cities, awarded for the first time in 2000. Since one of the criteria considered in the allocation of this latter prize is the adoption of an LA21 process, the award represents an indirect stimulus to LA21 diffusion.

Both ANPA and ENEA are evolving into significant LA21 actors. ANPA was set up in 1994 and each region was also requested to create an agency of its own (ARPAs), though not all regions have yet done so. Some ARPAs, such as the case of the Emilia-Romagna region, have decentralised their departments at the provincial level. ANPA has been indirectly stimulated by the existing LA21 experiences, and in 1998-99 promoted LA21-related initiatives. In particular, ANPA's activity focuses on the publication of a manual for LA21 implementation, which contains methodology suited to cities of different sizes (ANPA and Ambiente Italia, 2000); the creation of an observatory on local good practice; and the organisation of a series of seminars on LA21 for the professional training of officers working in ARPAs (ANPA, 1999; Cantoni and Colagrossi, 1999).

ENEA, originally the scientific agency for the development of nuclear energy, and then responsible for assisting public administrations – national, regional and local – in the fields of energy, environment and technological innovation, was recently allocated research tasks also related to sustainable development.[11] This recent change explains why ENEA is now involved in a number of activities linked to LA21, such as those included in the programme for the protection of the environment. In particular, ENEA is now working on the definition of an integrated system of urban indicators (SIAU), which will be successively tested in selected cities. Furthermore, the MoE and ENEA are developing a project with the National Association of Italian Municipalities (ANCI)[12] for a national observatory for the urban environment, which will also be responsible for collecting data and selecting indicators. In addition, ENEA has instituted a prize for sustainable development projects aimed at local administrations.

The local and the regional level

Local and regional authorities[13] hold a number of legal powers in fields relevant to LA21, such as environmental, social and land use policies. Such powers have increased over the last decade.[14] Thus, although constrained by limitations on the availability of human and financial resources, Italian local and regional authorities do, at least potentially, have the capacity to pursue policy options autonomously, including those concerning fields related to LA21.

There was little implementation of LA21 at the local level during the period from 1992 to 1995. Only the principal national environmental NGOs, some research institutions (such as the National Institute for Urban Planning (INU)), and a few pioneering local authorities appear to have been active (Berrini, 1999). National NGOs, such as WWF and Legambiente, played an important role in spreading the urban sustainability and Agenda 21 concepts among local authorities through various initiatives. Examples include initiatives concerning urban mobility and urban biodiversity launched by the WWF; and some of Legambiente's initiatives: the campaigns 'cities against global warming' and 'cities for waste recycling', the annual report on the urban ecosystem and the construction of a database on best practice with the Municipality of Ferrara. These also continued after 1996. In recent years, the same associations have also launched initiatives specific to LA21, for example, the organisation of congresses, workshops and training courses on LA21;[15] the initiative promoted by the WWF on the diffusion of LA21 within schools; and research and the publication of books, which have been instrumental in making both local and central levels more aware of the issue.

The Municipality of Rome appears to have been the first Italian authority to sign the Aalborg Charter in 1994 (ESCTC, 1994; Avanzi, 1999). A number of other municipal authorities also signed the Charter between 1994 and 1996, but it should be noted that signing the Charter and actually starting an LA21 process have rarely proven to be the same thing. It was only in 1996 and 1997 that the first LA21 processes actually started. Given the lack of any form of perceptible central support for LA21 initiatives, and considering the limited impact of NGO activities, the few LA21 processes that started in this period appear to have emerged independently. Apart from Modena provincial and municipal authorities and that of the Province of Crotone, all of the other processes began in the larger metropolitan areas such as Rome, Florence, Venice, Bologna and Genoa. LA21 processes have also gradually emerged in other smaller cities during the period 1999–2000. Furthermore, regional processes have begun in Tuscany, Liguria, Emilia-Romagna, Umbria, Bolzano and Trento[16] with provincial processes in Lucca, Turin, Reggio Emilia and Rimini.

In 1998, the WWF-Italy and Avanzi survey (1998) reported the presence of 24 local or regional authorities that claimed to have at least begun an LA21 initiative. The 1999 survey (Avanzi, 1999) indicates that there were 41 local or regional authorities[17] (6 regions, 6 provinces and 29 municipalities) actually involved in LA21 processes by June of that year, although many differences exist between both their degree of implementation and the interpretation of LA21. Various LA21 initiatives recorded in the 1999 survey were very much at the beginning of the process. A further six municipalities and two provinces signed the Aalborg Charter by June 1999, but have not yet started any concrete activities.

Even allowing for the possibility of differences in the samples or inaccurate data in the two surveys, it emerges that there has clearly been an acceleration in the initiation of LA21 processes over the 1998–99 period. The general impression is that the number of LA21 initiatives in Italy grew in the second half of 1999,[18] and an increased interest in LA21 is also indicated by the continuous growth in the number of participants in the LA21 coordination network.

With regard to the implementation of LA21, the 1999 survey shows that an action plan has been defined in only three cases. Seven have started a participation process through an LA21 forum, and only three have formed thematic working groups. Notwithstanding the small number of participation processes, in many LA21 experiences various public initiatives such as meetings, conferences and seminars have been promoted. The survey results show that the the participants are primarily environmental associations, schools and educational institutes, industry and trade associations, public bodies, environmental agencies, and voluntary organisations. There is little evidence of participation on the part of associations for women, young people or ethnic minorities.

The surveys also indicate that LA21 administrations are mainly concentrated in northern Italy (70 per cent of the cases), as opposed to 16 and 14 per cent respectively for central and southern Italy. Sancassiani (1999) suggests that this distribution is related to the degree of experience and attention historically paid to environmental policy and projects, in addition to the degree of implementation of regulations in the field of the environment and in situations that favour participatory processes. The relatively high number of initiatives in Emilia-Romagna (11 municipalities, 3 provinces and the region itself) and in Tuscany (4 municipalities) can also been interpreted from this perspective.

A number of local and regional authorities seem to have embraced the broad nature of LA21, viewing it as an opportunity to tackle economic, social and environmental issues. For example, in two municipalities (Cattolica and Rimini) and one province (Crotone) LA21 is explicitly related to the promotion of tourism. However, management of the LA21 process is usually entrusted to the environment department and to the MoE at the central level (Avanzi, 1999).

The LA21 process that distinguishes itself from the others in Italy in the 1999 survey is that of Modena, with support and involvement from both the municipal and provincial authorities. The Modena LA21 process displays many of the recognisable features of the Aalborg Charter and is, furthermore, the most advanced. Local stakeholder participation generated a preliminary action plan (Provincia di Modena, 1999) at the beginning of 1999. The city of Modena was awarded a certificate of distinction in 1999, along with ten other European cities, under the European city award established by the EU sustainable cities and towns campaign.

In early 1999, the concerted action of several LA21 administrations resulted in a highly relevant effort for the future of LA21, namely the creation of the Italian LA21 coordination network (see Box 10.2). In March and April 1999, the Province and the Municipality of Modena and the Municipality of Ferrara respectively organised the first two meetings for the creation of this network with the active participation of local administrations involved in or at least interested in LA21. Further meetings have since been held in Genoa and Rome.

BOX 10.2 ITALIAN LA21 COORDINATION NETWORK

- The Italian LA21 coordination network was established in 1999. This network is the work of the local and regional authorities involved in LA21. Today this represents the most important concerted effort being promoted at the local level.
- A meeting held in Ferrara in April 1999 formalised the establishment of the network through the approval of the Ferrara Charter. The Charter was signed by 45 local or regional authorities involved or interested in LA21.
- The Charter defines the objectives of the network, which is basically addressed to the promotion of LA21 and of partnerships among local governments; the monitoring of its development; the stimulation of pertinent research and the exchange of information.
- The Charter has established three internal working groups aimed at studying the relation between LA21 and other planning instruments.
- In January 2000 there were 119 members in the network.
- The Charter has gained support from national authorities. The ANPA has been able to establish a good relationship with this newly developed network. It has provided funding for some of the network activities and also offered technical support. The Minister of the Environment met with the network in the autumn of 1999 and committed the ministry to maintaining a permanent, open channel for consultation on various initiatives, including the national plan for sustainable development. The network initiative was also awarded the 1999 ENEA sustainable development prize.

INTERGOVERNMENTAL RELATIONS

LA21 implementation has travelled along two parallel pathways: that of the emergence of LA21 processes at the local level and the promotion and support for LA21 initiatives at the central level. Central-level initiatives, which became largely perceptible in the LA21 policy arena at the end of 1998, were previously scarcely visible during the period in which they made their way through MoE policy processes. In addition, the central level's commitment to LA21 has contributed to the very recent development of interactions between central-level institutions (MoE, ANPA, ENEA) and the local level.

Thus, it seems that the two separate pathways are starting to converge. The signs of this convergence can be found in some initiatives promoted by the central level which foresee the direct involvement of local authorities, such as the prize for sustainable cities and the financing of some

LA21 initiatives through the new programme for the protection of the environment. Some other initiatives, such as those promoted by ANPA (the practical manual, the creation of the initiative for good practice, and the organisation of training seminars on LA21), aim to provide tools for the implementation of LA21 processes. The very recent contacts between the Italian LA21 coordination network, whose creation represents the most important concerted effort promoted at the local level, and the MoE and ANPA, are also noted

Other interesting vertical governmental relationships have developed between regions, provinces and municipalities, in some cases even before the central level began to interact with the LA21 initiatives promoted at the local level. The 1999 survey highlighted that in a sample of 31 municipalities that had signed the Aalborg Charter by May 1999, 12 had collaborated with their regional authority and six with their provincial authority (Avanzi, 1999).

Some regions and provinces have chosen to coordinate the activities of LA21 processes taking place at lower levels of government as well as to promote LA21 and diffuse instruments inherent to the process rather than simply adopting an Agenda 21 of their own. The role of the region and province as active promoters of LA21 may have been determined in some cases (such as those of the regions of Liguria and Tuscany, as well as the Province of Turin) by the limited spontaneous development of LA21 initiatives at the lower levels of government. It may well be, however, that the contrary is the case in Emilia-Romagna, where the relatively high occurrence of LA21 initiatives may have influenced the region to place more emphasis on the technical aspects of LA21 rather than on encouraging the widespread initiation of LA21 processes. This region has, in fact, activated a technical coordinating group that has held various meetings on sustainability indicators since June 1998 and workshops on the participation process within the forum in October 1998. Various municipalities involved in LA21 processes have taken part in these activities.

A relevant and relatively long-standing initiative has also been promoted by the Tuscany Region, which passed the regional Act no 5 in 1995. This asserts that urban and rural planning must be oriented in the perspective of sustainable development. The most recent Regional Development Plan (PRS) was prepared in 1997, and was actually defined as the Regional Plan for Sustainable Development (PRSS) for the period 1998–2000.

Intergovernmental LA21-related interactions became more formalised in 1998 through the creation of a working group on sustainable development, which brought together various stakeholders and representatives of local administrations. The Municipality of Florence (1997) and the Province of Lucca (1999), have also initiated their own LA21 processes. The group has discussed the contents of the PRSS and proposed modifications (Regione Toscana, 1998). Within the PRSS, the regional programmes (PIR), Agenda 21, instruments for sustainable development and pilot actions for sustainable development identify actions and objectives aimed at testing instruments for sustainable development and directly promoting LA21 initiatives in Tuscany (Regione Toscana, 1998). During 1999, the region developed a number of specific instruments to be used in the pilot LA21 projects, such as a manual for the implementation of LA21 in Tuscany elaborated with Ambiente Italia. Furthermore, the region and the Tuscany ARPA organised a training programme on LA21 for the local administrators to be involved in pilot projects in three areas, which include several municipalities (Del Lungo, 1999). The results of the pilot projects will also provide essential information for the definition and implementation of the Regional Agenda 21 (Mugelli, 1999).

It would seem that the LA21-related initiatives on the part of the Tuscany region aim more at the provision of tools for the replication of LA21 processes in the territory and in facilitating the diffusion of LA21, rather than at a coordination of existing or potential LA21 initiatives.

The LA21 process launched by the province of Turin started in June 1998 and is another significant example in the context of intergovernmental relations. It directly aims to spread LA21 within the territory, to stimulate municipalities to get involved in LA21 processes and to promote a provincial coordination of these processes (De Leonardis, 1999). In March 1999, the province created a coordinating group that included 23 municipalities and three mountain communities interested in LA21. Some of these, such as the municipalities of Turin (1999) and Settimo Torinese (1999), have already started their own LA21 processes. Shortly after, the municipality of Turin, in collaboration with Ambiente Italia, developed a proposal for a Turin Province action plan (Ambiente Italia and Provincia di Torino, 1999), which constitutes the basis both for the drawing up, through a forum, of a final plan for the province, and for the activity of the municipalities involved in LA21. The Turin Province is also attempting to disseminate LA21 in the small alpine municipalities through the network Alliance for the Alps promoted by the International Commission for the Protection of the Alps (CIPRA). This network principally aims to facilitate the implementation of 'The Alps Treaty', endorsed by seven countries in 1991, which has the goal of promoting sustainable development in the alpine ecosystem.

It is difficult to say whether local interest in LA21, in the regions and provinces that have promoted LA21-related initiatives, has emerged only in response to their efforts, or as a consequence of other factors that are not investigated in depth in this chapter (such as political orientation, degree of administrative organisation, tradition of public participation and effectiveness of environmental policy). Nevertheless, from the analysis of the distribution of the LA21 processes and of the administrations that have taken part in the Italian LA21 coordination network, it emerges that these provinces and regions are characterised by a relatively high number of LA21 activities at the local level.

Horizontal interrelations: Networks and partnerships

It would appear that horizontal interactions have played a relevant role in the development of LA21 in Italy in two ways: namely, the dissemination process fostered by international, European and national networks, and the partnerships between public administrations, NGOs and other institutions.

With regard to the first, 42 Italian local authorities were members of the European sustainable cities and towns campaign in May 1999. This figure represents 9.5 per cent of the European total, thus making Italy one of the European countries with the highest relative membership (Avanzi, 1999). It should be noted, however, that 50 per cent of these members have made their commitment since 1998 (Avanzi, 1999). Networks such as this, in addition to the international and European networks of ICLEI, WHO, Eurocities, World Federation of United Cities (UTO) and Féderation Mondiale des Citées Unies (FMCU), have served to spread information and knowledge on urban sustainability initiatives in Italy.

Nor should we overlook the important role that internal networks, in the form of national NGOs (principally the Italian branch of the WWF and Legambiente), have played in the stimulus and dissemination of information pertinent to urban sustainability, both more recently and in the period before 1996 (Berrini, 1999). The efforts of NGOs have not only prompted specific activities at the local level but have also served to alert participants at the central level; for example, as mentioned above, the MoE's working group on sustainable cities was largely composed of NGO representatives.

The role of national umbrella associations for local authorities – such as ANCI, the Union of Italian Provinces (UPI) and the Italian Confederation of Local Public Services (CISPEL) – has generally been marginal, even since 1996. The function has largely been limited to supporting existing programmes related to LA21 initiatives, such as the sustainable cities and towns campaign. In 1996, ANCI, CISPEL and Legambiente organised various meetings in preparation for the Habitat II Conference in Istanbul, which produced a final document, the City Charter (ANCI, 1996), later presented at the Istanbul conference.

However, the most important coordinating initiative in relation to LA21 was the creation of the Italian LA21 coordination network in 1999. This has taken place in a decentralised manner and is the work of the local municipalities and provinces and regional authorities involved in LA21.

The lack of long-standing and visible national coordination of, or support for, LA21 at the central level, probably facilitated the development of a coordinating structure such as this. In addition, it seems that the international and European context has played an important, indirect role in stimulating its promotion, since it was during the Euro-Mediterranean conference on sustainable cities and towns held in Seville, in January 1999, that Italian participants recognised the need for a structure of this nature in Italy and thus began to mobilise themselves. This was further aided by the intent expressed by the Italian local and regional authorities involved in LA21 to present a unitary, integrated and coordinated contribution of Italian LA21 initiatives to the international networks (such as ICLEI, WHO, EUROCITIES, UTO and FMCU) and to the third conference on sustainable cities and towns, in Hanover in 2000.

In 1999 a meeting in Modena, which was aimed principally at the presentation of the Modena provincial–municipal LA21 guidelines for an action plan, was consequently exploited as an opportunity for the Italian LA21 initiatives to exchange experiences and to discuss the creation of a coordinating group.[19] A second meeting, held in Ferrara, formalised the establishment of the network through the approval of the Ferrara Charter, which was signed by 45 local or regional authorities involved or at least interested in LA21. The Charter defines the objectives of the network, which is basically addressed to the promotion of LA21 and of partnerships among local governments, the monitoring of its development, the stimulation of pertinent research and the exchange and dissemination of information. It furthermore establishes three internal working groups aimed at studying the relation between LA21 and other planning instruments; participation, management of the forum and definition of partnerships; and sustainability indicators. The LA21 coordination network initiative was awarded the 1999 'ENEA-sustainable development prize'. In January 2000 there were 119 members in the network.

Even if the activity of the Italian LA21 coordination network is in an early phase, it is likely that some of its objectives and consequent actions will be integrated with those of other bodies involved in LA21 issues, such as ENEA, the MoE or ANPA. It appears that ANPA, in particular, has been able to establish a good relationship with this newly developed network (Cantoni and Colagrossi, 1999), as indicated by its willingness to provide funding to some of the network activities (Avanzi, 1999). ANPA has also offered its technical support to the LA21 coordination network and will integrate some of the above-described activities in its projects. The Minister of the Environment met with the network in 1999 to ask it to play the role of collaborator and spokesman with participants at the local level in supporting the Ministry's policies concerning sustainability. The Minister also made a commitment to maintaining a permanent, open channel for consultation with the coordination network for various initiatives, including the national plan for sustainable development. At the same time, a twinning scheme, aimed at the transfer of sustainability-related experience between administrations in the north and the south of Italy was proposed (ag21L Italia, 1999).

It is still too early to judge the benefits deriving from this recent more cohesive approach to developing LA21 practice in Italy, and there are still organisational hurdles to overcome, such as the lack of a single official point of reference.

Some of the Italian LA21 experiences also feature partnerships that have played a significant role in the implementation process – the LA21 initiative resulting from the joining of forces on the part of the Modena provincial and municipal authorities is an example. Partnerships have also been developed in the form of coordinating bodies composed of members from different levels of government (regions, provinces and municipalities), as well as NGOs and the regional environmental protection agencies, for example in the Tuscany and Liguria regions.

Modena provincial authority signed the Aalborg Charter in 1996 and later, in 1997, the Lisbon action plan. In the same year, the Modena municipal authority signed the Aalborg Charter. In July 1997, the province made a formal commitment, passed by the council, to set up the forum for environment and sustainable development jointly with the municipality, which actually began in November of the same year. The LA21 forum was instituted and managed through the cooperation of the provincial and the municipal authorities. This is said to be due to the expected benefits created by greater combined human and financial resources, as well as because some of the environmental issues considered (such as water) must be managed at an inter-municipal level (Remitti, 1999). It is also likely that the long-standing cooperation between these two authorities (Lewanski, 1986) is another factor that has facilitated the joining of forces in the preparation and the implementation of the LA21 initiative.

During the course of the year in which the forum was held, there was a notable improvement in the understanding of LA21 and sustainable development. Subsequently, the work of four working groups was discussed in a plenary forum in January 1999 and formally concluded with the approval of the document *Guidelines for the Local Agenda 21 Action Plan* (Provincia di Modena, 1999).

The municipality of Modena intends to promote its own forum, which will follow on directly from the one generated in the previous provincial-municipal forum, and will focus on the implementation of the actions identified during 1998 and reported in the *Guidelines for the Local Agenda 21 Action Plan*. The province plans to follow up the forum and develop the contents of the guidelines by integrating suitable actions into the provincial departments' policies and projects, thus forming the operational LA21 action plan (Remitti and Nora, 1999).

The Modena province-municipality LA21 is regularly referred to as a model example, and presents a number of interesting features: the cooperative manner in which the province and municipality have approached LA21 and the emphasis on participation and communication. Furthermore, the Modena LA21 process seems to have stimulated LA21 initiatives in other municipalities within the province, such as those under development in the towns of Sassuolo and Carpi.

LA21 in Italy: What can we learn?

Before delineating the lessons that can be learned from the Italian case, it is worth making a snapshot characterisation of the LA21 implementation process in this country.

LA21 in Italy is superficial and weak. To date, little has occurred in terms of active implementation. No visible activities have been carried out at the national level until recently, and the number of local and regional administrations involved in LA21 initiatives is still limited. The geographical distribution of LA21 processes to date clearly follows the pattern that distinguishes north from south. In 1999, 70 per cent of LA21 processes in Italy were to be found in the north. This is not surprising if one considers that the performance of local administrations in the southern part of the country is, generally speaking, much more limited compared to the rest of Italy, and even more so in regard to policy actions related to the protection of the environment.

Implementation and coordination have emerged at the local level rather than being directed or fostered by the central state. LA21 initiatives have occurred spontaneously and autonomously at the local, and, to a lesser extent, at the regional level.

Compared to both the original timetable indicated by Chapter 28 of Agenda 21 and other more advanced European countries, the progress of Italian LA21 activities is running late. Its evolution has been fragmented and an integrated and cooperative LA21 network has been lacking until recently. Because of the less-developed environmental policy in Italy and the lack of resources, cooperation among different levels of government and other participants is an important condition for LA21 implementation. Though policy networks exist between some regions, provinces and municipalities and have contributed to positive developments, they are too small, too isolated and lack the resources necessary for fully developing their potential. The Italian LA21 coordination network, which includes the majority of local and regional authorities involved in LA21, may be able to overcome these problems.

LA21 has recently gained momentum at different levels of government. At the local level there is diffusion of LA21 initiatives, the creation of the coordination network, and the promotion of LA21 initiatives carried out by some provinces. Regionally there is the coordination and promotion of LA21 initiatives promoted by some regions; and nationally there is the institution of the prize for sustainable cities, the updating of the old national plan for sustainable development, the development of LA21 pilot initiatives in medium-sized cities, and ANPA and ENEA initiatives. These different LA21-related initiatives have contributed to determining a more fluid and dynamic situation in which their multiplication represents an important sign of positive change.

The Italian LA21 implementation model differs from that of many in northern Europe due to the fact it is characterised by the evolution of two parallel processes that have only recently started to converge. LA21 initiatives began in an isolated and autonomous manner, in a context of central LA21-related activity, which remained largely unperceived by those at the local level. In response to the question in the 1999 survey regarding the greatest difficulties encountered by the administrations in implementing an Agenda 21 process, the reply included, time and again, the lack of experience and technical know-how,[20] the lack of financial resources, and the lack of information. It is, therefore, not surprising that efforts were made along the local LA21 pathway to address these problems through the formation of partnerships and the participation in international and national networks.

Furthermore, in a number of cases, relationships between different levels of government are aimed at coordinating and promoting LA21 in order to address efficiency, and problems of information and organisation.

Regions and provinces that have chosen this strategy are characterised by a relatively higher presence of LA21 activity, although other factors may have played a role.

In this context, the fact that LA21 initiatives have slowly reached a critical mass at which they have been able to transform and organise themselves into an autonomous coordinating structure, namely the Italian LA21 coordination network, represents the most relevant event. Due to the inherently local nature of LA21, it could be argued that this coordination has developed as a reflection of the basic ethos. The creation of the Italian LA21 coordination network, and the activities promoted by and through it, can clearly be expected to have broader implications for the further diffusion and effectiveness of LA21 implementation in central and southern Italy.

The current picture indicates that the increased interest in sustainable development and LA21 at the central level of government can be greatly facilitated by the presence of this structure. The central level may gain in that it does not need to establish communication channels with each of the involved or potential administrations, but can instead take advantage of the existing communication channels within the network and the role of spokesman provided by it. The relationship between the two levels can be seen as a symbiotic one. In fact, the very nature of some of the recent plans and projects that are unfolding at the central level – such as an LA21 manual, seminars, financial support, prizes and a set of urban sustainability indicators – gives no indication of intentions to wrest control of LA21 activities from the coordination network, but rather, to 'leave well enough alone' and provide some of the much-needed support and implementation tools.

NOTES

1 The information needed for this chapter has been collected from different sources: surveys on LA21 initiatives in 1998 (WWF-Italy and Avanzi) and 1999 (Avanzi); personal interviews with representatives of the main institutions involved in the LA21 implementation process; analysis of case studies and official documents. The authors would like to thank W Sancassiani (Avanzi, Milan) and E Maini (DOSP, University of Bologna) for their help in collecting data and information on Italian LA21 initiatives and in analysing some of the 'best cases' discussed in this chapter. Special thanks also go to M Berrini (Ambiente Italia, Milan), B Dente (IRS, Milan), A Liberatore (Research Directorate-General, European Commission) and P Remitti (Municipality of Modena) for their useful comments on a previous version of this chapter.
2 L. 349/1986.
3 The second report also refers to the upcoming Earth Summit, but does not discuss Italy's positions on the topics in any detail, though references to topics such as climate change and biodiversity are made in other sections of the reports.
4 Delib CIPE 28.10.1993. The Convention on climate change was ratified by L 65/1994 and that on biodiversity by L. 124/1994.
5 Ambiente Italia is a research institute working closely with the environmental association Legambiente.
6 Which was foreseen by Art 2 of L. 662/1996.
7 DM 28.05.1998. The programme was partly modified by DM 26.11.1998; DM 23.9.1998 instituted the committee for the supervision of the programme for the protection of the environment.
8 ENEA and MoE officially signed a programme agreement, which defines the role of technical support of ENEA in relation to many of the projects defined by the programme for the protection of the environment, on 28 November 1998. The updating of the national plan for sustainable development is included in these projects.
9 This commission substitutes the obsolete coordinating committee established in 1993. CIPE has recently gone through a reorganisation of its structures and various commissions have been created within this body.
10 DM 3.08.98.
11 Dlgs 36/1999.
12 The National Association of Italian Municipalities.
13 Italy is divided into 20 regions: 15 ordinary and 5 with a special status. Each region is composed of provinces that represent a lower level of territorial governance. The total number of Italian provinces is 104. Each province is divided into municipalities. The total number of Italian municipalities is about 8100.
14 See, for example, the Act on local autonomy no 142/1990 and the so-called Bassanini Decrees: L 59/1997, L 127/1997 and Dlgs 112/1998.

15 For example, WWF organised the European conference *Agenda 21 Locale, La Partecipazione dei Cittadini nei Progetti di Sostenibilità* with the Municipality of Bologna in 1998.
16 It should be noted that Trento, together with Bolzano, has been granted special powers stronger than those of most regions, due to the special ethnic-linguistic context of the Trentino-Alto Adige Region (formed by the two special provinces). Thus, for all practical purposes these two provinces should be considered as regions rather than as normal provinces.
17 These numbers refer to those administrations that have actually started an LA21 process and thus also include those that have not signed the Aalborg Charter. It should be noted that the analysis of the data collected through the 1999 survey has only considered the regional and local administrations that signed the Aalborg Charter by May 1999, also including those that have not yet got off the ground.
18 The next survey on LA21 implementation was due to appear between June and September 2000.
19 It can been seen in the 1999 survey data (Avanzi, 1999) that public administrations with LA21s have been previously involved in informal exchange of information.
20 Thirty-nine per cent of administrations involved in LA21 have had to resort to external personnel in the management of the process (Avanzi, 1999).
21 'L' refers to act, 'DM' to ministerial decree, 'Dlgs' to legislative decree and 'Delib' to resolution.

References

ag21L Italia (1999) *Newsletter 2, La Campagna Europea per le Città Sostenibili in Italia*, October 1999, Ambiente Italia, Milan, Italy

Ambiente Italia and Provincia di Torino (1999) *Agenda XXI, Proposta di Piano d'Azione per la Sostenibilità Ambientale della Provincia di Torino*, March 1999, Torino

ANCI (Associazione Nazionale Comuni Italiani), CISPEL (Confederazione Italiana Servizi Pubblici Enti Locali) and Legambiente (1996) *Carta delle Città*, Italy

ANPA (Agenzia Nazionale per la Protezione dell'Ambiente) (1999) *Documenti e Presentazioni, Seminario di Confronto e Formazione sulle Agende 21 Locali per il Sistema Nazionale delle Agenzie per la Protezione dell'Ambiente*, 1–2 March and 11–12 March 1999, Roma, Italy

ANPA and Ambiente Italia (2000) *Linee Guida per la Realizzazione di Agende 21 Locali in Italia,* in print

Avanzi (1999) *Agenda 21 Locale in Italia, 1999, 2a Indagine sullo Stato di Attuazione – Campagna Europea Città Sostenibili,* Milano, Italy

Berrini, M (1999) *L'Italia a Confronto con le Iniziative Internazionali ed Europee su Ambiente Urbano, Sostenibilità Locale, Agende 21 Locali,* Contribution elaborated for the ENEA and MoE by Istituto Ambiente Italia

De Leonardis, D (1999) *Proposta di Piano d'Azione per la Sostenibilità Ambientale della Provincia di Torino,* paper presented at the conference Agenda XXI della Regione Liguria: Ambiente e Sviluppo Sostenibile, 13–15 October 1999, Genoa, Italy

Del Lungo, C (1999) *Esempi Italiani: Regione Toscana – PRS 1998–2000*, paper presented at the conference 'Agenda XXI della Regione Liguria: Ambiente e Sviluppo Sostenibile', 13–15 October 1999, Genoa, Italy

ESCTC (European Sustainable Cities and Towns Campaign) (1994) *Charter of European Cities and Towns Towards Sustainability*, Aalborg, Denmark

Lewanski, R (1986) 'Il Controllo degli Inquinanti delle Acque: L'attuazione di un apolitica pubblica', *Quaderni ISAP Saggi*, Giuffrè, Milan, Italy

Ministero dell'Ambiente (1989) *Relazione sullo Stato dell'Ambiente*, Istituto poligrafico e Zecca dello Stato, Rome, Italy

Ministero dell'Ambiente (1992) *Relazione sullo Stato dell'Ambiente*, Istituto poligrafico e Zecca dello Stato, Rome, Italy

Ministero dell'Ambiente (1998) *La Guida alle Città Sostenibili delle Bambine e dei Bambini*, Ministero dell'Ambiente, Rome, Italy

Provincia di Modena (1999) *Forum per l'Ambiente e lo Sviluppo Sostenibile di Modena, Piano d'Azione d'Indirizzo Agenda 21 Locale*, Centro Stampa, Modena, Italy

Ramieri, E and Fiorentini, F (1999) 'The Evolution of LA21: Obstacles, deficiencies and positive signs' in Lafferty, W M (ed) *Implementing Local Agenda 21 in Europe: New Initiatives for Sustainable Communities*, Grafmont, Oslo, Norway, pp219–239

Regione Toscana, Gruppo di Lavoro Sviluppo Sostenibile (1998) *Documento Conclusivo*, a cura dell'area extradipartimentale 'Sviluppo sostenibile e controllo ecologico', presented at 'Terza Conferenza sullo Stato Dell'ambiente in Toscana', 11–12 June 1998, Florence, Italy

Remitti, P and Nora, E (1999) *Esempi Italiani: Un Premio Europeo per Modena*, paper presented at the conference 'Agenda XXI della Regione Liguria: Ambiente e Sviluppo Sostenibile', 13–15 October 1999, Genoa, Italy

Sancasssiani, W (1999) *Lo Stato di Attuazione di Agenda 21 Locale in Italia, Risultati della Seconda Indagine Nazionale*, paper presented at the conference 'Agenda XXI della Regione Liguria: Ambiente e Sviluppo Sostenibile', 13–15 October 1999, Genoa, Italy

WCED (World Commission on Environment and Development) (1987) *Our Common Future*, Oxford University Press, Oxford, UK

WWF-Italy and Avanzi (1998) *Agenda 21 Locale in Italia. Indagine sullo Stato di Attuazione, Sintesi*, paper presented at the European Conference 'Agenda 21 Locale, La Partecipazione dei Cittadini nei Progetti di Sostenibilità', 13–14 February 1998, Bologna, Italy

INTERVIEWS

Cantoni, S and Colagrossi, M (1999) ANPA national environmental agency

Marzi, C (1999) ENEA national body for new technologies, the environment and energy

Mugelli, M (1999) Tuscany Regional Authority, extra-departmental area on sustainable development and environmental control

Remitti, P (1999) Municipality of Modena

Soprano, P (1999) Italian Ministry of the Environment, EIA department

LAWS REFERRED TO[21]

L 8.07.1986, n349: Istituzione del Ministero dell'Ambiente e norme in materia di danno ambientale. *Gazzetta Ufficiale Serie gen– n162 del 15.07.1986*

L 28.08.1989, n305: Programmazione triennale per la tutela dell'ambiente. *Gazzetta Ufficiale Serie gen – n205 del 2.09.1989*

L 8.06.1990, n142: Ordinamento delle autonomie locali. *Suppl ord alla Gazzetta Ufficiale Serie gen – n135 del 12.05.1990*

Delib CIPE 28.12.1993: Approvazione del Piano Nazionale per lo sviluppo sostenibile in attuazione dell'Agenda XXI. *Suppl ord alla Gazzetta Ufficiale Serie gen n47 del 26.02.1994*

L 15.01.1994, n65: Ratifica ed esecuzione della Convenzione quadro delle Nazioni Unite sui cambiamenti climatici, con allegati, fatta a New York il 9.05.1992. *Suppl ord alla Gazzetta Ufficiale Serie gen – n 23 del 29.01.1994*

L 14.02.1994, n124: Ratifica ed esecuzione della convenzione sulla biodiversità, con annessi, fatta a Rio de Janeiro il 5.06.1992. *Suppl ord alla Gazzetta Ufficiale Serie gen – n44 del 23.02.1994*

L 23.12.1996, n662: Misure di razionalizzazione della finanza pubblica. *Suppl ord alla Gazzetta Ufficiale Serie gen – n303 del 28.12.1996*

L 15.03.1997, n59: Delega al Governo per il conferimento di funzioni e compiti alle regioni ed enti locali, per la riforma della Pubblica Amministrazione e per la semplificazione amministrativa. *Gazzetta Ufficiale Serie gen – n63 del 17.03.1997*

L 15.05.1997, n127: Misure urgenti per lo snellimento dell'attività amministrativa e dei procedimenti di decisione e di controllo. *Suppl ord alla Gazzetta Ufficiale Serie gen – n113 del 17.05.1997*

L 8.10.1997, n344: Disposizione per lo sviluppo e la qualificazione degli interventi e dell'occupazione in campo ambientale. *Gazzetta Ufficiale Serie gen – n239 del 13.10.1997*

Dlgs 31.03.1998, n112: Conferimento di funzioni e compiti amministrativi dello Stato alle regioni e agli enti locali, in attuazione del capo I della legge 15 marzo 1997, n59. *Suppl ord alla Gazzetta Ufficiale Serie gen – n92 del 21.04.1998*

DM 28.05.1998. *DM GAB/DEC/780/98*

DM 3.08.1998: Istituzione del riconoscimento 'Città sostenibile delle bambine e dei bambini' da assegnarsi a comuni italiani. *Gazzetta Ufficiale Serie gen – n213 del 12-09-1998*

DM 23.09.1998. *DM GAB/DEC/831/98*

DM 26.11.1998 *DM GAB/DEC/844/98*

Dlgs 30.01.1999, n36: Riordino dell'Ente per le nuove tecnologie, l'energia e l'ambiente – ENREA a norma degli articoli 11, comma 1, e 18, comma 1, della legge 15 marzo 1997, n59 *Gazzetta Ufficiale Serie gen – n46 del 25.02.1999*

11. Spain
LA21: A question of institutional leadership?

Nuria Font, Francesca Gomila and Joan Subirats

INTRODUCTION

The 1992 Earth Summit, through the Agenda 21 document, encouraged governments to take actions towards sustainability. More specifically, in its Chapter 28, it encouraged local governments to adopt an LA21, which requires them to cooperate with social groups in order to design strategies for sustainable development. While most of the governments represented at the Summit broadly agreed upon these principles, the conversion of sustainability rhetoric into substantial praxis raises a number of difficulties in countries like Spain: a relatively low level of development of environmental policies; weak traditions of public participation and consultation among local communities and target groups; and a relatively limited handling capacity for local authorities. These factors place a number of difficulties in the way of adopting sustainable strategies at the local level of governance. Environmental protection is not high on the political agenda, and therefore confronts obstacles for penetrating other policy areas; most policy initiatives are top-down oriented and there is little room for community-based initiatives; and local authorities are too dependent on resources coming from regional and national administrations.

While these structural factors do not constitute optimal conditions for the adoption of LA21, a number of related initiatives have taken place over the last few years. This chapter aims at both analysing the type and depth of responses to LA21 and exploring the factors accounting for successful stories. The main argument is that the exchange of informational resources and, above all, the presence of institutional leaders broadly account for the adoption of LA21 in many towns and cities in Spain (Font and Subirats, 2000). This chapter is divided into four sections. The first section provides a general profile of LA21; the second broadly analyses the main trends characterising the policy, the process and the product of LA21;[1] the third explores the validity of two of the main factors accounting for the adoption of LA21, namely, the exchange of cognitive resources and the presence of institutional leadership; and the fourth, focusing on three outstanding examples of LA21 in Spain, highlights some of the positive and negative lessons emerging from the process.

LA21 IN SPAIN: A GENERAL PROFILE

The development of LA21 in Spain is at an emerging stage and only a few municipalities have adopted initiatives to promote sustainable development. There are at least three structural factors that account for this situation. First, Spanish environmental policy is comparatively less developed than that in other Western European countries (see Hanf and Jansen, 1998; Aguilar et al, 1999). While some countries adopted environmental initiatives at the end of the 1970s, Spanish environmental policy was included in the political agenda only recently in the 1990s, both in terms of the design of policy instruments and the allocation of financial resources. Second, the decentralisation process that has been implemented throughout the 1980s and 1990s, following the constitutional mandate, has clearly favoured regional governments both in terms of distribution of powers and resources. Compared to the regional level, municipalities are said to be the 'losers' in the process and have become dependent on national and regional administrations in obtaining resources and the adoption of sectoral policies.[2] And finally, since the celebration of the first democratic municipal elections in 1979, local governments have basically given priority to the adoption of social and urban policies while, in general terms, the issues of environmental protection, sustainability and public participation have only recently been included on the political agenda. Only a few municipalities, mostly those with large urban concentrations, have created effective instruments of public participation, and just a handful of local authorities have taken the first steps to adopt the model of sustainable city (see Font et al, 1999).

Within this general framework, responses to LA21 have been uneven among national, regional, provincial[3] and municipal administrations. National administration support to LA21 has been almost non-existent. The implicit argument held by the national authorities is that environmental protection policy is decentralised, and LA21 does not constitutionally fall under national but rather regional and local domains. The response of regional administration to LA21 has been uneven among the 17 Autonomous Communities: some of them – the Basque Country, Catalonia and Valencia, among others – have given technical or financial support to local administrations in order to allow them to take the first steps in the adoption of LA21, although most regional governments have not been involved at all. A few provinces have played an important role by promoting and supporting LA21 initiatives: Barcelona, Cordoba and

Soria being among the more outstanding cases. Finally, the wide range of municipalities in Spain (a total of 8000, among which 5000 have a population of less than 1000 inhabitants) leads to dramatically different types of responses at this level of government. Most large municipalities have taken some LA21-related actions and a proportionally lesser number of small- and medium-size municipalities have launched this initiative.

To sum up, national and regional support for LA21 has been minimal, with the vast majority of related initiatives emerging at the local and provincial levels of government. Thus far, approximately 100 municipalities have adopted some measures connected to LA21. The next section will look at the general trends characterising these processes.

POLICY, PROCESS AND PRODUCT

Given the large diversity of municipalities in Spain in terms of population, the analysis of LA21 initiatives distinguishes between large municipalities (those having a population of over 80,000 inhabitants) and small- to medium-size municipalities (those having a population of under 80,000 inhabitants). Regarding the larger municipalities, the number of LA21 processes initiated has dramatically increased in a very short period of time. Taking 1998 and 1999 as the years of reference, data show that the evolution of rates for municipalities ignoring LA21 – those acknowledging it, but not having taken action, and those having initiated some related actions – offers a very positive balance in favour of LA21.

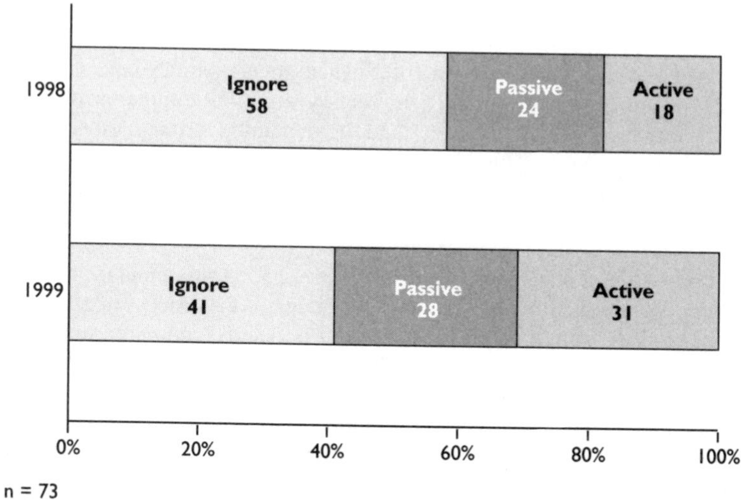

Figure 11.1 *Large municipalities involved in LA21, 1998–99*

As shown in Figure 11.1, in 1998 only 18 per cent of large municipalities had adopted any of the LA21-related initiatives – such as the signature of the Aalborg Charter, performance of a status assessment or the creation of consultation structures. In contrast, only one year later, this rate rose to 31 per cent. In addition, while the rate of municipalities that ignored LA21 in 1998 was unexpectedly high, representing 58 per cent, this rate decreased to 41 per cent only one year later. As shown in Figure 11.1, the percentage figure of large towns and cities moving towards LA21 dramatically increased in a short period of time. In contrast to large municipalities, the number of small- and medium-size municipalities having initiated the LA21 process represents a small proportion within this large category, and only about 1 per cent of small- and medium-size towns have initiated actions to adopt LA21.

One could argue that large municipalities play a leading role in the LA21 process in Spain when compared to small- and medium-size municipalities. Two of the reasons accounting for the apparent leading role played by large municipalities are their ability to be connected to national and international networks, on the one hand, and their pre-eminent institutional, socio-economic and strategic role in their respective regional landscapes, on the other. While these two factors may be crucial, the fact that large municipalities represent less than 1 per cent of the total number of municipalities in Spain makes it possible that single additions to LA21 initiatives substantially change the ratio – and the reverse is true for small and medium municipalities, as they represent 99 per cent of the total figure. Therefore, in order to assess LA21 responses in the two categories of municipalities, looking at positive LA21 processes rather than considering rates of the totals for each category will help to give a more accurate overview of LA21.

As mentioned above, about 100 Spanish municipalities have adopted some type of initiative on LA21 in recent years. About a quarter of them correspond to large municipalities and the remaining three-quarters correspond to small and medium municipalities. Furthermore, LA21 processes in small and medium municipalities are in a more advanced stage than those in large municipalities regarding the adoption of an action plan and the implementation of measures included in it. As Figure 11.2 shows, 15 per cent of small and medium municipalities had at this juncture already elaborated a pre-action plan and 44 per cent are in the process of adopting an action plan (which makes a total of 59 per cent), compared to the 11 per cent and 28 per cent, respectively, in the case of large municipalities (which makes a total of 39 per cent). In addition, all small and medium municipalities had considered the adoption of an action plan, while 6 per cent of large municipalities had not. A similar trend is found when analysing the extent to which municipalities have implemented any of the measures contained in the action plan. In this respect, 21 per cent of small and medium municipalities had not yet carried out any of the initiatives,

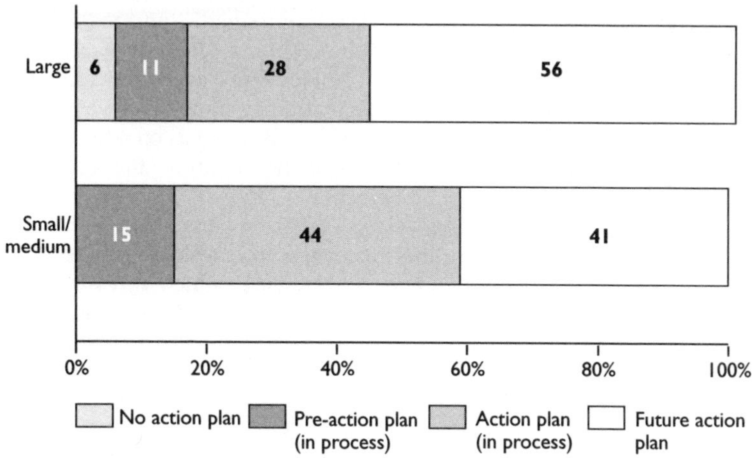

n = 64 (46 large, 18 small and medium); missing = 1

Figure 11.2 *Stage of adoption of the action plan, early 2000*

whereas 43 per cent of large municipalities had not done so (see Figure 11.3). This means that 79 per cent of small and medium municipalities have already implemented actions in some areas (for instance, environmental protection, urban and territorial planning, economic development and social affairs) or in all the areas included in the action plan, while only 57 per cent of the large municipalities have done so.

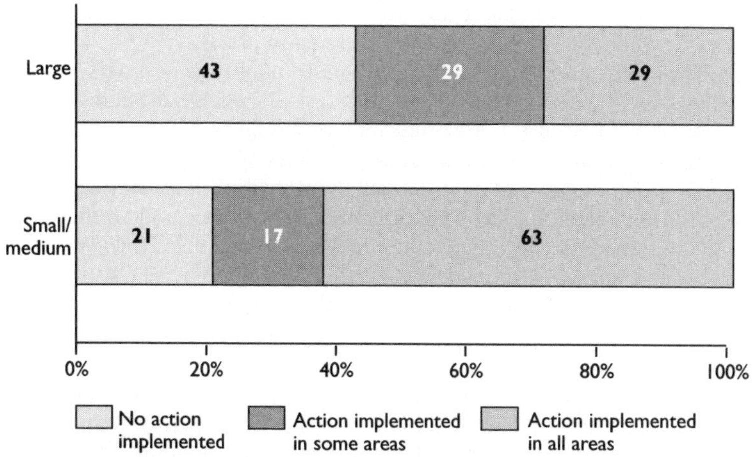

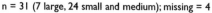

n = 31 (7 large, 24 small and medium); missing = 4

Figure 11.3 *Implementation of actions, early 2000*

Beyond these differences between large and small- and medium-size municipalities, identifying trends characterising LA21 process in all municipalities becomes an extremely complex task, given the wide diversity of experiences in terms of type, intensity and effective impact. However, some general trends can be traced and we focus on three components of LA21: the initial assessment of the situation, the system of indicators adopted, and public participation.

An initial assessment usually constitutes the first step taken in the LA21 process. In this respect, there are important cross-municipal differences regarding three considerations: the extent to which the process has been conducted following external criteria; the substantive contents of the assessment itself; and the use of the assessment within the LA21 process. Regarding the first consideration, the assessment is conducted in some cases by external audit-consultancy teams; in others by council experts in collaboration with social groups and external experts; and in a few cases only by internal experts. Regarding the second consideration, the assessment commonly deals with environmental aspects instead of sustainability in general. Regarding the third consideration, only 8 per cent of municipalities have planned to use the assessment to modify their urban, territorial or strategic plans, and 4 per cent will use it to modify sectoral plans. Again, the performance of small and medium municipalities on this issue is better than that of the larger ones.

In addition to the assessments, important cross-municipal variations are also identified when looking at the systems of indicators; not only in terms of the number of municipalities that have reached this stage of the process but, more importantly, in terms of the general import of the process. For most municipalities, the adoption of a system of environmental and sustainable indicators represents a necessary step in the LA21 process, while for some it constitutes an end in itself.

The main challenge seems to be the adoption of cross-sectoral policies. As Figure 11.4 shows, while a low percentage of municipalities (12 per cent) had at this juncture included indicators in the four local policy areas considered to be traditional (economic promotion, social affairs, urban policy and environmental protection), this rate reached 72 per cent in the action plan. This figure could be considered an indication of the increasingly integrated nature of LA21 initiatives. However, when those departments responsible for the adoption of LA21 were asked whether the other departments acknowledged the LA21 initiative, 50 per cent of them answered that they did not and 9 per cent ignored the question altogether (n = 65).

While local responses to the initiative vary significantly in terms of process, type and intensity, it could be argued that LA21 in Spain has stimulated social participation. There are two considerations that support this hypothesis. Most municipalities have created or reinforced pre-existing instruments of social participation. In other words, LA21 has activated

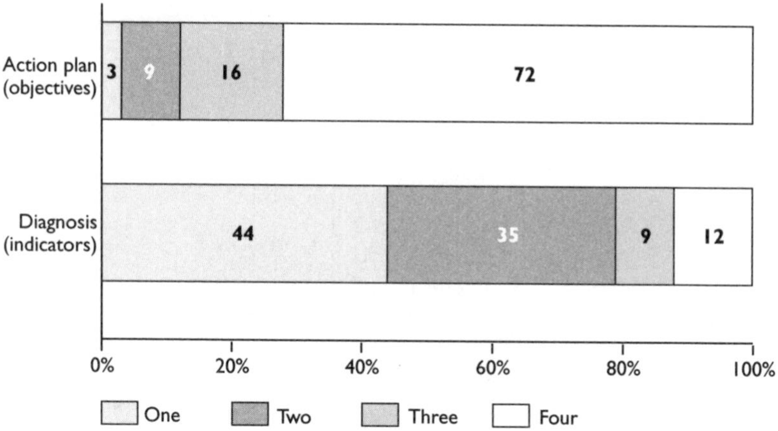

n (diagnosis) = 46, missing = 19; n (action plan) = 32, missing = 33

Figure 11.4 *Number of areas with indicators and objectives, early 2000*

participation at the local level of governance, and this is recognised by many local authorities. Thus, new forms and intensities of participatory structures connected to the goal of sustainable development have been set in motion over the last few years. Moreover, there are some signs of an emerging participatory culture at the local level, which, in some cases, might be partially due to the introduction of LA21. As a result of this initiative, some local authorities have conducted LA21 processes in cooperation with groups of external experts in the assessment stage; other local governments have created forums that gather many of the local social groups to discuss the technical documents and issues of interest; and many local administrations have surveyed the population in order to find out their opinions and perceived necessities.

Figure 11.5 shows the number of municipalities having promoted or planned to promote participation through the several phases of LA21 at the time of the survey. In general terms, the rate of participation in the LA21 process is relatively high. Around two-thirds of the municipalities have participated in assessments, the elaboration of the action plan and the follow-up and monitoring of the plan. In addition, around half of these municipalities have also participated in the establishment of the priorities, the definition of the system of indicators, and the elaboration and execution of the action plan. Therefore, groups and citizens are not equally present in all stages of LA21 in all municipalities, and their participation is higher in the assessment, the elaboration of the action plan and the monitoring phase. Apart from that, the rate of municipalities having no instruments of participation in the LA21 process is very low and represents just 5 per cent.

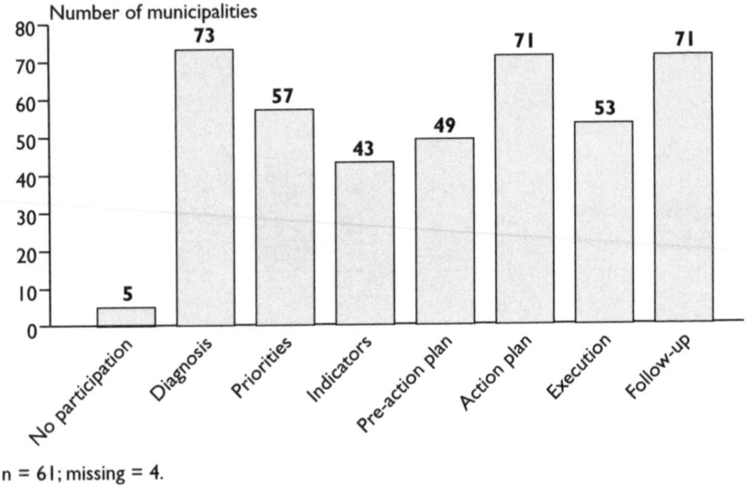

Figure 11.5 *Participation in LA21 stages, early 2000*

While there are different forms of public participation in the LA21 framework, a top-down approach seems to be the common denominator in most cases. Municipal administrations have adopted some instruments to involve the social base, but in general terms these instruments leave little room for key groups and the general public in the design of local strategies for sustainability. Furthermore, in many cases, participation has been limited to those organisations that have explicitly been invited by the municipal administration to do so, leaving the general public and other small groups outside. In addition, participation has generated discontinuous and uneven feedback between local governments and their communities. Therefore, the extent to which the LA21 processes conducted in Spain have integrated a new dialogue with citizens and social groups into local planning and politics is difficult to assess. As a general trend, LA21 has allowed the general public to have a voice in some local planning processes. The extent to which this voice turns into real input and co-responsibility in the implementation phase emerges as one of the most challenging aspects of LA21 in Spain.

Beyond cross-municipal variations regarding assessments, the system of indicators and public participation, the most outstanding cross-municipal difference probably refers to the actual scope of LA21. A few municipalities have taken first steps towards incorporating the LA21 philosophy – that is, using it as an instrument of strategic planning – while the vast majority of municipalities, probably driven by reasons of feasibility, have adopted isolated environmental issues, or have simply labelled pre-existing environmental policies as LA21.

In this sense, environmental departments within municipal administrations, which are those administrations commonly assuming the responsibility for developing LA21, are faced with the challenge of cooperating with sectoral departments dominating the institutional network and the political agenda.

When globally assessing municipal responses to LA21, one can conclude that municipalities are gradually progressing in the adoption of strategies of sustainability. Some differences between large, and small and medium municipalities can also be identified. The former have more rapidly included the LA21 initiative into their political agendas; but some of the best LA21 experiences are to be found in the category of small and medium municipalities.

The exchange of cognitive resources and institutional leadership

When trying to identify possible reasons for the increasing local responsiveness to LA21 in Spain, two types of factors seem to be particularly relevant: first, the diffusion and exchange of cognitive resources on LA21 processes among local authorities and experts that are shaping an emerging policy community; and second, the institutional leadership by local authorities or other actors involved in the LA21 process. It must be pointed out that support has been given not only by the local authorities directly involved, but also by an intermediate level of government. These two factors will be broadly elaborated by focusing on three of the most outstanding LA21 experiences in Spain.

First, there is the case of about 50 municipalities located in Barcelona Province, most of whose populations are lower than 100,000, which have already begun an LA21 process by following the initiative launched by the provincial administration. Secondly, there is the case of about 20 municipalities located in Soria Province, all of which have a population of less than 4000, and which have taken the first steps towards the adoption of an LA21. These 20 municipalities have followed the model designed by the Fundación Desarrollo y Naturaleza (DEYNA), an NGO founded in 1992 that works for sustainability and has a special focus on rural areas. Finally, there is the case of Calvià, a tourist municipality located on the island of Majorca, having a population of 35,000 inhabitants, which has been particularly proactive in relation to LA21.

The exchange of informational resources between local authorities has proved to be a crucial factor in the deployment of LA21. There are several aspects of the process which are of interest. On the one hand, the exchange of these resources refers to the informational and promotional action carried out by those municipalities that pioneered the adoption of

LA21 initiatives. The promotional roles played by Calvià city council, the Barcelona Province administration and DEYNA are remarkable. These institutions have been relatively successful in promoting their initiatives in inter-municipal forums and through the media, as well as in having these initiatives welcomed by the environmental community (environmental groups and scientific community). On the other hand, multilateral exchange among municipalities and certain institutions concerned with LA21 has been an increasingly outstanding trend by the end of the 1990s. An increasing number of municipalities have taken part in national and international forums, have exchanged experiences in formal and informal settings (such as conferences, courses, bilateral and multilateral contacts), and have promoted their LA21 experiences. In this multilateral exchange, Calvià city council, the Barcelona Province administration and DEYNA have played a prominent role at the local, regional and even international levels. As a result of both diffusion and exchange of information, LA21 has provoked a modest but noticeable mimetic effect among a wide range of municipalities.

This exchange of cognitive resources has thus contributed in promoting the LA21 initiative. However, while this factor has generated a certain climate of opinion among local authorities and has put local sustainability high on the agenda, the most outstanding responses to LA21 have come in those cases where a high institutional leadership has been apparent. This leadership means, in practice, the ability to mobilise resources, to gain political saliency and to search for new policy areas and new ways of gaining legitimacy. In other words, LA21 has generally been promoted in those cases where municipal, supra-municipal or social actors – whether institutional or not – have conceived that the adoption of LA21 could become an opportunity to both redefine the model of local development and gain institutional saliency. Again, Calvià local authority, the Barcelona province administration and DEYNA have all shown high levels of institutional leadership.

The institutional leadership exercised by the Barcelona province and DEYNA indicates that, given the size of Spanish municipalities, the role of an intermediate level of government or NGO is an important factor accounting for the start of a number of LA21 processes. Due to the small size of most Spanish municipalities, many of these units lack the technical skills to both acknowledge and set up an LA21 process. In this context, the role of an intermediate level that fills this gap becomes crucial in order to expand the number of LA21 initiatives and to spread the LA21 process. Together with supra-local initiatives, institutional leadership also emerges within the municipalities themselves. This is clearly the case in Calvià, where the local authority has politically committed to sustainability and LA21. The following section focuses on these initiatives, in particular the Barcelona province initiative, the Calvià process and the DEYNA model.

Barcelona Province and the Network of Sustainable Cities and Towns for Sustainability

The Barcelona province administration is an indirectly elected institution that aims at cooperating with municipalities in the development of their policies. With respect to LA21, this administration has played a leading role in defining policy objectives, the allocation of resources and the design of strategies. Regarding objectives, the provincial administration has put the issue of sustainable development high on the agenda since the 1995 municipal elections. Regarding resources, as a result of the former, this administration has the necessary financial and technical resources available to conduct a planned programme on LA21. Finally, regarding strategies, territorial networking has become central to the LA21 project. The two main instruments designed to promote and implement LA21 include the promotion of the Network of Sustainable Cities and Towns for Sustainability (Xarxa de Ciutats i Pobles cap a la Sostenibilitat, or XCPS) and the adoption of an eco-audit programme.

Regarding the XCPS, in July 1997, 120 municipalities of the Barcelona province created the network through the Manresa declaration. The XCPS is an association of towns and cities; more specifically, a municipal platform for cooperation and exchange between towns and city councils towards sustainability. The Manresa declaration formulates the network commitment, with a main goal to promote sustainable development through the implementation of LA21. The Barcelona province administration plays an active role regarding the XCPS. It promoted its creation, works on its diffusion and informational activity, and provides technical support to the local authorities willing to initiate an LA21. To date, the total number of members has risen to approximately 150 municipalities. This figure represents 15 per cent of the total number of Catalan municipalities and 90 per cent of Barcelona province municipalities (Diputació de Barcelona, 1998). The performance of the XCPS is so impressive that some municipalities belonging to the three Catalan provinces other than Barcelona (Girona, Lleida and Tarragona) have applied to become members of the network. The XCPS organisational framework includes an assembly, a monitoring commission, a technical secretariat and four working groups to promote internal debate and discussion. So far, the XCPS, under the auspices of the province administration, has organised two seminars, published a journal and circulated booklets and reports among the member municipalities.

In addition to the promotion of the XCPS, the Barcelona province administration has launched an eco-audit programme to be applied in those municipalities located in the province that are willing to carry out an LA21 process. This institution began playing an active role in LA21 in 1994. Between 1994 and the municipal elections in June 1995, the province administration co-financed and conducted pilot experiments in five municipalities – Igualada, Sant Celoni, Manlleu, Mataro and Viladecans. In 1995, after the municipal elections, the province administration took the political decision of including integrated environmental protection in the agenda. It was the aim of this institution to give priority to municipalities in the development of a strategy towards sustainability. In order to manage the programme, the administration created a separate unit for environmental protection. The main objectives of the programme include the holding of municipal environmental audits; establishing a starting point for the deployment of LA21; the provision of information to the municipalities; the establishment of integrated strategies to further a cross-sectoral approach; a move through local development towards the sustainable use of resources; and the provision to the environmental department of the province administration of assistance to help plan cooperation with municipalities.

The eco-audit process consists of a series of phases. During the preliminary phase, those municipalities interested in adopting the province model take the first steps to formalise their application. Once applicant municipalities have been selected, the LA21 process is segmented into four phases. Phase one deals with local information and data collection and treatment. In phase two, municipalities conduct an assessment and an analysis of the current situation of the city (identification of the main structural elements and environmental vectors), while in phase three an environmental action plan is adopted. During the last phase, a post-audit process is carried out in which a follow-up of both the environmental action and the social participation plans is carried out.

The implementation of this model is impressive: in 1999, 28 of the municipalities concluded the eco-audit; 10 were implementing the process; and 16 had formalised the necessary steps to initiate it immediately (see Figure 11.6). In addition, 25 more had submitted their applications.

The Barcelona province model has rapidly become a common tool available to all municipalities. The administration has redefined its policy objectives since the 1995 municipal elections, and has put LA21 high on the political agenda. LA21 has thus gained considerable political and material support at this institutional level. As a result, the implementation of the eco-audit programme has intensified relations between the province administration and municipalities. Local authorities have been encouraged to adopt LA21 initiatives and have found the necessary financial incentives to start related actions. In this respect, the total expenditure in eco-audit programmes monitored by the Barcelona province administration between 1995 and 1999 rose to 1.8 million euro. This figure has been sufficient to encourage many local governments to start rethinking local policies and planning in a more sustainable fashion. In turn, the province administration can register both substantive and institutional gains. Substantively, it has launched an initiative that has been closely followed

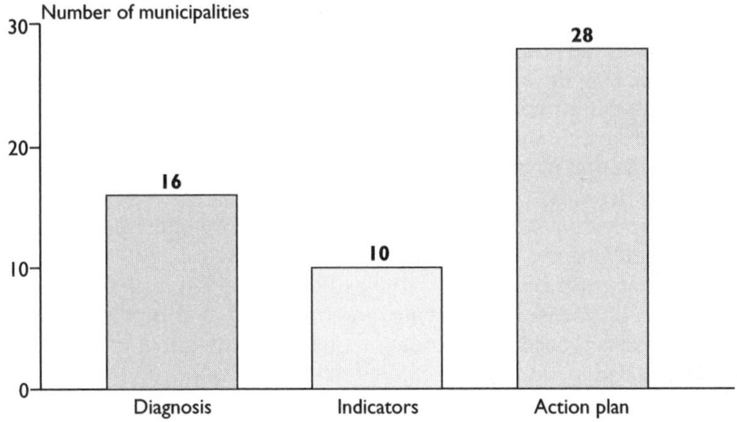

Source: Diputació de Barcelona

Figure 11.6 *Municipalities in Barcelona following the eco-audit model, 1999*

by local authorities. Institutionally, it has successfully demonstrated an otherwise unclear institutional task (since it is an indirectly elected body); it has gained institutional legitimacy among the municipalities in the province and, through its network strategy, it has extended its LA21 leadership beyond its territorial jurisdiction.

The Calvià case

In contrast to the initiative presented above, this section explores the case of Calvià, a small municipality located in the Balearic Islands that initiated an LA21 itself. Calvià is generally acknowledged as the most successful case of LA21 in Spain. The adoption of the LA21 initiative is the result of three factors: first, the increasing perception by the community that Calvià might lose attraction as a tourist centre due to environmental degradation; second, Calvià's status as one of the wealthiest municipalities in Spain, both in terms of GDP per capita and job creation; and third, and most importantly, the personal commitment and leadership of its mayor in the LA21 process. These three factors have been central to the development of LA21 in Calvià.

In order to understand the origins of the Calvià LA21, one must look first at some of the previously related initiatives adopted by the city council. During the 1980s and the beginning of the 1990s, the town council launched a series of programmes designed to both modernise and diversify the tourist industry and to protect the environment. Due to its limited success, at the beginning of 1995, in cooperation with the Ministry of Commerce and Tourism, the town council decided to unify the tasks in hand by freezing the approval of new urban plans and introducing Calvià LA21. With these two initiatives, the local authority aimed at developing a model of sustainable development (the Calvià Local Agenda 21 of 1995). The action plan, entitled *Local Agenda 21: The sustainability of a tourist municipality*, presented in February 1999, is the result of this working process, and its content and mode of action follow precisely the guidelines of Chapter 28 of Agenda 21.

First, the town council tried to play both a facilitating and coordinating role. In this sense, it distributed the first LA21 draft – with a vision, objectives and procedures – among target groups to allow them to give input to the plan. Second, it created several working groups, usually headed by independent experts, who conducted a diagnosis including environmental indicators, citizen assessment and alternative future plans. Finally, the results were presented in citizen forums, with the resulting action plans being voted on in a non-institutionalised referendum. The voting received a massive response, with more than 6000 citizens voting in favour.

In general terms, the LA21 process has encouraged the participation of social groups and citizens. While participation of target groups, experts and citizens is exceptional, local authorities have played a limited facilitating role. This is because the participatory process has been conducted in a relatively top-down perspective. Citizens and organisations who agreed to become members of the forum have participated in the process by, at most, making suggestions to the proposals, studies and campaigns presented to them, but have very rarely contributed to actually designing them.

Secondly, the phases through which an LA21 should be elaborated have been more or less accomplished. First, an initial period of information on the first draft, followed by diffusion and selective consultation, leading to an adaptation of LA21 to the local conditions of a tourist municipality. This work led to the definition of ten priorities or strategic lines, and to the adoption of 40 initiatives that form the action plan. In addition, a large number of evaluation indicators, which are the first step of the 'observatory of sustainability and local quality of life', have been established as implementation criteria.

Thirdly, LA21 aims at being a strategic plan covering all areas. The 40 initiatives mentioned above took aim at becoming the town council's governing programme and are the responsibility of different departments. For every initiative, the person responsible has definined its goals, content, the strategic line to which it belongs, the actors involved and the period of execution. Moreover, the coordination panel, which has the task of disseminating information and takes part in international panels, is directly dependent on the mayor. The mayor, and not the environmental department, has the political responsibility for the LA21. This arrangement reflects both the priority of launching the LA21 process and the aim of approaching sustainability and the LA21 process in a comprehensive and global perspective.

The efforts to involve citizens in the process did not result in a massive response and participation was dominated by representatives of organisations. However, it must be pointed out that some of the environmental organisations, such as Friends of the Earth, have been responsible for the implementation of some programmes (composting and recycling, for example). Apart from that, not all political and economic actors were equally receptive to the invitation to take part. Some politicians perceived LA21 as being a project of the governing party, especially of the mayor, whereas the main opposing party was hardly involved. Regarding the economic actors, those from the real-estate business were not integrated into the process and this circumstance could limit the success of the project. This is especially important in a municipality where town planning and the extensive construction of hotels and apartments have caused severe environmental degradation. In this sense, the community considers the possibility of changing the current tourist model and interrupting the process of intensive construction along the coast as a vital indicator for success of LA21 in Calvià.

The DEYNA model

DEYNA is an NGO founded in 1992 that works for sustainability particularly in rural areas, and has developed a model for developing LA21 in mainly rural municipalities. This model has been implemented in 20 municipalities of the Soria Province, a rural and sparsely populated region located in north-central Spain.

The DEYNA model is based on the assumption that LA21, given its complexity and lack of a specific 'vehicle' for all cases, will only be possible at the administrative and technical level and, therefore, will be deployed by a top-down approach, without reaching lay people or local organisations (DEYNA, 1999). DEYNA assumes the role of filling this gap by editing a guide to inform municipalities about LA21, showing that it can be simple, short, participatory and relatively easily circulated. The methodology it proposes is a process directed by the local council, but with an active participation of social groups. Therefore, a commission formed by local associations was to be created. This commission should meet every three months and exercise a consultative role regarding the LA21 and environmental policy in general. The LA21 document was to consist of a series of objectives to promote social and economic development and welfare of the citizens, and should propose a set of actions and a schedule to reach them.

The result was to be a short document that could be widely circulated and easily understood. The next phase would consist of assigning a budget to the actions, which would come not only from local government but also from citizens, institutions and associations. Providing publicity for the process and drawing up a balance every year was also to be required. Finally, exchange and collaboration with surrounding municipalities was considered a necessary component for the success of the process. This model has been adopted by 20 municipalities in the Soria Province, with populations ranging from 100 to 3600, and in every municipality between 5 and 15 people have participated. These municipalities account for 14 per cent of the inhabitants of the province and 11 per cent of the number of municipalities.

LESSONS FROM THE THREE EXPERIENCES

The Barcelona province initiative, the DEYNA model and the Calvià process are three of the most remarkable cases in the adoption of LA21 in Spain. As mentioned previously, institutional leadership is one of the crucial factors accounting for success. However, the underlying reasons motivating these institutions to promote LA21 are different. The Barcelona province administration aims to gain political saliency and legitimacy through the creation of a new 'policy space' LA21 as a window of opportunity. Calvià city council, on the other hand, aims for both identity-building, by making LA21 an example of good practice, and the redefinition of its tourism industry in strategic terms. Finally, DEYNA aims to become an actor in the policy process by promoting its own LA21 model (see Table 11.1).

What are the positive and negative lessons that can be learnt from these processes? In order to assess them, three considerations are taken into account: institutional leadership, the mobilisation of groups and citizens, and the interpretation of environment versus sustainable development (see Table 11.2).

There are clear differences between Barcelona province, the Sorian municipalities and the Calvià cases regarding institutional leadership. Barcelona is an indirectly elected institution that has no direct powers over local authorities, DEYNA is an NGO and Calvià city council directly controls the process. These distinctions may have both positive and negative impacts, especially in the Barcelona province and Calvià cases. Barcelona province is a meso-level administration and may thus play a neutral role when calling for municipal administrations to engage in its LA21 model. In many local authorities following the Barcelona model, the initiation of the LA21 process has been unanimously approved by all groups represented in the city council. Therefore, in general terms, the degree of political consensus on carrying out an LA21 in those munici-

Table 11.1 *Origin and institutional aim of LA21 initiatives*

	Origin of the initiative	*Institutional aim*
Barcelona Province	Supra-municipal administration Model applied in more than 50 industrial urban municipalities	Gaining political saliency Finding new policy space Gaining legitimacy
Calvià	City council Model applied in a tourist municipality	Identity-building Becoming an LA21 example Redefining the tourism industry in strategic terms Promoting Calvià internationally
DEYNA	NGO (supra-local) Model applied in 20 rural municipalities	Establishing itself as an actor in the process Promoting its LA21 model

palities is commonly high. In addition, as the LA21 process involves both municipal and higher administrations, the potential for exchanging information and mutual learning is very high. At the same time, however, the Barcelona province model presents some inconveniences. Given that the province has no direct control over the way the LA21 process is carried out, especially once the environmental audit has been concluded, the continuity of LA21 and its impact on local planning almost exclusively depends on the continued will of the municipal administration. While it is too early to assess the extent to which these administrations implement action plans, there are some signs that some local authorities have followed the first steps in the adoption of LA21, without, however, having a strong commitment to sustainability.

In contrast to the Barcelona province model, the case of Calvià has the advantage that its mayor is personally committed to LA21, and it is the mayor – and not the environmental department – who directs the process. This circumstance presents the advantage that there is a clear political commitment to LA21. While the personal commitment of the mayor may reinforce the LA21 process, this circumstance may have the inconvenience that it makes LA21 more vulnerable to political changes and politicisation. In fact, some of the opposing political groups on the city council consider LA21 to be too centralised in the hands of the mayor.

The extent to which the involvement of social groups and citizens improves the quality of dialogue between local authorities and their

Table 11.2 *Institutional Role, Environment versus Sustainability and participation*

	Institutional role	*Participation*	*Environment versus sustainability*
Barcelona Province	Neutral No direct control	Promotes its own participatory model (not compulsory) Participatory performance depends on local traditions	Focus on environmental protection More realistic, more feasible Risk of having pre-existing policies relabelled
Calvià	Strong political commitment Vulnerable to political changes	Uneven representation of interests High on environmental aspects; low development aspects	Goal of sustainability Risk of being too ambitious
DEYNA	Indirect control over the process	Relatively small size of the municipalities makes participation easier	Goal of comprehensive approach: socio-economic and welfare issues to be concluded

communities is difficult to assess. In the case of the municipalities that have followed the Barcelona province model, important variations have been identified. In general terms, LA21 has fostered participation. The Barcelona province has designed a participatory methodology that includes consultation and discussion with social groups from the beginning of the process. Once a technical assessment has been conducted, the results are presented and discussed within the 'Commission 21', and then discussed in different open meetings. The guidelines regarding the adoption of the action plan follow a similar rationale. A proposed action plan is presented to the public and, once it is discussed and agreed, is adopted by the city council. The Barcelona province administration recommends municipalities to initiate the eco-audit programme and follow its guidelines, but it cannot compel them to do so. In practice, there are important cross-municipal variations in terms of participatory performance. Some local authorities take all the steps recommended by the province administration, while others limit participation to the disclosure of the proposed action plan. Some city councils organise a number of informative sessions, while others set up a series of follow-up sectoral and thematic hearings. In most cases, these are accompanied by support measures, such as websites, information hot-lines, the distribution of a municipal newsletter, or the use of an opinion survey. In general, a wide range of municipalities recognise that the LA21 initiative has encouraged participation. Beyond these general trends, the extent to which LA21 in the Barcelona province encourages participation of social groups and citizens depends, in many cases, on the previous existence of participatory structures related to environmental policy and, ultimately, on local civic traditions. In those municipalities with stronger participatory traditions, like Mataró and El Prat del Llobregat, the articulation of participation in LA21 has been easier than in others with weaker participatory structures.

Participation in the Calvià case presents its own particular lesson. In general, some attempts to strengthen participation have been carried out. For instance, Friends of the Earth has assumed some responsibilities for the implementation of certain LA21 measures. However, some economic sectors, like the real estate business, have not actively taken part in the LA21 process. As LA21 in Calvià directly relates to the tourism industry, the exclusion of this sector could eventually have negative effects in the entire implementation process. In addition, the small size of the Sorian municipalities makes participation an easy process.

Finally, some slight differences may be found among the Barcelona province, Calvià and the Sorian cases regarding the interpretation of sustainability. Barcelona mostly relates the idea of sustainability to environmental protection. For instance, the assessment of the eco-audit programme refers almost exclusively to environmental issues. In addition, most LA21 processes are managed by the local department of the environment. As a result, many issues dealing, for instance, with immigration or social services are excluded from the LA21 agenda. In Calvià, it seems that some other issues are included in the LA21 process, mostly those related to the tourism industry. LA21 is, moreover, not managed by the environmental department but from the mayoral office itself. While the Calvià model seems more inclusive than that of the Barcelona province, it also involves a risk of being too ambitious if all the target-groups affected do not agree upon a new model of tourism development. In turn, the Barcelona province model, while seeming more feasible than that of Calvià, presents the risk that LA21 simply adds a label to pre-existing environmental policies. Finally, the goal of sustainability in the Sorian municipalities is quite clear and is not unrealistic considering that these are sparsely populated rural areas.

Conclusion

The introduction of LA21 in Spain has considerably increased over the last few years. Large municipalities have proportionally increased their adherence to LA21 to a great extent, although most LA21 initiatives correspond to small and medium municipalities. In addition, the latter are, in general, at a more advanced stage in the LA21 process. While there are deep structural and historical factors that make the adoption of strategies of local sustainability in Spain a difficult task to reach – for instance, late democratisation of the country as a whole; a relatively weak tradition of environmental policy-making; weak participatory traditions and the limited administrative capacity of local governments – there has been some progress regarding LA21. Among the factors accounting for this, two seem to be particularly relevant. On the one hand, the ability of local authorities to exchange cognitive resources and take part in national and international networks; and on the other, the ability of certain actors to become institutional leaders and consider LA21 as an opportunity – rather than a constraint – for achieving institutional saliency and legitimisation. This leading role has, in many cases, been played by intermediate, meso-level actors, for example by a province administration or by an NGO. In addition, these initiatives account for the existence of LA21 islands, for instance in the Barcelona and Soria provinces.

In order to assess LA21 outcomes, two dimensions must be taken into account: firstly, the tension between environmental protection and sustainability, and, secondly, the extent of participation. Regarding the first dimension, LA21 is normally promoted by environmental departments (with some clear exceptions, like Calvià) and this appears to be a constraint to promoting sustainable development due to the often peripheral position of environmental departments in town councils. This makes it difficult for these administrative units to penetrate or ally with other policy departments. Therefore, LA21 tends to be connected with traditional environmental policies rather than with sustainability. In general terms, sustainability does not guide local planning but may reinforce environmental policies.

Regarding participation, the adoption of LA21 has led to the creation of new forms of social participation or the reinforcement of pre-existing ones. The top-down approach to participation, according to which local authorities direct, control and define the type and depth of participation, could be considered a common denominator in most cases. This means that communication between local authorities and the community is often uneven and discontinuous. However, beyond this general trend, differences among both participatory formulae and local government commitment to participation have to be highlighted. In this respect, some municipalities consider that participation has to be a key component in LA21 from the very start of the process, while others adopt forms of consultation that have a marginal impact on the final decisions. In addition to procedures and formulae, the degree of commitment by the local community regarding participation makes the biggest difference among LA21 cases. Some local authorities seem truly committed to the idea of involving citizens and groups, while others seem to conceive participation as simply another formal and procedural LA21 requirement. In general terms, the different degree of commitment to participation in each case probably has its roots in causes other than LA21. Nevertheless, LA21 has contributed to both accelerating and emphasising the idea of social participation in some Spanish municipalities. The conversion of social participation and dynamic feedback into an input for sustainability, however, is difficult to assess, given the emerging nature of most LA21 processes in Spain. However, apart from isolated cases, it seems that LA21 is far from integrating a new dialogue with citizens and social groups into local planning and politics, and this seems to be one of the biggest challenges facing LA21 in Spain.

NOTES

1 The data contained in this chapter come from two sources: two rounds of phone interviews addressed to the largest municipalities (n = 73) in Spain and a questionnaire sent to the most active 100 municipalities in relation to LA21 (n = 65). Data included in Figure 11.1 result from phone interviews with representatives of municipal administrations. Figures are only indicative.

2 In 1980, the share of total public spending among administrations was: 88 per cent central administration and 12 per cent local authority; and in 1998: 61 per cent central administration, 27 per cent regional administration and 13 per cent local authority (INE, 1999).

3 Provinces are indirectly elected administrations and have diffuse powers. Their main task consists of supporting municipalities in the development of policies.

REFERENCES

Ajuntament de Calvià (1995) *Calvià A21L*, Calvià Municipality

Aguilar, S, Font, N and Subirats, J (eds) (1999) *Política Ambiental en España*, Tirant lo Blanch, Valencia

DEYNA (1999) *Modelo DEYNA de Agenda 21 Local*

Diputació de Barcelona (1998) *Environmental Municipal Audits Programme*, Diputació de Barcelona, Barcelona

Font, N and Subirats, J (2000) *Local y Sostenible*, Icaria, Barcelona

Font, N, Gomila, M F and Subirats, J (1999) 'Spain: From promise to reality?' in Lafferty, W (ed) *Implementing LA21 in Europe*, ProSus, Oslo

Hanf, K and Jansen, A-I (eds) (1998) *Governance and Environment in Western Europe*, Longman, Harlow

INE (1999) *España en Cifras*, Instituto Nacional de Estadística, Madrid

12. Conclusions and perspectives

William M Lafferty and Frans Coenen [1]

Having presented the 11 country reports from the SUSCOM project, we now formulate more general conclusions from a comparative perspective. We look first at some of the conceptual insights gained from the network dialogue and approach, and then go on to a summary overview of the implementation results across the 11 domains. This is followed by an update on the explanatory variables covered by the research protocol (see Lafferty, 1999, Chapter 1) along with policy implications from this analysis. Finally we consider some of the more general lessons learned with respect to viewing LA21 as a democratic reform, followed by a concluding word on the relevance of the study to the issue of subsidiarity.

CONCEPTS AND NORMS

LA21 as 'sustainable development'

Eight years after the Earth Summit, opinions vary considerably as to both its significance and the subsequent record of achievement. Was the Earth Summit a major turning point with respect to establishing a global agenda for sustainable development? And, if so, how has this agenda been pursued since? Are there notable signs of progress? Or have the nations of the world simply pursued business as usual within a different rhetorical framework?

From an academic point of view, these questions have become increasingly focused around a debate as to the nature of 'sustainable development' itself. In the immediate aftermath of the launching of the Brundtland Report (WCED,1987), the reaction in academic circles (predominantly British) was largely sceptical. Sustainable development was viewed as simply a veiled declaration for continued economic growth. Lacking what many academics viewed as necessary elements of a more radical political solution, the report became the brunt of widespread criticism. It was viewed more as a result of political expediency than a workable and effective approach to problems of environmental degradation: a technological fix, whereby countries both North and South could continue global competition for ever higher rates of GNP per capita – without serious consequences for the global environment.

Since the Earth Summit such views have attained a certain conceptual coherence within a discourse on 'ecological modernisation'. From several different points of view (Weale, 1992; Jänicke, 1992; Hajer, 1995; Jänicke and Weidner, 1997; Hanf and Jansen, 1998), there has emerged a common perspective which portrays the greening of public policy, business and technology as part of a necessary adaptation of advanced capitalism. An 'ecological' image is, in this view, seen as a functional adjunct of a necessary 'modernisation' of the means of production and distribution. Sustainable development is profiled – most particularly in the works of Hajer (1995) and Hanf and Jansen (1998) – as the most widely popularised version of such modernisation tendencies. Sustainable development is, in other words, ecological modernisation under a different flag, hoisted and saluted by global politicians and bureaucrats committed to continued economic growth and market liberalism, under the guise of environment and development.

The relevance of this particular discourse for the present study of LA21 in Europe is to provide a broad value-based backdrop for our concluding discussion of the implementation record. Given that Agenda 21 (United Nations, 1993) is specifically designed as an action plan for achieving sustainable development; and given further that Chapter 28 of the Agenda is a specific process-oriented admonition to local authorities, we raise the issue as to what a successful implementation implies. We have established within the SUSCOM project clear criteria as to what is to be understood as the key elements of an LA21 (Lafferty and Eckerberg, 1998; Lafferty, 1999). We believe also that these criteria are in line with both the intent of Agenda 21 as adopted at the Earth Summit, and the follow-up activities of interpretation and dissemination carried out by ICLEI and the European Commission (EC) within the European Sustainable Cities and Towns Campaign. The entire point of these criteria has been to stipulate benchmarks so as to be able to differentiate, monitor and assess specific LA21 activities in a European setting. As outlined in the introduction to the present work, these criteria differentiate not only between business as usual and green environmental change, but also between the latter and change for sustainable development.

The significance of this as a backdrop and point of introduction to our conclusions, is that we:

- acknowledge that the intentions of Chapter 28 of the action plan indicate a mode of integrated change – sustainable development – which is more far-reaching and radical than that implied by ecological modernisation;
- try to integrate this understanding into our criteria for empirical documentation (that is, what we in fact select for observation and analysis); but

- realise that definitive assessment is highly complicated due to the simple fact that much of what is *called* 'Local Agenda 21', is in fact traditional environmentalism under the guise of the Earth Summit label.

For many, these differentiations may appear arbitrary and irrelevant: the types of distinctions that academics find interesting, but which practitioners find tedious. Of importance is any change in a positive direction, rather than the name chosen to identify such change.

Indeed, if political programmes were as empirically distinct as roses, and social science as ancient and clever a discipline as botany, we could forgo the point. But neither being the case, we must stress the point since it underlies and colours all of our analytic perspectives. As pointed out in our initial assessment of eight countries (Lafferty and Eckerberg, 1998), national governments have consistently reported implementation results on LA21 which do not reflect the intentions of the Earth Summit and the follow-up by ICLEI.[2]

This raises issues of fundamental importance for democratic governance and legitimacy. If the quality of implementation of global accords is to be left up to the interests and idiosyncrasies of national administrative practice, we will rapidly experience a decline in the trust of and support for international agreements and bodies. Furthermore, we have seen how, within the concerted action itself, discussions as to what is really an instance of LA21 activity could lead to quite different assessments as to what is really happening. The fact that we were able, in the course of the initial year of our project, to achieve a relatively strong degree of consensus as to what we in fact were reporting on, is one of the key value-added results of the research effort.

In short, the point at issue reflects a fundamental problem of combining normative and descriptive categories in an evaluative study. By raising the issue here within the context of a differentiation between sustainable development and ecological modernisation, we want to make the reader aware of the alternative dimensions involved.

PROCESS, PLAN, POLICY OR PRODUCT

In addition to the problems of normative-empirical assessment, there has also emerged within the project an important underlying differentiation as to the stages and degrees of implementation. At the inception of the research network, we had to confront the issue as to whether we were reporting on 'process' or 'policy'. Was it the introduction of new procedures and forms of citizen and stakeholder mobilisation which was the key point of LA21? Or was it the achievement of new and different policies for achieving more fundamental change in the direction of sustainable development?

The debate continued throughout the duration of the project, leading – at an important 'dialogue conference' in Barcelona in November 1999 – to a more nuanced understanding in terms of 'process', 'policy' and 'product'. Further reflection on the issue has, however, led us to add yet another 'P' to the list of benchmarks: 'plan'. The logic behind this differentiation is as follows:

- Chapter 28 of Agenda 21 is by and large directed only towards process. The four key objectives set out in the chapter all involve either specific procedures, coordinating activities or standards of representation (see the introductory chapter here). Further, the most salient and distinctive admonition of the chapter is that local authorities should initiate and engage in a 'consultative process' with their 'local populations' – later specified in terms of both citizens and stakeholders and with a special mention of women and youth. Clearly, on a textual basis alone, the goal is one of a new process for achieving change.
- Chapter 28, however, is only one of 40 chapters in the Earth Summit action plan. LA21 is an integral part of Agenda 21, and the goal of Agenda 21 is to achieve a global partnership for sustainable development. This clearly indicates that the processes in question must be of a type to foster sustainable development, so that processes without new and different results do not alone reflect the intentions of the action plan. Clearly, the output of the process must also be included in the overall assessment.
- Given the fact, however, that change – particularly *substantial* change in the direction of sustainable development – takes time, it was necessary to differentiate further between 'policy' and 'product'. Adopting a specific policy for change within an LA21 framework is an important step in the prescribed direction – but it will usually take considerable time for a policy to produce the intended product in the form of real change. Assessments must be sensitive, therefore, to the prospect that effective change takes time, and that each step in the normal chain of democratic governance must be taken into account.
- Having established the three benchmarks of 'process', 'policy' and 'product', however, it quickly became clear that we should add a fourth 'P' – the adoption of a specific 'plan' within the LA21 context. The need for such an addition emerges in relation to the language of Chapter 28 itself, where a key objective is stipulated as an LA21; that is, a specific and comprehensive agenda for achieving sustainable development within the local community. It is also this goal that has led ICLEI and the European Sustainable Cities and Towns Campaign to stress the idea of a strategic plan within the model framework for action. The introduction of a specific plan raises, however, a slight problem for the logic of assessment. While a new plan clearly can

> emerge from a new process for mobilising citizens and stakeholders, and clearly should emerge as a rational basis for policy and the assessment of product, it is also clear that the threshold for producing and adopting such a plan is much higher than that for initiating individual policies which may have significant impacts for sustainable development, without having first been formulated in an overall plan. LA21-related policies for climate change and biodiversity would be but the most obvious cases in point.

What we are left with, therefore, is a basic evaluation whereby the logic of an idealised implementation sequence must be interpreted and applied without ranking the order of the different steps in the process. We must acknowledge, in other words, that the sequence of process–plan–policy–product is an ideal-type according to rational standards for democratic governance; but that all four 'P's may, in fact, be realisable independent of the other three.[3] Though this may appear as a relatively trivial insight, it is anything but trivial from the point of view of evaluative research and democratic theory – issues we return to below.

OVERALL ACHIEVEMENT: TIMING AND RATES OF IMPLEMENTATION

Any study of implementation is a study of achievement according to some set of pre-determined expectations; and any comparative study of implementation is a study of relative achievement. Analogies with competition and sport are thus inevitable; even if – as in the present case – local authorities in the countries represented are, for the most part, uninterested in LA21 as a competitive enterprise. That there are competitive aspects involved, however, is manifest in two ways: firstly, as an indirect consequence of the reporting obligations of national governments to the UNCSD; and, secondly, as a result of the fact that a number of local authorities have been clearly interested in using the LA21 initiative – both its symbol and relationship to the Earth Summit action plan – as a framework for promoting their own municipality, community or region. National authorities wish, in other words, to put their best foot forward when reporting to UN bodies (or at least not to be seen as laggards), and local authorities wish to be perceived (for a variety of economic and political reasons) as front-running green communities. Having discussed these issues in the research network, we arrived at an approach which was designed to grasp the essence of implementation differentials without giving undue emphasis to the competitive aspect. The results of this approach for the cross-country comparison were published in our 1999 report, which was mainly a descriptive overview of implementation up to that time (Lafferty, 1999). The essence of the comparative assessment was a categorisation of the 12 countries according to the timing and intensity of implementation. Given the fact that the relative placement of the now 11 countries has changed little since our original categorisation, we reproduce the table here (Table 12.1), and confine our comments to a summary overview of the situation.

Table 12.1 shows that Sweden has, from the beginning, been in a category by itself. It shows the earliest start of all countries monitored, and the highest proportion of local government units with LA21 activity.[4] Denmark was clearly slower to initiate activities, but, once the idea took root, moved toward a relatively high level of involvement within a brief period. The UK and The Netherlands also showed early signs of interest in the LA21 idea, but haven't managed the type of breadth visible in Sweden. Finland and Norway took significantly longer to get started, but once the idea took hold, initiatives began to appear across a broad front.

Looking at the trends for these six lead countries, we can discern from the updated country reports that the two most visible countries in the immediate post-Earth Summit phase – Sweden and the UK – have fallen off the pace, while both Finland and The Netherlands remain relatively flat (moving neither significantly upwards nor downwards). Denmark and Norway, on the other hand, have clearly picked up the momentum; in Norway primarily at the level of national support and regional coordination, and in Denmark at both the national and local levels.

At the lower levels of implementation, we find, first, Germany and Austria, both late getting started, but where there are increasing signs of interest and activity (particularly for Austria – data for Germany are only up to 1998)[5]. For the four most 'tardy' members of the sample – Ireland, Spain, Italy and France – we see that all four were still relatively weak in putting the idea into practice at the end of 1999. We notice, however, that, with the possible exception of France (where it is particularly difficult to get a comprehensive overview), the updates indicate varying degrees of increased activity. In Ireland particularly, there has been a marked increase in national support and LA21-related programmes – though this has not yet resulted in widespread activity at the local level.

It must also be pointed out, however, that for Spain, France and Italy, part of the difficulty in achieving a higher ranking lies in the sheer numbers of local authorities. Clearly it is much easier to transcend a threshold of 20 per cent if one is working with between 300 and 500 local authorities (as in Sweden, Finland, Norway and Denmark), than with a number between 8000 (in Spain) and 36,000 (in France). Were it not for the fact that most other indicators of activity are also low in the countries in question, this would be a major deficiency of simple quantitative comparison. As it stands, we feel that the rankings are roughly correct for overall national involvement, and that is all we are trying to reflect at this level of analysis.

Table 12.1 *The timing and breadth of LA21 activities in 12 European countries, 1992–99*

Relative number of initiatives	*Timing of active and broad-based implementation**		
	Early (1992–94)	*Later (1995–96)*	*Latest (1997–99)*
High (> 60 per cent)	Sweden ↘	Denmark ↑	
Medium (20–60 per cent)	United Kingdom ↘ The Netherlands ↔	Finland ↔ Norway ↗	
Low (< 20 per cent)		Austria ↗ Germany**	Spain ↗ Italy ↗ Ireland ↑ France ↔

* Arrows indicate general trends 1998–99
** Data for Germany only available up to 1998

NATIONAL PATTERNS AND KEY VARIABLES

Having provided detailed descriptive overviews of developments within each group of countries in our previous report (Lafferty, 1999), we here only summarise and update a list of possible key variables which appear to account for much of the variation across the countries.[6] In this connection we refer to the countries in four groupings, according to the timing and intensity of implementation:

1 *Early and many:* Sweden, the UK and The Netherlands.
2 *Later and many:* Denmark, Norway and Finland.
3 *Later and few:* Germany and Austria.
4 *Latest and least:* Spain, Italy, Ireland and France.

It should be noted that the variables in question are derived empirically, not theoretically. They constitute the categories of the initial reporting protocol of the network; categories which emerged from our earliest discussions of the implementation problem (Lafferty and Eckerberg, 1998) and which seemed to have relevance for an initial understanding of cross-national variation. In summarising their effects here, we want to provide a general understanding of the processes in question as a national phenomenon, so that we can then follow up with a brief discussion of policy implications at the EU level. The latter is particularly important, since most of the factors in question are either structural or historical in nature; that is, they involve effects which usually are not amenable to policies for change within normal national politics. They may, however, be amenable to direction from above, since one of the major advantages of supra-national governance is the potential to affect intra-national structural relations (as manifest, for example, by the use of structural funds). We follow up the discussion of key variables, therefore, with some brief perspective on how the EU might be able to contribute to a more successful implementation of LA21 at the national level.

Constitutional structure

By constitutional structure we refer to the basic institutional and procedural arrangements which seem to affect the implementation experience. A large part of the variance here seems to be related to the constitutional position of the national sub-units. Constitutional systems with relatively strong local authorities seem to provide better conditions for initiating and moving forward with LA21 than those with weaker systems of local governance. Using a scheme devised by Lidström (1996), we can distinguish four major models or types of local-government systems.[7]

1 The North European system (Sweden, Norway, Denmark, Finland): The local authorities in these countries have a high degree of autonomy supported by local tax revenues. They build upon historic traditions in which small-scale landowners played an important role, and where municipal powers have been progressively increased as a result of modern theories of public administration. After successive mergers of contiguous municipalities, the average size of the administrative-territorial unit has become larger, and the average scope of local governance broader.
2 The Anglo-Irish system (the UK, Ireland): Here the basic units (councils) tend to be somewhat larger, at least in terms of population. They generally lack, however, an independent and firm financial base, and are thus much more dependent on central government. The constitutional rule of competence – that the local authorities can only exert those powers endowed by Parliament – is in principle the same as for the North European system, but the transfer of power has, in fact, been much more restricted in this type of system.
3 The Middle European system (Germany, Austria): The federal structure divides the powers between at least three levels of government. The local authorities are thus rather small, and their size and authority varies within the federation. For instance, the office of mayor is accorded a more important role in the south of Germany than in the north. Historically, the local authorities have had a tradition of great local autonomy, but always within the scope of the prescribed powers.

4 The 'Napoleonic' system (France, Spain, Italy, The Netherlands): This model is characterised by a history with a relatively high degree of centralised state control. Local authorities tended to be supervised by mayors, who in turn were strongly associated with the central government. In general, local units can still be quite small, but there are also incidences of very large local authorities (particularly in Italy and France). There are often four levels of government, in which the middle levels (*départements*, provinces, regions) play an important role of coordination (France), and in some instances exert increasingly independent powers (Spain).

Two of these types – the North European and Middle European systems – can be characterised as having relatively strong local authorities. It would be expected that these systems should favour the development of LA21. The Anglo-Irish system is clearly the most centralised, and has even resisted the general European trend of increased administrative decentralisation in recent years. Whereas the state to a certain degree can affect the framework for local governance in the North European system (through regulation and sector-specific economic transfers), control is much more direct in the Anglo-Irish and Napoleonic systems. In the federal states, the exercise of local authority is more robust where allocated, but totally absent when not devolved.

In the assessment made above, we see that the four categories of 'early-and-many', 'later-and-many', 'later-and-few' and 'latest-and-least' correspond quite neatly with the four types of organisation of local authorities. All four of the North European countries appear in the two most advanced categories, while both of the 'later-and-few' countries are Middle European (federalist), and the 'latest-and-least' grouping contains three of the four Napoleonic systems. The major exceptions to the symmetry are The Netherlands and the UK, both of which belong to the 'early-and-many' category; and Ireland, which falls among the 'latest-and-least'. Interestingly enough, however, The Netherlands is clearly a hybrid Napoleonic system, while Ireland is just as clearly more Napoleonic than Great Britain within the UK. The fact that the UK in general performs (or at least performed) better than expected as a more centralised system is an anomaly with a lesson, since it appears that LA21 served one (political) function under the Conservative government, and another under the initial years of the Labour government.

Baseline conditions

By baseline conditions, we mean the general level of achievement already attained with respect to more traditional types of environmental policy, either in the area of nature conservation or pollution prevention. Both of these areas are pre-sustainable-development, and the record of implementation in a country here can be expected to affect the transition to a more comprehensive and demanding type of mobilisation and enactment.

The findings from the country reports seem to bear this out. Most of the leading LA21 countries had established active environmental policies early on, with the clear exception of the UK. The latter had a highly negative national reputation (the 'dirty man of Europe') throughout most of the previous Conservative government, but nonetheless performed strongly on LA21 immediately after the Earth Summit. Once again, the anomaly reflects the extremely politicised nature of LA21 in the UK: a situation where the colour of local politics strongly affected LA21 as an anti-centrist form of mobilisation. As such, the early interest in LA21 was as much a reflection of political ambitions at the local level as a reflection of active interest in and support for the UN initiative.

This generalisation is further reinforced when we turn to the 'latest-and-least' states. Here we find that the pre-LA21 record of environmental achievement is decidedly poorer than in the leading countries. What we see, therefore, is an apparent convergence between the constitutional factor and this one. It would thus appear that a well-founded record of environmental involvement favours LA21 implementation when the degree of local autonomy in general is higher. Such autonomy is not only, however, a question of constitutional arrangements. The data indicate two other important aspects of local autonomy:

1. the specific scope of autonomy with respect to the more popular LA21 themes and policy areas; and
2. the local capacity for action as measured by the resource levels and competencies of local authorities (Lafferty and Eckerberg, 1998).

By most indications, therefore, high autonomy in local authorities, coupled with a history of environmental concerns and actions, provides a solid basis for LA21 involvement.

No rule in social science is without at least one major exception, however. In this case the emphasis of most at the end of the last paragraph is warranted by individual case studies from Norway, Germany and Austria. Here we find evidence that past experience in green implementation is not always an advantage. The effect was perhaps strongest in Norway, where LA21 came on the scene just as a previous broad-scale reform was taking root. The Ministry of the Environment had sponsored the establishment of environmental officers in every municipality, with a mandate to represent and promote environmental concerns throughout the local administration (the so-called MIK-reform). The reform represented an enormous effort, both financially and administratively, so that Norway's local authorities were less than ecstatic about starting a new round of change related to LA21.

This points towards an understanding whereby it is openly acknowledged that all reforms demand excess energy and resources, and where there exists an important element of timing related to change. Whereas LA21 came into British politics at a very propitious time for politically motivated local councils, the entry into Norway was clearly out of phase with existing environmental efforts. It would appear, therefore, that the ideal baseline conditions for moving the agenda from traditional environmental policy towards sustainable development is a level of awareness and involvement that is high enough to appreciate the potential for more holistic change, but not so high as to be overly impressed with one's own recent accomplishments.

Involvement in the preparations for the Earth Summit

The Earth Summit action plan, Agenda 21, did not just 'appear'. Years of preparation and negotiations went into the document, and national delegations were involved in the development of respective sections and chapters. Clearly, a strong prior involvement would contribute to greater commitment politically, and, presumably, greater follow-up after the Earth Summit.

It is thus not surprising that all of the countries placed in the two most active categories of implementation played a more active role in the run-up to the Earth Summit and preparation of Chapter 28 than did the other countries surveyed. All four of the Nordic countries and The Netherlands played an active role both before and during the Summit. The Swedish, Norwegian, Danish and Dutch also played a very active role in the preparation of Chapter 28, particularly through the coordinating efforts of national umbrella organisations for local and regional authorities. Also in the UK, the LGMB was active in the preparations, providing a link to key local authorities who then became pioneers in LA21 implementation. Given the fact that these same countries also have been active in the IULA, and the highly influential ICLEI, we have a potential explanation for LA21 variation based on the ability of these countries to establish and maintain international policy networks which require organisational resources and a particular organisational culture which are perhaps less accessible to countries like Italy, Spain, France and Ireland.

Reactions of central government

Even though Chapter 28 is directed toward local authorities, the intentions of the chapter are clearly dependent on a more comprehensive national interest in Agenda 21 as a whole. The attention devoted to LA21 in Europe should not blind us to the fact that Chapter 28 is but one of 40 chapters of the action plan – central government involvement thus becomes a key variable. The manner by which relevant ministries and agencies interpret, communicate and facilitate the Earth Summit goals will have an important impact on how major groups in general, and local authorities in particular, react to the call for sustainable development.

The individual country studies show that, in every case but Spain, national governments have in fact accepted some form of responsibility for LA21 implementation.[8] Variations in the timing and degree of involvement have, however, been considerable. We can identify four broad forms of governmental reaction:

1 setting up an administrative focal point for coordination and information dissemination;
2 producing manuals, guidelines, books and training opportunities;
3 providing funding for research and pilot studies; and
4 providing direct funding for promoting LA21 initiatives.

These modes of involvement can be seen as forming a ladder of national support for local action, with earmarked funding for LA21 activities at the top. All of the countries studied, except Spain, have taken the first three steps on this ladder, although some to a very limited extent or only very recently. Only The Netherlands, Sweden, Norway and some German *Bundesländer* have earmarked funds for LA21 activities. There is a direct correlation between the intensity and seriousness of the central-government reaction and level of support, and the scope and depth of LA21 initiatives. It is thus obvious that the spread of the LA21 idea is highly dependent on national governments adopting a role as facilitator. The UK is, once again, an exception here, where the facilitating role was adopted mainly by NGOs and the LGMB, with little direct involvement by ministries.

Otherwise, it is clearly no accident that two of the earliest cases of active implementation, Sweden and The Netherlands, are in countries where LA21 was quickly integrated with national policies and support; or that national government involvement also provided take-off initiatives for two of the other front-runners, Denmark and Norway. One is reminded of the standard of equality in Orwell's *Animal Farm*:

> Local authorities: good.
> Local authorities + national support: better.

Local community reactions

It must not be overlooked, however, that it is at the level of the local community that the major responsibility lies, and it is at this level that

LA21 will either 'sink or swim'. And here we have found tremendous variations both within and across countries. There are, furthermore, clear variations as to how the different national umbrella organisations for local authorities have reacted. The relative inactivity of Austria, Spain and Italy, and the late involvement of Norway and Germany, are partly explained by uncharacteristically low levels of domestic activity within these bodies. It is also the case that what would normally be a positive factor for implementation (involvement of the national associations in negotiating Chapter 28 to begin with) can become negative if the same bodies fail to actively follow up at home.

However, it is also clear that simply having associations which aggregate and promote the interests of local and regional authorities as important authorities is a positive aspect. While such associations constitute powerful interest groups in Northern Europe and the UK, they are considerably less influential in, for example, France, Spain, Ireland and Italy, where relations between the national government and local domains are much more dependent on personal contacts and party politics. The associations of local authorities in several of these countries are also more regionally based, and this too, seemingly, affects their ability to promote LA21 on a national basis.

Looking more closely at the local authorities themselves, we find that the characteristics of pioneering municipalities seem to reflect a common pattern across the different national domains. This holds true despite the fact that such municipalities at first appear to have very different roots and motives. Some of the major common characteristics are:

- an active and politically mobilised population;
- interested and motivated civil servants;
- local politicians with a particular concern for environmental issues;
- positive international contacts and networks; and
- existing environment and development initiatives.

These characteristics are substantially the same as those revealed in the earlier eight-nation study (Lafferty and Eckerberg, 1998), and clearly constitute a form of 'critical mass' with respect to local-community forces. The most common underlying variable appears to be socio-political mobilisation and awareness with respect to environmental problems. Unless issues of nature conservation and pollution prevention – at a minimum – have been integrated into 'normal' politics and administrative responsibility, the prospects for moving towards the broader agenda implied by LA21 are clearly not good. For a local society to progress from a concern for nature conservation and pollution control, through the problem of resource use versus sustainable consumption, towards issues of global environment and development interdependence, clearly presupposes minimal standards of welfare and economic security, along with advanced standards of social learning and broader horizons of political responsibility. Success for LA21 as an issue and topic of mobilisation for an entire local community is primarily a question of value-added consciousness in relation to a series of pre-established values and stages of development.

NGOs and social partners

As key elements of civil society, both environmental NGOs and social partners have a vital role to play in the value-added process. With respect to the social partners – large and small businesses, professional organisations and labour unions – there has emerged a very clear difference. Whereas both business organisations and individual firms regularly appear as adjuncts to LA21-related processes, professional and labour organisations are – with the possible exceptions of the UK and Sweden – rarely involved.[9] This represents a significant insight into environment and development politics, as well as a point of departure for policy discourse.

With respect to environmental NGOs, we can discern two general types of involvement. In several countries, NGOs have been instrumental in coordinating activities and disseminating information,[10] and in others have played a more critical role where LA21 activities have been more limited.[11] NGOs also pursue a coordinating role at the national level, either within national forums or organisations for sustainable development,[12] or in more specific Agenda 21 organisations.[13] Two countries are exceptions: Spain, where NGOs have played a very marginal role,[14] and Norway, where virtually all of the 'running' has been carried out by two atypical organisations. In Norway, the Ideas Bank (Stiftelsen Idébanken) has specialised in the dissemination of information employing a broad spectrum of methods and media, and the Environmental Home Guard (Miljøheimevernet), an umbrella organisation organised in the wake of the Earth Summit for the purpose of promoting sustainable consumption in households and local communities, has played a major role.

In many ways, the picture of relative uniformity which emerges with respect to the role of NGOs is interesting, given the fact that there is so much diversity across the different organisations and national settings. Much of the NGO-related literature gives an impression of an organisational sector which is more-or-less uniform in its attitudes and approach to the global environment and development agenda. However, there is considerable variation both within and across national boundaries, and similar organisations seem to have different strategies and opinions as to the meaning and importance of the LA21 model. This also reflects a major underlying problem of the study: environmental protection is not the same as sustainable development, and factors associated with the one should not be taken for granted as factors affecting a transition to the other.

POLICY IMPLICATIONS

Viewing the diffusion of LA21 from the point of view of the EU, the pattern of variables summarised above gives rise to a number of policy implications. Assuming that the EU – as an independent signatory of the Earth Summit Accords – is actively interested in promoting LA21, what lessons and possible initiatives emerge from the SUSCOM project?

Constitutions matter

Clearly, constitutional structures and established procedures for decision-making and the allocation of resources play a major role in implementing a global policy such as LA21 within a European context. Since the end-users are local authorities, which are highly diversified within and across the different domains, implementation must be approached with a strong sensitivity for constitutional variation. No two national political systems are completely alike, yet there is enough similarity across sub-national systems to warrant a clustered policy approach.

Implementation of global policy prescriptions is more effective in unitary states than in federal states. Relationships between central and local government appear to be both more flexible and more integrated in unitary than in federal states. The scope for implementation by local authorities is viewed as a matter of adaptation to changing socio-economic and political realities, rather than a question of delimited 'sovereignties' between national and local or regional authorities. And they are more integrated in that changing responsibilities and functions are, as a rule, specifically made to adapt to existing groups. It is presumed, in other words, that there is continuity between new and established patterns of governance. By contrast, domains of responsibility are much more firmly established (and jealously guarded) in federated systems, so that the addition of new and level-specific tasks is always open to serious debate (and suspicion).

By recognising this difference with respect to LA21, EU bodies should be able to develop more specific remedial policies for overcoming the constitutional barriers of federal states. Directly, it should be possible to establish more systematic cooperative links and supportive programmes with local communities, providing them with a less onerous responsibility vis-à-vis global processes and the allocation of scarce local resources. Indirectly, it should also be possible for EU bodies to employ directives and other means of supra-national governance to empower national and regional authorities to do more to facilitate local involvement. In this way, EU intervention in global policy implementation can serve as a very specific mechanism for making subsidiarity work in practice – a topic we return to below.

Money helps – differentially

The comparative analysis shows a clear relationship between funding and LA21 activity. The more funds available to support different aspects and phases of LA21 initiatives, the broader the effect of the action, and the greater the potential for long-term involvement. Other factors – such as individuals who initiate activity and keep the process moving through personal effort and inspirational leadership, or a solid political majority for LA21 in the relevant local assembly – are equally important. But, given the ambitious goals of Chapter 28, it becomes clear that both time and special administrative and informational skills must be brought to bear. Since local budgets have a tendency to be overburdened and underfunded (especially in the midst of a clear trend towards decentralisation in public services and political-administrative responsibility), this usually means that local decision-making bodies must either alter priorities for spending, or secure external sources of funding.

In several of the cases studied, such external funding has come in the form of government programmes for directly promoting LA21. In several of these cases – principally Sweden, The Netherlands and Norway – the national authorities have pursued a dual function of providing financial assistance in conjunction with the role of active facilitator to move the agenda on Chapter 28.

In Sweden this role was seen and practised from the very start, with the amount of financial assistance actually being increased as LA21 became integrated into more comprehensive efforts to rejuvenate local economies. The Swedish model has, in many respects, been a classic social-democratic programme, with state authorities quickly taking a major responsibility for guiding the process, and then gradually co-opting it into an even more comprehensive state-supported effort for economic recovery and general social welfare.

In The Netherlands, the model was more in line with the very strong Dutch planning tradition, with a state-sponsored promotion of LA21 activities as an optional funding scheme in a new programme for municipal environmental improvement (the VOGM programme). Of particular interest with the Dutch model was the combination of available government funds with a need for the local community to choose between different steering tasks. This meant that LA21 became just one of several possible environmental management alternatives, a factor which possibly contributed to a fragmentation of LA21, rather than viewing it as an overarching effort for integrated and holistic planning for sustainable development.

Finally, in Norway, the funding model was completely different. Having just established environmental officers in all municipalities (the MIK-reform referred to above), the central environmental authorities felt that they had already financed a major environmental initiative at the local level. LA21 had, therefore, to first penetrate a mood of considerable self-righteousness before central government was willing to finance a new and broader effort for sustainable development. But once this role was seen (in 1995–96), the Ministry of the Environment was in a position to try something new. Instead of establishing a funding scheme for LA21 at the municipal level, it moved to set up regional 'nodes' for coordinating and supporting LA21 activities at the middle level of governance. Entering into a cooperative venture with NALRA, and also bringing in the environmental section of the county governor's office (Fylkesmannskontoret), a new constellation of facilitating forces was created for a more systematic promotion of LA21.

There are at least three major lessons to be learned from these funding initiatives:

1 That the provision of funds by a government unit at a higher level of responsibility is clearly an effective way to give LA21 a clearer and more substantial profile.
2 That there are many different models for how central authorities can execute a 'facilitator function' vis-à-vis local authorities.
3 That the choice of model should be made very carefully with respect to existing cultural, historical and political traditions in each country.

These results indicate that, should the EC – or more pointedly the Committee of the Regions (COR) – wish to promote the idea of subsidiarity more specifically by supporting the notion of LA21, one would want to look much more closely at the alternative methods of providing different kinds of assistance. An integration of the three models outlined above, whereby elements of traditional state-steering are combined with more selective aspects of democracy-and-planning along with 'middle-level' (regional) coordination and stakeholder integration, might result in a highly effective model for promoting 'sustainability through subsidiarity' within the EU mandate.

Global commitments promote local–global awareness

The potential advantage for European integration from such a model is apparent from a third insight that emerges from the cross-country comparison: the obvious learning effect that attaches to well-designed LA21 experiments. Where LA21 seems to take hold – as a new form of strategic dialogue related to sustainable development – there emerges a much clearer understanding of the interdependent nature of sustainable development. In other words, LA21 – above a certain minimum 'threshold' of institutional involvement and popular mobilisation – seems to promote a generalised learning effect as to the need for integrated multi-level governance in this area. As predicted by Robert Dahl in his 'pragmatic principles' for structuring democratic governance (1970), there is nothing so effective for nurturing respect and understanding for the need for higher levels of governance as a populist confrontation with serious problems of change at lower levels of governance.

LA21 serves as a clear analogy to the well-known learning processes developed and documented within earlier discourses on workplace democracy. As argued by Pateman (1970); modelled by Bernstein (1980); documented and generalised by Greenberg (1986), Lafferty (1989) and Heller (2000) – participation in serious decision-making at work leads to heightened consciousness as to the positive and negative aspects of decentralised power. Accepting a broader responsibility for local empowerment leads consequently to a heightened understanding of national, regional and global empowerment. Such lessons have always had an inherent potential in local democracy, but the major tendency has been to allow local jurisdictions to decide on local matters. With a successful introduction of LA21 as a mobilising force, the exigencies of the sustainable-development goals impinge on local consciousness, creating a recognition of the need for both supra-local and supra-national steering.

Complex change requires strategic alliances

Just as the exigencies of sustainable development appear to expand democratic awareness across the scale of governance, so too does a genuine LA21 initiative promote better cooperation among strategic actors. As this is, in fact, the principal *processual goal* of Chapter 28, it warrants attention as both norm and practice.

In the ideal LA21 situation, local authorities take responsibility for promulgating the basic goals of the Earth Summit and for mobilising citizens and strategic stakeholders in a new dialogue to convert and adapt the goals to individual communities. While the comparative analysis reveals relatively few genuine cases of this type, heightened interaction among authorities, NGOs and social partners is a central feature of the LA21 phenomena. Part of this interaction can be attributed to the more general interest in civil society and stakeholder democracy that has arisen in political contexts not directly connected to LA21. A case, however, can be made that most of these trends are related to a presumed undermining of the nation-state through diverse processes of globalisation, and to a general deconstruction of left–right politics.

It can be argued, however, that LA21 is actually related to these changes, since the politics of sustainable development are clearly the politics of increased global–local interdependence and the 'risk society'. LA21 provides a specific set of concepts, goals and principles for these processes, where a need for greater cooperation and strategic alliances among major groups is viewed as central to the Earth Summit action plan.[15] What our study reveals is a striking difference between the group of actors previously involved in the politics of industrialised society and the welfare-state, and those prevalent in the politics of sustainable development. Whereas business and labour tended to dominate interactions with government in the former – with NGOs in the wings – the latter reveals a strengthened involvement for NGOs (particularly those related to environment-and-development issues); a significant increase in the involvement of business associations; and a dramatic decrease in the involvement of labour.

These insights emerge as a direct result of the research design for the sustainable communities project, where LA21 has from the start been understood as a means for assessing different aspects of change across the 12 states. LA21 emerges as a common 'external carrier' for the new group: a generalised global–local model for what elsewhere has been identified as 'co-operative management regimes' (Lafferty and Meadowcroft, 1996; Meadowcroft, 1998). The clear attraction of the model in several of the more pronounced cases of best practice is acknowledged – for example, Albertslund in Denmark, Graz in Austria, Fredrikstad in Norway, and Modena in Italy, where the emergence of the model clearly documents a new spirit of constructive pragmatic cooperation – but we should also note that the internal discussions of the project point towards a number of potential difficulties with the model which warrant closer attention in a policy context.

First of all, the tendency to view the new cooperative regime as only positive is at best naive, and at worst a hindrance for effective change. An increasingly dominant focus on so-called 'win-win strategies', where all parts simultaneously enhance their own advantage and the cause of sustainable development through cooperative efforts, gives a decisive impression that change can be achieved without serious conflicts of interest. Since the model builds on varying degrees of consensus, and superficially appears to be relatively free of economic and social costs, there is a tendency to promote the model as the preferred alternative. This perception is, however, only partially correct. Clearly, the demanding nature of the sustainability transition requires relative losers as well as joint winners. While it is understandable that policy-makers and civil servants want to 'accentuate the positive, and eliminate the negative', there is a clear danger that the agenda for change can be narrowed to cover only those issues where there is a reasonable anticipation of cooperative success. In short, good governance for sustainable development implies a responsibility for managing fundamental conflicts of interest, as much as for facilitating win-win situations.

Secondly, another of the currently popular concepts related to the new cooperative approach – civil society – also contains numerous latent problems. As this study shows, there is considerable diversity in the way that NGOs react to, and become involved in, LA21 activities. Given the mobilisation of environment-and-development NGOs at the Rio Earth Summit – hailed universally as a defining event in the development of the new 'global civil society' – one would have assumed that the follow-up on an issue as popular as LA21 would have been more uniform and coordinated. This does not appear to be the case, however. Variations both within and across countries are great as to when, where and how NGOs relate to the idea. In several countries (for example, Finland, Denmark, Ireland and France) individual organisations took an independent lead, whereas in others (The Netherlands and Norway) the initiative became associated with new 'platforms' or umbrella organisations. If we, in addition, take into consideration the fact that the population of NGOs involved in this area is much broader and more diverse than just environment and development organisations, we have a situation which is anything but clear for 'cooperative-management' policy-makers.

There is at least one insight from the study that provides an important 'touchstone' for more systematic planning and initiatives. The success of LA21 appears to be principally related to the third objective of Chapter 28, namely that:

> *'By 1994, representatives of associations of cities and other local authorities should have increased levels of cooperation and coordination with the goal of enhancing the exchange of information and experience among local authorities.'*

There can be no doubt that without the mobilisation of national umbrella associations for local and regional authorities before the Earth Summit, and particularly the establishment of the ICLEI, there would be much less to celebrate with respect to Chapter 28.[16] This organisational group has provided a solid international network for supporting and promoting 'its' chapter from the action plan as soon as the Earth Summit was over. It has joined forces with several UN agencies; moved, in cooperation with the EC, to sponsor and administer the European Sustainable Cities and Towns Campaign; pushed through the highly influential Aalborg Charter; established and funded one of the most comprehensive and effective websites in NGO history; and engaged in widespread information dissemination and conducted training programmes for LA21 implementers.

What we can learn from this is that, on the one hand, such a 'global' organisational effort is indeed possible, constituting thereby a paradigm case for what might have been achieved in other Agenda 21 areas; while, on the other, the case in itself probably explains much of the variation (and seeming policy confusion on the issue) among environment-and-development NGOs in general. In other words, *this* particular group of

NGOs was so effective in taking over the running of LA21 that other more classic 'grass-roots' organisations were forced to either join up or quibble over the meaning of the new initiative.

Thirdly, the individual country reports confirm an increasingly widespread view of modern NGOs, that they are extremely diversified. Any attempt to associate the concept of 'civil society' with some kind of a homogeneous notion of 'NGOs', either as to thematic focus or moral intent, is clearly inappropriate. Even in an area so limited as LA21 – which in the eyes of many observers is prototypical for what 'environment-and-development' should be all about (at the local level) – there emerges a plethora of sizes, shapes and political colours.

There also emerges a more specific problem for public servants entrusted with implementation tasks, and ready to enter upon the path of cooperative management – democratic legitimacy. There is ample evidence that the relationship between the legally established channels of local political decision-making and the institutions of the new LA21 dialogue can come into serious conflict with each other. In this context, the overall democratic legitimacy of NGO representatives is an issue that, sooner or later, must be confronted and standardised within the UNCED system.

Finally, it is important to stress the clear difference between the organisational make-up of the new cooperative group mode and the more traditional mode of welfare–state politics. The LA21 experience across Europe is perhaps the best laboratory available for observing this difference in practice. In addition to the greater nuance that is required to negotiate and effectively structure the diversity of environmental NGOs, there is the challenge of having to relate to and 'manage' the very different type of NGOs represented by business, labour and other 'means-of-production' associations. Evidence emerges from all country reports of a business community that is much more interested in corporate–pluralist involvement with government decision-making than has traditionally been the case for industrial-welfare politics. This involvement is both more diversified, enthusiastic and proactive than before. It is a completely different 'game' from the relatively monolithic structures of those systems known for their 'corporate' solutions among the social partners (variously in Austria, The Netherlands, Scandinavia and Ireland), and a totally new phenomenon in those states where corporate pluralism has been traditionally weak (the UK, Germany, France, Italy and Spain).

Even more dramatic, however, is the lack of involvement on the part of labour in anything resembling LA21, with the exception of the UK and Denmark. This poses serious challenges for both politicians and public servants entrusted with implementation. Once again, one cannot expect 'win-win' strategies in an area where a crucial collective 'player' such as labour is only on the sidelines. Our monitoring of LA21 implementation illustrates the depth of potential conflict between business, labour and the public good in most of the serious challenges of sustainable development:

energy-use, land-use, greenhouse-gas emissions, preservation of biodiversity and sustainable production and consumption. We should all be aware that the more LA21 succeeds on the basis of the new constellation of organisations and interests, the deeper the potential conflicts with labour and other more traditional occupational interests may develop.

LA21 AND DEMOCRATIC PLANNING

As indicated earlier, questions related to planning and democratic participation have been of central interest for the SUSCOM project from the start. LA21 is by nature a planning and democratisation reform. Although the mandate of Chapter 28 does not explicitly demand that action plans or programmes should be the output of an LA21 process, it is clear that the purpose of the consultative process is to be a programme for change; a programme that eventually should be subjected to the normal demands of local decision-making and legal-administrative practice. The 'product' of sustainable development would be defeated if the 'process' remains external to normal party politics, or if the 'plan' and its resultant 'policies' are not connected to budgetary and other instruments of implementation.

Before turning to some of the more robust findings from the country studies, it is important to make explicit just why participation is thought to be so important for achieving sustainable development. A closer analysis of the UNCED process reveals both normative and functional arguments.

The normative perspective in Agenda 21 builds on arguments for direct democracy, stresses popular sovereignty and places emphasis on direct involvement in substantive decision-making on the part of the wider public. An LA21 aspires to shared responsibility, which means a redefinition of the relationship between government and societal actors. LA21 represents an attempt to expand the role of civil society in relation to both national and local authorities. As indicated above, there is clearly a potential tension with respect to more elitist democratic theories, since the latter clearly question both the ability of normal citizens to take an effective part in decision-making, as well as the legitimacy of expanded stakeholder democracy. Agenda 21 comes down solidly here on the part of participatory and stakeholder democracy.

Even more important is the functional logic underlying the reform. By explicitly focusing on the instrumental need for expanded participation by both citizens and strategic collective actors, Chapter 28 gives expression to well-established arguments for functional involvement (see Coenen et al, 1998). The greater degree of consensus and support for a plan of action, the easier it should be to realise the goals of the plan.

In the second place, participation is functional because it contributes to the quality of decision making. Extensive public consultation allows for a systematic identification of problems and their causes, so that these can then be subjected to alternative strategic options. In this way information and experiences from all sectors of the community will be mobilised into the preparation of local action plans.

Finally, there is the argument mentioned above as to empowerment and learning. Through participation, citizens and groups learn of the nature of sustainability problems in their communities, and of the conflicting interests and competing priorities that have to be reconciled.

Beyond these general arguments, Agenda 21 provides little guidance as to how local communities should proceed with the process. This gap has, however, been filled by ICLEI and the sustainable cities and towns campaign – particularly through the principles of the Aalborg Charter – so that shortly after the Earth Summit, there emerged ideal guidelines for an eight-stage model:

1 Recognition of the existing planning and financial frameworks as well as other plans and programmes.
2 Systematic identification, by means of extensive public consultation, of problems and their causes.
3 Prioritisation of tasks to address identified problems.
4 Creation of a vision for a sustainable community through a participatory process involving all sectors of the community.
5 Consideration and assessment of alternative strategic options.
6 The establishment of a long-term local action plan towards sustainability which includes measurable targets.
7 Programming of the implementation of the plan, including the preparation of a timetable and statement of allocation of responsibilities among the partners.
8 Establishment of systems and procedures for monitoring and reporting on the implementation of the plan (The Aalborg Charter, Part III).

As a paradigm for good LA21 practice, the Aalborg model presupposes active involvement from citizens and groups. What we have found in practice, however, are very diverse levels and phases of involvement. In the Graz case from Austria, for example, the generation of the plan and its vision was largely a top-down planning process dominated by experts, with a lack of active citizen participation. In the follow-up evaluation process, however, there has been broader participation. Similarly, the Spanish survey of the larger municipalities indicates very different levels of involvement at different phases of the process. In general, the country reports show a relationship between the availability of resources and guidelines on the one hand, and active involvement on the other. In the UK many LA21 processes produced participatory community visions that were useful and inspiring, but which had little chance of being implemented because of lack of funds and poor integration with normal politics.

In The Netherlands the system of earmarked funding, along with relatively specific guidelines from the environmental inspectorate, resulted in a more fragmented participatory profile, with emphasis on particular projects rather than the overall planning process.

In general, this was a familiar pattern across the original 12 countries, with LA21 becoming increasingly identified with specific environmental problems, rather than with the more ambitious and holistic views prescribed by sustainable development. An even more particular variant of this was visible in Finland and the UK, where LA21 became identified with consultancy-driven 'projects', with very little evidence of citizen involvement. In France we have seen signs of local authorities pointedly trying to delay participation until the plan was relatively well-formulated, and there has also been clear evidence of a lack of group resources and relevant knowledge for more active involvement.

We have also seen that an overall lack of participatory traditions and a participatory culture also influences the involvement profile. This was particularly true for France, Spain, Italy and Ireland. In France, for example, public participation in terms of involvement of the general public during the initial stages of planning and decision-making is relatively new and experimental. The dominant tradition of public participation is limited to more passive consultation and information procedures. Also, in Spain public participation has only recently been highlighted on the political agenda. The first municipal elections date back to only 1979, a clear reflection of the Franco era. In Ireland, the hindrance arises because of a strong tradition of local dependency, originally with respect to the national government, but more recently vis-à-vis the EU.

In Northern Europe there would in general appear to be a more activist orientation to issues of participation and consultation, with many pre-Earth Summit reforms in the area of participatory planning. These are most prevalent in Scandinavia and The Netherlands, where there is a strong tradition of consultation and consensus politics, such that many of the ideas which have been launched in the wake of the Summit as to enhanced participation in planning are in fact well known and, in isolated pilot cases, well tried.

Experiences from these reforms can, however, have both positive and negative effects. While the political culture is, on the whole, more supportive, there is also the problem mentioned earlier with respect to both reform tiredness and selected negative experiences. This is also the case in Germany, where experiments with more participatory urban planning (*Stadtenwicklungplanung*, STEP) have been less than successful, and in the UK, where the history of consultation in statutory planning has also been mixed.

In some countries we have seen a more specific link between the participatory aspects of recent environmental-policy reforms and LA21.

In the Austrian case, for example, the emphasis on the eco-social market economy has served as a particular variant of a sustainable development oriented reform which had already highlighted citizen involvement. This has contributed to relatively high levels of mobilisation in rural communities, which could then be channelled into LA21 activities when the idea finally gained attention. In Denmark there was a similar effect from the many experimental community projects in specific environmental policy areas (waste disposal, energy, transport), which provided models for the broader-based LA21 campaign which ultimately emerged. Likewise in The Netherlands, where the well-known target group approach served as a learning and implementation paradigm for the strategic group aspect of the LA21 model.

All of these findings have to do with factors which condition involvement in the different phases and levels of the stylised LA21 process. The issue can also be approached, however, on a more individual level in the form of thresholds for participatory involvement. In their standard overview of democratic participation, for example, Milbrath and Goel (1977) employ the analogy of a Roman arena for developing a typology of participants. There are always a very few gladiators willing and able to compete in the centre of the arena, with a much larger group of spectators in immediate attendance and the largest group of all outside the arena as apathetic citizens.

In our LA21-processes, gladiators can take the form of either citizens or collective actors, with (in most cases) relatively few of both. The Finnish study has perhaps the most specific data on the citizen aspect, pointing towards considerable apathy among the relevant populations as to the new idea. We have earlier pointed out how individual 'firebrands' have been the key in getting many LA21 processes up and running (Lafferty and Eckerberg, 1998), and the expanded pool of countries only serves to strengthen this impression. LA21 has, in many ways, arrived on the European scene at a most inauspicious time, when complaints as to declining turnouts in elections and dwindling memberships in voluntary organisations are common journalistic fare. Getting people into the LA21 arena has necessitated struggling with this general trend – at the same time that the demands in terms of knowledge and resources are much higher for substantive involvement in sustainable development than for normal electoral politics.

Yet the variation across countries is nonetheless significant. Focusing just on cases of best practice, we have seen that, in the Graz case, for example – despite major efforts by politicians and local public servants over a period of nearly five years – the awareness and follow-up by the community at large was weak. In the Danish Albertslund case, on the other hand, the involvement appears to be both widespread and sustainable.

The Albertslund case is probably the best single case in our study when it comes to documented participation. It also illustrates one of the most important conditioning factors for this variable: the make-up and general experience of the local population. The municipality in question had already gained a reputation from the 1970s as an innovative green community, such that there was a considerable pull for potential gladiators to this type of residential area. In short, the principle of 'build it and they will come' can clearly account for much of the later success in adapting to the LA21 imagery and focus. Getting LA21 up and running in communities with a more normal socio-economic mix is apparently a much more difficult prospect. Sticking to Denmark, we have seen – in a 1998 survey by the leading conservation NGO (Naturfredningsforeningen) – that over 50 per cent of active LA21 municipalities had initiated LA21 activities without extraordinary efforts for public consultation.

It should also be noted that, aside from the specific factor of an established green identity in a community, there is no clear connection between the size and cohesion of the community and an interest in LA21. Once again, in Austria pioneering communities are comparatively large and urban, while in general the majority of Austrian communities are relatively small. In France some of the more prominent pioneers are suburbs of larger cities were one would expect a lack of historical community roots and common interests; while in Finland it was noted that, due to the large size of urban communities, inhabitants are unfamiliar with each other and have, therefore, less of an interest in LA21 initiatives. Finally in Spain, particularly with the so-called DEYNA-initiative, the smallness of the municipalities is said to make participation easier.

The issue of citizen involvement can also be related to the question of representation. In France, LA21 steering committees bring together representatives of central government, local authorities, associations and experts, while average citizens are not directly associated or represented in these committees. In Spain, public participation is often limited to organisations explicitly invited by the municipality. Public involvement seems, in fact, to seldom represent a genuine cross-section of the community. In the UK, a specific area of concern is minorities, the poor, youth and the elderly; while in Finland there is an over-representation of upper-socio-economic status activists. In most countries there are widely varying proportions of different types of collective interests involved, and in both the UK and Norway debates have arisen as to the tension between participatory and representative democracy, with worries expressed as to the non-representative basis of many of the LA21 gladiators.

Assessing diversity: Standards and modes

In trying to gain an overall impression of both the practical and democratic aspects of LA21 as a new and different way to promote sustainable development at the local level, we can conclude our summary by construct-

Table 12.2 *Stylised modes of LA21 implementation in Europe*

Mode of implementation	*Emphasis placed on:* Process (new methods of mobilisation and cooperative governance for achieving SD)	Plan (adopting a strategic plan for SD with targets and indicators)	Policy (adoption of single-issue SD policies and programmes)	Product (achievement of confirmed SD-goals and targets)
Aalborg	Yes/strong	Yes/strong	Yes/strong	Probable/ strong
Paternal	No	Possible	Possible	Possible/weak
Integrated/ single-issue	Possible/ partial	Partial/ strong	Partial/ strong	Probable/ narrow
External/forum	Partial/strong	Possible/weak	No	Unlikely
External/ fragmented	Possible/ partial	No	No	Possible/ narrow

ing a simple typology over different modes of implementation (see Table 12.2). The different modes reflect sub-groupings of cases according to certain common traits that we have found in nearly all of the national contexts. The typology grasps, we believe, the essence of the variety encountered, and allows us to make a number of broader generalisations as to the lessons from the diffusion and realisation of LA21 thus far.

The Aalborg mode

This mode of implementation corresponds roughly with the eight-stage ideal type of the Aalborg Charter. As an ideal type it is meant to serve here as a benchmark for the other modes, since we cannot yet point to any single best case for this type of implementation. Several of the national studies have highlighted individual local communities that clearly aim at trying to achieve as much of the ideal model as possible. This applies (by way of illustration only) to Luleå and Gotland in Sweden, Åland in Finland, Albertslund in Denmark, Fredrikstad in Norway, Lancashire in the UK, and The Hague in Netherlands. These are all cases where strong political leadership tries to join with an ambitious and well-mobilised civil society in an attempt to achieve broad-based and politically integrated change. These communities have taken a solid in-depth look at the notion of LA21 as this has emerged from the UNCED process; they have understood and acknowledged the difference between processes and policies for environmental protection, and processes and policies for sustainable development; and they are seriously trying to adjust their own patterns of planning and governance in the direction of the new ideals.

This is not to say that these cases (or similar cases in other countries) have in fact achieved the procedural standards of the Aalborg Charter, or that they have fulfilled the ambitious goals inherent in the SUSCOM criteria. Their achievement is in demonstrating a willingness to take the commitments of the Earth Summit seriously, and stretching their own political and budgetary processes in the direction of difficult and controversial change. We also note, however, that these cases all point to pre-LA21 efforts which were apparently equally distinct with respect to the more traditional environmental policy paradigm.

This should not, however, be seen as some kind of a detraction with respect to LA21 achievement. We have seen in the Danish case that there are a number of communities that have been able to relate to LA21, not having made any previous mark as environmental front-runners. These communities can often appear as more genuine LA21 pioneers, since they can adopt the language and symbols of the ideal type more easily than communities with longer histories of more traditional environmental activities. It is important, therefore, to recognise such nuances as an important part of the implementation record. Just as these communities clearly needed front-runners to demonstrate LA21 in practice, so too will other, even less well-disposed communities, benefit from the examples of the less substantive followers-on. Clearly, this is how LA21, and for that matter all of Agenda 21, was meant to function – as an ongoing experiment in diffusion, social learning and change.

The paternal mode

Though it may sound like a contradiction in terms, the notion of a paternal LA21 is not without either interest or empirical foundation. The term paternal does not imply authoritarian as much as authoritative. Most fathers (in today's Europe at any rate) consult with their children – and then decide what is best for them. Though the analogy may sound out of place when dealing with change for sustainable development, this is far from the case. Several of our country studies have drawn attention to individual cases – in Finland, Austria and France, to name but the most explicit references – where relatively progressive authorities are unsure of the neo-democracy aspect of LA21 because they fear regressive input with respect to environment and development. The problem goes to the heart of the issues touched on above with respect to the normative and instrumental arguments for participation, and must be acknowledged as a problem since there is no guarantee that either increased citizen or stakeholder control will automatically result in greater sustainable development.

We need not pursue the issue in depth here, but must nonetheless make the point that an LA21 mode whereby an enlightened local political elite wishes to move faster and further on strategic plans, goals, targets and budgetary dispositions than the citizenry at large is clearly a possibility. That such a mode will have less chance of succeeding in promoting broad and lasting change for sustainable development derives from an ultimate conviction that in the end real change must be understood and supported by the broad mass of the population to be effective. This should not blind us, however, to issues of short-term versus long-term effectiveness, or to a need for differing modes of governance with respect to different types of sustainable development problems. An ethically based rejection of authoritarian solutions to such problems does not automatically preclude a discussion of more authoritative solutions; nor must we neglect the exigencies and foibles of entrenched materialist majorities. The notion that an intensity of democratisation is invariably positive for promoting sustainable development is both normatively flawed and empirically unsound (Lafferty, 2000).

The integrated/single-issue mode

This type of mode is more easily and widely documented and is much less controversial. The pattern is one where many of the aspects of the Aalborg model are present, but where the focus is narrowed to one dominant single issue. The most prevalent type is for climate change, with LA21 being connected to an existing campaign or initiative; but there are also instances of LA21s for local transport, tourism, pollution-control, recycling, education, and – in the UK and Norway at least – biodiversity. The common features are: retention of the idea of a new dialogue and mobilisation; development of a specific plan or set of objectives; an attempt to focus new instruments and steering strategies; and even to have built-in monitoring and follow-up mechanisms. Everything is, however, concentrated on a single major issue. Furthermore, most of these are instances of the LA21 idea and symbol being carried further by an existing initiative (for example within the Climate Alliance campaign). The fact that these initiatives are integrated into established decision-making and allocation structure gives them a potential for substantial results and change – but it will be within a clearly delimited area.

The external/forum mode

This type of implementation has been particularly popular in the UK, where anti-establishment attitudes are often very strong among local activists and NGOs. It builds on an interpretation of LA21 as an inherent grass-roots idea; a vehicle for mobilising local populations against party politics, local bureaucrats and big business. The image of an LA21 forum becomes a symbol for communitarian anti-politics – a populist meeting place for drawing up alternative plans and policies. Variations of this are mentioned in all of the Scandinavian reports, and there are signs of similar developments in France and Italy. The mode takes an idea which is specifically directed to local authorities and aims to turn it against those same authorities. It can have a strong mobilising potential, and can, in the most robust of cases, lead to comprehensive alternative plans. Having specifically chosen a separatist path, however – usually with few resources and few links to other strategic actors – the potential for achieving significant change (at least in the short, pragmatic, run) is quite small. On a positive note, however, the mode has probably served to enhance the symbolic value of LA21, giving the UN-based idea a prominence and staying power in settings that otherwise might not have been brought into the sustainable development discourse.

The external/fragmented mode

This mode is perhaps the most common type of all, and is particularly prevalent in those countries which have provided some form of funding for LA21 activities (The Netherlands, Sweden, Norway, Denmark, Finland). The pattern is to parcel out LA21 as sub-group projects, primarily within traditional small-scale areas such as composting, bicycling, street-and-traffic regulation, recycling and school projects. While there is potential for such projects to achieve significant individual results – based as they are on a strong moral emphasis on personal responsibility and mobilisation by imitation – the fragmented nature of the involvement and the lack of integration among projects, and between projects and major political and economic decisions, point to relatively narrow and superficial change. Once again, however, some involvement and change can be of benefit. Furthermore, it is within the scope of this mode that we see the strongest evidence of both citizen and strategic-group involvement and interaction; representatives from business and environmental NGOs and large numbers of citizens often make their first 'hands-on' acquaintance with the Earth Summit and its values and goals within the frame.

Summing up, we feel that this relatively simple typology of alternative modes of implementation captures yet another important facet of the LA21 experience. The typology reflects LA21 as it has evolved, rather than as it was designed to evolve. Clearly, only those cases which roughly approximate to the eight stages of the Aalborg Charter can qualify for full LA21 accreditation, and even these would have to be more closely scrutinised as to the quality of plans, policies and products with respect to the criteria of the SUSCOM project. Yet all of the modes outlined above are patterned from initiatives which relate to the LA21 idea. As self-conscious evaluators, we have to concede that all but one of these modes fall short of the ambitious intent of Chapter 28. But as empirical observers, we must concede that the large numbers of individuals, groups and local authorities involved in these efforts perceive themselves as doing LA21, regardless of ideal standards or Earth Summit/ICLEI goals.

Having established this understanding on the basis of comprehensive monitoring, reporting and comparative analysis, we have provided a new point of departure for the discourse on local sustainable development. We have reported results which are probably much less than those anticipated by the initiators and authors of Chapter 28, but which, on the other hand, are clearly far more interesting than those who would relegate the Earth Summit to a major non-event in the history of environment and development are willing to acknowledge.

LA21 AND SUBSIDIARITY

As outlined in the Introduction to this book, the implementation of LA21 in Europe would seem to touch directly on the issue of subsidiarity. Chapter 28 is formulated as a clear admonition to local authorities to improve conditions for democratically pursuing sustainable development, based on the understanding that it is at the local level of governance that many of the most vital issues of environment and development have their most immediate impact on individual citizens and local strategic actors. Local arenas are thus seen as constituting key settings for identifying and eventually remedying unsustainable practices. The wording and logic of the chapter raise clear associations with the relevant subsidiarity articles of the Treaty on European Union, where – at first reading – it appears that the principle requires that decisions be 'taken as closely as possible to the citizen'. In this light, Chapter 28, and the entire campaign related to LA21, could be seen as a potential effort to provide guidelines and examples for how decentralised decision-making can be strengthened within the EU.

The internal discussions of the SUSCOM network quickly revealed, however, that such an interpretation is not easily reconciled with the highly pliable nature of the subsidiarity principle. What at first appears to be a clear-cut norm in favour of decentralisation emerges on closer investigation as a very elastic norm in favour of integrated, multi-level pragmatic governance. While the superficial semantics of subsidiarity seem to encourage decentralisation and protection against downward penetration from the institutions of the EU, both the deeper logic of the wording and legal practice of the European Court point in an opposite direction. As a specific discourse, the history of subsidiarity (subsequent to the events which arose in connection with the ratification of the Maastricht Treaty) can be characterised as one of protecting the need for supra-national governance in and through an idiom of support for national and sub-national governance.[17] The most succinct expression of this 'double-speak' is the second section of Article 3b of the Treaty of European Union:

> *'In areas which do not fall within its exclusive competence, the Community shall take action, in accordance with the principle of subsidiarity, only if and in so far as the objectives of the proposed action cannot be sufficiently achieved by the Member States and can therefore, by reason of the scale or effects of the proposed action, be better achieved by the Community.'* (Treaty of European Union, Article 3b)

A close reading of this formulation indicates that, whereas the language appears to be protecting member-state prerogatives, the actual opening for new powers is upwards towards the Community. In short, the debate which arose in connection with the anti-Union signals that emerged during the referenda on Maastricht – and which culminated in the so-called 'Edinburgh Annex' of 1992 – was more a question of wording and imagery than a significant change in direction for EU governance. The debate and resultant changes in the language of EU documents clearly raised the level of awareness as to the issue of level-specific prerogatives, but they did not significantly hinder the potential for EU institutions to adopt policies which could incur on lower-level sovereignty in the service of Union objectives and overall efficiency.

Our discussions of subsidiarity within the SUSCOM project were an attempt to probe the relevance of the different national experiences on LA21 within the broader discourse on the principle. Given the many different perspectives that emerged in the course of our meetings and workshops, we were able to do no more than formulate a simple typology over the alternative understandings (Box 12.1). The scheme provides a rough vocabulary on subsidiarity, so that the different meanings can be distinguished when discussing the implications of LA21.[18]

What emerges – as expressed by the notion of instrumental subsidiarity – is a perspective on the problem of allocating responsibilities for governance. Within the context of SUSCOM, this means that the pursuit of sustainable development is inherently understood to be a challenge of governance along vertical and horizontal axes. Vertically, we have the numerous levels of decision-making jurisdictions, from the most decentralised local steering units within nation-states, up through national and regional jurisdictions to the EU, and beyond to the UN and other international conventions. Horizontally, we have the unlimited potential at each

Box 12.1 Alternative meanings of the principle of subsidiarity within the context of European integration

Supra-subsidiarity: The legitimation of a limited transfer of authority to a decision-making body at a level of governance higher (more comprehensive) than the unit or units in question.

National subsidiarity: The protection of national sovereignty from the incursion of binding governance by supra-national bodies and authorities.

Infra-subsidiarity: The enhancement or protection of local and regional decision-making prerogatives for purposes of effectiveness, efficiency or democratic legitimacy.

Functional subsidiarity: The sharing of governmental authority with representatives of strategic collectives ('stakeholders') and voluntary organisations.

Instrumental subsidiarity: The goal of maximising the effectiveness and legitimacy of governance through goal-directed, multi-level, multi-stakeholder public management.

vertical level for different cooperative management regimes between level-specific authorities and diverse partners for sustainable development.[19] Remembering that subsidiarity is – and must be – a principle, the challenge is to determine where, when and how the principle will be applied. As this can clearly never be a matter of 'fiat' with so complex a goal as sustainable development, there is no other recourse than to try to clarify the nature of the principle so as to enhance discussion and eventual consensus as to its application.

The issue of LA21 provides us here with illustrative material. While, on the one hand, the entire attempt to implement Chapter 28 appears as a strong endorsement of infra-subsidiarity, there are two vital caveats on this perspective.

First, the post-Edinburgh understanding of the principle can, in a legal context, only refer to national subsidiarity, not to infra-subsidiarity. The entire debate around the ratification (and later amendment) of the Maastricht Treaty is a debate as to competitive competences between the EU and its member-states. The EU cannot legislate subsidiarity for subnational jurisdictions. Thus while the imagery of subsidiarity in this context is to defend the interests of individual citizens and local communities, the constitutional substance of the debate is a matter of national versus EU jurisdiction. An overemphasis on LA21 as infra-subsidiarity thus fudges the ultimate (juridical) reality underlying the division of powers in question. That this is much more than an issue of principle is apparent in our country studies, where there has emerged in nearly all of the national jurisdictions (Sweden is the exception) serious debates as to the role of both national and local authorities vis-à-vis LA21.

Second, an over-emphasis on LA21 as infra-subsidiarity also glosses over the equally important fact that Chapter 28 is an integral, and highly dependent, part of Agenda 21, and that Agenda 21 represents an incidence of supra-subsidiarity for the EU. An application of the principle here, therefore, implies that the EC and European Parliament should be actively involved in honouring their obligations to supra-subsidiarity by promoting and integrating Agenda 21 throughout the EU. In this light, the supra-subsidiarity of the EU with respect to its sub-units is clearly enhanced by its adhesion to the Earth Summit accords; a perspective that has not been given notable emphasis by the EU in its follow-up. One can even make the argument here that the EU is missing a golden opportunity to enhance the legitimacy of its own supra-subsidiarity by not promoting the prescriptions of Agenda 21 across a much broader front. Pointedly enough, it can be further argued that it is the exception to this lack that makes the case: namely the EU's involvement in supporting LA21 initiatives through the sustainable cities and towns campaign.

Third, there is the issue of functional subsidiarity, where constituted authorities aim to achieve complex goals by sharing steering responsibility with organisations and groups from civil society. Two perspectives are of relevance. The first is that the extensive documentation of LA21 implementation provides a wealth of updated information on how such subsidiarity works in practice. The sheer amount of material provided by the individual national reports – along with the judiciously chosen storylines of national implementation profiles – should serve as a fruitful source of ideas and insights into the where and how of the new cooperative management regimes. Regardless of how one evaluates the overall effect of these efforts on achieving sustainable development, the fact cannot be denied that hundreds of experiments and programmes are being conducted under the banner of LA21. Efforts are being made, barriers are being broken down, and lessons are being learned.

Furthermore, at a higher level of generalisation, the evidence in question documents a legitimisation of functional subsidiarity which may point towards a distinct type of competitive advantage in the promotion and achievement of sustainable development. We noted above how certain European states have had a consistent history of corporate pluralism, and that this history and practice distinguishes these countries from either Anglo-Saxon or Asian modes of organisation. Through the microscope of LA21 monitoring, it now appears that this distinct European mode is not only becoming much more widespread across the European Community, but that it is particularly adaptable to the difficult challenge of the sustainability transition (O'Riordan, 1996; O'Riordan and Voisey, 1997). In other words, efforts to realise the aspirations of LA21 appear to have released a form of cooperative governance that is both more effective and more legitimate than alternative modes of governance in other regional settings.

Fourth, there is the vital issue of regions and subsidiarity. Several of our national case studies have documented an unexpected and highly interesting phenomenon in the shape of 'Regional Agenda 21'. Stated quite simply, we have seen a form of diffusionary shift, whereby key aspects of the LA21 idea have been taken on at:

- intermediate levels of government within states (Norway, Denmark, The Netherlands);
- broader agglomerations of existing sub-units within states (Finland, France, Spain and Ireland); and
- newly formed regional identities both within and across state borders (Austria, Sweden and Finland).

These developments represent forms of subsidiarity in the making, since it is the common driving force of the LA21 idea, and the more intricate demands of sustainable development, which inspire the incorporation of the idea unto a regional arena. Given the very high ambitions – but correspondingly low profile – of the Committee of the Regions within the EU, this development may prove to be the most significant yet to emerge from the LA21 experience.

Finally, there is a vital insight which can be documented in nearly all of the studies, but which has been made most explicit in the Norwegian profile. We refer to what appears to be a clear learning effect as to the need for supra-subsidiarity within the policy domain in question. It will be recalled that the Norwegian case placed specific emphasis on the issue of obstacles to achieving more sustainable production and consumption within the LA21 framework. The insights gained here were the result of a comprehensive empirical analysis of seven communities within a pilot study of sustainable local communities. In summary, the studies clearly showed that respondents perceived obstacles to local change and individual learning as relatively trivial, while obstacles at higher levels of governance were viewed as much more serious and recalcitrant. Most of these latter obstacles were formulated as resulting from either the direct effects of existing national policies and priorities, or from processes of internationalisation – processes beyond nation-state influence. In both of these cases, the results indicate a need for supra-national initiatives and steering to complement the work that can be done at the local level.

In sum – and by way of a concluding perspective – efforts to implement LA21 seem to function as an active stimulus for calling forth both the positive and negative potential for trying to deal with issues of sustainable development at the local level of governance. On the one hand, the enormous variety in different modes of implementation across the 12 countries studied indicates what can be accomplished at the local level; while, on the other, the frustration generated by confronting at first hand the obstacles to more effective change generates a clearer understanding of what cannot be achieved without additional (subsidiary) efforts at higher levels of governance.

The multifaceted LA21 experience serves, in other words, as a school in the need for subsidiarity, illustrating in a very clear way the essence of the problem that makes the principle both necessary and confused. It is necessary because the challenge of sustainable development requires all of the different aspects of the principle outlined above; and it is confused because the problem emerges, and must be solved, within an evolving context of insufficient and fragmented sovereignties. The widespread attempt to realise sustainable development through LA21 thus proves to be a vital catalyst for a deeper understanding of the necessity of European integration within this area.

NOTES

1 The authors of this chapter are grateful to several of their SUSCOM colleagues for helpful comments and suggestions – particularly Katarina Eckerberg and Rudy Lewanski. We wish to stress, however, that the conclusions and implications drawn in the chapter are primarily the responsibility of the two authors alone.

2 See the discussion on the differing standards and reports in the concluding chapter of Lafferty and Eckerberg (1998).

3 While most of the possibilities here will appear reasonable, some may react to the notion of a product that is achieved without prior LA21 process, plan or policy. Clearly, however, numerous results of a highly beneficial nature for sustainable development can be achieved through innovations and even policies that are not consciously aimed at achieving sustainable development. Technological change motivated by free-market competition is but the most obvious case. The differentiation is important since we are not saying that all positive change for sustainable development must result from the idealised logical sequence, merely that this type of non-purposive change is outside the scope of the Chapter 28 prescription.

4 It should be stressed here that when we use the term 'early' we are referring to the overall national reaction and initiative in support of the LA21 idea. Denmark had, for example, isolated cases of pioneer communities at an early stage, but cannot be said to have manifested a significant overall effort during the initial 1992–94 period.

5 We mention again the fact that Germany had to withdraw from the concerted action prior to the preparation of the final country reports. We have tried to include the data on Germany from the initial period so as not to lose the important perspectives, but do not have an update on either the general status of implementation or best-cases.

6 The previous status report – entitled *Implementing LA21 in Europe: New Initiatives for Sustainable Communities* – is available on request from ProSus: Post Box 1116 Blindern, University of Oslo, 0317 Oslo, Norway (e-mail: info@prosus.uio.no). It can also be ordered at the programme website: www.prosus.uio.no.

7 This categorisation is relatively conventional. Hesse and Sharpe (1991), for example, use roughly the same scheme, but they include the Northern European model with what is here referred to as the Middle European model.

8 In the Spanish case the environment ministry openly stated that it has no power to be involved in the implementation of LA21.

9 In the UK, labour organisations have, in certain local communities, been involved within the overall more politicised context of selected LA21 initiatives, and in Sweden the coupling of the LA21 idea with major financial initiatives to revive local economies has also had union support and involvement. In neither of these cases, however, do we see an active involvement with LA21 as a means toward sustainable development on its own terms. Agenda 21 has, of course, a separate chapter on 'Workers and Trade Unions', but we have found no evidence of any connection between activity in this area and LA21.

10 Especially in Sweden, where the Swedish Society for Conservation and Nature was a major driving force behind the rapid growth of LA21 (Eckerberg and Forsberg, 1998). In Finland (Finnish Nature Conservation and Friends of the Earth-Finland); the UK, (WWF and Friends of the Earth-UK); and Norway (The Environmental Home Guard), NGOs have played important roles at different phases of the implementation.

11 In Ireland, An Taisce; and in Italy, Legambiente, WWF.

12 In The Netherlands, NCDO; Germany, the Forum for Environment and Development; France, 4D; Sweden, q2000 and Austria, the Õkobureau.

13 In France, Comité 21; and Finland, Finland 21.

14 Greenpeace, Adena WWF and Friends of the Earth.

15 In many ways, Agenda 21 is a unique document in this respect. By devoting one of its four major sections to the roles and responsibilities of major groups, and by constantly referring to these groups throughout the other three sections, the document can be seen as one of the most specific corporate-pluralist political statements ever issued. By attributing such a central role to these collective actors – a role that is deemed to be vitally strategic, at the same time that their interaction and mobilisation are to be only cooperative and (ideally) consensual – the Earth Summit action plan gives voice to a group theory of governance which joins the more corporate tradition of Europe (with groups often given direct access to governmental decision-making) with the more pluralist tradition of the United States (with groups relegated to the lobbies of parliamentary assemblies). As indicated in the text, it is possible to distinguish a key difference between the corporate-pluralism of earlier group-theory discourses (in the 1970s and early 1980s) and the stakeholder democracy of current discourses.

16 For a brief overview of the history of ICLEI and its major activities, see Lafferty and Eckerberg (1998).

17 The most recent overview of the issue with respect to environment and development is available in a special issue of the *Journal of European Environmental Policy* (*European Environment*, 2000). For the general interpretation presented here, see particularly the articles and references by Jordan and Jeppesen ('EU Environmental Policy: Adapting to the Principle of Subsidiarity?') and Sharo, Nadin and Seaton ('The Application of Subsidiarity in the Making of European Environmental Law'). Other more general sources are Duff (1993), CEPR (1993) and CDLR (1994).

18 The list presented here is an amended version of a list which was first presented at a conference on 'Regions: Cornerstones of Sustainable Development', Joensuu, Finland, 13–14 September 1999.

19 Let it also be mentioned that problems of horizontal integration and the setting of priorities within and between governing institutions at the same level remain a major unsolved problem of governance for sustainable development.

REFERENCES

Bernstein, P (1980) *Workplace Democratization: Its Internal Dynamics*, Transaction Books, New Brunswick, NJ

CDLR (1994) *Definition and Limits of the Principle of Subsidiarity*, report prepared for the Steering Committee on Local and Regional Authorities, Council of Europe Press, Strasbourg

CEPR (1993) *Making Sense of Subsidiarity: How Much Centralization for Europe?* Centre for Economic Policy Research, London

Coenen, F, Huitema, D and O'Toole, L (1998) *Participation and the Quality of Environmental Decision-Making*, Kluwer, Dordrecht

Dahl, R (1970) *After the Revolution?* Yale University Press, New Haven and London

Duff, A (1993) *Subsidiarity within the European Community*, Federal Trust for Education and Support, London

Eckerberg, K and Forsberg, B (1998) 'Implementing Agenda 21 in Local Government: The Swedish experience', *Local Environment*, vol 3(3), pp335–349

European Environment (2000) Special Issue, 'Subsidiarity and Environmental Policy in the EU', *European Environment: The Journal of European Environmental Policy*

Greenberg, E S (1986) *Workplace Democracy: The Political Effects of Participation*, Cornell University Press, Ithaca

Hajer, M A (1995) *The Politics of Environmental Discourse: Ecological Modernisation and the Policy Process*, Clarendon Press, Oxford

Hanf, K and Jansen, A (1998) *Governance and Environment in Western Europe: Politics, Policy and Administration*. Longman, Harlow

Heller, F (2000) *Managing Democratic Organizations*, vols I and II, Ashgate Publishers, London

Hesse, J J and Sharpe, L J (1991) 'Local Government in International Perspective: Some comparative observations' in Hesse J J (ed) *Local*

Government and Urban Affairs in International Perspective, Nomos Verlagsgesellschaft, Baden-Baden
Jänicke, M (1992) 'Conditions for Environmental Policy Success', *The Environmentalist*, vol 12, pp47–58
Jänicke, M and Weidner, H (1997) *National Environmental Policies: A Comparative Study of Capacity Building*, Springer Verlag, Berlin
Lafferty, W M (1989) 'Work as Political Learning among Wage-Laborers and Lower-level Functionaries' in Sigel, R S (ed) *Political Learning in Adulthood*, University of Chicago Press, Chicago and London
Lafferty, W M (ed) (1999) *Implementing LA21 in Europe: New Initiatives for Sustainable Communities*, ProSus, Oslo
Lafferty, W M (2000) 'Democracy and Ecological Rationality: New trials for an old ceremony' in Lachapelle, G and Trent, J (eds) *Globalization, Governance and Identity: The Emergence of New Partnerships*, Les Presses de L'Université de Montréal, Montréal
Lafferty, W M and Meadowcroft, J (eds) (1996) *Democracy and the Environment: Problems and Prospects*, Edward Elgar, Cheltenham
Lafferty, W M and Eckerberg, K (eds) (1998) *From the Earth Summit to Local Agenda 21: Working Towards Sustainable Development*, Earthscan, London
Lidström, A (1996) *Kommunsystem i Europa* (*Local Authorities in Europe*), Publica, Norstedts Juridik AB, Stockholm
Meadowcroft, J (1998) 'Co-operative Management Regimes: A way forward?' in Glasbergen, P (ed) *Environmental Agreements*, Kluwer Academic, Dordrecht
Milbrath, L and Goel, M L (1977) *Political Participation: How and Why do People get Involved in Politics?* 2nd edition, Rand McNally, Chicago
O'Riordan, T (1996) 'Democracy and the Sustainability Transition' in Lafferty, W M and Meadowcroft, J (eds) *Democracy and the Environment*, Edward Elgar, Cheltenham
O'Riordan, T and Voisey, H (1997) *Sustainable Development in Western Europe: Coming to Terms with Agenda 21*, Frank Cass, London
Pateman, C (1970) *Participation and Democratic Theory*, Cambridge University Press, Cambridge
United Nations (1993) *Report of the United Nations Conference on Environment and Development, Rio de Janeiro, 3–14 June 1992, vol I*, United Nations, New York
WCED (World Commission on Environment and Development) (1987) *Our Common Future: Report of the World Commission on Environment and Development*, Oxford University Press, Oxford
Weale, A (1992) *The New Politics of Pollution*, Manchester University Press, Manchester

Index